Wood Deterioration and Its Prevention by Preservative Treatments

Volume I
Degradation and Protection of Wood

SYRACUSE WOOD SCIENCE SERIES, 5
Wilfred A. Côté, Editor

SYRACUSE WOOD SCIENCE SERIES

WILFRED A. CÔTÉ, *editor*

1 JOHN F. SIAU, *Flow in Wood*, 1971.

2 B. A. MEYLAN and B. G. BUTTERFIELD, *Three-Dimensional Structure of Wood*, 1972.

3 BENJAMIN A. JAYNE, editor, *Theory and Design of Wood and Fiber Composite Materials*, 1972.

4 CHRISTEN SKAAR, *Water in Wood*, 1972.

5 DARREL D. NICHOLAS, editor, *Wood Deterioration and Its Prevention by Preservative Treatments*, 1973.
Volume I: Degradation and Protection of Wood
Volume II: Preservatives and Preservative Systems

Wood Deterioration and Its Prevention by Preservative Treatments

DARREL D. NICHOLAS, *Editor*

with the assistance of WESLEY E. LOOS

Volume I
Degradation and Protection of Wood

SYRACUSE UNIVERSITY PRESS, 1973

FIRST EDITION

Library of Congress Cataloging in Publication Data

Nicholas, Darrel D.
    Wood deterioration and its prevention by preservative
treatments.

    (Syracuse wood science series, 5)
    CONTENTS: v. 1.   Degradation and protection of
wood.—v. 2.   Preservatives and preservative systems.
    Includes bibliographies.
    1. Wood—Preservation.   2. Wood preservatives.
I. Title. II. Series.
TA422.N53   674'.38   73-4640
ISBN 0-8156-5037-X (v. 1)

Printed in the United States of America

Foreword

In the 1970s there developed in the United States, as in many other parts of the world, an intense interest in the environment on which we are dependent for life itself. This rather sudden concern with ecological questions and for conservation of natural resources has been noted with particular interest by those who have made careers in forest science. The professional schools of forestry and wildlife conservation have been involved for decades in the struggle to preserve the environment. While effort originally was concentrated in the obvious areas of forestry, environmentalists now work at many levels—dealing with everything from submicroscopic organisms to *Sequoia gigantea* in size—and in many disciplines.

These activities are the subjects of this two-volume work, the first of which deals with wood deterioration and its causes, the second with preservation applications and processes. Between them, they cover everything from the historical development of discoveries and applications concerning wood to consideration of the control of pollution from wood-preserving processes.

Included are detailed analyses of the factors that lead to great losses of an important natural resource, wood, a material that is produced through a renewable resource, the forest. Wood deterioration brought about by decay, insect attack, heat, chemical degradation, marine-borer attack, weathering, and many other agencies is the source of huge financial losses—both to producer and consumer—in material and labor.

In a real sense, the contributors to these volumes are environmentalists who are working at a vital interface with the ecology, doing much more than proposing salvaging processes and operations. They are finding ways to circumvent losses of a basic and essential resource through research on its effective utilization and preservation. This is environmental science at a subtle level which until recently has been unappreciated by most laymen and even by many researchers and industrial processers. Yet, such activities should now more than ever be considered one of the major efforts for efficient use of the world's natural resources.

The well-balanced approach taken in this work gives the fundamental scientist a fair share of the responsibility for establishing the interdisciplinary background and yet allows the applications engineer to offer the practical solutions to preventing wood deterioration. From the initial chapter in Volume I to the last chapter in Volume II, this book is provocative of thought and action in the control not only of deterioration of processed wood but for a contribution to better future control of those resources vitally important to future generations—the forests, waters, and soil of the world.

Syracuse, New York
Spring, 1973

Wilfred A. Côté, *series editor*
Professor of Wood Technology
Director, Laboratory for
  Ultrastructure Studies
State University College of
  Environmental Science and
  Forestry

Preface

The field of wood preservation has been gradually evolving from the empirical to the scientific approach. That we are indeed well into the science-oriented concept will become apparent after reading this book. Nevertheless, the reader will have the feeling that there are many missing links in our knowledge of wood deterioration and methods of preservation. This is unquestionably true, and it is hoped that this book will lend a certain amount of direction to future research as well as provide an up-to-date review of this field.

In general, the field of wood preservation can be divided into two broad categories; namely the deterioration and protection of wood, and the treatment of wood with preservatives. Consequently, this book was separated into two volumes so that each subject could be covered in greater detail. This also will permit the reader to choose a single volume in the event his interest is confined to one particular area. The initial chapter of the first volume covers the history and purpose of wood preservation in order to provide the reader with a general background in the principal developments that have occurred since the beginning of recorded history. Following this, the major causes of wood deterioration—degradation by microorganisms, marine borers, insects, heat, and chemicals—are covered in detail. Because of its complexity and importance, the subject of degradation by microorganisms is encompassed in five chapters. Each chapter includes a discussion of the principles of protection of wood since it is inextricably related to degradation. The second volume deals primarily with the treatment of wood to protect it from degradation. This includes chapters on factors influencing the effectiveness of preservatives and treatability of wood as well as treating processes and properties of preservatives. Because of its increasing importance, water-pollution abatement and control is also covered in detail.

The multi-author approach was chosen because the field of wood preservation is entirely too diverse for any one individual to be an expert in all facets. As a result of this, each subject area in this book is covered in depth by individuals who have devoted many years, if not their entire lives, to a particular phase of the field. Each chapter includes a comprehensive review of the literature along with a thorough analysis and summary of the pertinent points. The authors have also indicated areas where additional research would be desirable.

In an endeavor of this type, many individuals provide assistance and it is especially true for this book. In the initial stages, Dr. Wesley E. Loos served as co-editor but because of unforeseen difficulties was forced to drop out before completion. Without his efforts, this book would not be a reality. The editor also wishes to thank Dr. Wilfred A. Côté for his co-operation, guidance, and enthusiasm. Support in the form of encouragement, secretarial assistance, mailing costs, and travel expenses were provided by Honolulu Wood Treating Co., Ltd., and the editor would like to express his gratitude to Mr. Clinton T. Hallsted for making this possible. Reviews by Mr. George B. Fahlstrom, Dr. Roy H. Baechler, and Dr. John F. Siau were helpful and are acknowledged.

This book is dedicated to the authors who participated in this endeavor. They have generously given their time and talents to summarize existing information and chart a future course for research in wood preservation.

DARREL D. NICHOLAS

Honolulu, Hawaii
Spring, 1973

Contents

Volume I: Degradation and Protection of Wood

Contents of Volume II
Preservatives and Preservative Systems

CONTENTS OF VOLUME II (continued)

Wood Deterioration and Its Prevention by Preservative Treatments

Volume I
Degradation and Protection of Wood

1. History of Wood Preservation

ROBERT D. GRAHAM

School of Forestry
Oregon State University, Corvallis, Oregon

1.1 Purpose

The improved utility of wood has been the sole purpose of wood preservation since man first elevated wood on stones to keep it dry or daubed wood with oil of cedar to prevent its decay. Construction that keeps wood dry remains the most important practice for preserving wood, while chemical treatments make possible its use under an ever increasing variety of service conditions.

Preservatives make wood toxic to organisms that use it for food or shelter, fire retardants reduce flame spread and prevent wood from supporting its own combustion, water repellents slow moisture changes in wood, while other chemicals make wood resistant to acids and alkalis or modify its characteristics for special applications. The increasing emphasis on aesthetics portends well for those preservative treatments that enhance its natural beauty. All enable wood to compete successfully in the marketplace with other materials.

Wood preservation can increase greatly the serviceability of wood; yet, we would do well to heed the philosophy on durability of materials expressed by Clark in 1868 [18]:

> Though sometimes, in ignorance, the perishable character of all surrounding things may be lamented, yet on the other hand, it must not be forgotten that perpetual destruction and perpetual renewal are in reality the essential causes of all life, beauty and harmony.

The degradable nature of wood, untreated or treated, may prove in the long run to be its greatest asset.

1.2 Development of Wood Technology, 2000 B.C.–1550 A.D.

Our history of wood preservation begins about 2000 B.C. at the eastern reaches of the Mediterranean where the first plows were being used to

1

cultivate the land, the potter's wheel was coming into widespread use, metallurgy was developing, writing and the alphabet were emerging, and sea trade was well established. The wooden ship had become, and was to remain, the principal means of transportation for nearly 4,000 years.

In the Nile Valley, the early Egyptian belief in life after death led to the erection of huge stone monuments and equally monumental efforts to preserve the bodies of men, birds, and animals. Their efforts to preserve wood by daubing with natural oils were feeble by comparison, but the secret preserving processes of ancient Egypt were too frequently rediscovered by shysters in the eighteenth and nineteenth centuries and, though still secret, haunted the development of wood preservation in Europe and the United States.

The rise of Greece about 1000 B.C. was accompanied by the increasing use of durable woods and construction practices to keep wood dry either by placing wooden pillars on stones or stones on top of pillars to shed water.

By 72 A.D. the records of Pliny the Elder [82], early Roman naturalist, show that a basis for wood technology and preservation had been established. Recognized were the susceptibility of sapwood to "rotting easily" and "liable to wood worm"; durability of cypress, cedar, ebony, lotus, box yew, and juniper that "do not experience decay and age"; that trees under water in the Red Sea continued "free from rot for 200 years" whereas wood in marine waters was attacked by borer-worms that "have a very large head in proportion to their size"; that openings made in wood permit "the chemical properties of the liquid to nourish the wood and keep the joins together"; that sound traveling through a beam of wood, however great its length, can be used to "detect whether the timber is twisted and interrupted by knots"; that teeth of saws are "bent each way in turn so as to get rid of the sawdust"; and that "timber well smeared with cedar oils does not suffer from maggot or decay."

A Roman architect records the use of lees of oil to preserve it from all manner of worms, that pitch is a defense to it against water, and that a wooden tower having been thoroughly bedaubed with alum would not take fire when under siege.

The continued expansion of people and shipping around the shores of the Mediterranean during the next 1,000 years led inevitably to a scarcity of shipbuilding timbers [67]. "A definite policy designed specifically to conserve and increase the oak groves was first formulated between 1470 and 1492" by the Venetians. Since "two hundred oars hardly sufficed for one voyage" and "from ten to twenty thousand oars were cut at a time," procurement of oarwood remained a persistent problem. A supply of beech was secured in 1548, and the Foreman of Oarmakers reported that it "would yield sufficient oarwood if properly preserved" (the preserving process was not described).

1.3 National Survival and Wood Preservation, 1550–1900 A.D.

Marine borers, which have always been and still remain a plague to wood in marine waters, were reported in 1560 to have caused some damage to wooden piles in the earthen dykes of Holland. By 1700, the damage was so extensive as to threaten the inundation of the country. In 1590, 100 ships of the Spanish Armada were destroyed by shipworms in the West Indies.

Meanwhile the Royal Navy of Great Britain was faced with a timber shortage that was aggravated by marine borers and decay. Albion [1] wrote:

> The timber problem was closely related to the durability of ships. Unsatisfactory wood could produce speedy decay. This not only reduced the efficiency of the Navy, but it greatly increased the demand for timber to replace the rotten material. Decay could come from external or internal sources. The external decay was usually produced by marine borers; the internal by dry rot. One of the advantages of oak was its strong tannic or gallic acid, which was distasteful to the teredo navalis, or sea-worm. In spite of this, these marine borers made leaky sieves of dozens of the King's ships by chewing the planking into veritable honeycombs, especially on the southern stations. Sheathing with tar, hair and fir boards was an ineffective remedy practiced for two centuries. Experiments with lead sheathing during the restoration was not satisfactory, but the general introduction of copper sheathing into the Navy during the American Revolution finally put an end to this external decay.
>
> The Navy hit upon no such simple remedy for the internal ravages of the dry rot which was the curse of wooden ships for centuries. Its results were very evident, for it sometimes pulverized whole fleets. There was never a time when at least a few warships were not feeling the effects of its ravages. It was a baffling enemy, and, after hundreds of suggestions and experiments of checking it, dry rot remained unmastered to the end.

The admiral of the flagship *Venerable,* which was to sink the following year (1804), wrote in the ship's log "...it was discovered to be so completely rotten as to be unfit for sea. We have been sailing for the last six months with only a copper sheet between us and eternity."

Albion also noted that "the timber problem was prominent among the causes of delay which helped the cause of American independence."

The interest in wood preservation, stimulated by the frantic search for solutions to the timber problems during the 200 years that national survival rested heavily on the durability of wooden vessels, was stimulated further in the early 1800s and maintained for another 100 years by the search for suitable preservatives for crossties to support the railway systems that spread throughout the world.

1.3.1 Burt (1853)

In London, the meetings of the Institute of Civil Engineers became the forum for papers on wood preservation, and its minutes faithfully presented the extended discussions of those papers. Developments in wood preservation were reviewed by Burt [14], and the discussions continued for three evenings. He noted that oxygen, moisture, and nitrogen favor decomposition of wood, whereas exclusion of water, low temperatures, and preservatives retard or prevent its decomposition; also that dry rot depends upon the growth of fungi which introduce water that causes fermentation, resulting in the slow combustion of wood. Another 20 years would pass before fungi were shown to be the cause, not the result, of decay in wood.

Burt discussed the durability of native and foreign woods, mentioned that in India some woods were destroyed by "white ants" (termites), reviewed the early patents on wood preservation, and described his "creosote works."

The early patents, beginning about 1737, dealt primarily with poisonous substances and coatings to shed water. The first successful preserving process by Kyan (1832), in which wood, rope, and canvas were soaked in dilute water solutions of mercuric chloride, was to be used by the first treating plant in the United States. In the Margary process (1837), wood was soaked in copper sulfate solutions. The Burnett process (1838), in which wood was impregnated under pressure with zinc chloride in water, eventually became the principal method for treating crossties in the U.S. until the 1920s.

Meantime, the use of creosote by Moll (1836) and numerous other inventors saw little application until Bethell's "Specification for Rendering Wood, Cork and Other Articles More Durable," less pervious to water, and less flammable was enrolled in 1839 "in the second year of the reign of Her Majesty Queen Victoria." Various mixtures of solutions were forced into the articles "either by means of hydrostatic or pneumatic pressure, aided in some cases by exhausting the pores of the articles of the atmospheric air contained therein." The application of an initial vacuum prior to impregnation with preservative became the "full-cell" process, and his patent became the basis for the pressure wood-preserving industry of the present.

The Payne process (1841)—in which wood was treated under pressure successively with iron sulphite, then carbonate of soda, to form an insoluble precipitate—did little to protect wood. A double-diffusion treatment for green posts that deposits toxic precipitates would be reported by Baechler [2] a century later.

Burt described his plant, consisting of 4 pressure vessels that treated 10,000 sleepers a week with creosote by the Bethell process, and remarked that the amount of creosote retained by the timber could be obtained by weighing "pieces in the charge or by the use of an accurately adjusted gauge in a reservoir." He condemned the London system of keeping timber in floats, predicted that artificial methods for dessication of timbers would be extensively adopted, and cautioned against the use of too high a temperature.

In response to questions, he suggested that oil treatments could be expedited by "removing the external ring of the timber, or to puncture it with numerous small holes," and he "considered 8 lbs. of creosote per cubic foot a full dose for timber for any situation." Bethell joined the discussion, stating his preference for "porous timber—it absorbed the creosote more readily, was more perfectly saturated," emphasizing that timbers should be thoroughly dried and recommending that "for railway works 7 lbs. per cubic foot would suffice, but that for marine works it was better not to have less than 10 lbs. per cubic foot."

1.3.2 Clark (1868)

Clark [18], discussing the durability of materials before the Institute of Civil Engineers, compared decay of wood to slow combustion and found the ultimate results "strikingly similar." During the discussion of Clark's paper, Boulton reviewed the results of recent marine tests of durability of creosote-treated wood in Holland, Belgium, and France, from which he concluded that "the timber should in all cases be thoroughly dry before creosoting," and "that for timber exposed to the action of marine insects, a much larger quantity of creosote was required than had usually been adopted in England." Tests of preservatives for marine use still continue, and creosote still remains the primary preservative for such harsh service.

1.3.3 Boulton (1884)

Boulton [11] was able to report to the Institute of Civil Engineers that "the process called creosoting, which consists in the injection of coal tar oils, has in this kingdom entirely, and in other countries to a very considerable extent, displaced the other well known processes" for preserving wood. This remarkable paper, "On the Antiseptic Treatment of Timber," reviews the history of wood preservation, theories on deterioration of wood, the origin of creosote, and the development of specifications for creosote, and describes his new process for seasoning wood as part of the pressure-treating process.

Distillation of coal tar, derived from the destructive distillation of coal, provided products that came over very nearly in order of their respective volatilities and inversely as their specific gravities: oils lighter than water, oils heavier than water, and pitch. Creosote, derived from the heavy oils, was and still is used alone for some purposes and mixed with coal tar for other uses. Considerable controversy raged about which was the "best" creosote—high-boiling heavy London oils, intermediate-boiling country oils, or low-boiling Scotch oils that were lightest of all. Some attributed the effectiveness of creosote to the presence of low-boiling fractions— especially carbolic acid, which had been used by Lister for the treatment of wounds. (Lister's adoption of the antiseptic system for surgical purposes in the early 1860s had revolutionized hospital practices.)

An early test with wood chips treated with various fractions of creosote and placed in a "putrefying pit" for 4 years proved the heavy fractions to be best. Extraction of creosote from sleepers that had been in service for years confirmed the absence of light ends. Boulton was a staunch advocate of heavier oils, and favored a specification for creosote requiring that 25 percent of the oil distilling above 600°F be present.

On the nature of decay of wood, Boulton cited Liebig's theory that fermentation was caused by slow combustion and Pasteur's theory of germ infection introduced in 1863. Pasteur's theory was confirmed by Tyndall in 1881, who showed by exposing tubes of agar that germs fall from the air. Boulton reasoned: "Let the comparison be made between the mouths of these tubes and the gaping orifice of a crack produced by the sun in a piece of timber. Through it the germs will descend and, if there is nothing to arrest their action, and if the crack is deeper than that portion of wood charged with antiseptic, they will carry destruction into the center of the log." Internal decay is still a problem in some large wood products.

Boulton was skeptical of metal salts as preservatives because "prolonged experience" had proven them not as permanent as the tar oils in moist situations. He questioned the prevailing theory that metal salts formed insoluble compounds with wood and cited research by Payen which substantiated earlier work by De Gimini in 1848, who had showed that copper sulfate "could be almost entirely removed from wood by repeated washings with water." He thought that copper sulphate might be found "useful in comparatively dry situations or as a protection against dry rot to timber under cover." On the other hand, he was impressed with the Boucherie process (1838) for injecting newly fallen timber with a copper sulphate solution "which was conducted through a pipe from a small reservoir fixed at a height of 30 or 40 feet. The tube was attached by an ingenious arrangement to the end or middle of the log; the antiseptic liquid expelled the sap from the softer parts of the timber, and took its place." Gurd and Lumsden [40] would report in 1967 on the 26-year performance of Douglas-fir poles treated by this process, using different inorganic salt solutions. The Boucherie process, modified to apply a vacuum at the exposed ends of the logs, is still used in Europe.

Boulton attributed the impregnation of wood by vacuum and pressure in a closed iron cylinder to Mr. Briant in 1831 and the improvement of this process to Bethell and his associate, Burt. Attempts to heat wood with vapors of creosote, which had a boiling-point range from a little below 400°F to about 760°F, usually proved disastrous—either the apparatus exploded or the wood was seriously weakened. Boulton noted that strength of wood was reduced at temperatures "much exceeding 250F."

In discussing the seasoning of wood, Boulton emphasized that the "hygrometric condition of timber at the time of injection" was all-important with the creosoting process. He noted that "wood fibre in itself is heavier than water, its specific gravity being generally considered as equal to 1.5, water being 1.0 (Paulet, 1874)." He preferred timbers and sleepers that had been "stacked" for 4–6 months, cautioned that "to subject timber to a dry heat, elevated enough to remove its moisture with the necessary rapidity, will invariably result in injury to the wood," and commented that a vacuum "assists the operation by withdrawing air from the pores of the wood, but it is a mistake to suppose that it has much effect in withdrawing moisture."

To rid the wood of moisture as part of the timber-preserving process without damage to the wood, Boulton described his new method of heating wood in creosote at a little above 212°F under a vacuum: "The water is speedily and effectually removed, and the creosote takes its place. If necessary, pressure can be used to obtain higher retentions." Boulton-drying was to become, and remains, an accepted procedure for drying woods in western United States.

1.3.4 Hartig (1894)

While chemists and engineers were developing preservatives and perfecting equipment for impregnating wood, pathologists were unraveling the nature of the decay process. One of these, Robert Hartig, would be recognized by Hubert in 1931 [55] as the father of forest pathology and as "the first investigator correctly to interpret the true relations of the fungus mycelium and the fruiting body to the decay process in the wood of trees." Hartig [43] wrote: "it was only after botanical science, by the aid of its chief instrument, the microscope, had obtained a clear insight into the normal structure and vital phenomena of plants, and especially after the study of fungi had been prosecuted in the last few decades by a series of distinguished investigators, that the examination of the phenomena of disease in the life of plants could be undertaken with a prospect of success." Success in identifying the cause of decay arrived in the early 1870s.

1.4 Wood Preservation in the United States, 1850–1971 A.D.

1.4.1 Railway expansion

Meanwhile, in the United States, the availability of unlimited supplies of wood and of durable chestnut, white oak, cedar, and bald-cypress slowed development of the wood-preserving industry until the late 1800s. The first commercial plant for Kyanizing wood with mercuric chloride was founded in 1848. The next year gold was found in California, and San Francisco Bay soon became "an immense forest stripped of its foliage" as 800 deserted ships provided a "fertile breeding ground for marine borers" [53]. By 1857 whole wharves were destroyed by shipworms, and replacement wharves met the same fate. Not until 1889 was the treatment of piles with 14 lb/cu ft of creosote initiated. Six years later, concrete was introduced into marine construction.

The gold rush of '49 and the westward movement gave added impetus to the construction of the continental railroad completed in 1869. Maintenance of this vast, expanding system soon led to the recognition of the need for more durable crossties.

In 1885, the year after Boulton presented his paper, the Committee on the Preservation of Timber chaired by Chanute [17] presented its report, 5 years in the making, to the American Society of Civil Engineers. The report recognized "that as a measure of both private and national economy it would soon become necessary for us to resort to the artificial preparation of wood against decay." To determine which methods of preserving timber against decay were most successful and which methods were best adapted to the needs and current practices in this country, the Committee sought facts through correspondence and from patents, pamphlets, and the results of some 147 experiments. "When the information began to come in, the committee found it very confusing. Not only were there the greatest possible differences in opinions which were expressed, but the facts seemed to contradict each other."

The Committee recognized the successful use of creosote in Europe, but was more interested in the less expensive processes using water-soluble chemicals. The dangers of some treatments became all too apparent from one experiment in which green ties were treated by placing a dry powder containing salt, arsenic, and mercuric chloride in holes: "The arsenic and corrosive sublimate effloresced from the ties. Cattle came and licked them for the sake of the salt and they died, so that the track for 10 miles was strewn with dead cattle."

The Committee was doubtful as to the value of double treatments to form insoluble precipitates in wood and of zinc chloride plus glue followed by Tannin (Wellhouse process) to prevent leaching of the zinc chloride. It concluded: "The method to be selected for preserving wood (if any) depends almost wholly upon its proposed subsequent exposure, and that it has been a mistake hitherto to look to a single process for all purposes."

For dry situations, "Kyanizing is a good practice to use" but "caution needs to be observed in carrying it on as corrosive sublimate is a violent poison."

Creosote only was recommended for marine waters at retentions of 10–12 pounds per cubic foot in northern waters and 14–20 pounds in southern waters, with the caution that "the selection of the oil, as well as the quantity, is of importance."

Burnettizing with zinc chloride was recommended as the "advisable process" for railway ties because of the lower cost.

To achieve success in wood preservation, the Committee suggested: (1) that the process should be consistent with the use of the product, (2) the use of the cheaper sappy woods, (3) seasoning as far as practicable, (4) correct steaming of green timber "at such heat and pressure as not to injure the fiber," (5) that enough preservative be used to accomplish the desired results, (6) draining the roadbed for ties, (7) "contract with none but reliable parties," and (8) "let there be no undue haste in carrying on the work." The Committee must have had in mind a previous comment: "The pressure was applied to the operators instead of to the cylinder and as a result, the timber was put through without sufficient preparation, some of it hard frozen in winter."

The Committee's recommendations found ready acceptance. Wood-preserving plants were constructed across the country, and the use of zinc chloride–treated ties mounted steadily upward for over 30 years as railroads spread throughout the land.

Formation of the American Wood-Preservers' Association (AWPA) in 1904 greatly stimulated the interest in wood preservation and the formation of similar organizations in other countries. Its annual meetings became, and remain, the forum for discussion and interchange of ideas by representatives of many disciplines and for standardization of specifications for preservatives and their application to wood. Virtually all significant advances in wood preservation would be published in its *Proceedings*.

The relative merits of zinc chloride and of creosote for crossties were debated by its members for over 20 years. By 1920, when about 100 plants were producing nearly 225 million cubic feet of ties annually, the need for longer tie life and the successful search for methods to reduce cost combined to turn the tide in favor of creosote solutions. Whereas the full-cell process used an initial vacuum before impregnation to obtain the maximum retention of zinc chloride, introduction of the Rueping and Lowry empty-cell processes reduced treating costs by permitting, for the same depth of penetration, lower retentions of creosote containing less expensive coal tar. The Rueping process (patented in 1902) used initial air pressures above atmospheric, whereas the Lowry process (patented in 1904) used atmospheric air pressure before impregnation to "kick back" excess preservative.

In 1913 Goltra [33] reviewed the many processes that had been developed to preserve wood and the development of the industry in Europe and the United States, and presented early statistics on treating plants and ties treated. Thorne [90] showed in 1918 that the average life of ties is obtained when 60 percent are renewed. This relationship, which was found to pertain also to the life of stakes, posts, and poles, provided a basis for predicting the service life of treated wood products in general. Eventually, tie plates were used to distribute the load, tie pads reduced wear, and bituminous coatings helped shed water and reduce checking. Substitutes for ties were tested in increasing numbers and, except for special locations, nearly all were discarded. In 1963 Blew [9] published results of 50 years of tie-service tests by the U.S. Forest Products Laboratory. By 1969, over 1 billion pressure-treated wood crossties supported and cushioned a 300,000-mile network of rails on rock ballast; the average life of the wood tie had increased from 12 years in 1900 to 35 years. Nonetheless, heavier equipment running at higher speeds on heavier multimile lengths of ribbon rail imposed increasingly severe demands on the wood tie and encouraged experimentation on a large scale with prestressed concrete ties.

1.4.2 Accelerated research

Establishment of the U.S. Forest Products Laboratory (USFPL) at the University of Wisconsin in 1910 launched an era of accelerated investigation in wood and wood preservation through "a new kind of venture, unique in a world where at the time the discoveries of scientists and science had not yet been recognized as fundamental to better living and fuller lives for mankind everywhere. This was the first research institution created anywhere in the world for the specific purpose of applying findings of science to the problems of the producers and users of forest products" [80]. Research in wood preservation remained an important segment of its program, and its representatives participated actively in the annual meetings and on committees of the AWPA.

The publication of *Preservation of Structural Timber* by Wiess in 1916 [101], formerly Director, USFPL, brought together and organized the scattered knowledge that had been accumulating on the protection of wood preservation. Bailey's observation that membranes of bordered pits in softwoods possess minute perforations was cited, but about 40 years of debate would continue before the electron microscope revealed in great detail the presence of these openings. Even though the role of these openings, of incrustations blocking them, and of aspiration of the central membrane of bordered pits helped to explain differences in permeability of woods, attempts to improve penetration of liquids into refractory heartwood would continue with little success.

As for the treatment of wood, Wiess believed "that considerable freedom should be given the operator as regards the details of the treatment and that only a few essential features need be required." These included sound wood with reasonable limitation on its characteristics, a clear statement of the composition of the preservative, a maximum temperature, a minimum retention of preservative, and as deep and uniform penetration as possible with complete penetration of sapwood.

Two decades later, *Wood Preservation* by Hunt and Garratt [60] became the principal general textbook in this field, having successfully "attempted to summarize the essential facts contained in the mass of available information and provide an easily accessible and orderly presentation of the fundamental principles." Much of the new information was developed at the USFPL, which Hunt joined soon after its founding and directed from 1946 to 1951. Bell Telephone Laboratories, Inc., the Canadian Forest Products Laboratory, and many other private and public research organizations contributed to the progress in wood preservation.

1.4.2.1 Wood-destroying agents

1.4.2.1.1 Marine borers

The onset of World War I slowed the growth of the wood-preserving industry but not the spread of marine borers in San Francisco Bay— especially the molluscan borers *Bankia* and *Teredo* which, by relentlessly rotating the small but finely serrated bivalve at their heads, riddled the interior of untreated piles [53]. Low rainfall in 1917, accentuated by the removal of river water for municipal supplies, rice culture, and irrigation, permitted salt water and the marine borers to advance up the northern tributaries into areas that had been considered safe for low-cost untreated piles. Continuation of low river discharge into the Bay "prepared conditions for the great destruction of wharves in 1919." By fall of that year "wharves began to collapse, and this continued throughout the following year. Impact of ships which would ordinarily be resisted by flexure of the piling, now caused the latter to break off in large groups; vibrations from various impact loads produced the same result; in some cases the wharves collapsed of their own dead weight. The destruction affected about fifty structures with a damage estimated at $15,000,000." By the end of 1921, marine borers would destroy an additional $6,000,000 of untreated wooden pile structures. The San Francisco Bay Marine Piling Committee, appointed in 1920 to survey the damage, study the distribution and growth of marine borers, and develop information on methods of protecting piles and substitutes, reported its findings annually to the AWPA and published its outstanding *Final Report* in 1927 [53].

The Committee estimated the service life of pressure-creosoted piles to range from 15 to 30 years, depending "partly on the severity of borer attack, but chiefly on the intelligence and care used to protect the integrity of the creosoted shell, throughout the whole course of the piling from the creosoting plant to its place in the structure, and thereafter in preventing pike pole inspections." It recommended that dogs should be unconditionally prohibited except within specified distances of either end of piles; that during driving, care should be taken against the always present danger of checking the piling under the hammer; the use of steel shoes and plates during hard driving; that timber piling should not be braced below the high-water line; and that cut-offs, bolt holes, and framing cuttings should be treated with hot creosote. These recommendations would continue to be ignored, to the detriment of marine timber pile construction.

Creosote protected wood against the shipworms, *Bankia* and *Teredo,* but, in warm-water ports, 4-mm-long crustaceans called *Limnoria* or "gribble" tunneled by the thousands just below the surface of even the best creosote-treated piles, biting off small particles of wood and gradually reducing the pile diameter in the intertidal zone. To solve this problem, extensive experiments have been carried on from the 1950s to the present, using small panels, $\frac{3}{4}$-inch cubes, and toothpick-size specimens. Colley [20], after reviewing the experimental evidence, recommended in 1967: "In areas where *Limnoria tripunctata* is rampant, or where it may be expected to attack, the use of a double treatment for piles, employing the copper-chrome-arsenic salts, or copper-arsenic salts, followed by creosote is apparently essential for economic service life." Hochman [54] concluded that service life of marine piles could be extended by addition of soluble components to creosote, by double treatment, and by use of metal or plastic barriers. Graham and Miller [37] found creosote, creosote-coal tar, and Chemonite (ammoniacal copper arsenite) to be effective for protecting wood in cool-water ports, and concluded that "a dual treatment of creosote or creosote–coal tar and Chemonite merits evaluation for severe exposure conditions." The dual treatment became an AWPA standard for severe marine exposure conditions, and marine testing of these and other treatments continued. Fahlstrom [29] reported promising results by the addition of tributyltin oxide and dieldrin to creosote in 1971.

1.4.2.1.2 Termites

The successful cooperative effort of the San Francisco Bay Marine Piling Committee led to the formation in 1927 of a Termite Investigations Committee to report on "the ravages of termites, which are becoming increasingly destructive, and if possible to prevent the introduction to the Pacific Coast of the more destructive oriental termites." Its extensive report, *Termites and Termite Control* [65], summarized the scientific investigations and technical advice of some 34 authors. Major emphasis was placed on the biology of termites, "with recommendations for prevention and control of termite damage by methods of construction and the use of chemically treated and unpalatable woods." Its recommendations stimulated both the revision of building regulations to reduce termite damage and, in some states, the licensing of persons engaged in the practice of repairing structures damaged by termites.

An International Termite Exposure Test was inaugurated in 1930 to study the effectiveness of different wood preservatives. Specimens were installed in the Panama Canal Zone, Australia, Hawaii, and the Union of South Africa, and the final report was published 27 years later [10]. Meanwhile, chlorinated hydrocarbons such as aldrin, chlordane, and dieldrin when uniformly mixed with soil proved to be effective barriers to termites for longer than 20 years, with but little movement into the adjacent untreated soil [64]. Soil poisoning became a standard procedure for protecting wooden buildings against subterranean termites, whereas plastic and asphaltic-paper ground covers, by reducing movement of water vapor from the soil into the structure above, helped to prevent decay [23]. The drywood termites, which do not require contact with the ground for survival, continued to increase their range.

1.4.2.1.3 Fire

Fire has always been the nemesis of wood construction, but fire retardants that protect wood from fire or prevent wood from supporting its own combustion have contributed greatly to the fire safety of wood. Tried first by the U.S. Navy in 1895, fire retardants were discontinued in 1902 because of their corrosiveness to metal fastenings [75]. Pre-

liminary research by Prince in 1919 [81] produced encouraging results
with inexpensive chemicals. The first of a series of five progress reports
of experiments in fireproofing wood at the USFPL during the 1930s [61]
discussed the shavings, timber, and crib tests used by the City of New
York, then described their fire-tube apparatus in which the loss in weight
of a $\frac{3}{8} \times \frac{3}{4} \times$ 40-inch specimen, suspended in a tube where it was exposed
to the flame of a Bunsen burner, could be determined during the test.
After presenting the second report in 1931, Hunt [62] commented: "It
seems to us that what is needed now more than anything else in the
fireproofing of wood is to take the mystery out of it, to find what facts
underlie the production of a good job of fireproofing, and make them
available to everyone." These comments applied equally as well in 1962
when Eickner [27] reported the plans to increase the research program of
the U.S. Forest Products Laboratory on fire performance of wood by
undertaking "a fundamental program to determine the values for the
basic thermal and chemical parameters for the pyrolysis and combustion
of wood and how these parameters are changed for wood treated with
known fire-retardant salts."

The fifth and final progress report in 1935 [92] discussed results of
tests of 130 single chemicals or combinations of which 17 were investigated intensively. Ammonium sulfate, diammonium phosphate, borax,
and boric acid became the most widely used components of fire-retardant
formulations for indoor use at relative humidities below 85 percent. Zinc
chloride imparted decay resistance and sodium dichromate reduced corrosiveness of some formulations. Under the leadership of Hartman [44],
the AWPA Special Committee on Processing of Wood in 1936 published
an extensive bibliography on the fireproofing of wood.

Strength of wood treated with hygroscopic fire-retardant chemicals has
long been suspect for, under a given set of conditions, strength of fire-
retardant-treated (FRT) wood should be lower by at least the amount
attributable to the increase in moisture content. In 1970 Gerhards [31]
reviewed studies on the effect of fire-retardant treatment on bending
strength of wood and concluded that, "in general, the reductions are
consistent with the 10 percent reduction in design stresses recommended
for fire-retardant treated lumber." Further research would show that kiln
drying, even at relatively low temperatures, could have an adverse effect
on strength of FRT wood.

St. Clair [87] introduced during 1969 the first fire-retardant treatment
for wood in outdoor exposure. Wood is impregnated with a water-
soluble monomer that is converted by heating to a polymer that resists
leaching. Strength tests showed that the treatment had little or no effect
on bending strength.

Although FRT wood was tested in different ways to evaluate its fire characteristics [93], the tunnel test was most widely used. Compared to asbestos-cement board (rating of 0) and red oak (rating of 100), FRT wood was given a fire-hazard classification by Underwriters Laboratories, Inc., based on flame spread, fuel contributed, and smoke developed. Fleischer [30] suggested that wood can be used to best advantage from the standpoint of flammability by employing fire retardants that reduce the rate of flame spread and make fires more easily extinguishable, by taking advantage of the self-insulating qualities of wood through heavy timber construction, by good building design that retards rate of spread of fire, and by the use of automatic water sprinkler systems.

1.4.2.1.4 Fungi

Despite the national attention caused by damage to wooden structures by marine borers, termites, and fire, fungi cause by far the greatest economic loss by discoloring and destroying wood. The worldwide practice of testing potential preservatives first against decay, then against other organisms, attests to the major economic importance of fungi.

The principal decay fungi attacking wood products were described by Hubert [55], Boyce [12], and, in greater detail, by Cartwright and Findlay [16]. In 1965 Duncan and Lombard [25] listed the fungi associated with decay of wood products in the United States and 5 years later Eslyn [28] described the Basidiomycetes associated with decay of utility poles.

Research on the role of diffusible enzyme systems that catalyze the dissolution of cell-wall substance and the progressive changes in properties of wood by white- and brown-rot fungi, spearheaded by Cowling [21], greatly expanded the knowledge of the biochemistry of the decay process. Wilcox [102] reviewed methods for studying the microbiological deterioration of wood, then later described in detail the sequence of changes that occur in wood undergoing attack by white- and brown-rot fungi [103].

Fungi that caused sap stain or blue stain had long plagued the lumber industry by discoloring sapwood of logs soon after trees were cut and of lumber during air seasoning. Huber [55] noted that "attempts to solve the sapstain problem in the United States date back to 1888 when lime in various forms was used on the boards and under the lumber piles." Dipping freshly cut pine lumber in a 5 percent water solution of sodium bicarbonate was initiated in 1903, but the use of a hot solution of sodium carbonate and sodium bicarbonate (soda ash) applied by dipping or spraying soon found favor in the industry. The introduction of water-soluble ethyl mercurials and chlorinated phenols finally provided effective control of sap stain in softwoods in the 1930s. Addition of borax improved sap-stain control in hardwoods. In 1940, *Stains of Sapwood and Sapwood Products and Their Control* by Scheffer and Lindgren [84]

described the stain fungi and results of extensive tests of chemicals and
became the "bible" for stain control. The authors cautioned that "stain-
free logs, prompt treatment, thorough coverage of the stock, adequate
concentration of chemical, protection of the treating solution and treated
stock from rain, and good seasoning methods are essential" for satisfactory results.

Spraying logs with a water emulsion of 0.5 percent gamma isomer
benzene hexachloride plus 2.5 percent sodium pentachlorophenate [63]
became an accepted practice for reducing stain and insect attack.

Upon the advice of the Minimum Standards Advisory Committee,
composed of industry and government personnel, the National Woodwork Manufacturers Association recommended standards for dip and
vacuum treatment of dry, precut millwork with a mineral spirits–pentachlorophenol–water repellent solution to prevent staining and to slow
swelling of windows and doors in use. These recommendations were
incorporated in U.S. Commercial Standard CS 262–63, "Water-repellent
preservative non-pressure treatment for millwork."

1.4.2.2 Wood preservatives

1.4.2.2.1 The search

Development of more effective preservatives demanded an explanation
of how these chemicals protect wood from fungi. Bateman [5] proposed
in 1920 that any preservative must be soluble in water at least to the
extent of producing a toxic water solution. He suggested that the nontoxic higher boiling fractions of creosote acted as a reservoir for the lower
boiling toxic constituents that were slightly water soluble. This stimulated
a series of experiments and discussions on the mechanism of the protection of wood by preservatives and the development of testing methods for
their evaluation.

Early evaluations measured the concentration of chemical required to
inhibit or to kill fungi placed on nutrient agar containing the chemical
(petri-dish test). To improve this screening method, treated wood blocks
were placed on glass supports resting on inoculated nutrient agar (agar-
block test) and the lowest retention of chemical to prevent decay (threshold value) was determined from loss of weight by the blocks. Von
Schrenk [96] reviewed the toxicity determinations from a practical standpoint and urged successfully in 1933 that the same procedures, same fungi,
and same strain of fungi be used so that results obtained by different
investigators could be compared.

Noting the rapid decay of wood in contact with soils while conducting
termite tests, Leutritz [68] placed treated wood blocks on feeder strips of
pine sapwood over moist soil inoculated with a decay fungus and mea-

sured the weight loss. He found that higher chemical retentions were needed to protect wood than were indicated by petri-dish tests and obtained good agreement between laboratory and field tests. The soil-block tests underwent extensive trials and improvements by Richards and Addoms [83] and Duncan and Richards [26] in the late 1940s and a series of developmental studies by Duncan [24] in the 1950s. Meanwhile, in the early 1950s, Colley [19] undertook a detailed review of the evaluation of preservatives and presented a correlation of the results obtained from soil-block tests, outdoor exposure tests on stakes and on pole-diameter posts as well as pole line experience. The soil-block method for evaluating preservatives was later adopted by AWPA and the American Society for Testing and Materials (ASTM). Respirometric methods that measured changes in concentration of carbon dioxide or of oxygen during decay of small wood blocks continued to receive attention as a means of accelerating laboratory testing of preservatives.

Although laboratory tests permitted rapid screening of preservatives, field tests provided a more rigorous and realistic evaluation. The USFPL began installing untreated and treated fence posts in 1908, and many other organizations initiated similar post tests in the years to follow. Extensive post service test results by these organizations were published in 1966 [66]. The USFPL later adopted 2 × 4-inch stakes for much of its routine testing. Bell Telephone Laboratories, Inc., began tests of pole-diameter posts in 1925 as one step of a program to develop adequately treated clean poles. The other steps included soil-block tests, $\frac{3}{4}$-inch square stakes, posts, and poles in test plots, and pole service records. Results of the 25 years of testing were discussed by Lumsden in 1952 [70]. To accelerate outdoor tests and to simulate round timbers, Waterman and Williams [100] used treated saplings. After intensive testing by many research organizations, tests with stakes and posts were adopted as standards by AWPA and ASTM.

1.4.2.2.2 New preservatives

From the search for preservatives that could provide adequate yet clean wood products, the chlorinated phenols began to emerge in the early 1930s. Hatfield [45,46], in petri-dish tests employing both decay and stain fungi, reported toxicity limits for tetrachlorophenol, its sodium salt, and pentachlorophenol. In a discussion of the practical significance of toxicity data, Bateman and Baechler [6] reported: "Of all the compounds that were found to kill our test organism, tetrachlorophenol and pentachlorophenol are the cheapest source of toxic action." Encouraged by these laboratory findings, they initiated service tests of 100 posts treated with a 3 percent solution and another 100 with a 5 percent solution of penta-

chlorophenol. The issuance of Federal Specification for Wood Preservative; Pentachlorophenol, TT–W0570, 1947, prompted Hatfield [47] in 1949
to declare "penta of age."

Used in heavy petroleum carriers, penta began replacing creosote for
poles, timbers, lumber, and other products in steadily increasing quantities
while penta in mineral spirits, with or without water repellents, provided
clean and, if properly applied, paintable wood products.

The national beautification program of the '60s gave added impetus to
the development of clean, paintable treatments for wood. Transmission
and distribution pole lines that once bespoke progress as they brought
electrical energy to the most remote areas, now became unsightly blem-
ishes on the landscape. Unable to replace a multibillion-dollar investment, utilities sought new rights-of-way hidden from the general public,
sculptured the vegetation along existing rights-of-way to make them less
noticeable, cleaned up the maze of wires and arms that cluttered poles,
created new pole designs, and turned to sky blue, hacienda grey, green,
or mottled poles that blended into the background.

To help meet the evolving appearance criteria, Henry [52] reported a
new process for impregnating wood with penta and a co-solvent in liq-
uified petroleum gas called Cellon® and, in 1971, Davies [22] documented
the durability of poles treated by this process. Penta carried in methylene
chloride soon came into commercial use. Waterborne preservatives with
superior leach resistance such as ammoniacal copper arsenite (ACA) and
chromated copper arsenate (CCA) that imparted a natural greenish-
brown color to wood were approved for poles by the AWPA. All provided clean products that could be colored, if necessary, to meet varying
environmental situations and helped to ease the demand that power lines
go underground.

Copper-8-quinolinolate, the only preservative to be approved for wood
in contact with foodstuffs, was introduced by Goldfarb in 1962 [32].

1.4.2.2.3 Penetration and retention requirements

Acceptance of pressure-treated wood products customarily had been
based on minimum requirements for penetration and retention of the
preservative, which varied with the product and service conditions. Penetration, measured on small cores removed with a hollow borer, was easily
determined with dark-colored preservatives while with others that imparted little or no color to wood, special chemicals caused a differential
staining of the treated portion. Retention of preservative was based on
the amount of preservative retained by a charge, as measured by gauging
tanks that contained the preservative before and after treatment with
appropriate corrections made for temperature differences (gauge reten-

tion). Retentions among pieces within a charge could vary greatly, depending on their sapwood content, moisture content, permeability, and other factors beyond the control of the plant operator.

In 1952 Lumsden [70] showed that the incidence of decay in pole-size posts treated with creosote to gauge retentions of 6–8 lbs/cu ft was correlated with their individual retentions as determined by assaying samples after treatment. To provide serviceable poles, he suggested that "the only answer is to specify charge retentions by some means that insure as far as practicable that 8.0 pounds actually is present in the wood itself. Such a plan entails results-type specifications." Hearn [51] noted that for a short period around 1930, assay retentions had been required in Douglas-fir poles based on the extraction of wood samples obtained with a brace and bit. Both he and Baechler [3] reported only fair agreement between gauge and assay retentions of creosote in pine poles, which led Hearn to recommend in 1954 that results-type specification be used for poles.

Interest in such specification mounted steadily; X-ray emission spectroscopy was introduced in 1957 [105] and later adopted for rapid analysis of treated wood and treating solutions. As data were developed, assay retentions were specified for designated zones in different products. By 1970 assay requirements were incorporated in standards for most treated wood products, usually at retentions of at least twice the threshold retentions found necessary to protect wood in laboratory tests.

1.4.2.3 Treating practices

1.4.2.3.1 Treating conditions

Research on temperature changes in wood initiated by Hunt in 1915 [57] was continued and expanded by MacLean to an intensive study of treating variables, the results of which were published regularly in the AWPA Proceedings and condensed in *Preservative Treatment of Wood by Pressure Processes* [71].

The damaging effect of steaming was authenticated frequently, and, over a 50-year period, AWPA treating standards gradually reduced both steaming temperatures and duration. The compromise between steaming—a rapid method for heating wood—and reduction in strength of wood gradually favored this increasingly valuable raw material. Steaming of Douglas-fir was prohibited or limited severely in the 1920s, but its effect on southern pine was not realized fully until strength tests were initiated under an ASTM Wood Pole Research Program. Results of this program published in 1960 [104] reported bending strength reductions of 20–40 percent for steamed pine poles, smaller strength reductions with diminished steaming temperatures and durations, reductions of 10 percent in strength of Boulton-dried Douglas-fir, and no reductions in strength for air-seasoned lodgepole pine and western redcedar. Steaming temperature and duration for pine poles were reduced in AWPA standards to prevent such severe losses in strength.

1.4.2.3.2 Seasoning

Air seasoning, the least expensive drying method where suitable climates prevail, posed a decay hazard to sapwood in the humid southern states and was limited to a portion of the year in the northern states. In all areas, it required large inventories. Boulton-drying, long an accelerated drying method in the Northwest, tied up valuable retort time with seasoning cycles of 40–60 hours for large green poles and piles. Vapor drying of wood at elevated temperatures in hydrocarbon solvents, introduced by Hudson in 1950 [56], tied up less retort time but has been limited largely to the drying of ties. To reduce costs, Vaughan [95] introduced controlled air seasoning by which poles were dried at low temperatures in low-cost kilns. Meanwhile, kiln drying of lumber and plywood treated with waterborne preservatives and fire retardants created additional interest in kiln drying of poles, ties, and piles. By the mid-1960s the dry kiln had become an indispensable part of many pressure-treating plants.

1.4.2.3.3 Incising

While the voracious marine borers were riddling piles in San Francisco Bay, holes were being punched in timbers near Portland, Oregon, to facilitate penetration of preservative into Pacific Coast Douglas-fir. By the early 1920s a staggered incising pattern was being made with equipment consisting of two vertical and two horizontal drums with chisellike teeth extending about 1 inch. By exposing end-grain for longitudinal flow of preservatives, incising permitted heartwood to be penetrated on side surfaces to depths up to $\frac{3}{4}$ inch. The Greenlee incisor, which became standard equipment at western plants, opened the markets for pressure-treated ties and timbers of the relatively thin-sapwood western species and, later, was used to improve treatment and reduce checking of eastern and southern hardwood ties.

Incising equipment that punched 3-foot-long rows of slits in the groundline zone of cedar poles as they were intermittently rotated aided the penetration of preservative into the sapwood during treatment by the hot-cold bath (Thermal) process. Butt-treating incised cedar poles with creosote or with penta in heavy petroleum more than doubled the average service life of 15–20 years of these naturally durable heartwood species.

Since "shell rot" of the untreated sapwood in moist climates created a hazard for linemen, full-length treatment of cedar poles was adopted after World War II. Flooding the untreated tops of butt-treated cedar poles in service with a 10 percent penta-petroleum solution later proved effective for arresting shell rot and in reducing the climbing hazard it caused.

By the late 1950s, full-length incising of poles had become a common practice. Incising devices used with peeling machines made incisions in the peeled wood as the poles were rotated. Peeled poles were pushed tip first through a multiwheeled machine that produced parallel rows of incisions that favored formation of many narrow, long checks. Incisions varied up to 1 inch in depth.

As the use of electricity surged ever upward during the 1960s, longer and still longer poles were required from the Pacific Northwest, which could supply the 70- to 125-foot lengths needed. Since the $1\frac{1}{2}$–2 inch average sapwood depth of the long Pacific Coast Douglas-fir poles left a large central core of untreated heartwood, 2.5-inch-deep incisions [8] and through perforations ($\frac{7}{16}$ inch in diameter) [13,38] were devised that permitted deep treatment of the critical groundline zone. Intermountain Douglas-fir (Cascades to the Rocky Mountains) was not deeply incised because its heartwood is refractory to treatment [73].

1.4.2.3.4 Kerfing

To minimize checking beyond the treated zone, a kerf to the center was made along the bottom of round, double-tapered Douglas-fir spar cross-arms [36], and from the butt end to 5 or more feet above the groundline of Douglas-fir poles [34]. In addition, 2 opposed $1\frac{1}{2}$-inch-deep kerfs extending about 18 inches down from the tops of the poles helped to prevent checking through predrilled bolt holes during treating.

1.4.2.4 Maintenance of treated wood structures

The steady increase in number and age of treated wood structures, and rising costs of labor and materials for replacements, focused attention on their maintenance, especially of large members such as poles that were used in great numbers and represented a major capital investment. Pole maintenance programs were developed by the Bell System in 1931, the Rural Electrification Administration in 1957, and by other pole users. The initiation in 1960 of wood pole conferences throughout the United States, some of which were continued at about 3-year intervals, increased the awareness of the need for pole maintenance programs. The increased interest was accompanied by a corresponding increase in research on new methods for increasing the service life of poles in line. In 1962 Mothers-

head and Graham [76] surveyed the literature and listed 406 publications
to show relationships that exist between the many disciplines involved and
to provide a basis for research necessary to develop improved methods
for inspecting and treating poles in service.

1.4.2.4.1 Inspection

Visual inspection told much about the condition of wood. Soft,
crumbly wood was evidence of advanced decay, a sawdust mound was a
sure sign of carpenter ants, round or elliptical holes of emerging adult
wood-boring beetles indicated internal damage, discarded wings or
earthen tunnels signified the presence of subterranean termites, and wood-
pecker holes were all too obvious.

Internal decay was detected by jabbing wood with pointed metal bars,
sounding with a hammer, by forcing a heavy needle into wood, and by
removing wood with a brace and bit or hollow borers. Too frequently,
inspection techniques left untreated wood exposed, thereby causing still
more deterioration.

Recognition of the need for standardized inspection procedures led to
the publication of "Recommendations for the Inspection of Treated
Poles in Service" in 1940 [41], which included (1) visual examination from
roof to ground, (2) sounding to locate internal decay, (3) examination
below-ground, (4) boring suspected areas for internal decay, and (5) exploration to determine the extent of decay. From decay-allowances
tables, the inspector could determine if the remaining sound wood was
sufficient to sustain the imposed load.

To speed and improve the reliability of inspection of cedar poles,
Detroit Edison Company financed development of a semiportable X-ray
unit during the 1940s which they used to inspect cedar poles [89]. The
application of radiography to inspection of wood products was discussed
by Mothershead and Stacey in 1965 [77]. Radiographs of Douglas-fir
poles were found to provide a good visual record of their internal condition [39].

Miller, Taylor, and Popeck [72] reported in 1965 the development of a
sonic testing device based on the delay in the passage of a sound wave
across a defective pole. They believed that the sonic device would replace
hammer sounding completely and eliminate 70 percent of X-ray testing.
Parrott [79] tested the Pol-Tek, the commercial version of the sonic device, and recommended its use for inspecting poles. Since the sonic device detects marked changes in density, boring of poles found to be defective is desirable to determine the nature of the defect. Walden and Trussell
[97] reported the results of 4 years of commercial sonic inspection of
marine piles in which sound waves transmitted by water to the pile at
one point are picked up at a higher point.

Although visual, boring, sonic, and X-ray inspection could detect advanced decay, Graham and Mothershead [76] believed that a bioassay procedure warranted consideration as an important phase of the inspection process. Growth of decay fungi from wood cores incubated on nutrient media permits detection of early stages of decay in poles that otherwise would be reported as sound. Supplemental treatments could be initiated before significant losses in wood strength take place.

1.4.2.4.2 Supplemental treatments

Early treatments for poles in service, many of which originated in Europe [58], were applied first in the United States to untreated cedar poles, then to older treated poles as preservative was depleted from the groundline zone. The usual procedure included digging out the pole to a depth of about 18 inches, scraping off the decayed wood, brushing the new wood surface with creosote or mixtures of creosote and other preservatives, and then backfilling around the pole. Some utilities preferred to char the surface of the pole before applying the preservative, to mix preservative with the backfill, or to pour preservative around the base of the pole.

The Cobra process injected preservative to depths of $1\frac{1}{2}$ inches or more through a hollow tooth ingeniously designed to leave the water-soluble preservative in the wood when the tooth was withdrawn. A long hollow handle containing the preservative provided leverage and a chain provided a fulcrum for the tooth beneath. The treated zone was coated with creosote before backfilling.

Eventually, asphalt paper or polyethylene film were wrapped around the preservative-treated groundline zone of poles to retard loss of the chemicals, and bandages incorporating the preservative in or on a wrapping material were developed for rapid application. Leutritz and Lumsden [69] found that formulations having a minimum of 15 percent creosote, 10 percent penta, and 15 percent sodium fluoride appeared most promising for application to pressure-treated southern pine poles.

Groundline treatments also were evaluated by Panek et al. in 1961 [78] and Smith and Cockcroft in 1967 [86], who found that bandage-type treatments increased preservative concentrations in the outer $\frac{1}{4}-\frac{1}{2}$ inch while the Cobra process gave deeper sapwood protection.

In recent investigations by Hand, Lindgren, and Wetsch [42], soil fumigants such as Vapam and chloropicrin poured into holes in Douglas-fir and western redcedar poles near the groundline appeared promising for arresting internal decay. Subsequent studies by Graham, Corden, and Scheffer [35] confirmed the ability of such fumigants to reduce greatly the population of decay fungi in distribution and transmission poles for at least several years.

1.4.2.5 Reviews of the literature

The appearance of the *Annual Report on Wood Protection, 1935* marked the beginning of a series of comprehensive reviews of the literature; the latest report abstracts literature for the years 1959–60 [7]. The first edition of the well-known textbook, *Wood Preservation,* by Hunt and Garratt was published in 1938 and the third edition in 1967 [60]. Van Groenou *et al.* [94] published in 1951 a worldwide summary of research in wood preservation and of the organizations engaged in research during the past 50 years.

In 1952 Hunt [59] presented a concise review, "A century of Engineering in Wood Preservations," to the American Society of Mechanical Engineers. Wood preservation figures prominently in reviews of "Materials of Construction: Wood" by Baechler in 1956 [4] and Stamm and Baechler in 1958 [88]. In 1960 Sedziak [85] summarized "New Preservatives and Treatment Methods" for the Fifth World Forestry Congress. Meanwhile, the Forest Products Research Society undertook to survey activities in major segments of the forest industries. During the latter 1950s and early 1960s, surveys on wood preservation were published in its *Journal* by Hatfield [48,49,50], Walters [98,99], Troxell [91], and Carter [15]. In 1967 Miller and Graham [74] reviewed research in wood preservation in the United States and Canada for the American Wood-Preservers' Association.

1.5 International Developments

Research by organizations throughout the world has contributed greatly to knowledge on the preservation of wood. The emergence, during recent years, of groups to encourage international cooperative programs on wood protection has been especially noteworthy.

1.5.1 International Union of Forest Research Organizations (IUFRO)

Its Working Group, Wood Protection, deals with the biology of organisms responsible for the deterioration of wood, chemistry of preservatives, and the technology of treating methods. Its objectives are: (1) to assess the present state of knowledge in the field of wood protection and to summarize worldwide current research; (2) to indicate the areas of needed research and their relative priorities; (3) to provide assistance in international standardization on methods of test and application of wood preservatives; and (4) to arrange for and participate in international conferences, to foster personal exchange of research results and needs, and to organize cooperation in research.

1.5.2 International Research Group on Wood Preservation (IRGWP)

The IRGWP was an outgrowth of the Organization for Economic Co-operation and Development. Its objectives are: (1) to gather information on the occurrence, distribution, and succession of deteriorating organisms of timber in soil, above soil, in the open, in buildings, and in fresh water; (2) to gather experience on the dependence of species and strains of organisms causing deterioration or loss in value on nutrient and climatic factors; (3) to contribute to the fundamental principles underlying comparative standards, methods, and their international unification, and to the evaluation of results obtained in laboratory and field tests; (4) to compare, on an international basis, results and experience on the efficacy and duration of wood preservatives under different conditions; and (5) to investigate the dependence of the efficacy of wood preservatives on wood species and treatment methods.

1.5.3 European Committee for the Homologation of Wood Preservatives

The aim of this committee, composed of representatives from several European countries, essentially is to agree on common methods for the acceptance and approval of wood preservatives. Its work compliments the fundamental work of the International Research Group on Wood Preservation.

1.5.4 Comité Européenne de Co-ordination des Normes

This committee is concerned with the preparation of unified methods for testing wood preservatives.

The development of international cooperation in wood preservation bodes well for the wise utilization of the wood resources of the world and for an improved standard of living for all mankind.

REFERENCES

1. Albion, R.G. 1926. *Forests and Sea Power: The Timber Problem of the Royal Navy, 1652–1862.* Vol. XXIX, Harvard Economic Studies. Harvard Univ. Press, Cambridge, Mass.
2. Baechler, R.H. 1941. "Resistance to leaching and decay protection of various precipitates formed in wood by double diffusion." *Proc., Am. Wood-Preservers' Assoc.* 37:23–44.
3. Baechler, R.H. 1954. "Relations between gage retention and amounts of creosote extractable from borings taken from treated pine poles." *Proc., Am. Wood-Preservers' Assoc.* 50:113–19.
4. Baechler, R.H. 1956. "Materials of construction: Wood." *Ind. Engr. Chem.* 48(9):1798–1801.

5. Bateman, E. 1920. "A theory on the mechanism of the protection of wood by preservatives." *Proc., Am. Wood-Preservers' Assoc.* 251–55.
6. Bateman, E. and Baechler, R.H. 1937. "Some toxicity data and their practical significance." *Proc., Am. Wood-Preservers' Assoc.* 33:91–104.
7. Becker, G. and Theden, G. 1969. *Annual Report on Wood Protection, 1959-60.*
   Springer-Verlag, Berlin.
8. Best, C.W. and Martin, G.E. 1969. "Deep treatment in Douglas fir poles." *Proc., Am.
   Wood-Preservers' Assoc.* 65:223–26.
9. Blew, J.O. Jr. 1963. "A half century of service testing crossties." *Proc., Am. Wood-
   Preservers' Assoc.* 59:138–46.
10. Blew, J.O. Jr. and Johnston, H.R. 1957. "An international termite exposure test—
    twenty-third and final report." *Proc., Am. Wood-Preservers' Assoc.* 53:225–34.
11. Boulton, S.B. 1884. "On the antiseptic treatment of timber." *Minutes of Proceedings,*
    Institution of Civil Engineers (London). 78:97–211.
12. Boyce, J.H. 1938. *Forest Pathology,* McGraw-Hill Book Co., N.Y. Revised 1961.
13. Brown, D.L. 1964. "Experience with the assay method of inspection on Douglas fir
    poles." *Proc., Am. Wood-Preservers' Assoc.* 60:98–104.
14. Burt, H.P. 1853. "On the nature and properties of timber, with descriptive particulars
    of several methods, now in use, for its preservation from decay." *Minutes of the
    Proceedings,* Institute of Civil Engineers (London). 12:206–43.
15. Carter, R.M. 1962. "Progress in wood preservation." *Forest Prod. J.* 12(4):155–57.
16. Cartwright, K.S.G. and Findlay, W.P.K. 1950. *Decay of Timber and Its Prevention.*
    Chemical Publishing Co., N.Y.
17. Chanute, O. 1885. "The preservation of timber: Report of Committee on the Preserva-
    tion of Timber." *Trans. Am. Soc. of Civil Eng.* 14:247–360.
18. Clark, E. 1868. "On engineering philosophy: The durability of materials." *Minutes of
    Proceedings,* Institution of Civil Engineers (London). 27:554–81.
19. Colley, R.H. 1953. "The Evaluation of Wood Preservatives." Monograph No. 2118,
    Bell Telephone System.
20. Colley, R.H. 1967. "Observations on experimental evidence of the effectiveness of
    creosote and creosote–coal tar solutions in preventing attack on marine piling by
    Limnoria tripunctata." *Proc., Am. Wood-Preservers' Assoc.* 63:151–62.
21. Cowling, E.B. 1961. "Comparative biochemistry of the decay of sweetgum sapwood
    by white-rot and brown-rot fungi." USDA Tech. Bull. No. 1258.
22. Davies, D.L. 1971. "Durability of poles treated with penta in an LP gas system."
    Proc., Am. Wood-Preservers' Assoc. 67:37–42.
23. Diller, J.D. 1958. "Moisture-barrier performance of general covers in basementless
    homes." Forest Res. Note No. 85, Northeastern Forest Exp. Sta.
24. Duncan, C.G. 1958. "Studies of the methodology of soil-block testing." U.S. Forest
    Serv., Forest Prod. Lab. Rept. No. 2114.
25. Duncan, C.G. and Lombard, F.F. 1965. "Fungi associated with principal decay in
    wood products in the United States." U.S. Forest Serv. Res. Paper WO–4.
26. Duncan, C.G. and Richards, C.A. 1948. "Methods for evaluating wood preserva-
    tives: Weathered impregnated wood blocks." *Proc., Am. Wood-Preservers' Assoc.*
    44:259–64.
27. Eickner, H.W. 1962. "Basic research on the pyrolysis and combustion of wood." *Forest
    Prod. J.* 7(4):194–99.
28. Eslyn, W.E. 1970. "Utility pole decay. II. Basidiomycetes associated with decay in
    poles." *Wood Sci. Tech.* 4:97–103.
29. Fahlstrom, G.B. 1971. "Additives to creosote for improved performance in marine
    piling." *Proc., Am. Wood-Preservers' Assoc.* 66:131–39.

30. Fleischer, H.O. 1960. "The performance of wood in fire." U.S. Forest Prod. Lab. Rept. No. 2202.
31. Gerhards, C.C. 1970. "Effect of fire-retardant treatment on bending strength of wood." U.S. Forest Serv., Forest Prod. Lab. Rept. No. 145.
32. Goldfarb, S. 1962. "Copper-8-quinolinolate (solubilized) as a wood preservative." *Proc., Am. Wood-Preservers' Assoc.* 58:166–69.
33. Goltra, W.F. 1913. "History of wood preservation." *Proc., Am. Wood-Preservers' Assoc.* 9:178–202.
34. Graham, R.D. 1968. "Special handling to insure better service: Deep incising and kerfing." *Proc.,* Wood Pole Inst., Colorado State Univ. 101–10.
35. Graham, R.D., Corden, M.E. and Scheffer, T.C. 1969–1971. "Improved Serviceability of Wood Products Used by Bonneville Power Administration: Reports of Work Accomplished from July 1, 1969 to September 30, 1971." Unpublished. Forest Research Lab., Oregon State Univ.
36. Graham, R.D. and Estep, E.M. 1966. "Effect of incising and saw kerfs on checking of pressure-treated Douglas-fir spar crossarms." *Proc., Am. Wood-Preservers' Assoc.* 62:155–58.
37. Graham, R.D. and Miller, D.J. 1968. "Ten-year exposure tests of pressure-treated Douglas fir and southern pine panels in U.S. coastal waters." *Proc., Am. Wood-Preservers Assoc.* 64:61–68.
38. Graham, R.D., Miller, D.J. and Kunesh, R.H. 1969. "Pressure treatment and strength of deeply perforated Pacific Coast Douglas fir poles." *Proc., Am. Wood-Preservers' Assoc.* 65:234–41.
39. Graham, R.D. and Mothershead, J.S. 1967. "Inspecting and treating western redcedar and douglas fir poles in service." Info. Cir. No. 21, Forest Research Lab., Oregon State Univ.
40. Gurd, J.M. and Lumsden, G.Q. 1967. "Twenty-six year performance of Douglas fir poles Boucherie treated with several inorganic salt solutions." *Proc., Am. Wood-Preservers' Assoc.* 63:80–87.
41. Haenseler, H.A., Chairman. 1940. "Recommendations for the inspection of treated poles in service." *Proc., Am. Wood-Preservers' Assoc.* 36:175–78.
42. Hand, O.F., Lindgren, P.A. and Wetsch, A.F. 1970. "The control of fungal decay and insects in transmission poles by gas phase treatment." Bonneville Power Adm., Vancouver, B.C.
43. Hartig, R. 1894. *Textbook of the Diseases of Trees.* Macmillan & Co. (translation from German by W. Sommerville).
44. Hartman, E.F., Chairman. 1936. "Report of special committee on processing of wood." *Proc., Am. Wood-Preservers' Assoc.* 425–28.
45. Hatfield, I. 1931. "Recent experiments with chemicals suggested for wood preservation." *Proc., Am. Wood-Preservers' Assoc.* 304–14.
46. Hatfield, I. 1932. "Further experiments with chemicals suggested as possible wood preservatives." *Proc., Am. Wood-Preservers' Assoc.* 330–39.
47. Hatfield, I. 1949. "Pentachlorophenol comes of age." *Proc., Am. Wood-Preservers' Assoc.* 45:84–89.
48. Hatfield, I. 1956. "Advances in wood preservation in 1954–1955." *Forest Prod. J.* 6(2):59–62.
49. Hatfield, I. 1957. "Activities in the field of wood preservation in the United States in 1955–56." *Forest Prod. J.* 7(2):54–60.
50. Hatfield, I. 1958. "Report on wood preservation activities, 1956–57." *Forest Prod. J.* 8(2):58–62.

51. Hearn, A.H. 1954. "Creosote retention as determined by toluene extraction of treated wood." *Proc., Am. Wood-Preservers' Assoc.* 50:122–33.
52. Henry, W.T. 1963. "A new method for impregnating wood with preservatives." *Proc., Am. Wood-Preservers' Assoc.* 59:68–76.
53. Hill, C.L. and Kofoid, C.A. 1927. *Marine Borers and their Relation to Marine Construction on the Pacific Coast: Final Report of the San Francisco Bay Marine Piling Committee.* Univ. of California Press, Berkeley, Calif.
54. Hochman, H. 1967. "Creosoted wood in a marine environment—A summary report." *Proc., Am. Wood-Preservers' Assoc.* 63:138–50.
55. Hubert, E.E. 1931. *An Outline of Forest Pathology.* John Wiley & Sons, Inc. N.Y.
56. Hudson, M.S. 1950. "Drying lumber by the vapor process." *Proc., Am. Wood-Preservers' Assoc.* 46:209–39.
57. Hunt, G.M. 1915. "Temperature changes in wood under treatment." *Proc., Am. Wood-Preservers' Assoc.* 11:85–99.
58. Hunt, G.M. 1927. "Notes on wood preservation and utilization in Europe." *Proc., Am. Wood-Preservers' Assoc.* 23:107–49.
59. Hunt, G.M. 1952. "A century of engineering in wood preservation." *Reprint,* The Am. Soc. of Mech. Engr., Paper No. 52-F-22.
60. Hunt, G.M. and Garratt, G.A. 1938. *Wood Preservation.* McGraw-Hill Book Co., N.Y. Revised 1953 and 1967.
61. Hunt, G.M., Truax, T.R. and Harrison, C.A. 1930. "Fire resistance of wood treated with zinc chloride and diammonium phosphate." *Proc., Am. Wood-Preservers' Assoc.* 26:130–59.
62. Hunt, G.M., Truax, T.R. and Harrison, C.A. 1931. "Additional experiments in fire-proofing wood." *Proc., Am. Wood-Preservers' Assoc.* 27:104–28.
63. Johnston, H.R. and Kowal, R.J. 1949. "New insecticides for the prevention of attack by ambrosia beetles on logs and lumber." *Southern Lumberman* 119:183–8.
64. Johnson, H.R., Smith, V.K. and Beal, R.H. 1971. "Chemicals for subterranean termite control: results of long-term tests." *J. Econ. Entomology* 64(3):754–48.
65. Kofoid, C.A., ed. 1934. *Termites and Termite Control.* Univ. of California Press, Berkeley, Calif.
66. Kulp, J.W., Chairman. 1966. "Report of Committee U–5, post service records." *Proc., Am. Wood-Preservers' Assoc.* 62:60–130.
67. Lane, F.C. 1934. *Venetian Ships and Shipbuilding of the Renaissance.* The Johns Hopkins Press, Baltimore, Md.
68. Leutritz, J.Jr. 1946. "A wood-soil contact culture technique for laboratory study of wood-destroying fungi, wood decay and wood preservation." *Bell System Tech. J.* 25(1):102–35.
69. Leutritz, J.Jr. and Lumsden, G.Q. 1962. "The groundline treatment of standing southern pine poles." *Proc., Am. Wood-Preservers' Assoc.* 58:79–86.
70. Lumsden, G.Q. 1952. "A quarter century of evaluation of wood preservatives in poles and posts at the Gulfport test plot." *Proc. Am. Wood-Preservers' Assoc.* 48:27–47.
71. MacLean, J.D. 1952. *Preservative Treatment of Wood by Pressure Methods.* USDA Agri. Handbook No. 40.
72. Miller, B.D., Taylor, F.L. and Popeck, R.A. 1965. "A sonic method for detecting decay in wood poles." *Proc., Am. Wood-Preservers' Assoc.* 61:109–13.
73. Miller, D.J. and Graham, R.D. 1963. "Treatability of Douglas fir from western United States." *Proc., Am. Wood-Preservers' Assoc.* 59:218–22.
74. Miller, D.J. and Graham, R.D. 1965. "Research in wood preservation in United States and Canada." *Proc., Am. Wood-Preservers' Assoc.* 63:65–79.
75. Moreel, B. 1939. "The Navy's experience with the use of treated wood." *Proc., Am. Wood-Preservers' Assoc.* 35:149–53.

76. Mothershead, J.S. and Graham, R.D. 1962. "Inspection and treatment of poles in service: A survey. Rept. No. P-6, Forest Research Lab., Oregon State Univ.

77. Mothershead, J.S. and Stacey, S.S. 1965. "Applicability of radiography to inspection of wood products." *Proc.,* Second Symposium on Non-destructive Testing of Wood, Spokane. 307-36.

78. Panek, E., Blew, J.O.Jr. and Baechler, R.H. 1961. "Study of groundline treatments applied to five pole species." U.S. Forest Serv., Forest Prod. Lab. Rept. No. 2227.

79. Parrott, R.E. 1969. "An evaluation of the 'pole-tek' sonic decay-detector." Unpublished. Forest Products Rept. No. 265, Forest Products Lab., Forest Research Inst. New Zealand.

80. Peterson, E.L. 1960. "Forestry research and creative forestry." In *The Forest Products Laboratory, A Golden Anniversary Record.*

81. Prince, R.E. 1914. "Preliminary work in fire proofing wood." *Proc., Am. Wood-Preservers' Assoc.* 10:158-72.

82. Rackham, H. 1945. *Pliny: Natural History.* Vol. 4. Harvard Univ. Press, Cambridge, Mass.

83. Richards, C.A. and Addoms, R.M. 1947. "Laboratory methods for evaluating wood preservatives: Preliminary comparison of agar and soil culture techniques using impregnated wood blocks." *Proc., Am. Wood-Preservers' Assoc.* 43:41-56.

84. Scheffer, T.C. and Lindgren, R.M. 1940. "Stains of sapwood and sapwood products and their control." USDA Tech. Bull. No. 714.

85. Sedziak, H.P. 1960. "New preservation and treatment methods." *Reprint,* Paper presented at the Fifth World Forestry Congress, Seattle.

86. Smith, D.H. and Cockroft, R. 1967. "The remedial treatment of telephone and electric transmission poles." *Reprint* Wood, September, October, and November.

87. St. Clair, W.E. 1969. "Leach resistant fire-retardant treated wood for outdoor exposure." *Proc., Am. Wood-Preservers' Assoc.* 65:250-59.

88. Stamm, A.J. and Baechler, R.H. 1958. "Materials of construction: Wood." *Ind. Engr. Chem.* 50(9):1496-98.

89. Stoker, R.S. 1948. "X-ray pole inspection." *Proc., Am. Wood-Preservers' Assoc.* 44:298-312.

90. Thorne, M.E. 1918. "Relation between average life of ties and percentage of renewals." *Proc., Am. Wood-Preservers' Assoc.* 14:150-59.

91. Troxell, H.E. 1961. "Progress in wood preservation, 1959-60." *Forest Prod. J.* 11(2):67-76.

92. Truax, T.R., Harrison, C.A. and Baechler, R.H. 1935. "Experiments in fireproofing wood—fifth progress report." *Proc., Am. Wood-Preservers' Assoc.* 31:231-45.

93. U.S. Forest Products Lab. 1965. "Test methods used in research at the Forest Products Lab." Report No. 1443. Revised 1965.

94. Van Groenou, H.B., Rischen, H.W.L. and Van Den Berge, J. 1951. *Wood Preservation During the Last 50 Years.* A.W. Sijthoff's Uitgeversmaatschappij N.V., Leiden, Netherlands.

95. Vaughan, J.A. 1954. "Controlled-air-seasoning." *Proc., Am. Wood-Preservers' Assoc.* 50:282-86.

96. Von Schrenk, H. 1933. "Significance of toxicity determinations from a practical standpoint." *Proc., Am. Wood-Preservers' Assoc.* 29:140-55.

97. Walden, C.C. and Trussell, P.C. 1965. "Sonic examination of marine piles: Report on four years' commercial experience." *The Dock and Harbour Authority* 66(535).

98. Walters, C.S. 1959. "Problems and practices in wood preservation, 1958." *Forest Prod. J.* 9(2):43-49.

99. Walters, C.S. 1960. "Problems and practices in wood preservation, 1958-59." *Forest Prod. J.* 10(2):73-81.

100. Waterman, R.E. and Williams, R.R. 1934. "Small sapling method of evaluating wood preservatives." *Ind. Engr. Chem.* 6:413–18.
101. Wiess, H.F. 1916. *The Preservation of Structural Timbers.* 2d ed. McGraw-Hill Book Co., N.Y.
102. Wilcox, W.W. 1964. "Some Methods Used in Studying Microbiological Deterioration of Wood." U.S. Forest Serv., Forest Prod. Lab. Rept. No. 063
103. Wilcox, W.W. 1968. "Changes in Wood Microstructure Through Progressive Stages of Decay." U.S. Forest Serv., Forest Prod. Lab. Rept. No. 70.
104. Wood, L.W., Erickson, E.C.O. and Dohr, A.W. 1960. "Strength and related properties of wood poles: Final report." American Society for Testing and Materials, Philadelphia.
105. Wright, J.P. and Storks, K.H. 1957. "X-ray fluorescent spectra for the analysis of preservatives in wood and paper products." *Proc., Am. Wood-Preservers' Assoc.* 53:57–61.

2. Microbiological Degradation and the Causal Organisms

THEODORE C. SCHEFFER
School of Forestry
Oregon State University, Corvallis, Oregon

2.1. Introduction

The subject of microbiological degradation of wood is quite complex and a single chapter on this subject would be too cumbersome. Consequently, the various facets of this subject are covered in Chapters 2 through 6 of this volume. This initial chapter deals with the general aspects of microbiological damage, its gross characteristics and importance, and the organisms responsible for the different forms of degradation.

2.1.1 Kinds of damage to wood by organisms

Organisms cause three major kinds of damage to wood that are conventionally referred to simply in terms of the kind of organism responsible for the particular damage. Wood in salt or brackish water incurs marine-borer damage, consisting of attack by marine animals, notably species of *Teredo* and *Limnoria*. Wood suffers severely from insect damage, especially by termites, wood-boring beetles, and carpenter ants. But the largest wood losses in the aggregate are microbiological, caused by microorganisms consisting of fungi and, to a relatively minor extent, bacteria. Marine, insect, and other forms of degradation are considered in later chapters.

2.1.2 Microbiological damage

Microorganisms that invade and degrade wood are, by definition, microscopic in size. Aggregates or specialized structures such as the fruit bodies of many fungi can be seen without magnification, but the individual vegetative parts can be observed clearly only through the microscope.

Wood-damaging fungi and bacteria are simple forms of plant life. They
have no chlorophyll, so must obtain their nourishment from energy-
supplying and tissue-building organic substances previously produced by
green, chlorophyll-bearing plants. Wood is such a substance, and it
constitutes virtually the sole source of food for many fungi. As an
interesting sidelight, the ultimate source of energy for the organisms that
use wood is the same as that for other living things—the sun.

Essentially all constituents of wood are utilizable by microorganisms of
some kind. The holocellulose (cellulose and hemicelluloses) and lignin
that together comprise the bulk of wood are broken down by enzymes
secreted by fungi and bacteria into simple compounds, such as sugars,
that can be absorbed and metabolized by the degrading organisms. Although all woods are subject to biodeterioration, some are more vulnerable than others. The more durable woods owe their resistance mainly to
their extractives, which serve as natural preservatives.

It is both convenient and practical to recognize five kinds of microbiological damage, namely, decay or rot, soft rot, stain (largely known as
"sap stain" or "blue stain"), and bacterial degradation. The distinction
between some of them often is not sharp, but typical examples of each are
usually not hard to identify by anyone having a little familiarity with the
differences. Decay, stain, mold, and most soft rot are caused by fungi.
Fungi enter and ramify within wood in the form of minute threads or fila-
ments, called hyphae, which consist of many cells joined end to end. The
bacteria develop mainly as single-celled plants, though one group of soft
rotters—the Actinomycetes—has chainlike linked cells.

The different kinds of fungus damage are caused largely by different
taxonomic groups or species of fungi. The causal fungus is sometimes the
ultimate criterion by which the kind of damage is assessed; for example,
decay and soft rot occasionally may not be clearly distinguishable except
by culturing and determining what fungus is involved.

Decay is by far the most serious kind of microbiological damage
because much of it causes structural failure—sometimes quite rapidly.
Soft rot also weakens wood but it is ordinarily much less serious because
it typically—thought not invariably—progresses slowly into wood from
the surface, and commonly does not go as deep. Sap stain and mold are
harmful chiefly because of the unattractive appearance they impart to
wood. Nevertheless, they may be objectionable in other ways, which will
be noted. By and large, bacterial degradation is not a serious problem,
though in some situations of extreme wetness the affected wood may be
made excessively permeable or even substantially reduced in strength.

Recognition of the major kinds of microbiological damage frequently
can be of distinct advantage. For example, one can accept moderately

sap-stained or molded wood for many uses where even slightly decayed material would not be strong enough. Thus, ability to identify stain or mold as something distinct from early decay makes it possible to avoid unwarranted rejection of infected material. Similarly, by recognizing as soft rot the surface softening of preservative-treated wood in the ground, one can avoid misinterpreting the damage as evidence of inadequate treatment against decay. If treating of wood with decay already established is to be avoided, it is, of course, essential that the wood preserver be able to recognize signs of decay in round stock, timbers, and lumber when received or after storage on the seasoning yard.

Knowledge of the specific organism or organisms causing damage can sometimes be helpful also. Some fungi may be a particular threat to certain preservatives, whereas others are not. For example, early failure of a group of experimentally treated fence posts was observed on a Wisconsin test site, whereas posts similarly treated were still sound on a Mississippi site where decay normally is much more severe. The difference in serviceability was traced to a decay fungus that was uniquely tolerant of the preservative and apparently present only on the Madison site. Diverse results among stake and post tests attributable to involvement of different fungi is to be expected, which emphasizes the desirability of reporting the fungi chiefly responsible for the decay in a field test as well as describing significant characteristics of the exposure site.

Likewise, knowledge of the chief fungi causing decay of a particular product can be helpful. As a case in point, the fungi mainly responsible for internal decay of utility poles in the United States were recently found to comprise but nine species [44], which simplifies greatly the problem of field detection of decay in poles on the basis of chemical changes in the wood. Knowledge of the organisms with which one is contending also can be broadly useful in selecting species most appropriate for pure-culture investigations of the physiological requirements of various individuals or types of organisms, of the biochemistry of the different forms of wood degradation, of the effects of the organisms on properties of wood and preservatives, and of the interactions between organisms when invading and degrading wood.

2.1.3 Economic impact of microbiological degradation

It is difficult to assess monetary losses accountable to destruction of wood products or to the impairment of their aesthetic qualities by microorganisms. Losses over a perior of years may be substantial, but rarely are they sufficiently distressing to induce keeping records of them. Commercial and public organizations concerned with maintenance of wood

structures may have records of their replacements costs, but these ordinarily are not published. Miscellaneous reported estimates and a variety of
observations, however, warrant concluding that annual costs of microbiological damage, especially decay, are very large in the aggregate.

Damage by decay to frame buildings in the United States probably
amounts to at least $200 million annually. This large sum has been mostly
unrecognized because the cost to individual homes (totaling about 55
million occupied housing units [145]), is not large enough to stimulate
concerted complaints. Frequently, repairs necessitated by decay are unrecognized in reports of damage by termites and carpenter ants, which
actually may have been of secondary importance. Annual damage by
decay and marine borers to waterfront properties has been estimated to
be a staggering $500 million [146]. A considerable part of the damage
comes from decay in planking and timbers of piers and wharves and in the
above-water portion of piles. A recent survey (unpublished) of naval
coastal facilities indicated that the service life of the general superstructure
of untreated piers and wharves commonly is terminated by decay in 10–15
years where the wood is Douglas-fir, and in 6 years or less where it is
southern pine (which is largely sapwood). Replacement costs are high
because of the large quantity of high-grade structural lumber and timber
used and because of the built-in structural complexities requiring a great
deal of labor and craft skills. Estimators at an eastern shipyard calculated
in 1966 that it cost about $4.50 per square foot of operating surface to
reconstruct one of the heavier piers or wharves down to the pile head.
Maintenance of wood bridges likewise is costly, and presents an expanding problem as the demand for access roads to timber and recreational areas increases. Other wood items incurring costly decay in total
are the millions of utility poles, railway ties, fence posts and rails, and
home and public recreational equipment.

Fungus staining, molding, and undesirable changes induced by bacteria
cause lesser but still serious monetary losses by degrading aesthetic and
utility values. Actual costs in these cases are largely indefinite, but a
figure has been given for blue staining of lumber. Blue stain of southern
pine lumber was once thought to cost southern lumber producers about
$10 million annually, a figure that should be valid for the country as a
whole today. Although staining has been curtailed by use of antistain
chemicals, that which occurs is more costly because of the increased value
of lumber.

Decay and other microbiological damage not only causes large monetary losses but it also results in indirect losses that have a heavy impact
on the national economy. There are the less tangible losses, for example,
represented in wasted timber and in rejection of wood items in favor of

substitutes that are both intrinsically less suitable and, unlike wood, are in the long run an irreplaceable resource. Cutting of forest stands to replace unserviceable wood entails a costly commitment of labor and of timber approaching critically short supply.

Until wood is more purposefully and widely protected against microbiological damage, direct and indirect losses will continue to be economically burdensome. Problems involved are deserving not only of increased research directed at improved means of protection but also of much better extension of existing information on the subject.

2.2. How Wood-Degrading Microorganisms Are Spread

2.2.1 Reproduction and dispersal

Fungi that harm wood reproduce largely by spores, which are analogous to seeds in the higher plants but much simpler in structure and microscopic in size. Spores consist of single or united cells, each capable of forming a new fungus. Many fungi also produce new individuals in abundance by fragmentation of the thread-like hyphae. The bacteria multiply merely by repeated division of the individual vegetative cells. Spores and new bacterial cells can be developed and liberated rapidly under favorable conditions.

Fungus spores are of two kinds—sexual and vegetative, and such features of the vegetative spores as appearance and manner in which they are positioned on the hyphae and the character of the structure in which the sexual spores are borne, serve to identify species. The structures in which sexual spores of decay fungi are borne (fruit bodies) are large enough to be easily seen. Familiar ones are certain of the mushrooms and the shelf- or bracketlike outgrowths on old logs, stumps, and sometimes trunks of trees—especially old ones. Millions of spores may be produced by a single fruit body.

The liberated spores are dispersed by wind, water, and insects, and are capable of germinating and starting new infections in wood that is suitably moist and warm (Figure 2.1). Wind dissemination has resulted in worldwide distribution of some species of fungi.

Wood-invading bacteria apparently are, to a considerable extent, dispersed in water since bacterial infestation is heaviest in wood that is kept wet—such as in log ponds, in sprinkled log decks, in cooling towers, and in underwater service.

Fungi also are dispersed by transportation of infected wood, as a fungus can grow from one piece of wood into another with which it is in contact if the latter is moist enough. Decay in the crawl spaces and occasionally in the walls of frame buildings and in exterior woodwork subject to rain

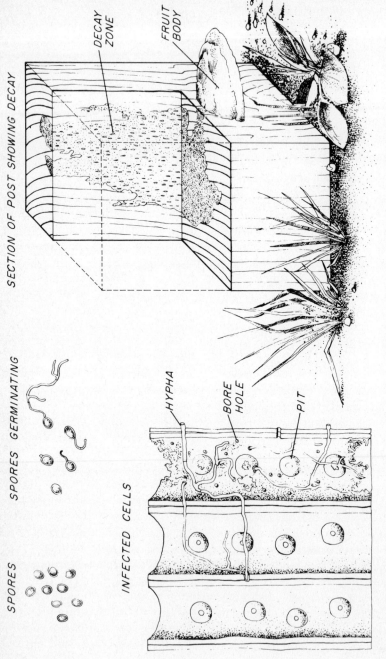

Figure 2.1. Cycle of decay: Spores produced by the fungus fruiting on wood undergoing decay are carried by wind or insects to other susceptible wood. They germinate under favorable conditions, producing hyphae that penetrate and proliferate in the wood causing additional decay. (Courtesy U.S. Forest Products Laboratory, Madison, Wis.)

wetting can sometimes be traced to infection incurred in this way. One of the most spectacular, though unique, examples of spreading of a decay fungus through infected lumber is the extension of the building-decay fungus, *Poria incrassata*, into northern areas far outside its natural range in the South. Widely scattered incidence of this fungus in buildings in the North, and the extreme rarity of its fruit bodies anywhere, attest to its dissemination northward largely in lumber shipped from the South [122].

As a guilding principle, it may be said that airborne spores and, to some extent, hyphal fragments of many wood-degrading microorganisms constitute a universal potential for new infections during mild weather. Blue stain and mold will develop early on susceptible wood no matter how far the wood may be from timberland, seasoning yards, or other areas where the fungi are abundant. Blue staining has been observed on green, solid-stacked lumber in less than a week after sawing, indicating that the infection must have occured during the few minutes between sawing and stacking. Decay normally gets established later than stain or mold infection, possibly because of a weaker initial competitive position of the decay fungi. The airborne spores of decay fungi are ordinarily far less numerous than those of the stains and molds, and they may require a more precisely favorable microclimate at the wood surface for the spores to germinate.

2.2.2 Start of new infections

Structures of essentially the same wood composition and design, and in what appears to be essentially the same environment, can vary substantially in their length of service. Those who have critically observed the incidence of decay in wood are especially aware of this. The explanation is elusive, but it may lie in obscure differences in the microclimate controlling infection of wood. Germination of spores of decay fungi may be favored not only by appropriate moisture and temperature, but also by such factors as acidic conditions and readily utilizable nutrients—especially sugars—at the wood surface, absence of intense light, and a certain amount of carbon dioxide. The presence of carbon dioxide seems to have considerable influence—perhaps more than oxygen [143,13]. A sugar such as glucose may be essential [94], and the availability of sugars could vary with different amounts of surface weathering. Poor spore germination on surfaces that have been leached attests to the need for one or more of the water-soluble wood constituents [100]. There is a suggestion in their frequent presence in advance of decay that bacteria and non-basidio-mycetous fungi may, by invading first, so condition wood as to increase its susceptibility to infection and degradation by decay fungi [54,72,138].

Wood in contact with the ground normally is much more subject to infection, hence more in need of preservative protection, than wood above-ground. The ground tends to retain moisture and thus keep the wood damp during dry periods. Also, it typically harbors a multitude of wood-attacking microorganisms that are able to grow directly into the wood from vegetative debris on which they are existing. Some soils also may provide chemicals conducive to attack.

Contact with soil not only presents optimal conditons for infection by microorganisms, but it also brings to bear on the wood a great variety of organisms and thereby increases the possibility that one or more kinds, species, or strains are present that are uniquely capable of tolerating a particular preservative. A variety of decay fungi—and especially of soft-rot species—molds, and bacteria usually is present in fertile soils.

2.3 Physiology of Wood-Degrading Microorganisms

2.3.1 Laboratory studies

Fungi and bacteria can be isolated from wood and grown in pure culture in the laboratory. Pure cultures make possible studies of the organisms to identify cultural characteristics, and to ascertain their physiological requirements and the biochemistry of their degradations. Pure cultures are also used in accelerated tests to determine the capacity of selected organisms to damage wood of various kinds or with particular preservative treatments.

Isolation of fungi usually is accomplished by aseptically transferring numerous small bits of the wood near the zone of visible damage to a nutrient medium in petri dishes or test tubes. Where more than one fungus is observed growing out of a piece of wood, the species can often be separated by promptly transferring fragments of the differing hyphae to separate containers. A widely used culture medium for wood-inhabiting fungi consists of 1.5–3.0 percent malt and 1.5–2.0 percent agar in water. The malt extract provides a broadly suitable natural mixture of required nutrients at a pH between about 4.5 and 5.5. Bacteria are favored by, or may require, a medium with pH nearer neutral and incorporating more nitrogen. Some fungi grow better if particles or an infusion of the wood substrate are incorporated in the medium.

Wood-degrading organisms have the same basic growth requirements as do green plants. These are a source of food, an adequate supply of water, favorable temperature, oxygen, and a suitable pH. As a general basis of reference, conditions suitable for good growth of familiar green plants are also conducive to vigorous aggression by wood-damaging fungi. Unlike the green plants, the fungi can grow without light, but some require it for normal reproduction. Organisms attacking treated wood must have, of course, some tolerance to the preservative.

2.3.2 Nutrition

The optimal nutritional needs of wood-damaging microorganisms vary, but all species obviously are able to get along with what is available in wood. Energy and most of the cell-building materials for the organism are supplied mainly by the carbohydrate fraction consisting of holocellulose, starches, and sugars, and, for some organisms, by the lignin fraction. Nitrogen and minerals are available, though in comparatively small amounts. A trace amount of thiamin, the vitamin B^1 of animal nutrition, apparently is needed by most decay fungi [67].

The cellulose, hemicelluloses, and lignin comprise more than 95 percent of the substance of most woods, so are sufficiently abundant to meet the requirements of organisms utilizing them. Nitrogen is extremely sparse, being present, according to Cowling, in amounts no greater than about 0.03–0.10 percent [25]. Nevertheless, these quantities are adequate for rapid decay of wood, indicating unique nitrogen-utilizing efficiency by the attacking fungi. Cowling's investigations suggest that this efficiency may derive in part from an ability of the fungi to solubilize the nitrogen in the protoplasm of their older hyphae and transport it to new zones of attack, where it supplements the nitrogen existing in the zones. Moderately greater rates of decay have been observed to be correlated with greater amounts of natural nitrogen, but there is conflicting evidence as to whether decay can be increased appreciably by artificially adding nitrogen to wood [25].

The ash content of domestic woods, although usually well below 1 percent, is more than adequate for microorganisms, which require only traces of certain minerals. Attempts to control decay by impregnating wood with chemicals such as a chelating compound—to "tie up" the scarcer but vitally needed minerals making them unavailable to the fungi—have not been promising.

Similarly discovering that most decay fungi seem to require thiamine has created interest in the possibility of protecting wood for service aboveground by alkaline treatments that destroy thiamin, and results of field trials of the method have been encouraging [56]. Laboratory probing of the fundamental nature of the protection thus provided indicates, however, that the observed decay control cannot be explained entirely by destruction of thiamin [60].

2.3.3 Need for moisture

As a general rule, microbiological degradation can occur only if the wood has a moisture content exceeding 20 percent of its ovendry weight. The most widely used and effective means of protecting wood is to dry it soon after it comes out of the tree, and thereafter handle it and put it into service with appropriate precautions to keep it dry. Where a safe moisture content cannot be reasonably assured, protection by preservative treatment ordinarily is the logical alternative.

Decay fungi can cause serious damage only when the moisture content is above the fiber-saturation (approximately 30 percent) level. This amount of moisture cannot be acquired merely from water vapor absorbed from humid air; it can come only in green wood or as a result of wetting by liquid water. Therefore, if initially dry wood is kept under shelter and protected against extraneous wetting, as by condensation or plumbing leaks, it will not decay. This generalization is true for wood with existing decay as well as for sound wood. Once the wetting has been corrected and the wood is permitted to dry, there can be no further progress of the decay so long as the dry condition is maintained.

The term "dry rot" is rather firmly entrenched, but is an unfortunate misnomer because it implies that wood can decay without being wet. The notion may have come from the dry, almost charred appearance of wood in an advanced stage of "brown rot." "Dry rot" can be used with some justification, however, to describe an extraordinary form of building decay, wherein the fungus itself wets the wood by transporting water from an external source, usually the ground, to the wood. The water is carried through special thick hyphal strands called "rhizomorphs," which resemble vines with a main stem that branches on the wood into relatively fine strands (Figure 2.2). This type of decay, caused chiefly by *Poria incrassata* in the Gulf states and Pacific Northwest in the United States, and in Europe by *Merulius lacrymans,* has been comprehensively described by Verrall [152] and by Cartwright and Findlay [15], respectively.

A reasonable objective in drying wood is to reduce the moisture content as soon as practicable to 20 percent or less. Although this is substantially below the approximate 30 percent minimum required by decay fungi, the lower figure is advisable because it provides a margin of safety in the event the material does not dry uniformly.

Mold and stain fungi also do best at wood moisture contents above the fiber-saturation point. But some molds can develop in the 20–30 percent range. Thus, in contrast to decay, some molding may take place in wood wetted strictly by the water vapor in air having a relative humidity of 90 percent or more.

Little is known about the minimum moisture requirements of fungi causing soft rot, but laboratory and field observations indicate that, for rapid attack, many soft rotters may require more moisture than do most decay fungi.

Bacteria does not become prominent in wood unless the moisture content is at least as high as that of the green wood. They have proved

Figure 2.2. Water-conducting strands (rhizomorphs) of *Poria incrassata* terminating in a mycelial "fan." This fungus appears to attack dry wood but in fact wets the wood first, by transporting water from an external source, usually the ground. (Courtesy U.S. Forest Products Laboratory, Madison, Wis.)

troublesome in ponded logs and in continuously wetted wood in cooling towers.

Wood is most susceptible to decay in a broad moisture range, possibly from as low as 40 percent to double this amount or more. White-rot fungi, such as *Polyporus versicolor,* may need more moisture for rapid decay than do brown-rot fungi such as *Poria monticola* [63]. The upper end of the optimal moisture range for decay varies with the wood density and size of the item, as these factors act in conjunction with an enlarged quantity of water in the cell cavities to limit diffusion of oxygen into the wood. The denser the wood and the deeper the zone of infection, the lower the maximum moisture content that will allow sufficient ingress of oxygen to support rapid decay.

Saturated wood is essentially immune to fungal attack except near surfaces exposed to the air. Near the surface, there may be sufficient penetration of air to support fungi despite the saturated condition. Shallow damage to very wet wood is characteristic of much soft rot. Among decay fungi, the white-rot species *Poria nigrescens* and *Peniophora mollis* have exhibited unusual tolerance of the very wet condition of cooling-tower slats [33].

Consideration of the moisture requirements of the organisms embraces not only their needs for growth but also their ability to survive in air-dry wood and resume attack when the wood is wet again. Some decay fungi have been found alive after 11 years in air-dry wood, but most seem able to survive no longer than 2 or 3 years [123]. *Poria incrassata* and *Coniophora cerebella,* both prominent in building decay, survived only 2 or 3 weeks. In the same study, stain fungi did not live as long as the majority of decay fungi. Experimental data and observations of wood in service indicate that the failure to protect wood against infection during drying and subsequent storage is a common cause of early decay in the vulnerable parts of wood structures.

2.3.4 Temperature requirements

Fungal degradation of wood is favored by the same moderate temperatures that support growth of green plants, though fungi can maintain growth at lower temperatures (Figure 2.3). Fungi differ in their optimum temperatures but for most, the range is from about 70–90°F. Decay is quite slow below 50°F and slightly above 90°F, and completely inhibited by temperatures near 32°F and 100°F. In many areas, temperatures from late fall to early spring are low enough to prevent decay or hold it to a negligible level.

Naturally occurring subzero temperatures do not harm fungi, but high temperatures sometimes incurred with direct heating by the sun or with

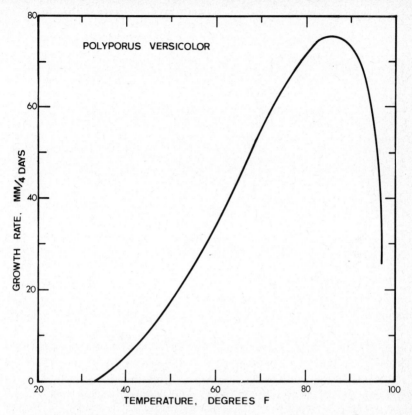

Figure 2.3. Relation of linear growth to temperature, observed with a culture of *Polyporus versicolor*. Growth of many decay fungi is prevented shortly above 32°F and near 100°F. (Courtesy U.S. Forest Products Laboratory, Madison, Wis.)

certain industrial processing of wood can be lethal. Temperatures and heating times ordinarily employed in kiln drying and in pressure treating green wood with a hot preservative usually will destroy existing infection. Combinations of temperature and time needed to kill decay fungi in green wood are given in Table 2.1.

2.3.5 Need for air

All wood-invading fungi require oxygen, which they get directly or indirectly from the air. They need comparatively little, however, and seem to be able to maintain near-normal development at oxygen levels far below the 20 percent present in air. Growth of decay fungi has been observed in as little as 1 percent oxygen at atmospheric pressure [132,68].

TABLE 2.1

Recommended Times at Various Temperatures
to Kill Decay Fungi in Green Wood*

Wood Heated in Steam or an Equivalent	
Temperature†	Time
°F	Min.
150	75
170	30
180	20
200	10
212	5

*From U.S. Forest Products Laboratory
Technical Note 259 (1956).
†Internal temperature reaching the fungus.

Jensen [68] has suggested that both depleted oxygen and an adverse effect of carbon dioxide produced by respiration of the causal fungus may automatically limit the rate of development of heartrot in trees. Experimental evidence [34] and the association of soft-rot fungi with very wet wood suggest that soft rotters in general may be even more tolerant of restricted oxygen than decay fungi. Because they require so little oxygen, the only practical means of controlling wood-degrading fungi by excluding air is to submerge the wood or set it in the ground below the water table, or—in the case of log storage—to keep it wet by spraying or sprinkling.

Wood submerged in water cannot receive enough oxygen to sustain serious fungus attack, though there may be shallow invasion by certain nondecaying species and slow bacterial degradation. Exclusion of air explains the long durability of untreated foundation piles driven below the permanent water table. An upsurge of decay in old foundation piles has been a problem in some localities where heavy consumption of underground water has dropped the water table below the pile tops. Wisely, foundation piles nowadays are routinely pressure-treated, irrespective of where they are to be driven. Logs can be protected against stain and decay by storing them in ponds or by keeping them wet in sprayed or sprinkled decks, and this is standard practice at many sawmills.

Stagnant ("dead") air is mistakenly thought by some to cause decay. Lack of circulation and the high humidity frequently associated with stagnant air retard drying of wood that becomes wet, and thus are conducive to decay; stagnant air per se is harmless so long as the wood associated with it remains dry.

2.3.6 pH relations

All wood-damaging fungi show, in their spore germination and growth, a distinct preference for an acid environment. Some are unable to grow if the substrate is much above the neutral point (pH 7). As normal wood has a pH well on the acid side, it is a favorable substrate for fungal invasion.

Cartwright and Findlay [15] reported a lower limit of pH 2.0 for growth of decay fungi but concluded that the optimum for most species lies between 4.5 and 5.5, which is within the normal range for wood. Comparable values, a limiting pH near 1.0 and an optimum range of 5.0–6.0, were reported recently in Russian observations [108]. Cartwright and Findlay noted further that fungi may change the pH of their substrate, possibly in the direction most suited to their growth, by acids they produce. The direction and extent of the fungus-induced change in pH varied according to the species of fungus. There was no evidence that alteration of the pH of wood by adding dilute acid or alkali can significantly increase the rate of decay. An appreciable change in the direction of lower pH provides a basis for detecting certain decay infections, the abnormal acidity being revealed by the color acquired by a liquid pH indicator applied to the wood.

2.3.7 Effect of light

All wood-destroying microorganisms grow well in the absence of light, as attested by their deep-seated invasions. Some light, nevertheless, is required for normal fruiting of many fungi. The absence or abortion of fruit bodies on rotting timbers in the dark environment of mines is striking evidence of a need of light for typical sexual reproduction among decay fungi. Strong light tends to retard growth of fungi, and to cause intensification of hyphal coloration in some.

The influence of light on decay fungi has practical application mainly for optimal handling of the fungi in the laboratory such as to produce fruit bodies in culture, to obtain vigorous and uniform growth, and to insure uniformity of activity in controlled laboratory studies or tests entailing comparisons of decay rate. Even at low intensity for short duration, light may influence the rate of decay by some species. In laboratory tests of decay resistance, using 0.75-inch cubical blocks in glass bottles, Duncan found that comparatively brief illumination by ordinary incandescent room light doubled the rate of decay by *Lenzites trabea* over that in total darkness [37]. The increase appeared to have been effected largely by the blue segment of the spectrum. This rather surprising phenomenon can be explained only by postulating a transfer of the decay-promoting factor, induced by light at the surface, through the fungus hyphae to the interior wood.

2.3.8 Tolerance of poisonous chemicals

The tolerance of the organisms for various chemicals is a physiological attribute closely pertinent to the subject of wood preservation. Microorganisms vary markedly in their tolerance of protective chemicals. Some fungi and bacteria may even denature or metabolize preservatives that are highly toxic to others. Species variation in tolerance of artificial and natural wood preservatives is sufficient to warrant identification of the principal fungi involved in field tests of preservatives. Also, for conducting pure-culture tests of decay resistance in the laboratory, both species and strain of test fungus should be selected to give results reasonably consistent with what is already known about the relative effectiveness of standard preservatives or the resistance of naturally durable woods. Different strains of some decay fungi can vary markedly in their tolerance of preservatives [50,136]. The subject of preservative tolerance is considered further in Chapter 5 of this volume.

2.4 Decay
2.4.1 Distinguishing features and diagnosis of decay
2.4.1.1 General

Advanced decay is characterized by three features: the deterioration extends deep into the wood, strength is much below normal, and the wood has an abnormal color. In addition, with some decay there are sunken areas of collapsed wood or, in extreme cases, general deformation of the affected piece resulting from uneven collapse and shrinkage. The color and presence or absence of areas of structural collapse varies with the fungus involved.

Two types of decay are generally recognized—brown rot and white rot. The distinction was based originally on a difference in the appearance between typical brown-rotted and white-rotted wood, but it is now known that there is also an underlying difference between the decays in the associated chemical changes and the fungi causing them. With brown rot, only the carbohydrate fraction is removed extensively and the residue becomes increasingly high in lignin. The wood acquires a brown color, often as though charred, tends to crack across the grain, collapse, and shrink abnormally (Figure 2.4). With typical white rot, both lignin and cellulose are depleted and the wood tends to lose color. Moreover, white-

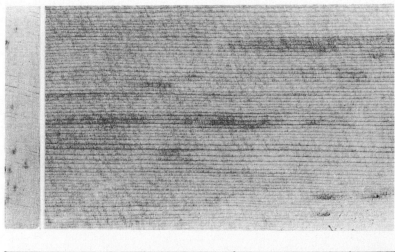

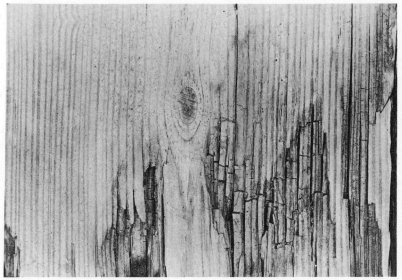

Figure 2.4. Typical brown rot. Top: Early stage, showing discoloration on side grain (right) and end grain (left) of the same board. Bottom: Late stage, with cracking across the grain and collapsed wood. (Courtesy U.S. Forest Products Laboratory, Madison, Wis.)

rotted wood does not crack across the grain and, unless very severely degraded, does not shrink abnormally or collapse (Figure 2.5).

Early or incipient decay may not be readily recognizable, but it should be looked for where circumstances require wood having normal strength or where there is the potential for decay to develop to serious proportions.

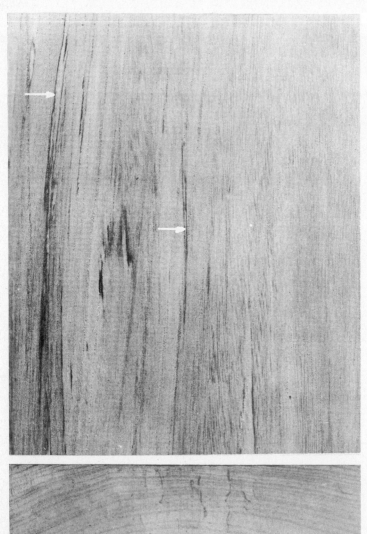

Figure 2.5. Typical intermediate stage of white rot. Left: Decay discoloration on end grain, characterized by mottling and dark "zone lines" (arrows) bordering the abnormally light-colored areas. Right: Decay discoloration on side grain of the same board. White rot softens but typically does not cause abnormal shrinking, crosschecking, or collapse. (Courtesy U.S. Forest Products Laboratory, Madison, Wis.)

Especially deserving of critical inspection for decay are items such as ladder stock, scaffolding, tool handles, structural members or products that will be highly stressed, products costly to replace like poles, piling, large sawed or laminated timbers, and lumber going into buildings at places subject to occasional wetting such as exteriors exposed to the weather and damp crawl spaces.

The signs of incipient decay are varied and often more than one symptom needs to be considered for a convincing diagnosis. Moreover, it is practically essential in the more difficult cases that one be familiar with the normal variations in appearance of sound wood of the kind inspected. Existence of decay frequently can be confirmed by examining the wood microscopically for the presence of hyphae or evidence of decomposition of the microstructure, or by incubating bits of wood on nutrient agar to see if a decay fungus will appear.

2.4.1.2 Change in luster and color

Visible manifestations of early decay are most readily observed on a smooth surface. One or more of the following abnormalities may be noted:

1. There is a lack of surface luster, giving the wood a dull or "dead" appearance.

2. With brown rot, the color of wood infected during storage or service tends to be an abnormal shade of brown.

3. With white rot developed in storage or service, the color tends toward an off-white, sometimes making the wood appear bleached. The bleaching occurs very early and is due to destruction of coloring materials in the wood, not to removal of lignin as once thought. If the wood is a hardwood, there also may be black "zone lines" in the light areas (Figure 2.5) which, no matter how small, are a positive sign of decay.

4. The appearance in lumber of rot originating in standing trees (heartrot) of North American timber species has been characterized by such discolorations as brownish, reddish, yellowish, bleached, bluish, purplish, and water soaked, varying with the tree species and fungus [9].

5. Infected areas have a mottled appearance. The discoloration more often than not is variable in shade and is irregularly distributed, giving the wood a mottled or variegated coloration. Such mottling commonly is more indicative of early decay than any particular color observed. Mottling coupled with definite loss of sheen is a strong indication of decay.

2.4.1.3 Reduced strength and presence of other organisms

In addition to luster and color changes, other accompaniments of decay may be noted:

1. Wet wood with appreciable decay infection will break brashly (abruptly) across the grain whereas sound wood splinters at the break. Brashness, reflecting reduced toughness, can be detected by breaking small pieces by hand or by lifting pieces of wood from the surface by means of a pointed tool—the "pick test" (Figure 2.6). The wood should be wet, otherwise it may break brashly even if sound. Decay-induced brashness is sometimes manifested by a conspicuously rough surface following sawing or planing. Brashness also is characteristic of compression wood, and so should be interpreted with this in mind.

Figure 2.6. The "pick test" for early decay. When wet wood is probed with a pick or comparable tool, it tends—if sound (left)—to lift out as a long sliver or it breaks by splintering; if infected (right), it tends to lift in short lengths and to break abruptly, without splintering. (Courtesy U.S. Forest Products Laboratory, Madison, Wis.)

2. The presence of numerous beetle holes originating in the log, heavy, nonuniform (blotchy) blue stain, or heavy mold is circumstantial evidence that the wood had been favorably situated for decay infection. Hence, wood having any of these imperfections should be regarded with suspicion if it is important that it be free of decay.

2.4.1.4 Microscopical and cultural evidence

Verification of early decay by microscopical examination of the wood depends largely on observation of bore holes through the walls of the wood cells made by the advancing hyphae. Numerous bore holes, if accompanied by colorless hyphae, are positive evidence of a decay fungus. Absence of bore holes does not necessarily indicate absence of decay, however, since with some fungi or conditions bore holes appear only in the later stages of decay.

Culturing of the wood can be helpful, especially if the species of decay fungi likely to be found are comparatively few and distinctive enough in culture or under the microscope to make them easily recognizable. This method of detection is being used to a limited extent commercially to inspect poles for internal decay. If microscopical examination of an isolated fungus discloses "clamp connections" on the hyphae, a decay species is positively indicated. In the absence of clamp connections, other cultural criteria must be relied on to decide whether or not the isolate is a decay fungus. To obtain cultures of decay fungi free of mold or bacterial contaminants, it often is necessary to culture many very small bits of the wood. Grant and Savory [52] have furnished general guidelines for isolating and identifying wood-destroying fungi. Culturing procedures can be simplified by circumventing aseptic handling of the wood prior to culturing. This can be safely done by enclosing the wood sample with crystals of paradichlorobenzene to prevent contamination until it is used, then briefly flaming the wood before placing it on nutrient agar [129].

2.4.1.5 Indirect diagnostic techniques

Simple, indirect means of detecting decay are being developed, but none so far is wholly adequate. A device that measures softening caused by decay, according to the resistance of wood to forceable penetration by a needle, was developed in Germany for use as a nondestructive means of detecting internal decay in utility poles [43]. The device shows also the depth of the sound shell of treated wood. Devices that reveal internal decay by a reduced rate of travel of sonic vibrations through the wood are being marketed for pole inspection. An original apparatus for this purpose was described by Miller and associates [99]. X-ray equipment for pole inspection is also available. The general applicability of radiography for inspecting wood products was discussed in a symposium report by Mothershead [102]. Both sonics and radiography respond reasonably well to voids or heavily decayed wood, but are considerably limited in capacity to reveal early decay. There seems to be little promise for detecting decay by ultrasonic response of the wood.

There has long been need of a chemical test, applicable in the field, whereby a solution brushed or sprayed onto wood being inspected would reveal the presence of decay infection by development of a distinctive color. A successful color test of limited applicability was devised by Lindgren [86] for detecting early decay in the sapwood of pine poles, piling, or timbers on the seasoning yard or in storage. A 0.75 percent water solution of sodium alizarine sulphate (Alizarine Red S), acting as a pH indicator, turns yellow on wood harboring *Peniophora gigantea*, the fungus mainly responsible for the decay. The alizarine test has not proved suitable for use on kiln-dried pine, nor for general application to a variety of decays and woods. A more broadly applicable color test, reported by Cowling and Sachs [26], is made with a 1 percent solution of osmium tetroxide. With a number of woods, the solution produces a black color much more rapidly if brown rot is present than if it is not. The test is not appropriate for white rot.

2.4.1.6 Chemical damage resembling decay

Wood sometimes is damaged by chemicals in such a way as to acquire an appearance superficially resembling decay. Prolonged contact with strong acids will hydrolyze cellulose and hemicellulose, giving wood some of the characteristics of brown rot. Strong alkalis attack lignin as well, which tends to give severely degraded wood a fibrous character somewhat resembling that of wood with certain white rots in an advanced stage. A simple pH test will usually reveal the nature of these abnormalities; a pH below 2.5 or above 7.0 is good evidence of chemical rather than fungus degradation [15].

Similarly, prolonged contact of wet wood with iron, notably nails, screws, bolts, and other fasteners, causes the wood to soften around the fastener. The affected wood and the surrounding area is also darkened, becoming almost black. The damage is known by some as "iron sickness." Degradation is caused by an alkaline conditon coupled with metal-catalyzed oxidation of the wood, both resulting from electrolytic action of dissimilar metals—especially in the presence of a strong electrolyte such as salt. The subject is treated in detail by Marian and Wissing [95], and particularly with reference to ship timbers by Pinion [109]. Use of nonferrous fasteners or other materials touching the wood will prevent most such trouble. Experience with minesweepers indicates that fasteners of an alloy such as bronze will greatly retard but not prevent softening of wood in salt water [64].

Wood close to the seacoast occasionally becomes coarsely shredded by salt spray, which gives it a fibrous appearance somewhat like advanced white rot. The damage is caused by intermittent wetting whereby particles of salt gradually accumulate and enlarge in the wood microstructure, rupturing bonds between the fibers. The same mechanism causing disintegration of rocks has been described [154]. Salt damage can usually be distinguished from decay by the near-normal tensile strength of the separated fibers when tested by hand; also, salt crystals may be seen in samples under magnification.

2.4.2 Effect of decay on physical properties

2.4.2.1 Strength

In comparison with all other strength properties, the toughness or capacity of wood to withstand shock loading is reduced rapidly. As much as a third to a half of its normal toughness may be lost by the time wood has decayed to a point barely detectable by loss of weight [117]. Because of this, toughness appraisal is the most sensitive means of detecting early decay and, correspondingly, it is most important that wood for uses requiring toughness should be free of decay.

Other strength properties such as resistance to bending and crushing are reduced more gradually but, nevertheless, may be diminished seriously before outward signs of decay are conspicuous. Several facets of difference in strength between sound and moderately decayed wood is given in the load-deflection curves of Figure 2.7, derived from specimens in static bending. Reflected by the area under the respective curves, toughness of the decayed wood was about 15 percent of that of the sound wood; the corresponding maximum load supported by the decayed specimen was about 60 percent of that of sound wood. Stiffness, denoted by the slope of the straight-line portion of curves (up to the proportional limit), was not reduced very much by the decay—which is a typical observation underlying a general conclusion that stiffness is a poor criterion of incipient decay. It is of further significance that whereas the sound wood failed gradually after the maximum load was reached, the decayed wood failed abruptly. This strikingly illustrates a danger inherent in decayed wood besides its weakness—it can fail abruptly without warning.

Strength losses from decay are caused by enzymatic degradation of cellulose and lignin. Chemical changes are discussed in Chapter 4. The pronounced early reductions in toughness are caused by very subtle changes that are not apparent in conventional chemical analyses. Very early toughness losses also are caused by blue-stain and mold fungi [17,59], which suggests that the changes underlying toughness degradation are readily affected by biochemical processes common to a variety of wood microorganisms. From experiments with different fungi and findings of others, Henningsson [59] concluded that early reductions in impact bending strength (toughness measure) may be caused by splitting of linkages between lignin and carbohydrates.

2.4.2.2 Permeability and absorptivity

Decayed wood is more permeable and absorptive than comparable sound wood due to openings and enlargements in its microstructure made by the invading fungus as it moves from cell to cell. Pit openings are enlarged through removal of portions of the pit membrane and any occlud-

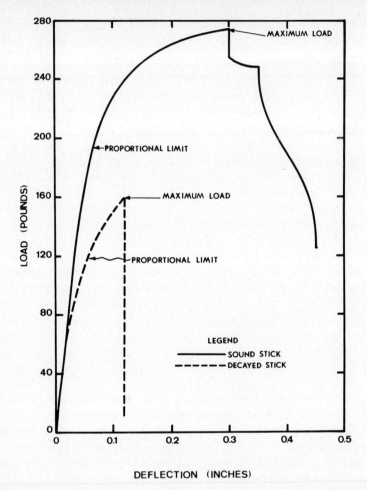

Figure 2.7. Load-deflection curves of small specimen tests for strength in static bending: One specimen had incurred an 18-percent loss in specific gravity from decay by *Polyporus versicolor,* the other was its sound, matched control. (Courtesy U.S. Forest Products Laboratory, Madison, Wis.)

ing substances. In addition, cells comprising the wood rays commonly are destroyed, thus promoting radial flow of liquids into the wood. As decay progresses, wood substance also is removed which correspondingly enlarges or even creates void spaces and thereby increases the liquid-holding capacity of the wood.

Infected wood, because of its greater permeability and absorptivity, tends to stay wet and thus become increasingly subject to continued decay if exposed to rain wetting. These qualities also can present difficulties with preservative treating. Poles, piling, or timbers with incipient decay tend, if dry, to absorb an excessive amount of treating solution and, conversely, if wetted by rain shortly before treating they may not receive preservative well. In either case, serious variations in retention can occur between pieces in a treating charge.

2.4.2.3 Hygroscopicity

The hygroscopicity of wood—its capacity to absorb and retain moisture from the air—apparently is but slightly altered by decay; at least this seems to be true if the decay is not greatly advanced. There is limited evidence that the equilibrium moisture content of moderately decayed wood, whether with brown or white rot, may sometimes be as much as one or two percentage values lower than that of comparable sound wood; or, perhaps rarely, it may be slightly higher [117]. The change seems to occur more through chemical alterations than from removal of wood constituents. It has little practical significance other than for laboratory studies in which equilibrium weights of sound and decayed woods are compared.

2.4.2.4 Drying characteristics and dimensional stability

The drying characteristics and dimensional stability of decayed wood have received little attention, probably because the matter is of small practical interest compared to the weakening effect of decay. In drying from the green condition, lumber with brown rot may shrink unevenly and develop localized areas of collapsed wood, depending on how far the decay has progressed. Brown rot originating in the standing tree presents no problem of nonuniform lumber dimensions if the rot is in the incipient stage, denoted merely by discoloration of the wood. Lumber with white rot dries without conspicuous shrinkage abnormalities, reflecting—as noted earlier—the different chemical action of this type of decay as compared with brown rot.

2.4.3 Fungi that cause decay

2.4.3.1 Systematic position of decay fungi

The decay fungi belong to the most advanced class of fungi in the evolutionary scale, the Basidiomycetes. This class name and that of a subdivision containing the decay-producing species, the Hymenomycetes, are increasingly seen in semitechnical literature on the subject of wood decay. The names derive, respectively, from the microscopic structure on which the sexual spores of the fungus are borne—the basidium—and the nature of the surface on which the basidia develop—the hymenium. The great bulk of wood-destroying Hymenomycetes have fruit bodies, technically known as sporophores or basidiocarps, that are easily seen. Those of the most destructive species generally appear in such forms as crustlike structures closely appressed to the surface of the wood, or as shelflike or bracket-shaped bodies that are tough, leathery, corky, or woody when mature, and stand out horizontally from the wood (Figures 2.1 and 2.8).

Figure 2.8. Bract-type fruit bodies of decay fungus. *Lenzites berkeleyi.* (Courtesy U.S. Forest Products Laboratory, Madison, Wis.)

Another very familiar form of fruit body, but with fewer representatives among the wood destroyers, is the stalk-and-cap structure, like that of mushrooms.

2.4.3.2 Identification of decay fungi

Different species of decay fungi can be identified from the outward appearance and, if necessary, the detailed structure of the fruit body.

Guides for identifying North American species in this way are available. Selected publications can be suggested, in which the species are dealt with in general and by botanical families: general [49,18]; Polyporaceae [106,90]; Thelephoraceae [12,140,80]; Hydnaceae [98]; Meruliaceae [11]; and Agaricaceae [73,77].

Usually, the presence of a fruit body is evidence of rather advanced decay in the wood beneath. There are situations, however, in which the fruiting fungus is not the one causing the major rot. Where there is any doubt about the relation, or where there is no fruit body (as is more often the case), the principal fungus frequently can be identified by planting bits of the wood on a nutrient medium, as described earlier, and observing certain distinguishing characteristics of the fungus developed in laboratory culture. Cultural identification entails skilled observations, including microscopical, of a combination of growth characteristics and physiological responses. The most widely used system for the purpose was devised by Nobles [104]. Käärik [71] has provided an interesting and rapid supplementary procedure based on observations of the production of laccase- and tyrosinase-type enzymes by different species. An ideal means of identification would be to grow fruit bodies of the fungi in the laboratory, but so far this has been done successfully only with a comparatively few species.

2.4.3.3 Variations with wood species, product, and environment

Some decay fungi are rather specialized with regard to the wood or product they invade or the external environment in which they grow; others occur comparatively broadly in relation to these factors. Knowledge of the dominant associations between fungi and situations in which they may be most serious can be helpful in such matters as selecting species most appropriate for laboratory studies aimed at improved protection of wood materials and structures, in understanding some of the variations in practical problems of protection, and in improving means of detecting and diagnosing decay.

A comprehensive report by the U.S. Forest Service summarizes fungus–wood species–product associations and geographical distribution of decay fungi in the United States observed by or brought to the attention of staff members over a period of nearly 30 years [40]. The species listed number 152; over 70 percent of them are in 5 genera: *Coniophora, Lentinus, Lenzites, Polyporus,* and *Poria.* The genus *Poria* was two to three times as frequent as any of the other four. Species most encountered were *Coniophora arida, C. puteana, Lenzites sepiaria, L. trabea, Polyporus versicolor, Poria incrassata, P. monticola, P. vaillantii, P. xantha,* and *Lentinus lepideus.* Their frequencies of occurrence on various types of products are shown in Table 2.2. All but *P. versicolor* are brown rotters. *L. trabea* was indicated to have been associated with a greater variety of products than any other one fungus. It has long been recognized as the dominant fungus causing decay of exterior woodwork of buildings, and because of this it has been considered the only species necessary to incorporate in the National Woodwork Manufacturers Association standard NWMA-M-1-60 for bioassaying woodwork preservatives [103]. It also is the fungus specified in the toxicity test of U.S. Commercial Standard CS 262-63 for "Water-Repellent Preservatives Non-Pressure Treatment for Millwork" [147]. The fungus next most prevalent on a variety of products was *P. monticola*. It and *L. trabea* are the brown-rot representatives in the standard laboratory bioassay of the American Society for Testing and Materials, in D1413 for appraising preservatives [1] and in D2017 for evaluating natural decay resistance [2]. *P. versicolor* is the white-rot representative in these ASTM standards, and was chosen for its ubiquity on wood of broad-leaved species—denoted by the prevalence of its fruit bodies, and evidence in laboratory tests of its capacity to decay a wide variety of hardwoods.

Other fungus–product associations are also of practical interest. *P. incrassata,* which causes spectacularly rapid decay of buildings in the humid coastal regions of the South, East, and West, is of negligible consequence on products other than buildings and lumber. Its counterpart in northern Europe, *Merulius lacrymans,* similarly causes very rapid decay in buildings and is virtually unknown away from human habitations [15]. *L. lepideus* seems to be the major cause of interior decay in pine poles [40,44]. In a special survey of pole-decay fungi, Eslyn found one or more of six species in 71 percent of the infected pine poles sampled, namely *L. lepideus* (49 percent), *Peniophora* sp., *L. sepiaria, L. trabea, Peniophora gigantea,* and *Poria radiculosa* [44]. In the same study, *Poria carbonica* was most often isolated from Douglas-fir poles (56 percent) and it and three other species—*P. monticola, L. lepideus,* and *P. xantha*—accounted for the decay in about 85 percent of the poles. *L. trabea* was indicated to be the chief cause of shell rot in cedar poles.

Some of the most marked specificity between decay fungus and wood species is found in the heartrots of coniferous timber having high natural fungus resistance. Some of the brown rots of the pocket type ("pocket rot"), in which scattered pockets of advanced decay are separated by comparatively firm wood, are caused by fungi that have become so specialized that they invade only one timber species. Notable examples are the pocket rot of incense cedar (by *Polyporus amarus*), pecky cypress (by *Stereum* sp.), western redcedar (by *Poria asiatica*), and redwood (by *P. sequoia*).

The foregoing and most other fungi in the heartwood of living trees

TABLE 2.2

Species of Decay Fungi Most Prevalent in the Duncan-Lombard Survey and Products on Which They Occurred

Fungus	Times Encountered					Experimental Material		Total
	Unseasoned Raw Products	Posts, Poles, Piling, Ties	Chiefly Boats	Buildings	Miscellaneous	Above-ground	Below-ground	
Coniophora arida	0	0	0	2	0	0	69	71
C. puteana	3	2	1	12	4	1	25	48
Lentinus lepideus	4	103	2	0	0	0	40	149
Lenzites sepiaria	6	9	13	5	8	13	38	92
L. trabea	6	20	54	44	7	1	8	140
Polyporus versicolor	12	3	12	0	6	1	8	42
Poria incrassata	15	0	0	83	1	0	7	106
P. monticola	5	10	42	12	5	1	25	100
P. vaillantii	0	4	0	18	2	0	31	55
P. xantha	4	6	26	4	3	0	12	55

usually do little damage to wood after it has been placed in service. Consequently, fungi originating in the tree generally do not constitute the same danger to a structure in service as those that get established after the wood is out of the tree. The relatively few examples of hazardous tree infections would include lumber containing *P. monticola,* which invades trees of western conifers—especially hemlock; and *Daedalea quercina* and *Stereum frustulosum,* in hardwood timber. These last two are prominent among fungi found in boats [40]. Hubert lists a few heartrot species as extending their attack to ties and mine timbers in service [65], but most of the species mentioned are not considered to be generally harmful to products.

The kind of wood and whether it is above- or below-ground often determine whether decay may be by a brown-rot or a white-rot fungus. In general, hardwoods in aboveground service are much more susceptible to white rot than brown rot, and softwoods are more susceptible to brown rot [40,24]. There is no satisfactory explanation for this difference. It does not exist with wood in ground contact; in the ground, hardwoods and softwoods are attacked extensively by both brown rotters and white rotters, and not uncommonly the white rotters will predominate even in a softwood. Perhaps factors inherent in the two kinds of wood that make each more subject to one or the other kind of fungus are counteracted or neutralized by nutrient substances in the soils, by wood-moisture levels determined by the soil, or by nondecay soil microorganisms that get into the wood first.

Some decay fungi can be more aggressive than others in unfavorable environments. In experimentally treated stakes, *Coniophora arida* exhibited unusually broad preservative tolerance, being found with 13 of 15 tested preservatives, whereas most of the other identified fungi were associated with only 4 or fewer preservatives [40]. *Poria nigrescens* and *Peniophora mollis* apparently far surpass most other Basidiomycetes in ability to damage wood that is consistently very wet—as in parts of cooling towers [34]. The prevalence of *L. trabea* in exterior millwork and similar material situated aboveground is thought to be attributable, at least in part, to a superior ability of the fungus to tolerate high temperatures commonly produced in the wood by direct sunlight. It has been established in laboratory studies that *L. trabea* tends to have a substantially higher temperature maximum for growth than the majority of decay species. Even moderate temperature differences possibly account for much of the world variation in geographical distribution of decay fungi. For example, *M. lacrymans* is widely distributed throughout northern Europe but occurs in North America mainly only outside the southern states. Some *M. lacrymans* will scarcely grow at ordinary room temperature.

2.5 Soft Rot

In 1950 Findlay and Savory [47] reported a form of wood deterioration resembling brown rot but which differed from it in certain significant details. Later, observing that the deterioration could result in unusual softening of the wood, Savory [112,113] applied to it the term "soft rot." Although as prevalent as decay, soft rot generally is less distinctive and damaging, which accounts for the fact that it was not recognized earlier as a unique kind of deterioration and one that in some situations could in itself be serious.

2.5.1 Recognition

Soft rot differs from decay in several respects: it is caused by a different group of fungi, the physical and chemical character of its attack on the wood cells differ, and prevalently only the outer wood is severely damaged. Although in some circumstances it may go deep into the wood like decay, soft rot more commonly tends to be concentrated toward the outside. It can often be identified in several ways. As revealed by probing with a knife, the conspicuously degraded wood may be comparatively shallow and the transition between it and the underlying firm wood quite abrupt. When wet, the wood may be so decomposed that it can be scraped from the surface with the fingernail. When dry, the surface of the wood may appear as though it has been lightly charred, and there will be profuse fine cracking and fissuring—both with and across the grain—like that one sees on old, unpainted boards long exposed to the weather (Figure 2.9).

The presence of soft rot usually is confirmed if microscopical examination reveals an abundance of cavities lying entirely with the cell wall. Seen in radial or tangential section, the cavities are elongated and spindle-shaped and follow the angle of the cellulose fibrils [22,81], (Figure 2.10). Isolation and identification of the causal fungus in culture can serve the same purpose.

2.5.2 Effects of soft rot

Where soft rot occurs in a comparatively thin item, as in the fill members of cooling towers, shallow damage can cause serious weakening. Also, the rot occasionally may penetrate deep into the wood, causing loss of serviceability in even large items. Such damage has been observed in Germany in inadequately treated poles of coniferous timber [51] and in hardwood crossties [137]. These observations showed that hardwoods tend to be more subject to soft rot than softwoods, and that wood margin-

Figure 2.9. (and facing page). Typical surface checking of soft-rotted wood when dry. In these samples, as in much soft-rotted wood, the deterioration was comparatively shallow and the wood beneath was quite firm, as though little affected. (Courtesy U.S. Forest Products Laboratory, Madison, Wis.)

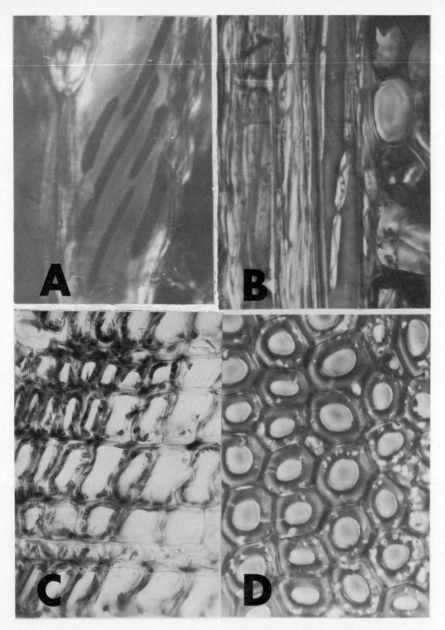

Figure 2.10. Microscopical sections of soft-rotted wood. (A) Typical spiral orientation of cavities produced by the fungus within the secondary wall. (B) Enlarged view of a cavity showing the fungus inside. (C and D) Appearance of the cavities in cross section. (Courtesy U.S. Forest Products Laboratory, Madison, Wis.)

ally treated with a salt preservative such as the German UA fluorine-chromium-arsenic type is more susceptible than one treated with creosote.

A number of experiments have clearly demonstrated an ability of soft rot and mold fungi to detoxify or destroy preservatives, at least if they are in marginal concentrations, rendering the chemicals less effective against decay [38,92,96,144,93,111,27].

Perhaps the most conspicuous effect of soft rot is its contribution to the slow weathering of wood surfaces. Weather elements alone—alternating rain and sunshine which produces cyclic swelling and shrinking, freezing and thawing of the wet surface, and chemical weakening by the actinic rays of the sun—all can cause shallow degradation. Nevertheless, fungi of the soft-rot type seem to be invariably prevalent in the degraded wood and this association, together with the appearance of the wood, suggests that the fungi are an additional and possibly major factor of weathering.

Soft-rot fungi are suspected of contributing occasionally to paint failure by exerting pressure beneath the paint film or by weakening the under-lying surface fibers causing them, with their covering of paint, to become detached [35].

2.5.3 Soft-rot fungi

2.5.3.1 Systematic position

Soft-rot fungi belong to the Ascomycetes and Fungi Imperfecti or Deuteromycetes, the latter being the less common term, which are botanical groups distinctly different from the Basidiomycetes—in which the decay-producing species occur. Except for lacking a known stage of sexual reproduction, the Fungi Imperfecti resemble Ascomycetes. Familiar Ascomycetes are yeasts, bread mold, many common black and green molds, and the morels and truffles prized by some for eating. In culture or viewed microscopically in wood, soft rotters having colorless mycelium can easily be mistaken for decay-producing Basidiomycetes.

In a taxonomic study of soft-rot fungi received at the U.S. Forest Products Laboratory, 69 species were identified [39]. Although not uniformly destructive, Duncan found that most of them could cause substantial degradation of sweetgum (*Liquidambar styraciflua*) sapwood [33]. One of the best known of the more damaging species, *Chaetomium globosum*, has been studied worldwide and used for testing resistance to soft rot.

2.5.3.2 Unique characteristics

Besides the way in which they attack wood, the soft rotters have a number of distinctive physiological and ecological characteristics. Exemplified by *C. globosum*, they differ from decay fungi in the way they modify the wood chemically, resembling white-rot fungi in causing a comparatively small increase in alkali solubility yet behaving like brown-rot species in being unable to utilize the wood lignin extensively [115,82]. According to Duncan [33], soft-rot fungi are more prevalent in hardwoods than softwoods. This coincides with the observation widely reported in the literature that species such as *C. globosum* can be much more easily grown in the laboratory on hardwoods than on softwoods. However, no wood is fully resistant to soft rot, and coniferous woods also are highly vulnerable to many of the fungi if they are in or on damp fertile soil or are wetted in conjunction with suitable nutrient minerals and vitamins.

Partial weakening of the lignin-carbohydrate complex, such as occurs in wood cooling towers wetted by water containing chlorine, will increase susceptibility to soft rot. Similar weakening of the complex is produced on wood surfaces by the mechanical and chemical elements of climate, and probably promotes the initial involvement of soft-rot fungi in weathering. The greater vulnerability of mildly delignified softwoods led Bailey and associates [4] to postulate that soft rotters may lack as efficient a precellulolytic enzyme system as the brown rotters.

The Duncan studies also showed that soft-rot species can, as a group, tolerate certain greater extremes of environment than species causing decay; this hardiness was exhibited in tolerance of higher temperatures, higher pH's, tolerance of preservative chemicals [33], and ability to grow with restricted oxygen [34].

The temperature optima of the soft rotters tended to be considerably higher than those for most wood-destroying Basidiomycetes: for 40 percent of them it was 93°F (34°C), and for 6 percent it was 100°F (38°C). Isolates from cooling towers exhibited temperature optima high enough to suggest that they might represent an ecological group especially able to tolerate warm water passing through the towers. Tolerance of both comparatively high temperatures and dessication must be ascribed to species capable of enduring the microclimate of wood surfaces undergoing weathering on a southern exposure.

The optimum pH for many of the soft rotters tended to center around 6.0, which also is favorable for many decay fungi. Markedly different from the decay fungi, however, was a capacity exhibited by about half the species to maintain maximum growth at pH 7 and some at pH 8. Growth was retarded but not prevented by pH 9.

Tolerance of preservatives by the soft rotters was generally equal to or greater than that of Basidiomycetes. It was much greater for sodium arsenate, sodium chromate, sodium fluoride, and zinc chloride; moderately greater for coal-tar creosote (low residue); and similar for sodium pentachlorophenate, copper sulfate, and mercuric chloride.

Many soft rotters isolated from cooling towers—but not from other sources—possessed a greater capacity than Basidiomycetes to gain weight in culture under severely restricted aeration. This finding supports the general assumption that the prevalence of soft rot but near-absence of ordinary decay in the wet wood of cooling towers is attributable at least in part to a superior tolerance of oxygen deficiency by the rotters involved.

2.5.4 Marine fungi

What essentially is soft rot also occurs in wood submerged in marine waters and, to some extent, in fresh water [5,70,97]. The character of the affected wood is like soft rot, and the causal fungi also are Ascomycetes and Fungi Imperfecti. Such underwater deterioration is slow and typically rather shallow, having negligible direct effect on the serviceability of the infected items. A question has been raised, however, as to whether the fungi may significantly contribute to marine-borer attack by conditioning the wood surface so as to make it more susceptible to the borers [97,110]. Salt-water bacteria conceivably could do the same. Also, either or both they and the fungi might degrade preservatives as noted for the microorganisms on land. The situation in these respects is yet to be clarified.

2.6 Stain

2.6.1 Occurrence and recognition of fungus stain

Next to decay, fungus staining has been the chief target of commercial control measures against microbiological damage to wood. Although far less harmful, decay stains can be very troublesome in some woods; because of their objectionable appearance, the discolored products frequently are rejected by wood users or they are accepted only at a reduced price. Blue stain or sap stain is the most prevalent and economically important of the fungus stains. It is largely a problem with unseasoned raw or primary products such as stored logs and pulpwood, lumber during air seasoning (Figure 2.11) or being held in green packages, and pine poles and piling on the seasoning yard. Lumber once dried is still subject to staining if rewetted, but seems to be less vulnerable than when green. Dark blue staining of seasoned wood is seen now and then in the lower corners of pine window frames that have been wetted by cold-weather condensate running off the glass panes. This staining was once of considerable concern until woodwork manufacturers adopted the practice of dipping or vacuum-treating the frames.

The sapwood of most, if not all, woods is subject to staining, but losses

Figure 2.11. Rough sweetgum lumber with blue stain that developed on the air-seasoning yard alongside lumber that had been protected by dipping with antistain chemical. (Courtesy U.S. Forest Products Laboratory, Madison, Wis.)

through degradation of stained wood in the United States and Canada are greatest with pine lumber and timbers, and with some hardwoods in the South—most notably sweetgum. Blue staining is prevalent under poor drying conditions in western softwoods other than pines, but generally is less disfiguring in these species—partly because of their thinner sapwood but more because the discoloration usually is less intense. Of Pacific Northwest species, Sitka spruce has been reported to be more subject to staining than the true firs (*Abies* spp.), Douglas-fir, western hemlock, or western redcedar [131]. Blue stain has been troublesome in shipments of green-packaged western hemlock and Douglas-fir lumber.

In northern latitudes, blue stain usually is not a problem with either logs or lumber of hardwood species. During the summer months, when it is most vulnerable to infection, unseasoned wood of northern hardwoods such as birches, maples, and beech typically incurs decay so soon after cutting that there is little opportunity for conspicuous development of blue stain.

In species and seasons in which blue stain is prevalent, infection takes place rapidly. Staining typically precedes noticeable decay, and may in the end be the only significant fungus defect. But wood that remains moist and warm for a few weeks or longer, as is often the case with round products and green-packaged lumber, is bound to acquire decay as well as stain.

Blue stain results mainly from the dark color of the fungus hyphae themselves, as seen en masse through the surface layers of the wood. It is essentially limited to sapwood, giving it a dark color that generally goes deep into the wood. The discoloration on softwood products ranges from bluish black to steel gray, and on hardwoods these colors commonly are modified by brown shades. The discoloration may be faint or intense, depending on the conditions of its development and the species of wood. Since typical blue stain goes deep, surfacing will not remove it. Another feature, observed on freshly exposed cross sections of softwood lumber, logs, and other round material, is a marked tendency of the stain to appear in radial streaks or wedge-shaped areas (Figure 2.12). This pattern results from the movement of discoloring fungi inward along the wood rays. Except for color, these features are found with other fungal sap stains also. The radial pattern of discoloration is not often seen in hardwoods because stain fungi are not especially prevalent in the rays, but are more diffusely distributed and occupy many of the longitudinal elements of the wood [14].

Sometimes the interior but not the surface of lumber is discolored (Figure 2.13). Interior stain can be unusually costly because it may not be noticed until the rough lumber has been shipped to a manufacturing

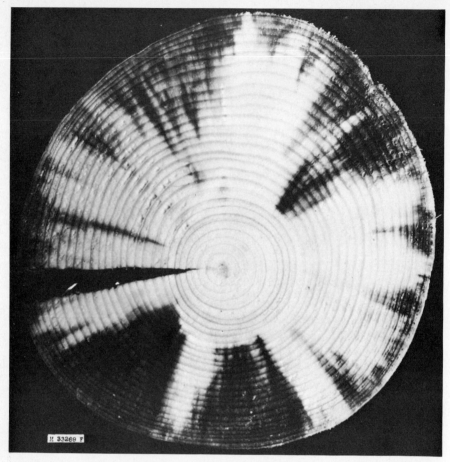

Figure 2.12. Typical wedge-shaped distribution of blue stain in roundwood, resulting from infection of the lateral surface and movement of the fungus inward along the rays. (Courtesy U.S. Forest Products Laboratory, Madison, Wis.)

plant and surfaced. It occurs when infected lumber becomes dry near the surface soon enough to prevent hyphae of the stain fungus in the outer wood from acquiring their dark color but not soon enough to prevent them from reaching the moist interior of the lumber where they can continue to advance and develop color. Interior stain can occur similarly in green lumber that is not surface treated with antistain chemical promptly enough after sawing. The delay permits the fungus to reach the unprotected interior wood although the chemical stops its growth in the outer wood.

Other deep-penetrating fungus stains are of considerably less economic

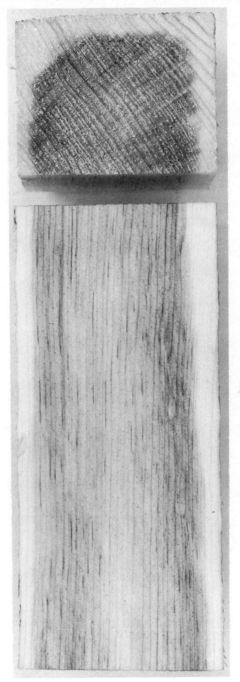

Figure 2.13. Interior stain in lumber. A result of arrested development of the fungus near the surface—by drying or surface treating, but not soon enough to prevent the fungus from getting established deeper in the wood. (Courtesy U.S. Forest Products Laboratory, Madison, Wis.)

importance than blue stain. Many are relatively bright-colored in shades of red, purple, and yellow [131]. Most, but not all, are in sapwood; some are found in trees as well as products. Differing from blue stain, the colors are produced largely by diffusible pigments released by the fungus and taken up by the wood cells. Among the more troublesome minor fungus stains are "brick-red stain," found primarily in both the sapwood and heartwood of Pacific Coast softwood lumber [31], and "brown stain" in pine sapwood, especially in western and northern species of the hard pine group [48]. The brick-red stain is typically rather shallow, but has proved more difficult than blue stain to control by dipping with conventional antistain chemicals. The brown stain has been sufficiently conspicuous and unsightly on pine poles in Canada to create, for a time, concern about its possible effect on the wood strength [48]. This stain closely resembles, and can easily be confused with, a chocolate-brown nonfungus (chemical) stain that develops on some pines in the course of drying.

There are several publications on blue-stain characteristics and control pertinent to the situation in North America. One of the first, and still useful, comprehensive accounts of stain development and influencing factors—mainly in lumber and logs—was given by Scheffer and Lindgren [131]. Subsequently, Verrall and Mook studied and reported on a large number of variables affecting successful chemical control of stain and decay in green lumber [153]. A broad review of the subject was prepared by Findlay [46]. A comparatively recent description of successful chemical measures for controlling blue staining of pine logs in Britain is given by Savory and others [116]. A review of means of log protection in North America appeared in 1969 [120]. According to Cserjesi and Roff [28], the problem of stain in green-packaged Canadian lumber can be reduced to a large extent by dip treating the freshly cut lumber. Evidence by Savory [114], indicates this practice may be generally adequate for shipments received in England if suitable additional precautions are observed, such as avoiding infected lumber to begin with and not holding the lumber in the package for too many months.

Protection of lumber against sap stain and such decay as may be incurred with it is largely accomplished by kiln drying or, temporarily, by surface treating with a water solution of conventional antistain fungicide, applied by brief dipping or spraying. Commonly used fungicides are one or more of sodium pentachlorophenate, borax, and an organic mercurial. Where insect infestation must also be controlled, as is sometimes the case, the treating solution must include an insecticide as well as the fungicide.

Logs in the woods or on the storage site also can be chemically protected by spraying with the same chemicals, but stronger solutions than are generally used on lumber are required. Oil solutions of pentachlorophenol are preferred where an insecticide is to be incorporated. For the longer storage periods, coating the log ends to prevent checking gives maximum protection. Peeled round products such as poles and piling cannot be reliably protected by ordinary dipping or spraying. Such superficial treating can keep the surface bright, which may be an advantage if appearance is of considerable importance but, because of subsequent development of seasoning checks, the untreated interior wood becomes exposed to infection. Good protection against fungus damage to these products on the seasoning yard, nevertheless, can be accomplished by comparatively simple diffusion treatment with ammonium bifluoride that gets the fungicide deep into the sapwood [107].

2.6.2 Physical properties of blue-stained wood

2.6.2.1 Strength

Blue stain ordinarily is accompanied by very little reduction of wood strength except for toughness or shock resistance. Chapman and Scheffer [17] concluded that in intensely stained pine sapwood there might commonly be reductions of 1–2 percent in specific gravity, 2–10 percent in surface hardness, 1–5 percent in bending and crushing strength, and 15–30 percent in toughness. Similar mild reductions in strength other than toughness also seem to be generally characteristic of staining in the hardwoods [14]. Cartwright and Findlay [15] reported a 20 percent reduction in bending strength and 43 percent reduction in toughness of a stained tropical hardwood, but the accompanying drop in specific gravity was about 12 percent, suggesting that the stain fungus in this case had progressed so far as to initiate soft rot. Some stain and mold fungi can cause soft rot if conditions favorable to their development are sufficiently prolonged, but this would be a rather uncommon occurrence in properly handled logs and lumber.

Thus, wood with strictly blue stain should be strong enough for any use except that in which shock resistance is a prime requirement. Severe stain would be undesirable in items expected to withstand repeated jars, jolts, and blows such as are given baseball bats, some tool handles, and certain moving machine parts made of wood. It would be undesirable, moreover, in products such as ladders and scaffolding that must be depended on for the safety of the user. Consideration of the strength of blue-stained wood should always include recognition that intense stain, especially that in a mottled pattern, may be accompanied by hidden incipient decay since prominent staining is evidence that conditions have also been suitable for decay.

2.6.2.2 Permeability

Blue-stained wood is more porous and permeable than comparable sound wood because of openings in its microstructure made by the penetrating fungus. Thus, staining can facilitate uptake of preservative solution into dry wood [88]. If the wood is exposed to rain wetting, however, staining may—like decay infection—have an opposite effect. Because of its greater permeability, stained wood tends to absorb more water than bright wood and thus be more liable to undertreatment.

2.6.2.3 Drying characteristics

Blue stain does not retard air drying of lumber protected by a pile cover, but rather may slightly reduce the drying time; moreover, any differences in the final equilibrium moisture content are negligibly small [131].

2.6.2.4 Decay vulnerability

Staining does not alter natural decay resistance significantly, but it can, nevertheless, make wood more vulnerable to decay by increasing its permeability and resulting susceptibility to serious rain wetting. Consequently, in the wetter climates one can justifiably avoid building with stained millwork that is to be exposed to the weather.

2.6.3 Stain fungi

2.6.3.1 Species and wood associations

Stain fungi belong to the same botanical groups as those responsible for soft rot, namely, the Ascomycetes and Fungi Imperfecti. Verrall [149] concluded from extensive isolations and confirmatory inoculations that the majority of stain damage to lumber and logs in the South is by eight species. Three are mainly in pine—*Ceratocystis pilifera, C. ips.,* and *Diplodia* sp.—and four in hardwoods—*C. virescens, C. plurianulata, C. moniliformis,* and *Graphium rigidum.* One species, *D. natelensis,* is prevalent on both pines and hardwoods. These fungi produce primary spores on tiny stalk- or bristlelike structures that can easily be recognized with the aid of hand lens. The spores are disseminated by air currents, insects, and milling machinery, the relative importance of these vectors varying somewhat with the fungus species [150]. Verrall found no significant differences between species occurring in lumber and in logs or species in dipped or in undipped lumber. Perhaps uniquely, some of the stain caused by *D. natelensis* is derived from an infection source other than wood—the cotton plant, which suffers from boll rot by this fungus. The principal western blue stainers apparently are not the same as those in the South. Davidson [30] identified two common and conspicuous species on western coniferous lumber: one, *C. coerulescens,* and the other, *C. piceae.* The predominant blue stainer of window frames wetted by condensation is *Aureobasidium pullulans.* The prominent brown fungus stain in lumber across the northern United States and Canada is caused by a single species, *Cytospora* sp. [48]. The occasionally troublesome brick-red stain of lumber of some northern softwoods is caused by *Cephaloascus fragrans* (*Ascocybe grovesii*).

2.6.3.2 Unique characteristics

Physiological studies by Lindgren showed that certain prominent *Ceratocystis* species, although able to invade slightly drier wood, could not develop their normal dark color—producing stain—unless the moisture content was above the fiber-saturation point [84]. Thus, in their moisture requirements for serious discoloration these fungi were comparable to decay fungi. Temperature relations were also comparable. Lindgren's studies also showed that the stainers investigated could penetrate into pine sapwood at daily rates of 0.5, 1.0, and 4.5 mm in the tangential, radial, and longitudinal directions, respectively. Penetrations in 48 hours at these rates were below the depths ordinarily reached by fungicidal solutions conventionally applied by dipping or spraying—which coincides with practical experience that when temperatures are optimal for staining, surface treating for temporary protection of logs and green lumber or timbers should not be delayed longer than approximately one day following cutting or sawing.

Unlike decay fungi, the stainers ordinarily do not initially attack the strength-giving cell walls of the wood, which accounts for the generally adequate strength of stained wood. The principal species depend for their early nourishment on parenchymatous tissue—as in the wood rays—and on sugars and starch in the cells. They may make some bore holes in traversing cell walls, but it is only with prolonged favorable conditions that some are able to enter the cell wall and cause soft rot.

The virtual absence of blue staining in heartwood seems to be attributable chiefly to a shortage of relatively easily metabolized carbohydrates rather than to inhibitory heartwood extractives.

2.6.4 Chemical stain

Green sapwood of many woods, chiefly hardwoods, also is subject to discolorations that often resemble those of fungus origin but actually are independent of microorganisms. This kind of discoloration is caused by oxidation of certain of the wood constituents on exposure to air, hence its name, chemical stain (or oxidation stain). Analogous staining is the browning of apple tissue on exposure to the air. Chemical staining, like fungus staining, is troublesome largely in logs and in lumber that is dried too slowly in warm weather. Favorable factors are temperatures above about 50°F and wood moisture above 30 percent.

One of the more costly chemical stains of hardwoods, resembling interior blue stain, occurs in lumber of some of the red oaks [19]. Similar staining occurs in lumber of tupelo gum, magnolia, birch, maple, basswood, and other hardwoods. Sometimes the stain may occur only under cross sticks separating the lumber during drying, because of retarded drying at these areas. A reddish or rust-colored stain developing progressively inward from the ends of birch logs can be serious in northern United States and Canada during summer months. A yellowish-to-reddish staining of logs and lumber is a problem with western alder in the Pacific Northwest.

The principal chemical staining of softwoods is a brown discoloration in lumber of northern white pine, sugar pine, and ponderosa pine. Chemical brown stain of pines is unique in that it occurs more in heartwood than sapwood. It is accentuated by high dry-kiln temperatures. Development and control are described by Stutz and by Cech [142,16]. A similar discoloration of western pines which occurs only in the sapwood, is initiated by bacterial infestation of ponded logs and is termed "sour-log" stain [142]. Another chemical or oxidation stain recognized commercially in softwoods is a shallow brown discoloration of sapwood on the ends and sides of western hemlock lumber ("hemlock brown stain") [6].

The oxidation type of chemical staining of hardwood logs can be minimized by rapid conversion in mild weather or by excluding air, as by ponding or water spraying. Staining of lumber can be reduced on the seasoning yard by getting the stock air dry as quickly as possible. Kiln drying will prevent staining of some hardwoods, using where necessary as mild a schedule (low temperature) as practicable. Control of discoloration of some hardwoods can be accomplished by heating the wood promptly after sawing to a high temperature (e.g., 200°F for oak [19]), which destroys the oxidizing enzymes. Chemical brown stain of pines can be controlled by dipping or spraying the lumber immediately after sawing with sodium azide or sodium fluoride solutions, which inhibit the oxidizing enzymes. The hemlock brown stain is shallow and can be eliminated by planing, providing the lumber remains dry [6].

Wet wood can also discolor by contact with iron. Iron stain often resembles blue stain, the color ranging from pale gray to intense bluish black—depending on the amount of iron and the duration of contact.

The stain in this case is produced by reaction between the iron and tannins in the wood, forming iron tannate—a material sometimes used in making black ink. Iron stain may appear faintly in the wood of logs stored for a long time in water having a comparatively high iron content. Dark staining is common on lumber and plywood at places that have been in contact with iron fasteners or equipment, or in spots where iron particles have settled. The familiar dark streaks extending from nails in wetted wood is iron stain. Copper or copper alloys will form copper tannate, producing a reddish rather than black discoloration.

Some of the chemical stains resemble blue stain, and some tend to resemble one another. Table 2.3 summarizes some of the similarities and differences between various stains or kinds of stains. A feature that identifies many chemical stains of the oxidation type is a comparatively shallow and uniform depth of penetration, reflecting limited and uniform penetration of air. In contrast, blue stain and other fungus stains typically are comparatively deep and irregular (Figure 2.12). Iron, copper, and the oxidation stains of hardwoods can quickly be partially or wholly eradicated with a strong solution of bleaching agent such as oxalic acid, whereas blue stain can be removed practically only with stronger bleaches accompanied by heating. Iron stain can be confirmed by positive color response to the sensitive potassium ferrocyanide test for iron, *i.e.*, 19 percent hydrochloric acid followed by a 12 percent solution of potassium ferrocyanide.

Except for the iron and copper stains, the chemical discolorations are not accompanied by significant alteration of the wood other than for color. Iron-stained wood of some species is known to have less natural decay resistance than normal wood [76], presumably because fungus-inhibitory extractives are inactivated by reaction with the iron. Also, as observed, prolonged action of iron or copper may cause chemical breakdown of the wood structure.

2.7 Mold

2.7.1 Occurrence and recognition

Mold, like blue stain, is a discoloring blemish primarily of sapwood. Antistain chemicals for lumber generally are formulated to protect against both mold and stain. Mold differs from typical fungus stains in its comparatively shallow discoloration; mold fungi regularly penetrate deep into wood, but the discoloration occurs mostly at or near the surface. Visible molding of softwoods is produced chiefly by surface development of masses of colored spores (Figure 2.14). Predominant colors are shades of green, but black is common and occasionally orange and other light

TABLE 2.3

Common Discolorations of Native Woods and Their Causes

Color of Stain	Designation and Miscellaneous Characteristics	Items in Which It Commonly Occurs	Common Cause
	Fungus Discolorations		
Steel gray to bluish black, principally: brown shades common on hardwoods.	Blue stain (sap stain). Occurs in spots, streaks, or patches which cover all or part of the sapwood. Moldlike growths of causal fungi often present on surface of stained areas. Generally penetrates deeply.	Lumber and logs of practically all commercial wood species. Wetted millwork, e.g., window frames (sapwood).	Dark hyphae of species of *Ceratocystis, Diplodia, Graphium,* and *Aureobasidium.*
Dull brown to gray or black	Mold stain. Discoloration persisting in surface layers of molded wood after surfacing or brushing. Usually spotty and comparatively shallow.	Lumber and veneer of hardwoods (sapwood primarily).	Soluble pigment of mold fungi; sometimes sporulation of the fungi in vessels near the surface of the wood
Various, green predominating, black common	Surface mold. Colored fungus growths present on surface of wood. On softwoods, it generally can be removed by planing and sometimes by brushing.	Various products of all commercial wood species (sapwood primarily).	Presence of *Trichoderma, Penicillium, Gliocladium, Aspergillus, Monilia,* and other fungi sporulating on the surface of the wood
Chocolate brown chiefly	Fungus brown stain. Occurs much like blue stain except for color. Color closely resembles that of chemical brown stain.	Poles and lumber. Especially in western and northern species of the hard pine group (sapwood).	Mainly soluble pigment of *Cytospora* sp.; also some dark hyphae.
Purple to pink	Bright-colored fungus stain. Occurs usually as blotches or small streaks. May penetrate deeply.	Southern pine and red gum lumber and logs (sapwood).	Soluble pigment and colored hyphae of *Fusarium moniliforme, F. solani, F. viride,* and *F. roseum.*

Pink to cinnamon brown	Brick-red stain. Usually in spots but may cover large areas. Usually relatively shallow. More resistant than blue-stain fungi to some anti-stain chemicals.	Logs and lumber of northern and Pacific Coast softwoods (sapwood and heartwood).	Soluble pigment of *Cephaloascus fragrans*.
Crimson to orange	Bright-colored fungus stain. Occurs usually as blotches or small streaks. May penetrate deeply.	Southern pine, gum, oak, and other hardwood lumber and logs (sapwood).	Soluble pigment of *Penicillium roseum* and *P. aureum*.
Crimson to orange	Bright-colored fungus stain. Occurs usually as blotches or small streaks. May penetrate deeply.	Southern pine, southern cypress, and oak lumber (sapwood and heartwood).	Soluble pigment of *Geotrichum* sp.
Pale yellow	Bright-colored fungus stain. Occurs usually as blotches or small streaks. May penetrate deeply.	Lumber and logs of oak, birch, hickory, and maple (sapwood and heartwood).	Soluble pigment of *Penicillium divaricatum*.
Deep yellow	Bright-colored fungus stain. Occurs usually as blotches or small streaks. May penetrate deeply.	Southern pine and red gum lumber and logs (sapwood).	Colored hyphae and to some extent soluble pigment of a *Gymnoscus*-like fungus.

Chemical Discolorations—Oxidation Type

Pale blue and brown	Chemical (oxidation) stain of hardwoods. Most common as a general interior stain and may not be observed until lumber is surfaced. Frequently resembles light blue stain. Sometimes appears only under seasoning stickers. Usually shallow and of uniform depth but can penetrate deeply.	Oak, birch, maple, basswood, tupelo gum, magnolia, and other hardwood lumber (sapwood).	Oxidation of certain wood substances on exposure to air during air seasoning or kiln drying.

TABLE 2.3 continued

Common Discolorations of Native Woods and Their Causes

Color of Stain	Designation and Miscellaneous Characteristics	Items in Which It Commonly Occurs	Common Cause
Chocolate-brown chiefly.	Chemical brown stain of lumber of western and eastern pines. Narrow margins of bright wood common at board surfaces and at juncture of heartwood and sapwood. May penetrate deeply.	White pine, ponderosa pine, and sugar pine lumber (sapwood and heartwood).	Oxidation of certain wood substances during air seasoning or kiln drying.
Brown	Hemlock brown stain. Mainly on ends and sides of lumber. Very shallow.	Lumber of western hemlock (sapwood).	Oxidation of tanninlike substances accumulated near the surface during drying.
Greenish black	Chemical stain of persimmon. Occurs as a general discoloration. May penetrate deeply.	Persimmon blocks (sapwood).	Oxidation of certain wood substances exposed to air during seasoning.
Yellowish to red	Bright-colored chemical stain of alder. Appears more or less as a general discoloration. May penetrate deeply.	Western alder logs and lumber (sapwood).	Oxidation of certain wood substances on exposure to air
Reddish yellow to rusty	Bright-colored chemical stain of birch. Appears more or less as a general discoloration. May penetrate deeply.	Birch logs (sapwood).	Oxidation of certain wood substances on exposure to air. Mainly a problem of warm weather.

Other Discolorations

Pale gray to black	Iron stain. Inklike streaks, blotches, or spots where nails or iron equipment or particles have contacted wet wood. May develop as general, light gray discoloration in logs stored a long time in water containing considerable iron. Can be confirmed by potassium ferrocyanide test for iron.	Lumber and various wood products with necessary tannin content (in both heartwood and sapwood).	Chemical reaction between iron and tannins in the wood, forming iron tannate.
Rust or copper shade	Copper stain. Like iron stain except for color.	As for iron stain. Observed in wood wetted by salt water.	Chemical reaction between copper, usually in copper alloys, and tannin in the wood.
Greenish brown	Mineral stain. Occurs in lenticular streaks of all sizes or as a general discoloration.	Living hardwood trees—prominent in hard maples and sweetgum lumber and veneer (sapwood and heartwood).	Unknown. Can be initiated by injuries.
Brown	Kiln burn and machine burn. Surface of lumber has a scorched appearance. Usually shallow penetration.	All lumber (sapwood and heartwood).	Light burning of wood due to excessive kiln temperature or to heat developed by planer knives.

Figure 2.14. Molded sweetgum veneer. Sheet 2: Typical mold discoloration by masses of spores. Sheet 6 (facing page): Shallow staining as well as superficial blemishing, as often produced by molding of hardwoods. (Courtesy U.S. Forest Products Laboratory, Madison, Wis.)

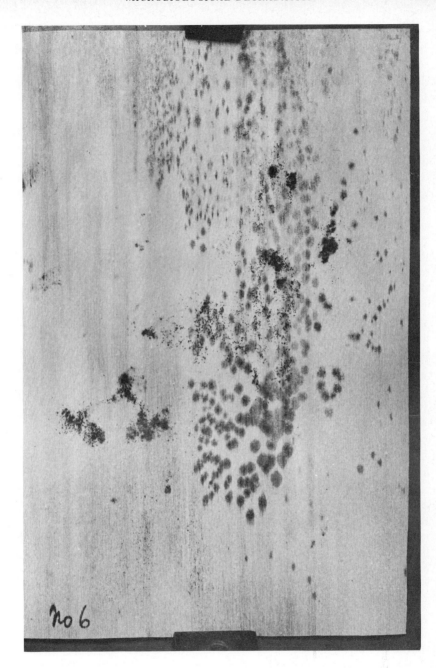

shades are seen. The discoloration imparted by spore masses can generally be removed by planing or even brushing. On hardwoods, molding often causes shallow staining in addition to the surface discoloration (Figure 2.14). This staining usually is dark-colored and spotty, and is very objectionable on some of the more valuable products such as plywood face veneer.

Molds frequently occur with other fungi, which often makes it difficult to isolate decay fungi or blue stainers in pure culture because the molds tend to overrun and mask the others.

Molding is heaviest on wood that has never been dried. Green lumber, timbers, round wood, and veneer are very susceptible. Hardwood veneer bulk piled ahead of the drier may mold objectionably over a long weekend. Shipments of green lumber containing much sapwood may mold and stain severely and often begin to decay before they reach their destination.

Furniture and other interior wood in homes may mold during very warm and humid weather if ventilation is restricted. Certain finishes seem to accentuate this. Some waterborne preservatives, though effective against decay, will not prevent development of certain molds.

2.7.2 Effects of molding

Mold fungi behave much like most blue stainers in their invasion of wood. Except where prolonged favorable conditions permit certain of them to damage the cell wall, causing soft rot, they attack mainly the more readily utilizable material—the parenchymatous elements, starches, and sugars—affecting only the appearance and permeability of the wood. Species able to cause soft rot could be classified both as mold and soft rot, the distinction being according to the kind of damage rather than botanical.

Strength other than toughness is little affected by molding, but the permeability of the wood may be greatly increased. In pioneering field studies of the influence of molding on permeability, Lindgren [85] and Harvey [87] observed nonpressure absorptions of oil preservative into heavily molded southern pine posts 8 or 9 times greater, and radial penetrations 30–40 times greater, than those obtained in essentially fungus-free posts. In Douglas-fir posts, absorptions were 3–6 times greater, and penetrations comparably greater, in heavily molded than in fungicidally protected control posts [89]. Similarly, Schulz [135] obtained absorptions and penetrations in soak-treated and in pressure-treated spruce and aspen that were usually 3–5 times greater in heavily molded than in uninfected wood. The heaviest molding in these studies was by a green mold, *Trichoderma viride,* growth of which was stimulated by dipping or spraying the green wood with a fluoride solution.

The greater permeability of molded wood can, like that noted for blue-stained wood, have adverse effects of causing uneven or variable uptake of preservatives and of making rain-wetted millwork vulnerable to decay over longer periods.

As noted in discussing soft rot, molds have been observed to degrade preservatives.

2.7.3 Mold fungi (molds)

The mold fungi also belong to the Ascomycetes and Fungi Imperfecti, as might be suspected from characteristics they share with blue stainers and soft rotters. Familiar molds in the home are the fungus growths that occur in unrefrigerated foodstuffs. Most troublesome of the wood molds are species of *Trichoderma, Gliocladium,* and *Penicillium,* all of which discolor surfaces with their green spores. Species of *Alternaria* and *Aspergillus* are responsible for much of the black mold. Perhaps all wood molds also grow on other substrates, and a variety of molds that occur mainly on other materials will at times extend their range to wood. Molds can be useful as well as damaging, notable examples being those used to make different kinds of cheese and to produce many indispensable antibiotics such as penicillin.

The wood molds, like soft-rot species, seem as a group to be more highly adaptable to or tolerant of unfavorable conditions or materials than decay fungi. Some molds can develop on air-dry wood with a moisture content in the 20 percent range. Thus, a susceptible wood can become noticeably molded simply as a result of exposure to air in which the relative humidity is about 90 percent or above. This accounts for occasional molding of furniture or other interior wood during humid weather.

One of the most striking manifestations of mold tolerance is the capacity to grow in contact with, or even degrade, toxic chemicals. Verrall has called attention to several molds on pine lumber that are capable of tolerating, or that even may be stimulated by, chemical treatments that are effective in controlling most wood-inhabiting fungi [151]. There is hardly a chemical regarded as poisonous that some species of mold cannot withstand in a concentration that would be lethal to most other organisms. *Trichoderma* will grow luxuriantly on pine sapwood treated with sodium fluoride or ammonium bifluoride—seemingly to the virtual exclusion of other fungi [85]. The ubiquitous presence of a "creosote fungus," *Hormodendron resinae,* in creosoted wood that has been in service for a time has long been known [96].

Many molds also have superior tolerance of higher temperatures. This can be a problem in kiln drying with a low-temperature schedule, unless the lumber is first surface treated. Such broad tolerance presumably arises from the predominance of molds among world fungi, and the profusion of spores borne by them—resulting in an infinite variety of strains and the accompanying very wide range of physiological attributes.

2.8 Bacterial Degradation

2.8.1 Occurrence of bacteria in wood

Bacteria are common in wood products, and often are associated with fungi. The possibility has been noted that they may sometimes favor invasion of decay fungi by conditioning the wood in some way. It is not unlikely that they contribute significantly at some point in the process to the ultimate biological breakdown of wood. In general, they do relatively little harm except in rather special circumstances, or over very long periods. Although bacteria have long been known to destroy pure cellulose, it was only rather recently that it became apparent that some are capable of seriously damaging lignified tissues if favored by appropriate conditions or time in which to act. The factor most conducive to bacterial damage to wood is high moisture content—as high as or higher than can be tolerated by most fungi.

Bacteria accumulate in logs that are ponded for several weeks or months [75], and their presence may be evidenced by a sour smell of the logs and green lumber. Bacteria also can infest veneer bolts of susceptible woods kept for an extended time in a holding tank or under a water spray [91,61,134]. The more stagnant the water, the greater the accumulation of nutrient debris which favors a build-up of bacteria. Limited trials of biocides in the water to control bacterial invasion of ponded logs have not been promising. It may be possible to protect tank-stored veneer bolts, but only if the logs are free of bacteria when placed in the tank [61].

Since most soils teem with bacteria, untreated wood in contact with wet or damp ground will in time practically always contain bacteria. Extremely wet wood, as in piles located below the water table, typically will contain bacteria but no active fungi. Similarly, bacteria usually can be found, though not necessarily in deep penetration, in submerged portions of wood structures in fresh water or sea water. Like soft-rot fungi, they also may invade the wetter elements of cooling towers. Some even enter living trees, producing what is known as wet wood [58,155].

2.8.2 Characteristics of wood invaded by bacteria

Bacterial inhabitants of wood have been troublesome in North America, chiefly by causing abnormal absorptivity of the sapwood in ponded logs of western pines [41,75]. Millwork of such wood, when preservative treated by short soaking or vacuum process, tends to acquire an excessive quantity of solution. Such wood retains so much of the preservative solvent that it cannot be safely painted, so must be held off the market until "dry." Comparable abnormal absorptions could be expected also in pressure-treated lumber.

Knuth concluded [74] that the primary way by which bacteria make wood abnormally permeable is through damage to the pit membrane— creating passageways from cell to cell. This conclusion has been supported in observations by Liese and Karnop [83], Johnson and Gjovik [69], and others. The pits in pines may be generally more vulnerable to bacteria than those in some other woods such as hemlock and Douglas-fir, which have encrustations on the membranes [7]. Bacteria also directly facilitate radial penetration by opening up the wood rays, and the horizontal resin ducts in softwoods.

Bacteria ordinarily do not weaken wood appreciably. Nevertheless, strength sometimes is seriously reduced; the extent to which this occurs and the conducive factors are receiving increasing attention. Prolonged infestation by some species may bring about severe degradation of the wood cell walls, with over-all weakening depending on the size of the item and the depth to which the wood is affected. Micromorphological changes in the walls differing from those caused by fungi have been observed [139,57,23,54,55].

Considerable weakening by bacteria of small wood specimens can occur in the laboratory within a few months, although this result cannot always be assured. Little effect beyond opening up of the microstructure was obtained in extensive culturing of wood specimens by Knuth [74]; in contrast, Siefert [139] obtained weight losses amounting to 7 percent in pine sapwood and Bauch et al. [7] obtained a 75 percent reduction in impact bending strength (toughness). Combinations of species, wood, and specific culture conditions required for sizable weakening by bacteria have not been established.

Wood submerged in fresh water or in mud is not, as once thought, necessarily immune to biological degradation. Even a large item such as a pile can eventually be considerably weakened by bacteria. This was recently noted with southern pine piles that had supported a bridge over the Potomac River for 62 years. The crushing strength of the sampled wood above the mud line had been reduced by approximately 60 percent and of that below by 20 percent [126]. Evidence in microscopical damage or strength tests of long-term bacterial weakening has also been reported for foundation piles of pine and spruce after 75 years of service in Stockholm [8] and 90 years in Copenhagen [57].

Comparatively thin items may be objectionably weakened by bacteria within a few years, or even months. In this regard, Greaves [54] observed treated cooling-tower slats in Australia that had been damaged by bacteria, though fungal attack had been largely prevented.

In a critical examination of pine veneer from bacteria-infested logs that had been summer-stored under a water spray, and from bolts tank-stored for 6 months in warm water, Lutz and associates found no significant loss of strength [91]. A loss in toughness near 10 percent was measured by Scheld and DeGroot [134] in wood of summer-cut longleaf pine logs stored for 4 and 8 months with continuous sprinkling. Occasionally, one may yet find veneer from tank-stored bolts that will show, simply by breaking in the hand, extreme bacterial weakening. Such a variation in damage suggests involvement of different species of bacteria resulting from unknown variables of bolt source, manner of handling, or of the tank water. Veneer that is not materially weakened by long wet storage, nevertheless, may have abnormally high permeability, affecting somewhat the characteristics of rotary cutting and of the veneer produced [91].

It was noted in discussing chemical or oxidation staining that bacteria developing in stored logs can produce materials that turn brown on exposure to the air, thereby discoloring the sapwood of affected lumber [142,45].

It should also be recognized that bacteria may, like some fungi, inactivate or destroy preservatives. Their possible role in this respect seems to have been investigated only for marine inhabitants. Drisko [32] and Duncan discovered that bacteria could strikingly reduce the decay-inhibiting potency of creosote (unpublished). But whatever preservatives bacteria may be able to degrade, general experience suggests that the harm done to well-treated wood must be quite small. Nevertheless, the matter deserves some further consideration.

2.8.3 Species and unique characteristics of bacteria

Many species of bacteria are capable of developing in wood, and the environment and kind of wood presumably dominate in determining just which ones are present in a particular item. Knuth [74] in a comprehensive exploratory survey of bacteria in wood products, traced 198 isolates to species of *Bacillus, Aerobacter,* and *Pseudomonas*—all common soil and water inhabitants. The species responsible for most of the excessive permeability in millwork from ponded logs of western pines was identified as *Bacillus polymyxa* [75]. Research by Harmsen and Nissen [57] and others disclosed that Actinomycetes also may be common wood modifiers.

In pure culture, Knuth's isolates caused a slight weight loss and a large increase in sapwood permeability, thus demonstrating a broad spectrum of capability among bacteria for at least mildly degrading wood. Some isolates were able to degrade heartwood also, which suggests a possible means of improving heartwood permeability to preservatives. Sapwood may normally be more easily affected by bacteria because of its starch content which, together with other contents of the ray parenchyma, seems to be an influential initial source of nutrition for the invading organisms [74].

Bacteria penetrate from cell to cell through the pits by rupturing the pit membrane. Their rapid invasion along the entire length of ponded logs appears to be largely by radial penetration, beginning at the inner bark and progressing inward through the rays and transverse resin canals [75]. The prevalence of bacteria in deeply submerged, water-saturated wood denotes a special ability of the organisms to develop with extremely little oxygen; some can develop anaerobically [75]. Bacteria as a class may be as remarkable as some of the soft rotters and molds in their tolerance of toxic chemicals. Besides their ability to detoxify creosote, bacteria have shown a high tolerance of copper-chrome-arsenic, creosote, penta-chlorophenol, and tributyltin oxide [53].

2.9 Natural Decay Resistance of Wood

2.9.1 Source of resistance

The heartwood of many timber species is highly resistant to decay and will give long service under conditions of severe decay hazard. Though there are measurable species differences, the sapwood has negligible decay resistance. The durability of heartwood is derived from extractive con-stituents acting as natural preservatives (Figure 2.15). These, like the ex-tractives that give heartwood its darker color, are created largely during the transformation of sapwood to heartwood.

The known decay-inhibiting extractives are phenolic compounds, with effectiveness determined by the kinds and amounts present, their chemi-cal stability, and resistance to depletion by leaching, volatilization, or microbial degradation. In some woods, more than one inhibitory com-pound may be acting—possibly synergistically. Indication of synergistic action was found, for example, in incense cedar, in which six fungi-toxic chemicals were discovered [3].

Density or other physical characteristics of wood does not affect decay resistance appreciably. Superior decay resistance is associated with greater weight in many tropical hardwoods, but this is a reflection of relatively large extractive contents—including decay inhibitors—rather than of the greater density contributed by wood substance. The fundamentals of natural decay resistance have been summarized by Scheffer and Cowling [124].

Figure 2.15. Growth of a decay fungus on malt-agar medium containing progressively greater (left to right) amounts of water-soluble extractive from black locust heartwood. (Courtesy U.S. Forest Products Laboratory, Madison, Wis.)

2.9.2 Natural decay resistance of wood species

Species differences in decay resistance are, like the differences in wood structure and other botanical characteristics, genetically determined. Greatest resistance occurs in some of the hardwoods. Black locust fence posts, for example, are known to have served for as long as 100 years on eastern farms. Posts of osage orange probably are comparably durable. Outstandingly durable wood is especially common among tropical hardwoods [124]. Woods such as greenheart and teak are universally renowned for superior durability, and many other durable species less familiar in North America might be mentioned.

Of domestic woods commonly used for structural purposes, the only hardwood species having substantial decay resistance are in the white oak group. White oak has long been used for boat framing because it combines both strength and comparatively good durability. The cedars and redwood are the only native softwood species available for those wanting decay resistance without preservative treating. Baldcypress, the "wood eternal," was once widely used, but all-heartwood lumber or timbers of the species are no longer obtainable in quantity.

Table 2.4 gives the comparative decay resistance of the more common domestic woods. Quantitative results of tests of resistance of a number of native species are available; pines [20], Douglas-fir [127], pole species [42], western redcedar [118], black locust [130], and oaks [128].

The list of tropical woods known to be durable is growing as increasing attention is directed to their utilization. Near the end of World War II, 41 Central American and Ecuadorian hardwoods being considered for bridge timbers were tested for decay resistance, and about a fourth to a third of them warranted classification as very resistant [125]. The relative durability and other properties of imported tropical woods have been conveniently reported by Kukachka for more than 100 species [79]. An earlier, expanded version of the report incorporating 174 species also is available [78]. Brown [10] has furnished durability ratings and a listing of other properties and uses of 118 tropical hardwoods in the United Kingdom. Osborne [105] provided tabular summaries of relative decay resistance of more than 150 species of Southwest Pacific rain-forest timbers. Reports of specific tests incorporating additional tropical woods include U.S. imports for exterior use [21], mahoganies [101], Peruvian woods [62], and miscellaneous [14]. Tests by Moses [101] showed that true mahogany (*Swetenia* spp.) has greater decay resistance than the African (*Khaya* spp.) and Philippine (chiefly *Shorea* spp.) mahoganies.

A classification of durability based simply on general experience or the reputation of a wood for serviceability may reflect termite as well as decay resistance. High decay resistance does not denote comparable termite re-

TABLE 2.4

Comparative Decay Resistance of the Heartwood of Some Common Native Species

Resistant or Very Resistant	Moderately Resistant	Slightly or Nonresistant
Baldcypress (old growth)*	Baldcypress (young growth)*	Alder
Catalpa	Douglas-fir	Ashes
Cedars	Honey locust[†]	Aspens
Cherry, black	Larch, western	Basswood
Chestnut	Oak, swamp chestnut	Beech
Cypress, Arizona	Pine, eastern white*	Birches
Junipers	Pine, longleaf*	Buckeye[†]
Locust, black[‡]	Pine, slash*	Butternut
Mulberry, red[‡]	Tamarack	Cottonwood
Oak, burr		Elms
Oak, chestnut		Hackberry
Oak, Gambel		Hemlocks
Oak, Oregon white		Hickories
Oak, post		Magnolia
Oak, white		Maples
Osage-orange[‡]		Oak (red and black species)[†]
Redwood		Pines (most other species)[†]
Sassafras		Poplar
Walnut, black		Spruces
Yew, Pacific[‡]		Sweetgum[†]
		Sycamore
		Willows
		Yellow-poplar

*The southern and eastern pines and baldcypress are now largely second growth, with a large proportion of sapwood. Consequently, it is no longer practicable to obtain substantial quantities of heartwood lumber in these species for general building purposes.

[†]These species, or certain species within the groups, are indicated to have higher decay resistance than most of the other woods in their respective categories.

[‡]These woods have exceptionally high decay resistance.

sistance, but low decay resistance and low termite resistance invariably go together. Of our readily available domestic woods, only foundation-grade coast redwood is considered to have useful termite resistance; it is not immune, however.

2.9.3 Resistance variability within a species

Although heartwood of a particular wood species may be relatively durable on the whole, individual selections of the wood may differ markedly in decay resistance. Differences in resistance among trees of the same species may sometimes be as large as species differences. This is strikingly illustrated in comparisons of decay resistance among oaks [128], pines [20], and western redcedar [118]. Such variability among trees of the same species seems, like species differences, to be genetically determined, and the character of the site on which the wood is grown has very little effect [130,128].

Natural decay resistance of heartwood also may vary substantially within individual trees. The variation tends to follow broadly a pattern in relation to such factors as the size and age of the tree—or, perhaps more specifically, of the heartwood—and the location of the wood in the trunk. General features of the pattern found in many durable woods are shown in the curves of Figure 2.16 for black locust. Decay resistance is greatest in the outer heartwood and decreases from there to the pith. Furthermore, this radial spread in resistance is larger as the heartwood diameter increases, with the most resistant wood being in the outer heartwood and the least resistant in the central heartwood at the base of the largest trees. Intermediate levels of resistance are found higher in the trunk or in smaller trees.

Experimental evidence suggests that the radial decrease in resistance may be largely due to a gradual conversion of the fungus-inhibitory phenolic compounds to less toxic materials as the wood ages [3]. Some of the literature cited on decay resistance includes additional data on factors of resistance variation within trees. Associations between tree character-

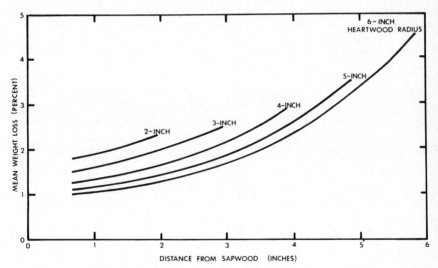

Figure 2.16. Radial trends of decay resistance—inversely related to weight loss of specimens in test—observed in the Shipmast variety of black locust trees of different sizes. (Courtesy U.S. Forest Products Laboratory, Madison, Wis.)

istics and resistance of teak heartwood were reported by Da Costa and associates [29].

The fact that decay resistance can vary both among trees and within individual trees of a species explains much of the familiar variation in usefulness of untreated wood of the same species when placed in comparable conditions of service. Insofar as decay resistance of a species conforms to the general pattern of Figure 2.16, the outer heartwood from second-growth timber can be expected to be somewhat less resistant than that from virgin timber with its larger trees. Split fence posts comprising a large proportion of outer heartwood should generally be more durable than round posts of the same size taken from smaller trees or from higher in the trunk. A notable case of lesser resistance in wood of the upper trunk was found in intermountain western redcedar, the outer heartwood in the upper third of pole-size trees being little more decay resistant than that in the lower trunk of comparable Douglas-fir trees [42]. Even before it was established experimentally, it was recognized by shipbuilders and other users of large-dimension materials that the central heartwood provided the least decay resistance. Consequently, wood with "boxed heart" (incorporating the pith area) was widely excluded where maximum resistance in the species was needed. As a general guide to meet a need for the highest natural decay resistance available in a nominally durable species, heartwood from the lower trunk of the larger trees is to be preferred.

2.9.4 Treated versus naturally durable wood

Those who have access to economical sources of naturally decay-resistant woods, such as redwood and the cedars, sometimes ask about the relative serviceability of these woods compared with wood that is preservative treated. Material pressure treated according to appropriate standards ordinarily is much to be preferred for service entailing contact with damp ground or risk of decay to an item that would be costly to replace. Although construction standards and specifications have commonly permitted both kinds of wood, it is now clear that for domestic woods the two are not equally permanent in situations conducive to decay. The desired level and permanence of protection can be much more positively and uniformly provided by pressure-treated wood than by naturally durable heartwood. Treated wood has an even greater advantage in resistance to termites, being virtually indispensable where safety against termites must be assured.

Untreated cedar or redwood heartwood is acceptable for service entailing comparatively small decay hazard, provided the cost of replacing the item would be moderate. Under such conditions, these woods might reasonably be used alternatively with wood protected by short-soak ("dip") treating—as by Commercial Standard CS 263–63.

A simple formula has been developed for estimating decay hazard imposed by climate on wood used above ground, based on standard U.S. Weather Bureau rainfall and temperature summaries [121]:

$$\text{Climate Index} = \frac{\sum_{\text{Jan.}}^{\text{Dec.}} [(T = 35)(D = 3)]}{30}$$

where T is the mean monthly temperature (°F); D, the mean number of days in the month with 0.01 inch or more of precipitation; and $\sum_{\text{Jan.}}^{\text{Dec.}}$ the summation of products for the respective months, January through December. The hazard is comparatively small where the climate index is less than 35.

2.10 Future Research on Wood-Degrading Organisms

Although much is known about wood-degrading microorganisms and the kinds of damage they do, many facets of potentially useful information remain to be developed in these fundamentals of wood protection. Most facets are more elusive than preceding ones, but are challenging in their potentials for leading to improved usefulness of wood.

General areas of effort might well include:

1. Making more effective use of wood-inhabiting microorganisms in the laboratory to assess preservative qualities.

2. Enhancing universal analysis and comparison of results of field tests, through more extensive recognition of and attention to the specific microorganisms involved in the tests.

3. Determining more comprehensively, and with due consideration of aboveground as well as below-ground environments, the tolerance of various microorganisms to preservatives of different kinds.

4. Enlarging our understanding of both the individual and combined roles of nondecay organisms in degrading wood, through their own attacks or by rendering the wood more subject to invasion by decay fungi (Basidiomycetes).

5. Using nominally harmless microorganisms to improve the treatability of wood, or to protect the wood by producing antibiotic chemicals.

6. Studying requirements of the Basidiomycetes for micro-elements in wood, such as thiamine, with a view to preservation by making these unavailable.

7. Improving means of detecting incipient decay in wood in service.

Basic to all these areas is a much broader knowledge of the species of microorganisms and of their relative prevalence and destructive capacities in various woods, products, and environments. Many species already identified have yet to be assessed as to the manner and amount of their damage. Molds, soft-rot fungi, and bacteria in wood have been examined least in this respect.

Especially helpful would be simpler procedures for obtaining pure cultures of microorganisms isolated in mixture, and more comprehensive, possibly simpler, means of identifying the Basidiomycete wood destroyers. Toward the latter objective, a broader basis for keying out species through distinctive physiological responses deserves consideration. Procedures for consistently developing fruiting bodies of most species in the laboratory would be immensely helpful.

Improved isolation techniques and means of cultural identification would make possible routine reporting of the fungi chiefly involved in major field tests. The information would help explain differences in test results caused by involvement of different fungi, which may be present even on small test plots [119], and facilitate worldwide comparison of field-test data and selection of fungi for laboratory testing.

More precise information is needed about the tolerance of decay fungi to different preservatives, including mixtures, under service conditions. Much of the present data on fungus–preservative associations lacks recognition of whether the fungus entered an item by attacking treated wood or merely bypassing the treated zone by invading through a seasoning check or other opening. Superior tolerance could, of course, be concluded if well-treated wood was destructively attacked. Experiments to ascertain which fungi are capable of doing this in different climates and soils have been established [40].

Examination of preservative tolerance might profitably include learning what surface concentrations of the various preservatives are needed to prevent infection by air- and insect-borne spores or hyphal fragments of decay fungi. This aspect of wood preservation has particular significance for the protection of wood with very shallow preservative protection for aboveground use. Typical examples are the many seasoning or weather checks above grade in poles and the lateral surfaces of dip- and vacuum-treated items. It is surprising in the case of Douglas-fir poles, for example, that heartwood deep within seasoning checks, which were formed prior to treating, can resist invasion by decay fungi despite an extremely thin layer of protected wood in the checks. An even greater mystery is limited evidence that seasoning checks formed after treating may be protected by fungistatic traces of preservative leaching into them. What may have been protection of this kind was suggested in the long "serviceability" observed in experimental flooring having extremely shallow protection provided by dip treating [133]. The possibility that checks may be protected by slight leaching of preservative from the treated zone poses a related question: to what extent can the shallow penetrations afforded by surface treating of exterior millwork be compensated for by use of extra strong treating solutions?

Comprehensive studies of preservative tolerance might well include the wood extractives responsible for natural decay resistance. The extremely high decay resistance of some woods, and the diversity of inhibitory compounds in the wood species already analyzed for this quality, encourages speculation that continued exploration might reveal chemicals that would be guides to improved commercial preservatives. Tropical hardwoods probably provide the best opportunity for success because of the great variety of species with known outstanding decay resistance.

More should be known about the sequences and mixtures of microorganisms in wood undergoing decay. It should be clearer to what extent molds, soft rotters, and bacteria may facilitate attack by the wood destroyers. A study by Käärik [72] of the succession of fungi in poles illustrates a tendency of non-basidiomycetous fungi to predominate at first. These fungi may bring about certain initial chemical changes in the wood, making it more readily metabolized by major degradative organisms that follow or, in the case of treated wood, by acting on the preservative to reduce its toxicity. Some microorganisms may favor decay by introducing into the wood needed thiamine or biotin, which the Basidiomycetes are unable to produce themselves. The question of whether advance infection by marine fungi may promote attack by marine borers has not yet been decisively answered.

Although experiments and general experience suggest that microorganisms do little damage to preservatives if the quality and initial retention meet recognized standards, their effects in this respect cannot yet be said to be insignificant. The practical significance of slow biodegradation of preservatives on the service life of treated items especially merits additional study. The question pertains chiefly to wood in contact with ground or water, and embraces such variables as kind of preservative, initial retention, wood species, and kinds of microorganisms on the exposure site. The extent to which invasion by nondecay microorganisms prior to treating may promote loss of preservative by making the wood more permeable also warrants attention.

Comparatively little is known about the prevalence of bacterial attack on cell walls sufficient to cause objectionable weakening. This and the factors governing the incidence and degree of bacterial weakening of wood in items such as piles, logs stored in water or under spray, tank-stored peeler bolts, and cooling-tower slats are largely still to be determined.

Similarly, there is much yet to be learned about the practical impact of degradation by soft-rot fungi. Severe soft rot is common in the outer-most zone of even well-treated wood in contact with the ground, but considerable uncertainty exists as to how commonly and under what conditions the rot may go deeper and constitute a threat to serviceability, or possibly make the wood more vulnerable to invasion by decay fungi. It is still not clear why some waterborne preservatives have failed conspicuously against deep damage by soft rot, why hardwoods tend to be more vulnerable than softwoods, or why damaging soft rot can be produced in the laboratory more easily in wood kept in soil than in equally wet wood not in soil. There also is more to be learned about the significance of soft-rot species as a contributor to paint failure and the weathering degradation of natural finishes.

The possibility that wood serving aboveground might be protected by destroying some micro-element in it needed for nutrition of decay fungi is a facet of fungus vulnerability that opens up a fresh area for exploration. Further basic research along this line might entail an expanded study of nutritional requirements of the fungi, with emphasis on the fungi while growing in wood. The studies could appropriately include consideration of whether nondecay organisms entering the wood might provide vital accessory food elements such as thiamine, which decay fungi cannot themselves produce, and thus nullify destruction of the element as a protective measure.

A broadly applicable, simple field method of reliably detecting early decay has long been desired. A color test based on reaction between an applied chemical and some product of the fungus metabolism might be developed for the purpose. Color indicators of pH changes have not proved suitable for dealing with a variety of decays. However, success with the method for detecting early decay in pine by *P. gigantea* [86] suggests that colorometric testing of the wood pH might be useful in other situations where the inspection is similarly directed at a single combination of fungus and wood species. For broader application of chemical detectors, it may be necessary to search empirically for color reactants as Cowling and Sachs did [26] in finding that osmium tetroxide will reveal many brown rots. Methods such as X-ray or gamma-ray, and sonic detection have not been promising for disclosing early decay, but can be useful with more advanced decay that has caused sizable loss of wood substance.

Only the surface has been probed regarding possible use of wood micro-organisms to better protect wood. A paramount need for better treating is to obtain deeper penetration of the preservative than is conventionally provided in the more refractory woods. Pretreatment infection of wood by molds or bacteria to increase permeability—by opening up pits, wood rays, and resin ducts—has been only briefly explored, but the results have been sufficiently promising to warrant further research. Needed are relatively harmless species or strains that would invade heartwood as well as sapwood. For practical application of the method, due consideration should, of course, be given to the effect of increased permeability on the permanence of the preservative.

Another possible biological means of better protection is to find harmless fungi that will penetrate deeply and also will inhibit decay fungi by producing antibiotic chemicals or by removing the most easily utilizable carbohydrates such as sugars and starch [66]. Although such a method has shown comparatively limited promise, it merits further consideration, particularly for temporary protection of stored roundwood such as logs, poles and piling, and pulpwood. It is uniquely attractive in that it would be consistent with efforts to minimize possibilities of chemical pollution. Long-term, antibiotic protection of wood in service would necessitate either continuing production of the antibiotic without harmful degradation of wood strength or permanence of the antibiotic initially produced —neither of which seem likely.

REFERENCES

1. American Society for Testing and Materials. 1961. "Standard method of testing wood preservatives by laboratory soil-block cultures." ASTM Standard D1413–61. Am. Soc. for Testing and Materials, Philadelphia.
2. American Society for Testing and Materials. 1963. "Standard method for accelerated laboratory test of natural decay resistance of woods." ASTM Standard D2017–63. Am. Soc. for Testing and Materials, Philadelphia.
3. Anderson, A.B., Scheffer, T.C., and Duncan, C.G. 1963. "Chemistry of decay resistance and its decrease with heartwood aging in incense cedar (*Libocedrus decurrens* Torrey)." *Holzforschung* 17(1):1–5.
4. Bailey, P.J., Liese, W. and Rösch, R. 1968. "Some aspects of cellulose degradation in lignified cell walls." Proceedings of 1st International Biodeterioration Symposium, Southhampton. 546–57.
5. Barghoorn, E.S. and Linder, D.H. 1944. "Marine fungi: their taxonomy and biology." *Farlowia* 1:396–497.
6. Barton, G.M. and Gardner, J.A.F. 1966. "Brown stain formation and the phenolic extractives of western hemlock (*Tsuga heterophylla* (Raf.) Sarg.)." Canadian Dept. of Forestry Pub. No. 1147.
7. Bauch, J., Liese, W. and Berndt, H. 1970. "Biological investigations for the improvement of the permeability of softwoods." *Holzforschung* 24(6):199–205.
8. Bautelje, J.B. and Bravery, A.F. 1968. "Observations on the bacterial attack of piles supporting a Stockholm building." *J. Inst. Wood Sci.* 4(2) No. 20(47–57).
9. Boyce, J.S. 1961. *Forest Pathology* (3d ed.), McGraw-Hill Book Co., N.Y.
10. Brown, W.H. 1969. "Properties and uses of tropical hardwoods in the United Kingdom." Proc., Conference on Tropical Hardwoods. State Univ. College of Forestry at Syracuse Univ., Syracuse, N.Y.

11. Burt, E.A. 1917. "Merulius in North America." *Ann. Mo. Bot. Garden* 4:305–62.
12. Burt, E.E. 1914–1926. "Thelephoraceae of North America I–XV." *Ann. Mo. Bot. Garden* 1–13.
13. Buston, H.W., Moss, M.O., and Tyrrell, D. 1966. "The influence of carbon dioxide on growth and sporulation of *Chaetomium globosum*." *Trans. B. Mycol. Soc.* 49(2)387–96.
14. Campbell, R.N. 1959. "Fungus sap-stains of hardwoods." *Southern Lumberman* 199(2489):115–20.
15. Cartwright, K.St.G. and Findlay, W.P.K. 1958. *Decay of Timber and Its Prevention.* H.M. Stationery Office, London
16. Cech, M.Y. 1966. "New treatment to prevent brown stain in white pine." *Forest Prod. J.* 16(11):23–27.
17. Chapman, A.D. and Scheffer, T.C. 1940. "Effect of blue stain on specific gravity and strength of southern pine." *J. Agr. Res.* 61:125–34.
18. Christiansen, C.M. 1970. *Common Fleshy Fungi* (4th printing). Burgess Publishing Co., Minneapolis, Minn.
19. Clark, J.W. 1956. "A gray non-fungus seasoning discoloration of certain red oaks." *Southern Lumberman* 193(2417):35–38.
20. Clark, J. 1957. "Comparative decay resistance of some common pines, hemlock, spruce, and true fir." *Forest Sci.* 3(4):314–20.
21. Clark, J.W. 1969. "Natural decay resistance of fifteen exotic woods imported for exterior use." U.S. Forest Serv., Forest Prod. Lab. Rept. No. 103.
22. Corbett, N.H. 1965. "Micro-morphological studies on the degradation of lignified cell walls by Ascomycetes and Fungi imperfecti." *J. Inst. Wood Sci.* 14:18–29.
23. Courtois, H. 1966. "Bacterial decomposition of cell walls in softwood." *Holzforschung* 20(5):148–54. CSIRO Translation No. 9220.
24. Cowling, E.B. 1957. "A partial list of fungi associated with decay of wood products in the United States." USDA Plant Dis. Rptr. 41:894–96.
25. Cowling, E.B. 1970. "Nitrogen in forest trees and its role in wood deterioration." Abstracts of Uppsala Dissertations in Science.
26. Cowling, E.B. and Sachs, I.B. 1960. "Detection of brown rot with osmium tetroxide stain." *Forest Prod. J.* 10(11):594–96.
27. Cserjesi, A.J. 1967. "The adaptation of fungi to pentachlorophenol and its bio-degradation." *Can. J. Microbiol.* 13:1243–49.
28. Cserjesi, A.J. and Roff, J.W. 1966. "Sapstain and Mould Prevention by Spraying and Dipping." *British Columbia Lumberman* 50(6):64–66.
29. Da Costa, E.W.B., Rudman, P. and Gay, F.J. 1961. "Relationship of growth rate and related factors to durability in *Tectona grandis*." *Emp. For. Rev.* 40(4):308–19.
30. Davidson, R.W. 1953. "Two common lumber-staining fungi in the Western United States." *Mycologia* 45:579–86.
31. Davidson, R.W. and Lombard, R. 1954. "Brick red stain of Sitka spruce and other wood substrata." *Phytopathology* 44(10):606–607.
32. Drisko, R.W., O'Neill, T.B. and Hochman, H. 1962. "Metabolism of creosote by certain marine microorganisms." U.S. Naval Civil Eng. Lab. Tech. Rept. No. R230.
33. Duncan, C.G. 1960. "Soft rot in wood, and toxicity studies on causal fungi." *Proc., Am. Wood-Preservers' Assoc.* 56:27–35.
34. Duncan, C.G. 1961. "Relative aeration requirements by soft rot and Basidiomycete wood-destroying fungi." U.S. Forest Serv., Forest Prod. Lab. Rept. No. 2218.
35. Duncan, C.G. 1963. "Role of microorganisms in weathering of wood and degradation of exterior finishes." *Official Digest Federation of Societies of Paint Technology.* (10):1003–12.

36. Duncan, C.G. 1965. "Determining resistance to soft-rot fungi." U.S. Forest Serv., Forest Prod. Lab. Rept. No. 48.

37. Duncan, C.G. 1967. "Effect of light on the rate of decay of three wood-destroying fungi." *Phytopathology* 57(10):1121–25.

38. Duncan, C.G. and Deverall, F.J. 1964. "Degradation of wood preservatives by fungi." *J. Appl. Microbiol.* 12(1):57–62.

39. Duncan, C.G. and Eslyn, W.E. 1966. "Wood decaying Ascomycetes and Fungi Imperfecti." *Mycologia* 58(4):642–45.

40. Duncan, C.G. and Lombard, F.F. 1965. "Fungi associated with principal decays in wood products in the United States." U.S. Forest Serv., Forest Prod. Lab. Rept. No. W0–4.

41. Ellwood, E.L. and Ecklund, B.A. 1959. "Bacterial attack on pine logs in pond storage." *Forest Prod. J.* 9(9):283–92.

42. Englerth, G.H. and Scheffer, T.C. 1955. "Tests of decay resistance of four western pole species." *J. Forestry* 53(8):556–61.

43. Eslyn, W.E. 1968. "Utility pole decay. I: Appraisal of a device for nondestructive detection of decay." *Wood Sci. Tech.* 2:128–37.

44. Eslyn, W.E. 1970. "Utility pole decay. II: Basidiomycetes associated with decay in poles." *Wood Sci. Tech.* 4:97–103.

45. Evans, R.S. and Halvorson, H.N. 1962. "Cause and control of brown stain in western hemlock." *Forest Prod. J.* 12(8):367–73.

46. Findlay, W.P.K. 1959. "Sap-stain of timber." *Forestry Abstracts* 20(1,2):1–14.

47. Findlay, W.P.K. and Savory, J.G. 1950. "Breakdown of timber in water-cooling towers." *Proc. International Botanical Congress* 7:315–16.

48. Fritz, C.W. 1952. "Brown stain in pine sapwood caused by *Cytospora* sp." *Can. J. Bot.* (30):349–59.

49. Fergus, C.L. 1960. *Illustrated Genera of Wood Decaying Fungi.* Burgess Publishing Co., Minneapolis, Minn.

50. Gersonde, M. 1958. "Uber die Giftempfindlichkeit verschiedener Stämme holzzerstörender Pilze." (The sensitivity to toxicity of different strains of wood-destroying fungi). *Holz als Roh- und Werkstoff* 16(6):221–26.

51. Gersonde, M. and Meyer, R. 1964. "Das Vorkommen von Moderfäule in Holzmasten." (Occurrence of soft rot in poles). *Holz als Roh- und Werkstoff* 22(2):42–47.

52. Grant, C. and Savory, J.G. 1968. "Methods for isolation and identification of fungi on wood." Forest Products Research Lab., Princes Risborough, Aylesbury, Bucks.

53. Greaves, H. 1969. "Micromorphology of the bacterial attack of wood." *Wood Sci. Tech.* 3(2):150–66.

54. Greaves, H. 1971. "The bacterial factor in wood decay." *Wood Sci. Tech.* 5(1):6–16.

55. Greaves, H. and Foster, R.C. 1970. "The fine structure of bacterial attack on wood." *J. Inst. Wood Sci.* 5(1)25:18–27.

56. Gjovik, L.R. and Baechler, R.H. 1968. "Field tests on wood dethiaminized for protection against decay." *Forest Prod. J.* 18(1):25–27.

57. Harmsen, L. and Nissen, T. 1965. "Der Bakterienangriff auf Holz." *Holz als Roh- und Werkstoff* 23(10):389–93. (Translation U.S. Forest Serv. FPL–657.)

58. Hartley, C., Davidson, R.W. and Crandall, B.S. 1961. "Wetwood, bacteria, and increased pH in trees." U.S. Forest Serv., Forest Prod. Lab. Rept. No. 2215.

59. Henningsson, B. 1967. "Changes in impact bending strength, weight and alkali solubility following fungal attack on birch wood." Studia Forestalia Suecia No. 41. Stockholm.

60. Highley, T. 1970. "Decay resistance of four wood species treated to destroy thiamine." *Phytopathology* 60(11):1660–61.

61. Highley, T.L. and Lutz, J.F. 1970. "Bacterial attack in water-stored bolts." *Forest Prod. J.* 20(4):43–44.
62. Highley, T.L. and Scheffer, T.C. 1970. "Natural decay resistance of 30 Peruvian woods." U.S. Forest Serv., Forest Prod. Lab. Rept. No. 143.
63. Highley, T.L. and Scheffer, T.C. 1970. "A need for modifying the soil-block method of testing natural resistance to white rot." *Material und Organismen* 5(4):281–92.
64. Highley, T.L., Scheffer, T.C. and Selbo, M.L. 1971. "Wood minesweepers are sound after 15 years of service." *Forest Prod. J.* 21(5):46–48.
65. Hubert, E.E. 1931. *An Outline of Forest Pathology.* John Wiley & Sons, N.Y.
66. Hulme, M.A. and Shields, J.K. 1970. "Biological control of decay fungi in wood by competition for non-structural carbohydrates." *Nature* 227(5255):300–301.
67. Jennison, M.W., Newcomb, M.D. and Henderson, R. 1955. "Physiology of the wood-rotting basidiomycetes. I. Growth and nutrition in submerged culture in synthetic media." *Mycologia* 47(3):275–304.
68. Jensen, K.F. 1967. "Oxygen and carbon dioxide affect the growth of wood-decaying fungi." *Forest Sci.* 13:384–89.
69. Johnson, B.R. and Gjovik, L.R. 1970. "Effect of *Trichoderma viride* and a contaminating bacterium on microstructure and permeability of loblolly pine and Douglas-fir." *Proc., Am. Wood-Preservers' Assoc.* 66:234–40.
70. Jones, E.B.G. 1963. "Observations on the fungal succession on wood test blocks submerged in the sea." *J. Inst. Wood Sci.* 11:14–23.
71. Käärik, A. 1965. "The identification of the mycelia of wood-decay fungi by their oxidation reaction with phenolic compounds." Studia Forestalia Suecia No. 31. Stockholm.
72. Käärik, A. 1968. "Colonization of pine and spruce poles by soil fungi after twelve and eighteen months." *Materials und Organismen* 3(3):185–98.
73. Kaufman, C.H. 1918. *"The Agaricaceae of Michigan."* Michigan Geol. and Biol. Survey Publ. No. 26, Biol. Ser. S. 2 vols.
74. Knuth, D.T. 1964. "Bacteria associated with wood products and their effects on certain chemical and physical properties of wood." Ph.D. dissertation, Univ. of Wisconsin, Madison, Wis.
75. Knuth, D.T. and McCoy, E. 1962. "Bacterial deterioration of pine logs in pond storage." *Forest Prod. J.* 12(9):437–42.
76. Krause, R.L. 1954. "Iron stain from metal fastenings may accelerate decay in some woods." *J. For. Prod. Res. Soc.* 4(2):103–11.
77. Krieger, L.C. 1967. *The Mushroom Handbook.* Dover Publications, N.Y.
78. Kukachka, B.F. 1969. "Properties of imported tropical woods." Proc. Conference on Tropical Hardwoods, State Univ. College of Forestry at Syracuse Univ., Syracuse, N.Y.
79. Kukachka, B.F. 1970. "Properties of imported tropical woods." U.S. Forest Serv. Res. Paper FPL–125.
80. Lentz, P.L. 1955. "Stereum and Allied Genera of Fungi in the Mississippi Valley." USDA Monograph No. 24.
81. Levy, J. 1965. "Soft rot fungi: Their mode of action and significance in the degradation of wood." *Advances in Botanical Research.* Vol. 2. Academic Press, N.Y. 323–57.
82. Levy, J. and Preston, R.D. 1965. "A chemical and microscopic examination of the action of the soft-rot fungus *Chaetomium globosum* on beechwood (*Fagus sylv.*)" *Holzforschung* 19(6):183–90.
83. Liese, W. and Karnop, G. 1968. "Attack on softwood by bacteria." *Holz als Roh- und Werkstoff* 26(6):202–208.

84. Lindgren, R.M. 1942. "Temperature, moisture, and penetration studies of wood-staining Ceratostomellae in relation to their control." USDA Bull. No. 807.

85. Lindgren, R.M. 1952. "Permeability of southern pine as affected by mold growth and other fungus infection." *Proc., Am. Wood-Preservers' Assoc.* 48:158–74.

86. Lindgren, R.M. 1955. "Color test for early storage decay in southern pine." U.S. Forest Serv., Forest Prod. Lab. Rept. No. 2037.

87. Lindgren, R.M. and Harvey, G.M. 1952. "Decay control and increased permeability in southern pine sprayed with fluoride solutions." *J. For. Prod. Res. Soc.* 2:250–56.

88. Lindgren, R.M. and Scheffer, T.C. 1939. "Effect of blue stain on the penetration of liquids into air-dry southern pine wood." *Proc., Am. Wood-Preservers' Assoc.* 35:325–36.

89. Lindgren, R.M. and Wright, E. 1954. "Increased absorptiveness of molded Douglas-fir posts." *J. For. Prod. Res. Soc.* 4(4):162–64.

90. Lowe, J.L. 1966. "The genus *Poria* in North America." State Univ. College of Forestry at Syracuse Univ., Tech. Pub. No. 90.

91. Lutz, J.F., Duncan, C.G. and Scheffer, T.C. 1966. "Some effects of bacterial action on rotary-cut southern pine veneer." *Forest Prod. J.* 16(8):23–28.

92. Lyr, H. 1963. "Enzymatische Detoxefikation chlorierter phenole." *Phytopathologische Zeitschrift* 47(1):73–83. (Also 1962, in English, in *Nature* 195(4838):289–90.

93. Madhosingh, C. 1961. "The metabolic detoxification of 2,4-dinitrophenol by *Fusarium oxysporium.*" *Can. J. Microbiol.* 7:553–67.

94. Manion, P.D. and French, D.W. 1969. "The role of glucose in stimulating germination of *Fomes igniarius* var. *populinus* basidiospores." *Phytopathology* 59(3):293–96.

95. Marian, J.E. and Wissing, A. 1960. "The chemical and mechanical deterioration of wood in contact with iron." Parts 1, 2, 3. *Svensk Papperstidning* 63(3):47–57; (4):98–106; (5):130–83.

96. Marsden, D.H. 1954. "Studies of the creosote fungus, *Hormodendrum resinae.*" *Mycologia,* 46(2):161–83.

97. Meyers, S.P. and Reynolds, E.S. 1957. "Incidence of marine fungi in relation to wood borer attack." *Science* 126(3280):969.

98. Miller, L.W. and Boyle, J.S. 1943. "The Hydraceae of Iowa." Univ. of Iowa Studies in Natural History. 18(2):1–92.

99. Miller, B.D., Taylor, F.L. and Popkek, R.A. 1965. "A sonic method for detecting decay in wood poles." *Proc., Am. Wood-Preservers' Assoc.* 1965:109–15.

100. Morton, H.L. and French, D.W. 1966. "Factors affecting germination of spores of wood-rotting fungi on wood." *Forest Prod. J.* 16(3):25–30.

101. Moses, C.S. 1955. "Laboratory decay resistance of some commercial species of mahogany." *Forest Prod. J.* 5(2):149–52.

102. Mothershead, J.S. and Stacey, S.S. 1965. "Applicability of radiography to inspection of wood products." Proc. 2nd Symposium on Nondestructive Testing of Wood. Spokane, Washington, April 1965:307–36. Pub. by Washington State Univ., Pullman, Wash.

103. National Woodwork Manufacturers Assn. 1960. N.W.M.A. Soil Block Test. Standard N.W.M.A. methods for testing the preservative property of oil-soluble wood preservatives by using wood specimens uniformly impregnated. N.W.M.A. Standard NWMA–M–1–60, National Woodwork Manufacturers Assn. Chicago, Ill.

104. Nobles, M.K. 1965. "Identification of cultures of wood inhabiting hymenomycetes." *Can. J. Bot.* 43(9):1097–1139.

105. Osborne, L.D. 1970. "Decay resistance of Southwest Pacific Rain-forest timbers." Div. of Forest Prod. Tech. Paper No. 56. CSIRO.

106. Overholts, L.O. 1957. *Polyporaceae of the United States, Alaska, and Canada.* Univ. of Michigan Press, Ann Arbor, Mich.

107. Panek, E. 1963. "Pretreatments for the protection of southern yellow pine poles during air-seasoning." *Proc., Am. Wood-Preservers' Assoc.* 59:189–95.

108. Petrenko, I.A. 1966. "Effect of acidity of synthetic nutrient medium on the growth of certain types of wood-destroying fungi." Pages 95–105 in *Properties and Preservation of Wood and New Materials from Wood.* V.A. Bazhenov, ed. and trans. Pub. for USDA, 1970.

109. Pinion, L.C. 1970. "The degradation of wood by metal fastenings and fittings." Timberlab Papers No. 27–1970, Forest Products Research Lab., Princes Risborough, Aylesbury, Bucks.

110. Ray, D.L. 1959. "Marine fungi and wood borer attack." *Proc. Am. Wood-Preservers' Assoc.* 55:147–54.

111. Rich, S. and Horsfall, J.G. 1954. "Relation of polyphenol oxidases to fungitoxicity." *Proc. Nat. Acad. Sci.* 40:139–45.

112. Savory, J.G. 1954. "Damage to wood caused by microorganisms." *J. Appl. Bacteriol.* (London) 17:213–18.

113. Savory, J.G. 1954. "Breakdown of timber by Ascomycetes and fungi imperfecti." *Ann. Appl. Biol.* 41(2):336–47.

114. Savory, J.G. 1967. "Avoiding deterioration in packaged softwoods during shipment and storage." Ministry of Technology, Forest Products Research Laboratory, England. May 1967.

115. Savory, J.G. and Pinion, L.C. 1958. "Chemical aspects of decay of beechwood by *Chaetomium globosum.*" *Holzforschung* 12(4):99–103.

116. Savory, J.G., Pawsey, R.G. and Lawrence, J.S. 1965. "Prevention of blue-stain in unpeeled Scots pine logs." *Forestry* 38(1):59–81.

117. Scheffer, T.C. 1936. "Progressive effects of *Polyporus versicolor* on the physical and chemical properties of red gum sapwood." USDA Tech. Bull. No. 527.

118. Scheffer, T.C. 1957. "Decay resistance of western redcedar." *J. Forestry* 55(6):434–42.

119. Scheffer, T.C. 1964. "Biological observations of significance for improved preservative treatment." *Holzforschung* 18(3):88–94.

120. Scheffer, T.C. 1969. "Protecting stored logs and pulpwood in North America." *Material und Organismen* 4(3):167–99.

121. Scheffer, T.C. 1971. "A climate index for estimating potential for decay in wood structures above ground." *Forest Prod. J.* 21(10):25–31.

122. Scheffer, T.C. and Chidester, M.S. 1943. "Significance of air-dry wood in controlling rot caused by *Poria incrassata.*" *Southern Lumberman* 166(2091):53–55.

123. Scheffer, T.C. and Chidester, M.S. 1948. "Survival of decay and blue-stain fungi in air-dry wood." *Southern Lumberman* 177:110–12.

124. Scheffer, T.C. and Cowling, E.B. 1966. "Natural resistance of wood to microbial deterioration." *Ann. Rev. Phytopathol.* 4:147–70.

125. Scheffer, T.C. and Duncan, C.G. 1947. "The decay resistance of certain Central American and Ecuadorian Woods." *Tropical Woods* 92:1–24.

126. Scheffer, T.C., Duncan, C.G., and Wilkinson, T. 1969. "Condition of pine piling submerged 62 years in river water." *Wood Preserving* 47(1):22–24.

127. Scheffer, T.C. and Englerth, G.H. 1952. "Decay resistance of second-growth Douglas-fir." *J. Forestry* 50(6):439–42.

128. Scheffer, T.C., Englerth, G.H. and Duncan, C.G. 1949. "Decay resistance of seven native oaks." *J. Agr. Res.* 78(5–6):129–52.

129. Scheffer, T.C. and Graham, R.D. 1972. "Paradichlorobenzene for temporary protection of wood against fungus contamination." *Forest Prod. J.* 22(8):40–41.

130. Scheffer, T.C. and Hopp, J. 1949. "Decay resistance of black locust wood." USDA Tech. Bull. No. 984.

131. Scheffer, T.C. and Lindgren, R.M. 1940. "Stains of sapwood and sapwood products and their control." USDA Tech. Bull. No. 714.

132. Scheffer, T.C. and Livingston, B.C. 1937. "Relation of oxygen pressure and temperature to growth and carbon-dioxide production in the fungus *Polystictus versicolor*." *Am. J. Bot.* 24(3):109–19.

133. Scheffer, T.C., Verrall, A.F. and Harvey, G. 1971. "Fifteen-year appraisal of dip treating for protecting exterior woodwork: effectiveness on different wood species and in different climates." *Material und Organismen* 6(1):27–44.

134. Scheld, H.W. and DeGroot, R.C. 1971. "Toughness of sapwood in water-sprayed longleaf pine logs." *Forest Prod. J.* 21(4):33–34.

135. Schulz, G. 1956. "Exploratory tests to increase preservative penetration in spruce and aspen by mold infection." *Forest Prod. J.* 6(2):77–80.

136. Schulz, G. 1958. "Vergleichende Untersuchungen mit verscheidenen Stammen von *Lentinius lepideus*, gleichzeitig ein Beitrag sum Soil-Block-Verfahren." (Comparative investigations with different isolates of *Lentinus lepideus*, a contribution to the soil-block method). *Holz als Roh- und Werkstoff* 16(11):435–44.

137. Schulz, G. 1964. "Versuche mit salzgetränkten Holzschwellen." (Service and laboratory tests with salt-treated wooden sleepers.) *Holz als Roh- und Werkstoff* 22(2):57–64.

138. Shigo, A.L. 1967. "Successions of organisms in discoloration and decay of wood." *Intern. Review of For. Res.* Vol. 2.

139. Siefert, Karl. 1967. "Uber den Holzabbau durch Bacterien." (Bacterial deterioration of wood). *Holz als Roh- und Werkstoff* 25(10):377–79.

140. Slysh, A. 1960. "The genus Peniophora in New York State and adjacent regions." State Univ. College of Forestry at Syracuse Univ. Tech. Publ. No. 83.

141. Smith, D.N. 1959. "The natural durability of timber." Dept. of Scient. and Ind. Res. For. Prod. Res. Record No. 30. 2d ed.

142. Stutz, R.E. 1959. "Control of brown stain in sugar pine with sodium azide." *Forest Prod. J.* 9(11):459–64.

143. Tabak, H.H. and Cooke, W.B. 1968. "The effects of gaseous environment on the growth and metabolism of fungi." *Botanical Review* 34(2):126–252.

144. Unligil, H.H. 1968. "Depletion of pentachlorophenol by fungi." *Forest Prod. J.* 18(2):45–50.

145. U.S. Bureau of the Census. 1970. "Statistical Abstract of the United States." Government Printing Office, Washington, D.C.

146. U.S. Department of the Navy. 1965. *Marine Biology Operational Handbook*, Nav. Docks MO–311, Dept. of the Navy, Washington, D.C.

147. U.S. Government. 1963. "U.S. Commercial Standard Water-Repellent preservative non-pressure treatment for millwork." U.S. Commercial Standard CS262–63, Government Printing Office, Washington, D.C.

148. U.S. Forest Service. 1956. "Temperatures necessary to kill fungi in wood." U.S. Forest Serv., Forest Prod. Lab. Rept. No. 259.

149. Verrall, A.F. 1939. "Relative importance and seasonal prevalence of wood-staining fungi in the Southern States." *Phytopathology* 29(12):1031–51.

150. Verrall, A.F. 1941. "Dissemination of fungi that stain logs and lumber." *J. Agr. Res.* 63(9):549–58.

151. Verrall, A.F. 1949. "Some molds on wood favored by certain toxicants." *J. Agr. Res.* 78(12):695–703.

152. Verrall, A.F. 1968. "*Poria incrassata* rot: prevention and control in buildings." USDA Tech. Bull. No. 1385.

153. Verrall, A.F. and Mook, P.V. 1951. "Research on control of fungi in green lumber, 1940–51." USDA Tech. Bull. No. 1046.
154. Wellman, H.W. and Wilson, A.T. 1965. "Salt weathering, a neglected geological erosive agent in coastal and arid environments." *Nature* 205(4976):1097–98.
155. Wilcox, W.W. 1971. "Absorptivity and pit structure as related to wetwood in white fir." *Wood and Fiber* 2(4):373–79.

3. Degradation in Relation to Wood Structure

W. WAYNE WILCOX

Forest Products Laboratory
University of California, Richmond, California

3.1 Introduction

The various species of wood have certain unique characteristics that allow one species to be differentiated from another, and the same is true of microorganisms which inhabit and degrade wood. Microscopical patterns of such degradation are, however, a result of the combination of properties of these two participating components. The structure and composition of a particular wood may determine certain aspects of its decomposition, and the properties and activities of the microorganism may determine others, but within these limits the form of the deterioration is a resultant of the combination of all these properties. Therefore, detailed study of microscopical changes in wood undergoing microbiological degradation requires an understanding of the properties of the attacking organism and its substrate.

The modes of degradation of wood by fungi and bacteria can be grouped into several descriptive categories according to the form and severity of the attack. Interestingly enough, these categories conform closely to the taxonomic divisions applied to the causal organisms. However, in taxonomy some organisms defy categorization—they may have properties assigned to several groups. The same is true for different types of wood degradation. This is an inevitable problem when attempting to apply a discrete classification system to a continuous phenomenon, and the categories used in this chapter must be accepted with that in mind. Generalizations can be made about the groups of microorganisms and their effects on wood if it is understood that some organisms may behave as though they were members of more than one group, depending upon

Portions of this chapter appeared in an article in *Botanical Review* 36(1):1–28.

the conditions under which degradation occurs (including variations in the type of wood under attack). Microscopical changes induced in wood by wood-destroying microorganisms have been the subject of several reviews [67,118]; the reader is referred to them for a more detailed treatment.

The purpose of this chapter is to explore the various types of microscopical changes induced in wood by wood-destroying microorganisms. Because structure and composition of the wood itself play such an integral role in determining the form of decomposition, some treatment of this subject must be included. The coverage will be brief and general; textbooks and reviews of these subjects provide more detailed information [12,22,50,93,112]. Furthermore, before ascribing a typical action to a particular microorganism, it would be well for one to consider how much the wood involved differs from the general description which follows.

3.2 Wood Structure and Composition

Wood structure varies between species and to some extent within species and individual trees. The characteristics and distribution of cells even vary with the season in which they were formed, and this variation parallels the changes in activity of the tree during various portions of the growing season. Thus, in temperate regions in the spring when transpiration stream flow is high, the longitudinally conductive cells tend to be predominantly larger with large lumina and correspondingly thinner walls (earlywood), while toward the end of the growing season smaller, thicker-walled cells tend to predominate (latewood). This results in formation of concentric zones of greater or lesser density of cell-wall substance which are apparent macroscopically as growth, or annual, rings (Figure 3.1). The impact of these two types of tissue upon microorganisms may be great, as earlywood may provide greater access to longitudinal distribution while latewood provides a greater concentration of cell-wall material. Some organisms appear to prefer one type of tissue over the other.

Another differentiation observable in xylem tissue is the difference between sapwood and heartwood (Figure 3.2). Many tree species develop at the center of the stem a zone of wood which is darker (heartwood) than the surrounding light-colored tissue (sapwood). In durable woods, the heartwood contains toxic extractives which contribute to the color change and are responsible for the resistance of this wood to attrack by microorganisms. Sapwood, lacking these extractives, is not resistant to degradation even in those species with durable heartwood. Sapwood may also contain storage materials such as starch, which may make it more attractive to invading microorganisms.

Wood is made up of several different types of cells. The structure of

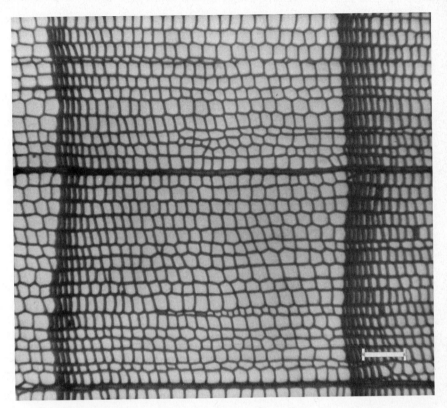

Figure 3.1. Cross section of incense cedar (*Libocedrus decurrens* Torr.) showing one complete annual ring (scale = 100 μm).

softwoods is less complex than that of hardwoods, which have more cell types (Figure 3.3). Tracheids make up the majority of the longitudinal elements of softwoods; they function both as conductive and strength-providing tissues simply through changes in cell diameter, lumen diameter, and cell-wall thickness across each growth ring. Because of this, most microscopical effects of degradation by microorganisms in softwoods will be observed in the tracheids and it is decomposition of these elements—particularly the thick-walled latewood tracheids—that most greatly affects mechanical properties of the wood. A small proportion of the longitudinal elements of some softwoods consists of parenchyma cells, either distributed among the tracheids or aggregated to form the walls of resin ducts. These elements may be important in the degradation process because they provide ready avenues for longitudinal distribution (resin ducts) or because they contain storage materials and possess thin cell

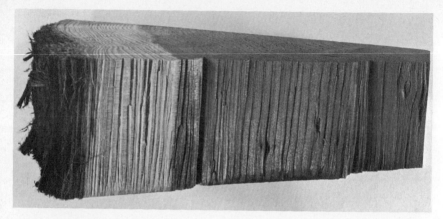

Figure 3.2. Portion of a cross-sectional disk of redwood [*Sequoia sempervirens* (D. Don) Endl.] showing the dark-colored heartwood at the center of the tree and light-colored sapwood nearest the bark.

walls (longitudinal parenchyma). Other softwood structures of importance in wood degradation are the rays, which provide avenues of transverse distribution and often large quantities of storage materials. Rays may consist of both parenchyma and tracheid cell types. Removal of storage material from rays, or destruction of ray cell walls, may have profound effects upon transverse movement of liquids within the wood.

Although the functions of tissues in hardwoods is the same as in softwoods, they are carried out by a large number of specialized cell types (Figure 3.4). Longitudinal conduction occurs through very large-lumened, thin-walled vessels, the diameter of which may vary from quite large in earlywood to relatively small in latewood. These structures provide ready access to longitudinal distribution for attacking microorganisms. The bulk of the cell-wall material in most hardwoods is contained in several types of fibers having relatively small diameters, narrow lumina, and thick walls. Like latewood tracheids in softwoods, fibers in hardwoods are the elements in which the effects of degradation by microorganisms often are most conspicuous and have the greatest effect upon mechanical properties of the wood. As in softwoods, longitudinal parenchyma cells and rays are also present in hardwoods and have the same significance with regard to degradation. The rays in most hardwoods consist entirely of parenchymatous cells and sometimes become very large through aggregation of many layers of parenchyma cells into a single ray.

One structural feature of the walls of all wood cells which is of considerable importance in degradation is the pit (see Figures 4.2 and 4.3 in Chapter 4 of Volume II). The structure of the wall in which the pit is

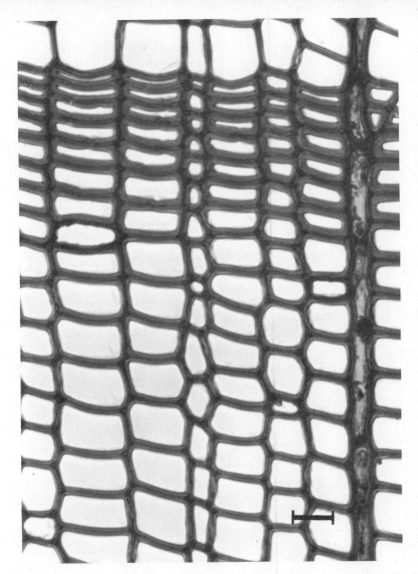

Figure 3.3. Cross section of the softwood incense cedar (*Libocedrus decurrens* Torr.). The wood structure consists primarily of tracheids. (scale = 25 μm)

formed largely determines the structure of the pit itself, but, in general, it consists of a hole through the cell wall at least partially blocked by a membrane. In cells having a well-developed secondary wall, such as tracheids and fibers, the pit is of the bordered type with the border consisting of a

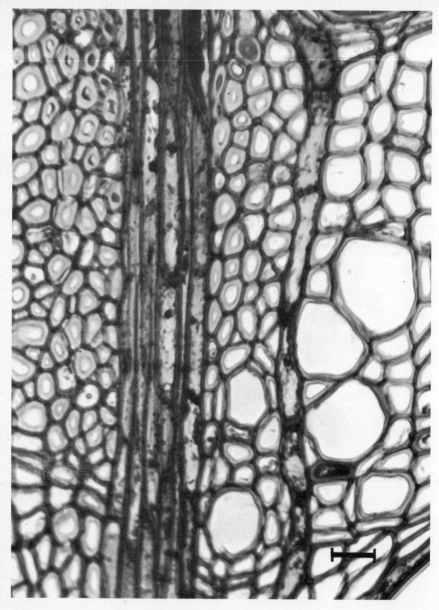

Figure 3.4. Cross section of the hardwood white oak (*Quercus alba* L.) showing the number of different types of cells which comprise the wood structure. (scale = 25 μm)

saucer-shaped flap formed over most of the pit by the secondary wall. In parenchymatous cells, the pits are of the simple type and consist simply of a gap in the wall occluded by a thin membrane. The pits play an important role in wood degradation. They provide avenues for distribution between cells for those organisms which have limited capabilities for direct penetration of the cell wall. Their condition also has a profound effect upon the movement of liquids in wood.

With regard to chemical composition, Bauch *et al.* [6] reported that tori of coniferous-bordered pits in sapwood consisted mainly of pectin with a small amount of cellulose and hemicellulose, the addition of lignin not occurring until the pits were incorporated into the heartwood. Enzymatic evidence of a significant amount of pectin in both pit membranes and ray parenchyma cell walls was presented by Nicholas and Thomas [90]. If this is true of soft woods in general, it could help explain increases in liquid permeability associated with attack of microorganisms, such as some wood-inhabiting bacteria thought to be incapable of lignin decomposition.

Although the various types of wood elements differ widely with regard to size and shape, they share some similarity with regard to cell-wall ultrastructure. This is particularly true of softwood tracheids and hardwood fibers. Because of this, and because of the importance of these two elements to degradation by microorganisms, a generalized structure for these elements will be discussed. Other elements may differ from this generalized picture by lacking some of the wall layers, by having additional layers, or by having variations in microfibrillar orientation or chemical composition.

A typical cell wall of a tracheid or fiber consists of the following layers: middle lamella (ML); primary wall (P); and secondary wall consisting of an outer (S1), middle (S2), and inner (S3) layer, and in some cases a warty layer or tertiary lamella on the lumen surface of the S3 (Figure 3.5). Two adjacent primary walls and the included middle lamella are commonly known as the compound middle lamella (CML). The primary walls are those first formed by division of the cambial initial and are cemented together by the middle lamella.

At its formation, the middle lamella consists largely of pectic substances, but as lignification occurs it becomes the cell-wall layer with the highest lignin content; at either of these stages, however, it is composed of amorphous materials. The other layers of the cell wall (excepting the warty layer) contain cellulose, and because of this they have at least some degree of crystallinity. Cellulose, a long-chain molecule, tends to aggregate into bundles known as microfibrils. Within each microfibril the cellulose molecules undergo various degrees of parallel orientation, producing zones called crystallites in regions of high molecular parallelism

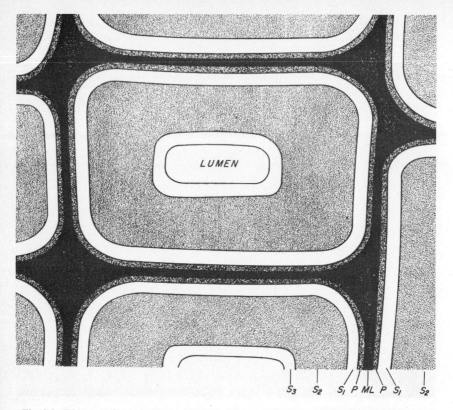

Fig. 3.5. Diagram of a typical cell wall [117]. (Courtesy U.S. Forest Products Laboratory)

and zones called amorphous regions where molecular orientation is more random. It is the crystallite regions that give the cellulose-containing walls their crystalline properties. The crystallite and amorphous regions also may display different degrees of resistance to enzymatic attack [26].

The primary wall contains some cellulose; however, since it is present throughout cell enlargement, the microfibrils are more sparsely distributed and randomly oriented than in the secondary-wall layers. Lignin content of the primary wall is much higher than that of the secondary wall.

The layers of the secondary wall are formed after cell enlargement has been completed. The secondary wall is made up primarily of carbo- hydrate (cellulose and hemicellulose), although it also contains some lignin. The lignin content generally is highest in the S1 layer next to the primary wall and decreases toward the lumen; in some hardwoods, the lignin content appears to increase again slightly in the S3 layer. Micro- fibrils of the secondary wall are highly oriented and the axis of orientation differs in the three layers, which is fundamental to their differentiation. The microfibrillar orientation tends to be nearly parallel to the longitudinal cell axis in the S2 (which usually is the thickest of the three layers) and to be nearly perpendicular to the longitudinal axis in the S1 and S3 layers. These differences in microfibril angle and in lignin distribution apparently greatly influence some types of microbiological degradation.

The warty layer, which may contain lignin and some protein, is believed to result from deposition of protoplasmic residue at the time of cell death. Few reports in the literature ascribe significance to the presence of the warty layer with regard to microbiological cell-wall decomposition.

3.3 Mode of Attack on Softwoods and Hardwoods by Decay Fungi

The term "decay" will be applied here strictly to effects produced in wood by the action of fungi belonging to the class Basiodiomycetes. Two major types of decay are recognized, and these are based on action within the wood and on reaction of the causal fungus to tests for extracellular oxidase [91]. In brown rot, only the carbohydrate fraction of the wood is removed to a significant degree while, in white rot, both the carbohydrate and lignin fractions of the wood are eventually removed. More detailed classifications of rot types have been proposed but will not be used here [9,81]. Earlier reviews of literature on the microscopical characteristics of decay were presented by Cartwright and Findlay [16,17] and Wilhelmsen [120].

In general, it appears that hyphal distribution is not a function of the type of decay produced by the particular fungus, since both uniform and irregular distributions have been reported for fungi causing white rot as well as for those causing brown rot. However, the anatomical effects of decay on the wood appear to be more uniform with white rot than with brown rot. Some fungi of both decay types preferentially penetrate pits in early stages of decay, but most decay fungi produce bore holes in the cell wall at some stage of decay. Both types of fungi are capable of producing cavities more or less parallel to the microfibrils of the secondary wall, or to the cell axis. The action of white-rot fungi on hardwood fibers and softwood tracheids most often involves progressive decomposition of both lignin and cellulose from the lumen outward (resulting in a progressive thinning of the wall), although the rate of decomposition of the two components may differ. Action of brown-rot fungi on cellulose occurs in a diffuse manner through the entire wall, with residual lignin maintaining the cell shape so that little damage to the wall is apparent until late stages of decay when the residual wall materials collapse. Differences in susceptibility to decay of various tissues, cell types, and wall layers appear to be correlated with differences in chemical composition—primarily with lignin content.

3.3.1 Hyphal distribution

In order for fungi to degrade wood, the enzymes which they produce must contact the substrate to be decomposed for use as food. For enzymes which can diffuse considerable distances from the hyphae which produce them, the distribution of the hyphae probably has little consequence on the progress of decomposition. However, for enzymes which remain close to the hyphae, the hyphal distribution has a profound effect upon the course of degradation. Because of its importance to our over-all understanding of the decay process, the research which has been conducted on distribution patterns of hyphae during the early stages of decay will be reviewed.

Since wood is a porous material, the elements of which vary greatly in relative size, one might anticipate that the fungi would move into the wood via the path of least resistance, which is through the largest, most open elements. This appears to be the case in many instances because it has been observed that certain white-rot and brown-rot fungi first extensively colonize the vessels or rays during attack of hardwoods [7,26, 37,104], and resin canals or rays during the attack of coniferous woods [117]. Hyphae of both types of fungi have been observed, however, in almost all cells of both types of wood early in decay [26,94,117]. If one were to search the literature on hyphal distribution in an attempt to find a characteristic which would differentiate white-rot from brown-rot fungi in early stages of decay, it would appear that hyphae of brown-rotters tend to be present in the wood as single hyphae in nearly every cell, or at least may be more uniformly distributed than the hyphae of white-rot fungi [26,30,81,94,116,117].

It seems logical to conclude that the distribution and number of hyphae can be used as an indicator of the severity of decay. However, this does not appear to be the case, since a study designed to test just that hypothesis found no correlation between the quantity of hyphae visible in spruce tracheids and the amount of wood deterioration indicated by loss in toughness [116].

3.3.2 Hyphal penetration

Since wood is essentially a closed system, fungal hyphae must penetrate through the cell walls or pit membranes in order to completely infiltrate the wood structure. This section reviews the modes and possible mechanisms by which decay fungi accomplish such penetration.

Hubert suggested that production of bore holes (holes directly through the cell wall perpendicular to the cell axis and produced by the passage of hyphae) is a characteristic that can be used to distinguish most decay fungi from other wood-inhabiting fungi [41]. In general, this appears to be true, and, as we will see in later sections of this chapter, production of bore holes is closely correlated with the ability of fungal groups to degrade wood substance. However, this is not always a reliable characteristic. In early stages of decay, some fungi of both the white-rot and brown-rot decay types have been observed to penetrate through pits instead of producing bore holes [7,15,26,37,94,104,106,117]. Nevertheless, in most of these cases the fungi did produce bore holes in later stages of decay. If bore holes are characteristic of wood-decomposing fungi, one might expect that the number of bore holes could be an indicator of the stage of decay. Apparently, this is true in some cases [116,125]. Other work, however, indicates only a rough correlation between degree of decay and the amount of mycelium or the condition of the cell wall [18]. Wilcox [119] found approximately the same number of bore holes inside and outside of advanced decay pockets caused by a brown-pocket-rot fungus. There seems to be no consistent difference between brown-rot and white-rot fungi with regard to the number of bore holes produced; they have been reported to be more numerous in advanced stages of brown rot [26,116], and vice versa [117]. It has also been pointed out that pit cavities were enlarged in white rot [46,76,117], and that enlarged pits and bore holes became indistinguishable in advanced stages of decay [117]. In the latter case, it would be difficult to distinguish between fungi which produced bore holes and those which penetrated through pits when the stage of decay was well advanced. In addition to the formation of holes perpendicular to the cell axis, there is one report of hyphae of brown-rot fungi growing longitudinally within the S2 layer [81], and cavities of axial orientation have been observed in both white rot and brown rot [24,64,74,111,114,117].

The mechanism by which fungi penetrate wood cell walls is important to the understanding and control of the decay process. As will be seen in this and later sections of this chapter, there appears to be a relationship between the mechanism of penetration and the relative ability of a fungus to degrade wood substance. On this basis, one might expect that the decay fungi—the most aggressive of the wood-attacking microorganisms —would all course through wood with relative ease. However, there appears to be considerable variation in mechanisms of bore-hole formation even within this group of fungi. As one might expect, both white-rot and brown-rot fungi appear capable of producing enzymes at the tip of the penetrating hyphae which digest bore holes in advance of actual passage of the hyphae [2,15,92,96,111]. Wall-deteriorating enzymes apparently are not liberated exclusively at hyphal tips, however, but are also exuded from lateral hyphal surfaces as indicated by the enlargement of bore holes to several times the diameter of the penetrating hyphae after penetration has been completed [2,15,16,26,92,116]. Further evidence of ability to secrete enzymes along the length of the hyphae was provided by Liese [64,66,72,74], who observed evidence of local wall dissolution around hyphae of white-rot fungi lying on wall surfaces. Not all decay fungi, though, appear to have such an easy time in penetrating through cell walls. While some hyphae remain the same diameter both inside and outside the bore holes [2,15], some have been observed to swell slightly before and after penetration [7] or to be constricted into a fine thread to perform the actual penetration [81,92,111]. Liese and Schmid [74,107] have even observed specialized structures formed at the tip of *Trametes (Fomes) pini* (Thore ex Fr.) Fr. hyphae. These structures, which they called microhyphae, were similar to structures formed by fungi believed to penetrate primarily by mechanical means. These structures appeared to function in bore-hole production, possibly in a mechanical role. Hyphae that originally were sharply constricted during the process of wall penetration were observed to fill out to their normal size following enlargement of the bore holes [92]. This suggests that these fungi have the capability of producing large bore holes but do not use it during initial penetration.

3.3.3 Microstructural changes

A major difference between white rot and brown rot lies in the microscopical appearance of the residual cell wall following removal of wall substance. White-rot fungi have most frequently been described as producing a progressive thinning of the secondary wall, beginning at the lumen and progressing outward toward the middle lamella (Figure 3.6) [16,26,41,46,71,81,104,106,116,117]. No such progressive thinning has been observed in brown rot, at least until very late stages of decay [16,71,94]. This difference occurs despite the fact that proportionate amounts of cell-wall material are being removed in both types of decay, as indicated by an increasing loss in weight as decay progresses. This observation leads to the concept that decomposition in white rot takes place on exposed cell-wall surfaces and is relatively complete before moving on to new surfaces, while decomposition in brown rot is generally spread throughout the cell wall and is incomplete at any particular location. There is strong chemical and microscopical evidence to substantiate such a hypothesis [26,117]. Similarly, Pechmann and Schaile [94] observed that strength loss in residual brown-rotted wood far exceeded the visible effects upon the wall, while in white-rotted wood, strength losses closely

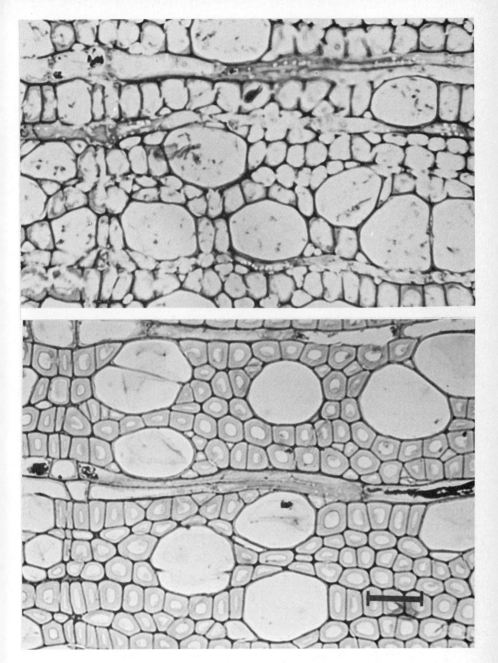

Figure 3.6. Cross sections of sweetgum (*Liquidambar styraciflua* L.) in the sound condition (bottom) and after having sustained 50 percent weight loss due to white rot (top) showing the characteristic thinning of the secondary wall. (scale = 50 μm)

paralleled the visible effects. Another general difference between white rot and brown rot is that in white rot the effects upon cell walls appear quite uniform within each cell and from cell to cell [26,104], while in brown rot, wall decomposition within a given cell or between adjacent cells is often very irregular [109,117]. Thus, although the end-result (decomposition of the wood substance) is the same in both white rot and brown rot, the means for achieving this result appear to be considerably different in the two types of decay. Because of this difference, the microscopical changes occurring in each type of decay will be reviewed separately.

White Rot. Fungi which produce white rot are capable of metabolizing all of the major components of wood—both the lignin and carbohydrate fractions. Theoretically, then, they are capable of achieving complete degradation of the wood substance. With this in mind, it would perhaps be expected that they would produce a uniform thinning or progressive removal of the wood cell wall. The situation, however, is not as simple and straightforward as one might expect. In fact, there appear to be two different types of white-rot fungi: those which decompose lignin and cellulose simultaneously throughout decay and those which decompose lignin preferentially in early stages of decay [9,81].

Of the white-rot fungi reported to attack only lignin first, *Panus stipticus* (Bull.) Fr. begins its deterioration of wood by delignifying the cells progressively from the S3 to the middle lamella, finally causing a loosening of the bond between cells [44]. It has been reported in other work, however, that this same organism entirely destroyed the S3 layer early in decay [85,89], suggesting that some action on the wood other than strictly lignin deterioration was occurring. Meier [81] found that *Trametes (Fomes) pini* (Thore ex Fr.) Fr. completely delignified spruce and birch wood progressively from lumen to middle lamella, before significant decomposition of cellulose became apparent. Long [76] reported delignification of ray cells and tracheids and destruction of the middle lamella of vessels and rays in the early stages of white rot caused by *Ganoderma (Polyporus) Curtisii* (Berk.) Murr. in oak. Lutz [78,79] reported that cell-wall lignin was completely destroyed before the cellulose was attacked in the early stages of several studies of white rots, but attack on the middle lamella was not observed until cellulose decomposition was nearly complete. Even in advanced stages of white rot, in contrast to brown rot, little or no wood shrinkage or collapse of cells occurred and the original shape and outward appearance of the wood were maintained [16,104,117]. Greaves and Levy [37] reported an exception to this generalization, however, in that they found a loss of structure in advanced stages of white rot in beech.

Among the organisms reputed to decompose lignin and cellulose simultaneously, *Polyporus versicolor* L. ex Fr. has probably received the most study.   Chemical investigations have revealed a remarkable proportionality between the rates of lignin and cellulose decomposition throughout all stages of decay by this fungus [26,104].   However, although this fungus follows the typical white-rot pattern of decomposing each wall layer successively from the S3 to the middle lamella, microscopical evidence suggests that the action of the lignin-destroying enzymes of this fungus precedes the destruction of cellulose in the cell wall [78,79,117]. Results of fluorescent staining experiments may indicate the same thing for other white-rot fungi [1].   The apparent disagreement between the chemical and microscopical results of study of *Polyporus versicolor* L. ex Fr. can be resolved by examining the distribution of lignin and cellulose within the cell-wall layers. Cell-wall lignin is primarily located in the compound middle lamella, with relatively little distributed throughout the secondary wall, while the bulk of the cellulose resides in the secondary wall. Therefore, in order for the relative proportions of lignin and cellulose to remain constant, as they appear to do during attack by *Polyporus versicolor* L. ex Fr., the lignin-destroying enzymes must travel farther into the wall structure than the cellulose-decomposing enzymes in order to reach the required amount of substrate. In fact, in a wood which contains relatively high amounts of lignin in the secondary wall, lignin decomposition by this fungus was found not to precede cellulose decomposition substantially [117].   In line with their ability to completely decompose wood, white-rot fungi have been observed to decompose ray cells progressively [7,13,37,116] and, in addition to their thinning of the cell walls, to cause great enlargement of pit canals and bore holes [26,104,117].

Although progressive cell-wall thinning is the typical manifestation of white rot throughout all stages of decay, often other features are more prominent in very early stages. Radial cracks or checks in the secondary walls have been reported in early stages of white rot [46,117] and have been interpreted as evidence of penetration of enzymes into the wall in advance of complete destruction [46]. A separation between cells within or adjacent to the compound middle lamella has also been observed in early stages of white rot [88,117]. Necesany and Cetlova [88] found a correlation between the amount of cell separation along the middle lamella and loss in lignin content. Such cell separation has even been observed in late stages of white rot caused by *Trametes (Fomes) pini* (Thore ex Fr.) Fr. [74].   Pit-cavity enlargement, wall checking, and cell separation were the only microscopical changes observed by Jurasek [46] in a white-rotted coniferous wood, even at moderate stages of decay.

The generalization that our knowledge of a phenomenon is intimately related to our ability to perceive the phenomenon is as true with the present subject matter as it is for others. Where white-rotted wood may appear largely unchanged to the naked eye throughout decay—with the exception of differences in color and weight—and decomposition appears progressive and uniform under the light microscope, observation with the electron microscope reveals the process not to be nearly as regular and uniform as we had previously suspected. For example, at the submicroscopical level, the thinning of individual cell walls may appear less uniform than as reported by a number of authors [26,81]. Minute pockets, indicating the removal of cell-wall material, have been observed in white-rotted wood [13,26,71,106]. Rhomboid cavities similar to, but smaller than, those typically procuded by soft-rot fungi have been reported in the secondary walls of wood attacked by white-rot fungi [64,72,74,106]. Some of the cavities observed were produced in the S2 layer of the secondary wall, even where no hyphae were present, and it was presumed that the fungal cellulase had diffused through the S3 layer to produce this effect [72,74]. Results of chemical analysis of white-rotted wood have also suggested that the enzymes of a white-rot fungus are capable of diffusing and acting some distance from the producing hyphae [26].

One means by which differentiation of fungi of the white-rot and brown-rot types in culture has been attempted is the color reaction produced by contact with a guaiacol reagent. The color change that occurs with white-rot fungi is presumed to be an indication of the presence of lignin-destroying enzymes. Since the color reaction is stronger with some cultures than with others, one might suspect that the intensity of color change when applied to white-rotted wood might indicate the extent of wood decomposition. However, research on this question revealed no such quantitative relationship [87].

Brown Rot. Fungi which produce brown rot are capable of metabolizing only the carbohydrate fraction of the wood. Unlike white rot, then, the maximum weight loss to be expected in brown-rotted wood would be 65–70 percent. Furthermore, the uniform, progressive, cell-wall thinning typical of white rot has not been observed in brown rot [46,71,94,117], the form of the cells being maintained by the residual lignin framework [16,46,81,94]. Changes in the cell wall in advanced stages of brown rot have been described as collapse rather than thinning [27,117], with the wall retaining its general appearance in earlier stages of decay even though cellulose removal occurs throughout. The wall collapse observed in advanced stages of decay presumably occurs when the residual material no longer possesses the strength to maintain the original form, resulting both in decreased cell size and wall thickness (Figure 3.7). Even in advanced stages of decay, however, brown rot does not display the microscopical

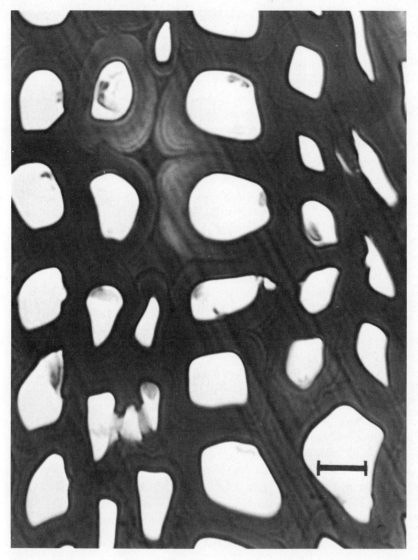

Figure 3.7. Cross section of southern pine (*Pinus sp.*) which has sustained 65 percent weight loss due to brown rot, showing the collapse of the residual lignin framework in cells with advanced decay and resulting in distortion and decrease in cell size. (scale = 10 μm)

uniformity characteristic of white rot. The degree of wall collapse can vary greatly between adjacent cells and even in various portions of the wall of any given cell. This irregular destruction has been offered as an explanation for the cracked appearance of brown-rotted wood [109].

Not only is brown rot less uniform than white rot in terms of the microscopical appearance of the decay, but differences between the modes of attack on hardwood and softwood have been reported to a far greater degree in brown rot than white rot. While cellulose decomposition in brown-rotted coniferous woods has been observed to leave the wall intact until actual collapse in advanced stages of decay [46,117], decomposition in a hardwood resulted in complete destruction of the various layers of the secondary wall, while leaving the general outline of the cell unchanged [117]. These results conflict with an early observation by Cartwright [15], who reported attack on coniferous tracheid walls by the brown-rot fungus *Trametes serialis* Fr. similar to that caused by white-rot fungi in that the attack began at the lumen. Meier [81] observed that the effects of two different brown-rot fungi were similar whether the attack was on a softwood (spruce) or a hardwood (birch). In both of these cases, however, decomposition was unlike that caused by white-rot fungi because it began in the S2 layer of the secondary wall rather than at the lumen boundary.

In contrast to the progressive removal of cell-wall layers typical of white rot, brown-rot fungi appear to attack various internal layers of the secondary wall first. Here again, however, the nonuniformity of brown rot is apparent. It has been observed that secondary-wall decomposition may begin by the formation of cavities in, or the complete destruction of, the S2 layer while the S3 layer remains essentially intact [44,81,117]. Some of the cavities in the S2 layer have been observed to take on a rhomboid shape [24,64,72] similar to that formed by soft-rot fungi and also observed occasionally in white rot. Two workers who found cavity production in the S2 layer of hardwoods, but not of softwoods, hypothesized that this difference might be due to a higher lignin content in the S2 layer of the softwoods [81,117]. Following complete removal of cellulose from the S2 layer in birch, the S3 layer was found to be decomposed next [81]; in other hardwoods, the S1 layer was attacked before the S3 [44,117]. Liese [64,66,72] also found that the S3 layer resisted degradation while the S2 layer was being destroyed, even when hyphae were in the lumen and lying against the S3. In contrast, however, Courtois [24] observed attack of the S3 layer prior to that of the S2, and Cowling [26] found an increased submicroscopical cell-wall porosity similar to that observed in white-rotted wood. As in the case of white rot, extensive cracking within the cell wall has been observed in early stages of brown rot [94,117] and appears to be characteristic of early stages of both types of decay.

The foregoing observations have involved changes primarily in tracheids of coniferous woods and fibers of hardwoods. This is understandable for several reasons. These elements are primarily responsible for wood strength; they also contain the thickest secondary walls so that changes in the cell wall are more readily apparent. It is also possible that changes may occur in cell walls of these elements much earlier than in other wood elements [117]. However, cell-wall changes resulting from decay have been observed in other wood elements as well. In one study, ray parenchyma cells were attacked in early stages of brown rot and walls were completely destroyed in advanced stages [94]. Wilcox [117] found thinning of ray cell walls in brown rot of a coniferous wood but noted little effect on ray cells in a hardwood. Greaves and Levy [37] also observed destruction of ray cells in advanced stages of brown rot in a coniferous wood. In brown-rotted beech, the cellulose of pit borders was attacked in early or intermediate stages of decay; in advanced stages the vessel walls had disintegrated completely while cells other than the early-wood fibers showed no signs of attack [37]. In advanced stages of brown rot in birch, cellulose decomposition was detected in all cells except the latewood fibers [37].

Szuleta's results [113] appear to be contradicted by current knowledge. Although reporting on the effects of brown-rot fungi—*Poria vaporaria* Fr., *P. vaillantii* (DC.) Fr., and *Merulius lacrymans* Fr.—Szuleta indicated that decomposition began in the region of the compound middle lamella and moved to the secondary wall only in late stages of decay; early decomposition reportedly consisted of the removal of lignin. Such activity presumably could occur with lignin-decomposing white-rot fungi, but would not be expected with brown rot.

3.3.4 Relative resistance of wood elements and cell-wall layers to decay

Most of the differences reported in the previous section, with regard to the degree and order of attack of different wood elements and cell-wall layers, are probably due to differing modes of action of the fungi involved or to different environmental conditions. However, some of the variations may be due to intrinsic differences in relative resistance of these elements and layers to decay. Identification of such resistance is important to our understanding of the mode of action of the decay fungi and is fundamental to a broad understanding of decay resistance and its contribution to our knowledge of the decay process and its prevention. Therefore, in this section information pertinent to decay resistance of individual elements and cell-wall layers will be cataloged on this basis rather than on the basis of the type of degradation involved.

It has been reported that the S3 layer of the secondary wall of some woods is highly resistant to degradation by brown-rot fungi [45,46,63,81, 86,117]; it also appears to be resistant to the action of acids and alkalis [56,63,115]. This resistance may be due to a greater degree of order in the cellulose microfibrils [55,81], to a higher concentration of lignin or other incrusting materials [44,45,46,63,117], or to differences in the chemical composition of the microfibrils [81]. The S3 layer appears to retain its resistance to the action of brown-rot fungi, even when it has first been delignified chemically [81]. Meier [81] reported that the S3 layer showed resistance even to the action of certain white-rot fungi. Necesany [86] found that the microfibrils of the S3 layer were resistant to degradation by white-rot fungi, particularly in early stages of decay, but even in advanced stages of white rot the microfibrils appeared more intact than those of brown-rotted wood. The S2 appeared to be the layer least resistant to the action of brown-rot fungi [81]; Necesany [85] suggested that it had greater resistance to lignin-destroying enzymes than to cellulose-destroying enzymes. However, Wilcox [117] found evidence of action of lignin-destroying enzymes of a white-rot fungus ahead of the action of the cellulolytic enzymes in the secondary walls of sweetgum fibers, probably due more to the difference in quantity of these two substrates than to intrinsic resistance to attack. The S1 layer has been reported resistant to attack by both white- and brown-rot fungi [81]; this was attributed to a greater density in the S1 layer than the S2, or to differences in chemical composition [81,82]. Yazawa [123] reported that brown-rot fungi destroyed the birefringence of the secondary wall, while a white-rot fungus did not. However, it could not be determined if Yazawa observed that all secondary wall layers retained their birefringence or if only the S1 was involved. Similarly, Schulze et al. [110] found that the X-ray interference due to cellulose disappeared gradually in wood decayed by several brown-rot fungi but remained in white-rotted wood. These results could be explained by the progressive action of white rot on wall surfaces, observed by Cowling [26] and Wilcox [117], which would allow residual cellulose to retain its crystallinity.

Meier [81] found that some of the differences between the effects upon wood of white-rot and brown-rot fungi disappeared if wood to be decayed was first macerated. He subjected macerated spruce wood (which he considered to be essentially pure cellulose) to attack by several brown-rot and white-rot fungi, and observed that both types of fungi decomposed this material at approximately the same rate and with similar morphological effects.

The compound middle lamella appears to be the region most resistant to attack of both white-rot and brown-rot fungi [26,81,117]. Nevertheless, this region was eventually attacked in advanced stages of white rot [81,117]. The thickened areas of the middle lamella at the cell corners resisted degradation the longest [81,117]. However, attack on the pit membranes was the only decomposition of the middle lamella by a white-rot fungus observed by Cowling [26] in sweetgum at weight losses up to 79 percent. In birch, Meier [81] found that the vessels also were resistant to the attack of brown-rot fungi, while in sweetgum, both vessels and rays were resistant to attack of a white-rot and a brown-rot fungus [117].

On the basis of a differential swelling rate, Kisser and Lohwag [47] concluded that the walls of earlywood tracheids and radial walls of late-wood tracheids had a denser structure than did tangential walls of late-wood tracheids. This was offered as the explanation for the fact that the white-rot fungus *Fomes Hartigii* (Allesch.) Sacc. and Trav. attacked principally the latewood and dissolved the tangential walls first. Liese and Schmid [74] found bore holes of the white-rot fungus *Trametes (Fomes) pini* (Thore ex Fr.) Fr. more prevalent on tangential than on radial tracheid walls, and attributed this to differences in lignification. They observed the first signs of deterioration to be the shrinkage of the tangential walls of the first few rows of latewood tracheids [74].

Differences in decay resistance of various regions within annual rings also have been reported. Schulze and Theden [109] observed that early-wood of pine and spruce was more resistant to brown rot than was late-wood. Conversely, Meier [81] reported that latewood of spruce was more resistant to the action of brown-rot fungi than was earlywood, but that earlywood was more resistant to white-rot fungi than was latewood.

3.4 Mode of Attack on Softwoods and Hardwoods by Soft-Rot Fungi

The type of cell-wall decomposition typical of soft rot was observed microscopically and attributed to fungus action as early as 1863 [103]. For some time it was considered simply as incipient decay [3]. The relationship of this type of wood deterioration to non-Basidiomycete fungi was surmised by Bailey and Vestal [4] and confirmed culturally by Barghoorn and Linder [5]. In 1954, Savory clearly described the occurrence of this form of deterioration and its symptoms and coined the term "soft rot" [102]. Various aspects of the type of wood decomposition known as soft rot have been reviewed by Bellmann [8], Cartwright and Findlay [17], Levy [59], and Wilhelmsen [120].

Although fungi causing soft rot have been clearly differentiated from Basidiomycetes which cause decay, the distinction between them and other non-Basidiomycete wood-inhabiting fungi has not been clear. Soft-rot fungi appear to belong to both the Ascomycetes and the Fungi Imperfecti, but so do those fungi which cause stain and mold. Differentiation has been based upon the anatomical aspects of the deterioration: the distinctive, often diamond-shaped, spiraling cavities in the S2 wall layer, and the extent to which the wood is degraded. This type of distinction has led to some confusion, and there is increasing evidence that it will lead to more if the definition of soft rot is not made more precise.

For example, Krapivina [52] reported studies on fungi that, because of their pigmentation, produced stain in wood, while the anatomical changes that they produced were described in terms appropriate to classical definitions of soft rot. Merrill [83] indicated that some species of mold fungi, such as *Trichoderma viride* Pers., were capable of producing a few diamond-shaped cavities in the secondary walls of some wood species and not of others. Duncan [28] found fine, spiraling cavities in the secondary wall which were produced by the white-rotting Basidiomycete *Poria nigrescens* Bres., and diamond- or rhomboid-shaped cavities have been found in the walls of both white-rotted and brown-rotted wood by Liese [64,72,74]. In fact, although such cavities have long been considered typical of soft rot, Liese and Schmid [64,72] concluded that, more accurately, they should be considered typical of fungi which hydrolyze cellulose regardless of classification. Corbett [19] has evaluated the soft-rot fungi as intermediate in properties and action between the stain and decay fungi, because they can sometimes display properties of both. Levi and Preston [58] concluded that if differences between soft-rot fungal action and that of other wood-inhabiting fungi are due to quantitative differences in enzymes, the soft-rotters are most like the brown-rot fungi; however, if due to qualitative differences, they constitute a distinct group of wood destroyers. Soft rot differs from both decay and stain because it is primarily a surface form of deterioration starting in outer layers of exposed wood and moving inward as outer surfaces are destroyed [21,23]. The decomposition occasionally extends somewhat more deeply into the wood in tracheids adjacent to rays [21]. However, under certain conditions [62,108], penetration and destruction of the wood may occur even more rapidly than would be expected with Basidiomycetes.

In degree of wood decomposition and aggressiveness of the causal fungi, soft rot appears to be intermediate between stain and decay. Fungi that cause soft rot penetrate through pits and live on storage material during early stages of their development in wood, which, of course, may be true of some decay fungi too. After these substances are no longer available, they may begin to penetrate and dissolve cell-wall material, but even then there is evidence that early wall penetration may sometimes be mechanical rather than enzymatic. Decomposition consists of localized cavities in the vicinity of the hyphae, primarily on the surface exposed to the lumen in hardwoods and within the S2 wall layer in softwoods. Wall decomposition is often limited to exposed surfaces of deteriorating wood rather than being distributed throughout, as in the case of decay. A characteristic of soft rot, particularly in softwoods, is the abundance of chains of conically tipped or diamond-shaped cavities in the S2 wall layer running helically around the cell axis, often approximately parallel to the microfibrils. Similar cavities have been observed in wood decomposed by other types of cellulose-destroying fungi, but not with the frequency with which these features are found in soft rot.

3.4.1 Hyphal distribution

Where enzyme activity can take place some distance from the producing hyphae, as appears to be the case with at least some of the decay fungi, the distribution of these hyphae may not be critically important to the progress of decomposition. In the case of soft-rot fungi, on the other hand, where decomposition appears to be closely tied to the presence of hyphae in the developing cavities, hyphal distribution would be expected to play a major role in the determination of the progress of decomposition. However, in the small amount of work done in this area, the activity and distribution of the hyphae of soft-rot fungi appeared similar to those of decay fungi in early stages of deterioration [37]. Hyphae traveled through cell lumina, becoming most numerous first in the rays in several species studied [19,37,60,61]. Vessels were the first elements attacked in beech [37], while Courtois [23] found that fibers were attacked first, followed by parenchyma cells and finally vessels. According to Greaves and Levy [37], it was not until bore-hole formation (their "active penetration" phase) that differences between soft-rot and decay fungi appeared [37].

It is interesting to note that the wood face exposed to decomposition may affect the relative rate at which fungi enter and distribute themselves throughout the wood. For example, Corbett [19] found that decomposition of test blocks occurred at a different rate, depending on which block face was placed in contact with the fungal culture. The order of the effect of the contacting face upon rate of decomposition (from fastest to slowest) was transverse, tangential, and radial. A higher lignin content of the radial walls was considered a possible explanation for their slow destruction [19].

3.4.2 Hyphal penetration

Since bore holes are considered primarily a characteristic of decay fungi, we would expect that soft-rot fungi would not produce them. On the other hand, if soft-rot fungi can produce cavities in the secondary wall, they presumably have the cell-wall decomposing capability necessary for bore-hole production. Nevertheless, it has been reported that penetration in early stages of soft rot was primarily through pits [37,60, 61]. After destruction of storage materials in the cell lumina, bore-hole formation began [37,52]. Pits continued to be the primary passageways for tangential spread [19], although bore hyphae can grow tangentially as well as radially [65]. The hyphae running longitudinally through cell lumina were relatively large and thick-walled, and formed fine, hyaline branches at right angles to the hyphal axis, which penetrated the cell wall through bore holes the same size as the fine hyphae [19,21,52,60,61]. These tiny bore holes did not appear to increase in size after penetration [19]. The penetrating branches often passed through the double cell wall and branched again in the adjacent lumen to form another thickened longitudinal hypha [19,21,52,60]. The cavities in the secondary wall may arise in several ways: branching of a penetrating hypha in the S2 layer, or change in direction of a hypha passing through a pit [57,58]. The penetrating hypha may branch in the S2 layer and form a T, with the two branches growing at the same rate in opposite directions and approximately parallel to the microfibrils [19,21,52,60]. In some studies, the penetrating hyphae usually passed through the first S2 layer encountered and formed the T-branch in the second contiguous S2 [19,21,61,65]. However, Levy and Stevens [61] found T-branching also in the first S2 layer encountered by the penetrating hypha, and Liese [65] observed that several cells might be penetrated before branching occurred. Penetration of soft-rot fungi was considered identical with that of stain fungi up to the point of T-branch formation [21].

Several theories have been suggested to explain the abrupt change in direction involved in the formation of T-branches selectively in the S2 layer [58]. First, certain properties of the S3 layer, such as degree of crystallinity, high degree of polymerization, the presence of an inhibitory substance, etc., may cause it to act as a barrier. Second, bore hyphae may be passing through plasmodesmata or other capillaries that may be blind. Third, there may be localized regions in the S2 layer that readily support hyphal growth.

T-branching was rarely found in hardwoods, and the predominant form of decomposition consisted of V-shaped notches in the secondary wall with fine hyphae passing through the wall connecting notches in adjacent fibers [19].

3.4.3 Microstructural changes

Where a major portion of wood decomposition is accomplished as part of the process of the distribution of hyphae through the wood, as is the case in soft rot, it is not possible to completely separate discussions of hyphal penetration and microstructural changes. However, all cell-wall degradation, regardless of whether it occurs at the time of initial penetration or subsequently, is a necessary part of any discussion of the effects of soft rot on wood properties.

Corbett [19] recognized two types of degradation produced by soft-rot fungi. Type 2, which occurred predominantly in hardwoods, consisted of erosion of the wall along hyphae lying in the lumen and formation of V-shaped notches at branches from the longitudinal hyphae [19,60,61]. These notches penetrated as far as the S1 layer or to the compound middle lamella, and notches in adjacent fibers often were connected by a fine hyphal branch passing through the cell wall at right angles to the fiber axis. The fine side branches reportedly became bulbous before forming a fine penetration hypha [61] in a manner similar to the formation of a transpressorium, as reported by Liese and Schmid [73] for blue-stain fungi. This suggests that the initial penetration of soft-rot fungi may be mechanical [61]. It also suggested to Levy and Stevens [61] that the hyphae of soft-rot fungi obtain their nutrition by direct wall erosion when the boundary layer can be decomposed enzymatically; where it cannot, the hyphae penetrate the barrier mechanically until they reach an area of the wall that can be attacked enzymatically. This theory could provide an explanation for the difference between the Type 1 and Type 2 forms of attack.

Corbett's Type 1 deterioration, the classical form of deterioration attributed to soft-rot fungi, is the primary form of attack in softwoods [19]. This type occurs after formation of T-shaped vertical branches in the S2 wall layer, or the entrance into the S2 layer of a hypha in a pit chamber. The two vertical branches of the T grow in length at about the same rate [19]. As the vertical hyphae extend through the S2 layer, cavities form around them at the tip [19,52]. The rate of hyphal extension may be reduced while the cavities enlarge laterally [19], or the cavities may enlarge as the hypha grows [52]. The tapered or conical tips of cavities (Figure 3.8) arise as the cavities enlarge [21,23]. The vertical hyphae may branch and give rise to branching chains of cavities [21,52]. Length of cavities appears to be inversely related to the diameter, with the longest cavities having the smallest diameter [19]. Formation of cavities appears closely related to hyphal growth because, unlike the deterioration caused by Basidiomycetes, there appears to be limited diffusion of enzymes away from hyphal surfaces [57,65,81] and hyphae must actually be present in the cell before deterioration occurs [59]. Fracture lines at the cavity ends suggested at least limited diffusion and action of the enzymes outside the cavities [65]. Levi and Preston [58] concluded, from evidence of loss of microfibrillar structure at a distance from hyphae, that diffusion of enzymes to significant distances from the hyphae must occur in late stages of decomposition.

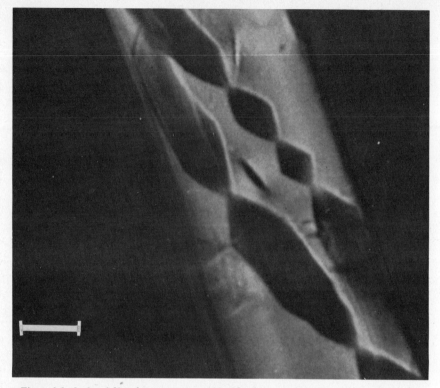

Figure 3.8. Isolated fiber from sweetgum (*Liquidambar styraciflua* L.) which had been at-tacked by a soft-rot fungus, showing the diamond-shaped cavities in the S2 wall layer typical of soft rot. Fiber was photographed in polarized light. (scale = 10 μm)

Courtois [23] recognized 14 types of soft-rot attack, basing the differen-tiations upon shape, orientation, and location of cavities in the wall. The characteristics of these types were influenced more by properties of the cell wall—such as fine structure, thickness, cell type, and chemical composi-tion—than by the species of soft-rot fungus involved.

The classical location for soft-rot cavities is the S2 wall layer, although both the S2 and S3 are involved in hardwood decomposition [19,23]. The S3 layer of softwoods is more resistant to attack than the S2 [23,66], but it may also be attacked in later stages of decomposition [23]. Corbett [20] found that soft-rot attack of tension wood fibers and cotton fibers, which contained essentially no lignin, produced a general attack (sculp-turing or thinning) along the exposed wall surfaces, suggesting that S3 layer resistance and the formation of discrete cavities may be controlled at least in part by lignin content or distribution. However, there is evidence that at least some soft-rot fungi can decompose lignin to a limited degree [52, 57, 58].

Most workers have reported that, in cases where cavities in the S2 layer are formed by soft-rot fungi, the cavities spiral along the cell axis with their sides approximately parallel to the microfibrils [28,81]. Liese [65] found that cavities paralleled microfibrils only in the more aggressive species of fungi; however, Courtois [23] concluded that cavity orientation was controlled more by the properties of the cell wall than by the species of fungus, and Willeitner [121] observed different cavity shapes when the same species of fungus attacked three different species of wood. The conical tips of the cavities form a fairly constant angle to the microfibril axis—23° as measured by Meier [81]. Such a constant angle has been attributed to enzymatic decomposition along given hydrolysis planes in the cellulose molecule [31,32], or to a faster rate of diffusion of a limited quantity of enzyme along the dissolving microfibrils rather than across them [98]. Liese [65] reported that the cavities enlarged more tangentially with regard to each cell than they did radially, leading to an oval shape. The regularity of this shape suggested that it was controlled by enzyme diffusion [65].

There are several possible explanations for the narrowing between each cavity in a chain (the formation of conical cavity tips) even though the hypha that formed them runs continuously through each one. One explanation could be based on Corbett's observation [19] that hyphal elongation slows down while the cavity behind the tip enlarges. Possibly, two different locations of enzyme secretions might be alternately involved in the processes of elongation and cavity enlargement [58]. Another theory is that the shape of the cavities is due to morphological or chemical properties of the cell wall [65]. This explanation would not, however, seem applicable to situations where cavities enlarge to the point of coalescence and general destruction of the S2 layer [57,61]. Perhaps the most plausible theory assumes restricted release of cellulolytic enzymes along certain portions of the hyphae, possibly at septa [57,58,65]. Levi [57] postulated that the rate of deterioration, and presumably the cavity shape, might be controlled by the rate of lignin modification rather than the rate of cellulose decomposition. Therefore, longitudinal enzyme diffusion would be between microfibrils, and transverse diffusion would be through the lignin between crystalline regions [57].

Cavities have been reported to be more conspicuous in latewood than in earlywood, especially in softwoods [28,102], while Levy and Stevens [61] reported them more prevalent in earlywood than in latewood in hardwoods.

3.5 Mode of Attack on Softwoods and Hardwoods by Mold and Stain Fungi

Mold and stain are considered together because of the similarity of action of the causal fungi on wood microstructure. Mold and stain (along with soft rot) are caused by members of the Ascomycetes and Fungi Imperfecti. Duncan [28] and Krapivina [52] showed that some fungi previously known as stain or mold producers can also cause soft rot under proper conditions. Merrill [83] reported that some mold fungi that produced little effect on the cell walls of poplar wood were known to produce typical soft rot in oak. It is probable that given the right conditions, other mold and stain fungi also may be able to produce soft rot. The difference in action is one of the level of aggressiveness upon the wood substance. In soft rot, a significant portion of the wood substance is decomposed by the fungus. With mold and stain, the fungus uses the wood substance primarily as a habitat and draws most of its food from stored materials in the wood. The major portion of the deterioration attributable to mold and stain is not decomposition but discoloration caused by pigment within the penetrating hyphae (in the case of stains), or by pigments only in the surface-formed conidia (in the case of molds). In either case, the attack on the wood is similar to early stages of soft rot—except that if deterioration is considered to be mold or stain, it does not proceed beyond the stage of fine bore-hole formation into a phase of cell-wall decomposition.

Mold and stain fungi apparently cause little damage to the structure of wood they inhabit, provided their action does not reach a more aggressive stage where it would be considered soft rot. Hyphae may be present in most wood elements, but are often more numerous in ray parenchyma cells. Penetration is primarily through pits, with hyphae passing directly through the membrane, but bore holes are formed through tracheids and fibers. The bore hypha is considerably smaller than the rest of the hypha and may actually arise from an appressorium. The bore holes apparently do not enlarge after formation. There is evidence that penetration through pit tori and cell walls may be primarily mechanical.

3.5.1 Hyphal distribution

Since the damage caused by mold and stain fungi is primarily the result of the presence of pigmented portions of the fungi themselves, the distribution of the hyphae, at least in the case of stain, is probably the most important aspect of the degradation to be considered. Hyphae of blue-stain fungi have been observed to occupy primarily the rays [51,70,105] (Figure 3.9). The hyphae tended to follow the rays into the wood [70,105], passing primarily through the ray parenchyma cells and occur-

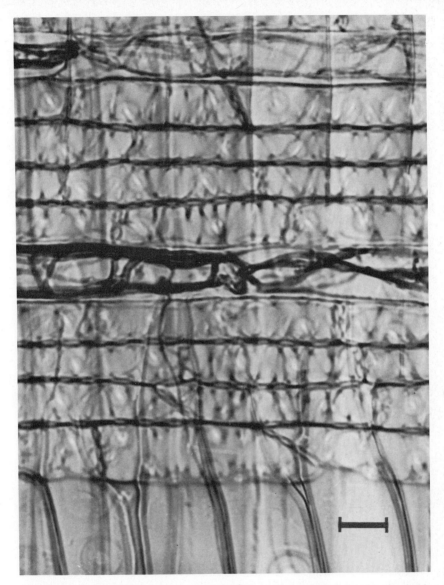

Figure 3.9. Radial section of ponderosa pine (*Pinus ponderosa* Laws.) showing the darkly pigmented hyphae of a blue-stain fungus in two rows of ray parenchyma cells. (scale = 25 μm)

ring only rarely in ray tracheids [70]. Hyphae also were present in fibers and tracheids and, although not as abundant, they were able to advance through the wood more rapidly in these elements [68,70,105]. Krapivina [53] reported differences in distribution of the hyphae of mold fungi within the annual ring, with species of *Fusarium* fairly uniformly distributed within both earlywood and latewood while species of *Penicillium* and *Verticillium* were limited primarily to the earlywood. A stain fungus that attacks the heartwood of living balsam fir was found to develop mainly in the tracheids [95].

Most studies of blue stain have been directed to that in coniferous wood; however, stains also occur in hardwoods. Only one report of the anatomical study of hardwood blue stain is known to the author. Fungi causing stain in hardwood were found to colonize primarily the vessels during early stages of infection and to occur only to a limited extent in the rays [14]. As stain progressed, hyphae became more abundant in vessels and fibers but not in rays. The ray cells generally were occupied by hyphae that were finer and lighter colored than those present in vessels and fibers. The absence of heavily pigmented hyphae in the rays is in striking contrast to the situation that occurs in softwood blue stain.

3.5.2 Hyphal penetration

Since mold and stain fungi do not physically destroy the wood they inhabit, one might presume that the damage they would do in passing through the wood would be minimal. As a matter of fact, hyphae of mold and stain fungi have been observed to penetrate primarily through pits [14,42,51,53,70,72,105], but occasionally most have been shown to produce bore holes as well [14,16,42,53,70,101]. Pit penetration appears to involve passage through the torus rather than the margo of the pit membrane [53,68,70,72]. Liese and Schmid [70,72] observed no appressorium, no hyphal constriction in passing through the torus, and no other evidence of enzyme action; this, along with detection of crushing of the pit membrane [70], indicated that penetration must be mechanical. However, Krapivina [53] observed extensive torus decomposition resulting from the penetration of mold hyphae, suggesting enzymatic action. In the genus *Pestalotia,* which also has been shown to produce soft rot [28,102], directional branching toward pits by means of specialized, naked protoplasmic outgrowths was observed [97]. Liese and Schmid [70] observed branch formation opposite pits, but once branching had occurred there was no apparent directional effect of pits on hyphal growth.

The formation of bore holes through tracheid walls appears to be a more complex process than pit penetration. Prior to bore-hole formation, the hyphal tip swells and forms an appressorium [16,54,64,66,70,72,

107]. A fine, bore hypha that penetrates the wall [54,64,70,72] is formed from the appressorium. This structure is so distinctive that Liese and Schmid [73] coined the term "transpressorium" to describe it. Although Krapivina [53] found histochemical evidence of enzymatic action during bore-hole formation by several mold fungi, and Liese [66] considered penetration by stain fungi to involve both mechanical and enzymatic processes, most workers have observed little or no evidence of enzymatic action and they believe that at least initial penetration is by mechanical means [16,54,70,72,73,105]. Liese and Schmid [73] reported mechanical penetration of metal foils by the bore hyphae of stain fungi. The bore hyphae produced by appressoria, which were about $\frac{1}{5}$ the size of normal hyphae, did not grow from the tip but were pushed into the cell wall by intercalary growth of the appressorium [70]. Other workers have reported extreme constriction of hyphae forming bore holes through tracheids [42, 99,105,112], which may be another interpretation of the same phenomenon. In an electron-microscopical study of elm xylem tissue invaded by *Ceratocystis ulmi* (Buism.) C. Moreau, MacDonald and McNabb [80] found minute bore holes which were not visible with the light microscope. Liese and Schmid [70] observed more bore holes in sapwood near the cambium than they did in older parts of the sapwood.

3.5.3 Microstructural changes

Although there is evidence that most mold and stain fungi do not attack the walls of tracheids and fibers other than by bore holes, they apparently can attack parenchyma cells. Hyphae have been observed growing within the walls of ray parenchyma cells [70], and in some cases they have partly or completely destroyed ray parenchyma cell walls [75,101,105] and the parenchyma cells in longitudinal resin ducts [105]. Degradation of the walls of both fibers and longitudinal parenchyma cells has been reported for *Ceratocystis fagacearum* (Bretz) Hunt [101].

Extensive microstructural changes probably are simply an indication that the mold or stain fungus is acting as a soft rotter. For example, Liese [65] reported formation of lysis zones in tracheid walls around the hyphae of *Alternaria* sp. which involved both the S3 and S2 of conifers in a manner similar to that of some soft-rot fungi, and Krapivina [53] reported an alteration of the secondary wall indicated by differences in staining reaction. Merrill [83,84] observed a few diamond-shaped cavities in the cell walls of wood attacked by the common mold *Trichoderma viride* Pers., and Johnson and Gjovik [43] found destruction of pit membranes in ray parenchyma cells of pine and interference with pit aspiration to be associated with hyphae of the same fungus. Merrill and French [84] reported that occasional attack on lumen surfaces was the only evidence of attack by mold fungi that was visible, even up to 20 percent weight loss in particle board. The gelatinous layer in tension wood fibers was partially decomposed by mold fungi [84,124]. Many workers, however, have reported no effects upon tracheid cell walls by hyphae of stain and mold fungi other than the formation of bore holes [66,68,70,72]. Liese and Hartmann-Fahnenbrock [68] reported the possibility of hyphae in the middle lamella, but the observation was not confirmed [70], and Krapivina [53] reported a weakening of the middle lamella. The fungus *Ceratocystis fagacearum* (Bretz) Hunt, which invades living oaks, was found to degrade both the secondary wall and the compound middle lamella during penetration [100,101]. The large openings in the pit tori (formed by passage of hyphae), and the extensive damage to ray parenchyma cell walls, could account for increased permeability to liquids in stained or molded wood [68,75].

3.6 Mode of Attack on Softwoods and Hardwoods by Bacteria

Although deterioration produced by bacteria in wood does not seriously affect most wood properties, it does represent another step in the continuum of aggressiveness of wood decomposition by wood-inhabiting microorganisms. Bacteria appear to focus their major effects upon the parenchyma cells of the rays and tori of bordered pits. Only when bacterial action on the rays is well advanced do effects on other elements usually appear, if then. The major effect upon wood properties produced by bacteria appears to be an increase in permeability to liquids. This may be accomplished by destruction of storage material in the rays, by destruction or alteration of pit membranes, or by decomposition of ray parenchyma cell walls.

3.6.1 Distribution

Bacterial cells in wood appear to be associated primarily with parenchymatous tissues, regardless of the type of wood. Bacterial cells have been found to accumulate in rays [25,33,35,37] and in resin ducts and other parenchyma cells [11,25,48]. They eventually move from these parenchyma cells to surrounding prosenchyma [25,33,37]. They have been observed to accumulate in pit chambers, and they show an affinity for the S3 layer in softwood tracheids and hardwood fibers and vessels [48]. In a review of numerous observations, Greaves [34] reported that all wood elements may be colonized by bacteria and are equally susceptible to attack, despite differences in lignification. Pine and eucalypt heartwood extractives reportedly had little effect on the growth of a number of bacteria [35].

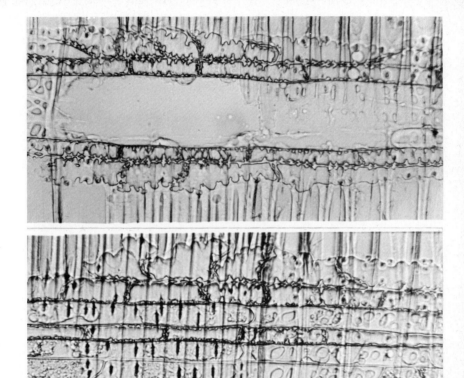

Figure 3.10. Radial sections of ponderosa pine (*Pinus ponderosa* Laws.) showing an intact ray (bottom) and one in which the ray parenchyma cell walls were destroyed by bacteria (top) [29]. (Courtesy *Forest Products Journal*)

3.6.2 Microstructural changes

The first change produced by bacteria appears to be decomposition of storage material in the rays [11,29,34,35,37,48]. Following this, the walls of the ray parenchyma cells may be attacked and destroyed [10,29,33,34, 35,37,40,48,77] (Figure 3.10). The walls of ray parenchyma cells in pine reportedly were decomposed, but not those in sweetgum or yellow-poplar [40,48]. Greaves and Levy [37], on the other hand, reported similar ray decomposition in pine, beech, and birch. The attack on ray parenchyma cell walls was found to involve a progressive attack on crystalline cellulose, beginning at the lumen and working outward [33,37]. Many workers reported no effects upon the walls of tracheids, ray tracheids, and fibers

[29,48,69,77]. Except for their pits, vessels were rarely attacked [34]. However, attack by bacteria on tracheid cell walls has been observed [10, 25], and attack on both tracheids and fibers was reported by Greaves [34,35].

Courtois [25] found depressions in the walls of tracheids underneath places where bacterial colonies had adhered to the wall. As the colonies enlarged, both S3 and S2 wall layers were attacked and the cavities became irregular etchings. The affinity of colonies for the S3 layer of longitudinal elements observed by Knuth [48] could be similar to the observations of Courtois, but representative of an earlier stage because of the wide difference in incubation times in the two studies. Courtois [25] observed that decomposition sometimes began in the rays and moved outward through the compound middle lamella to attack the secondary walls of tracheids. The middle lamella was resistant at first but was eventually attacked, so that all wall layers were subject to decomposition. Because decomposition was limited to portions of the wall in contact with bacterial colonies, and because the stage of decomposition varied widely in adjacent cells, it was concluded that enzyme diffusion from the bacterial cells was restricted and that actual contact between the cells and the walls was necessary for decomposition. It also was observed that the latewood was more resistant to bacterial attack than was earlywood.

Greaves [34,35,36] reported attack on both tracheids and fibers, the most common effect being erosion zones extending into the wall as far as the middle lamella. Attack on the middle lamella occurred primarily as an extension of attack on pit membranes [34]. Under long-term exposure, complete thinning of the secondary wall was observed, involving both the S2 and S3 cell-wall layers; such decomposition often occurred in patches associated with rays and vessels [34]. Unpublished data were cited that provided evidence that some bacterial enzymes are able to diffuse freely from the site of production in the lumen, through the S3, and into the S2 [34]. Later work [36] indicated that although enzyme diffusion apparently does occur, decomposition is limited to the near-vicinity of bacterial cells and consists of troughlike lysis zones approximately equal in depth to the diameter of the organism, but considerably wider.

Harmsen and Nissen [38,39] observed conical depressions in tracheids extending from the lumen into the secondary wall but not affecting the middle lamella. They isolated a bacterium and an Actinomycete from the material, but were unable to reproduce the observed effects in culture even though the organisms were cellulolytic; therefore, they could not positively ascribe the damage to bacterial attack [38,39].

The most common effect of bacterial infection upon wood properties appears to be a striking increase in porosity or liquid permeability [29,33,

37,48,49,69]. Several effects of bacterial infection could account for the increased permeability. Several workers reported bacterial attack on pit membranes [40,43,48,69]. Membranes of sweetgum were thinned significantly, and the tori of pine were destroyed and the margo disrupted [48]. Using light microscopes, Greaves [33,37] observed no effect on pits and concluded that increased permeability resulted from alteration of cellulose structure in ray parenchyma cell walls. However, in a later paper, Greaves [34] reported that pit degradation, including destruction of the border and even the margo and torus, was common. Johnson and Gjovik [43] found that bacteria destroyed bordered pit membranes in pine, and Highley and Lutz [40] found a loss in ruthenium red staining (a stain often used to detect pectin) of pit membranes in pine and yellow-poplar as a result of bacterial attack. This observation could well be significant in light of the report that the tori of coniferous pits may consist largely of pectin, with lignification of the tori not occurring until heartwood formation [6].

3.7 Opportunities for Future Research

One of the most important reasons for looking at the past is to chart the course of the future. Therefore, no review of literature would be complete without attempting to point out and organize the gaps in existing knowledge which have been revealed. There is much which remains a mystery to us with regard to the ways in which microorganisms attack and degrade wood. For example, what accounts for the apparent restriction of cellulolytic enzymes of white-rot fungi to exposed surfaces while the cellulases of brown-rot fungi appear to be capable of penetrating and acting throughout the cell wall? For those enzymes which do diffuse away from the producing hyphae, how far away from the hyphae are they able to go and still remain active? Furthermore, is there any correlation between location of enzyme production (*e.g.,* hyphal tip versus lateral) and diffusibility and enzyme activity? What is the role played in cell-wall penetration by special hyphal appendages and do they possess some special function in enzyme production or dissemination? Does chemical composition of the wood exert an influence on wood-attacking fungi by directly affecting enzyme diffusion and activity? In this same vein, what are the effects of natural and introduced fungitoxic compounds when studied at the cellular level? What is the source of the often-observed preferences of some decay fungi between hardwoods and softwoods as substrates or, perhaps of even more fundamental interest, what is the source of differences in susceptibility of the sapwood of various wood species which presumably contains no fungitoxic or fungistatic materials at all? It is possible that basic differences in the chemical or physical makeup of the wood cells may be responsible for such phenomena? Other differences of a similar nature also remain unexplained: differences in decay resistance of various cell-wall layers, of radial versus tangential cell walls, and of earlywood versus latewood. Is it possible that variation in chemical composition (*e.g.,* the quantity and distribution of lignin and hemicelluloses) or of the physical structure (*e.g.,* cellulose crystallinity and microfibrillar structure) may hold the key to the explanation?

By pooling the results of a number of observers, it can be concluded that members of all the groups of wood-inhabiting fungi—white rot, brown rot, soft rot, mold, and stain—are known to produce bore holes in lignocellulose cell walls. However, many of these fungi are known not to utilize lignin to any significant degree. What are the properties of lignin in the cell-wall complex or, conversely, of the non-lignin-destroying organisms, that allow such organisms to dissolve holes through substrate containing significant proportions of a substance they are incapable of destroying? Or, does mechanical penetration play a greater role in the movement of some of these organisms than has been suspected?

Although cavities parallel to the microfibrils have been considered characteristic of soft-rot fungi, it has been shown that some Basidiomycetes produce these as well. Why do some fungi produce such cavities while others do not? Does the microstructure or chemical composition of the wood affect the development of such cavities? Is the curious rhomboid shape of the longitudinal cavities formed by some fungi—primarily the soft rotters—caused by some property of the fungus, or of the wood, or both? Although theoretical bases for the occurrence of such cavities have been developed, based upon the crystalline structure and organization of the cell-wall cellulose, these theories still do not adequately explain why the shape can vary so significantly in similar woods or with different fungi. Another unexplained phenomenon which occurs in soft rot is the abrupt change in direction of hyphae when they form T-shaped branches in the wall. What are the causes of such unique behavior?

Finally, the bacteria have relatively recently been recognized as wood-attacking organisms of significant consequence. Considerable additional work is necessary to document the effects that bacteria may have on structural and mechanical properties of wood, to elucidate their probable role in discoloration and stain, and to determine their significance and to what degree they may function as predisposing agents to the action of wood-inhabiting fungi, for example, in the breakdown of chemicals responsible for natural decay resistance and of introduced preservatives. Clearly the numerous challenges that lie ahead, in this one small field, are as exciting as those that have been investigated before.

REFERENCES

1. Aufsess, H. von, Pechmann, H. von and Graessle, E. 1968. "Fluoreszenzmikroskopische Beobachtungen an pilzbefallenem Holz." *Holz als Roh- und Werkstoff* 26:50–61.
2. Bailey, A.J. 1934. "The penetration of fungi through wood." *J. Forestry,* 32:1010–11.
3. Bailey, I.W. 1913. "The preservative treatment of wood. I. The validity of certain theories concerning the penetration of gases and preservatives into seasoned wood." *For. Quart.* 11:5–11.
4. Bailey, I.W. and Vestal, M.R. 1937. "The significance of certain wood-destroying fungi in the study of the enzymatic hydrolysis of cellulose." *J. Arnold Arboretum* 18:196–205.
5. Barghoorn, E.S. and Linder, D.H. 1944. "Marine fungi: their taxonomy and biology." *Farlowia* 1:395–467.
6. Bauch, J., Liese, W. and Scholz, F. 1968. Uber die Entwicklung und Stoffiiche Zusammensetzung der Hoftüpfelmembranen von Längstracheiden in Conifern." *Holzforschung* 22:144–53.
7. Bayliss, J.S. 1908. "The biology of *Polystictus versicolor* Fries." *J. Econ. Biol.* 3:1–24.
8. Bellmann, H. 1961. "Zur Kenntnis der Zerstörung von Nadelhölzern durch Moderfäule-Pilze." *Holz als Roh- und Werkstoff* 19:429–34. (Translation CSIRO No. 5875).
9. Björkman, E., Samuelson, O., Ringström, E., Bergek, T. and Malm, E. 1949. "Om rötskador i granskog och deras betydelse vid framställning av kemisk papersmassa och silkemassa." *Kungliga Skogshögskolans Skrifter* 4, Stockholm. (From English summary.)
10. Boutelje, J.B. and Bravery, A.F. 1968. "Observations on the bacterial attack of piles supporting a Stockholm building." *J. Inst. Wood Sci.* 20:47–57.
11. Boutelje, J.B. and Kiessling, H. 1964. "On water-stored oak timber and its decay by fungi and bacteria." *Archiv für Mikrobiologie* 49:305–14.
12. Browning, B.L. (ed.). 1963. *The Chemistry of Wood.* Interscience, N.Y.
13. Buro, A. 1954. "Untersuchungen über den Abbau von Kiefern-und Buchenholz durch holzzerstörende Pilze und deren Einfluss auf einige physikalische Eigenschaften des Holzes." *Holz als Roh- und Werkstoff* 12:258–67. (From German summary.)
14. Campbell, R.N. 1959. "Fungus sap-stain of hardwoods." *Southern Lumberman* 199 (2489):155–20.
15. Cartwright, K. St. G. 1930. "A decay of Sitka spruce timber, caused by *Trametes serialis,* Fr. A cultural study of the fungus." Dept. Scientific and Industrial Res. Forest Prod. Res. Bull. No. 4 (London).
16. Cartwright, K. St. G. and Findlay, W.P.K. 1943. "Timber decay." *Biological Revs.* 18:145–58.
17. Cartwright, K. St. G. and Findlay, W.P.K. 1958. *Decay of Timber and Its Prevention.* 2d ed. H.M. Stationery Office.
18. Cartwright, K. St. G., Findlay, W.P.K., Chaplin, C.J. and Campbell, W.G. 1931. "The effect of progressive decay by *Trametes serialis* Fr. on the mechanical strength of the wood of Sitka spruce." Dept. Scientific and Industrial Res. Forest Prod. Res. Bull. No. 11 (London).
19. Corbett, N.H. 1965. "Micro-morphological studies on the degradation of lignified cell walls by Ascomycetes and Fungi Imperfecti." *J. Inst. Wood Sci.* No. 14:18–29.
20. Corbett, N.H. 1967. "Fungal breakdown of cellulosic plant fibers." *Naturwissenschaften* 54:350–51.
21. Corbett, N.H. and Levy, J.F. 1963. Penetration of tracheid walls of *Pinus sylvestris* L. (Scots Pine) by *Chaetomium globosum* Kunz." *Nature* 198:1322–23.

22. Côté, W. A. Jr., (ed.). 1965. *Cellular Ultrastructure of Woody Plants.* Syracuse Univ. Press, Syracuse, N.Y.

23. Courtois, H. 1963. "Mikromorphologische Befallsymptome biem Holzabbau durch Moderfäulepilze." *Holzforschung und Holzverwertung* 15:88–101. (Trans. Gt. Brit., Dept. Sci. Ind. Res. No. 111.)

24. Courtois, H. 1965. "Mikromorphologische Veränderungen verholzter Zellwände durch Basidiomyceten (Braunfäuleerreger)." *Material und Organismen* 1:41–53.

25. Courtois, H. 1966. "Uber den Zellwandabbau durch Bakterien im Nadelholz." *Holzforschung* 20:148–54. (Translation CSIRO No. 9220.)

26. Cowling, E.B. 1961. "Comparative biochemistry of the decay of sweetgum sapwood by white-rot and brown-rot fungi." USDA Tech. Bull. No. 1258.

27. Cowling, E.B. 1965. "Microorganisms and microbial enzyme systems as selective tools in wood anatomy." In *Cellular Ultrastructure of Woody Plants.* (W.A. Côté, Jr., ed.). Syracuse Univ. Press, Syracuse, N.Y. 341–68.

28. Duncan, C.G. 1960. "Wood-attacking capacities and physiology of soft-rot fungi." U.S. Forest Serv., Forest Prod. Lab. Rept. No. 2173.

29. Ellwood, E.L. and Ecklund, B.A. 1959. "Bacterial attack of pine logs in pond storage." *Forest Prod. J.* 9:283–92.

30. Falck, R. 1919. Berichte der Deutschen Botanischen Gesellschaft (General versammlung) 37:(8)–(14).

31. Frey-Wyssling, A. 1938. "Submikroskopische Struktur und Mazerationsbilder nativer Cellulosefasern." *Der Papierfabrikant* 36:212–27.

32. Frey-Wyssling, A. 1956. "Nachtrag zu P.A. Roelofsen, Eine mögliche Erklärung der typischen Korrosionsfiguren der Holzfasern bei Moderfäule." *Holz als Roh- und Werkstoff* 14:210.

33. Greaves, H. 1965. "The effect of bacterial action on some wood cubes in shake culture." *Material und Organismen* 1:61–67.

34. Greaves, H. 1969. "Micromorphology of the bacterial attack of wood." *Wood Sci. Tech.* 3:150–66.

35. Greaves, H. 1970. "The effect of some wood-inhabiting bacteria on the permeability characteristics and microscopic features of *Eucalyptus regnans* and *Pinus radiata* sapwood and heartwood." *Holzforschung* 24 (1):6–14.

36. Greaves, H. and Foster, R.C. 1970. "The fine structure of bacterial attack of wood." *J. Inst. Wood Sci.* 5(1):18–27.

37. Greaves, H. and Levy, J.F. 1965. "Comparative degradation of the sapwood of scots pine, beech, and birch by *Lenzites trabea, Polystictus versicolor, Chaetomium globosum* and *Bacillus polymyxa.*" *J. Inst. Wood Sci.* 15:55–63.

38. Harmsen, L. and Nissen, T.V. 1965. "Timber decay caused by bacteria." *Nature* 206:319.

39. Harmsen, L. and Nissen, T.V. 1965. "Der Bakterienangriff auf Holz." *Holz als Roh-und Werkstoff* 23:389–93. (Translation Joint Pub. Res. Serv.: U.S. Dept. Com. FPL–657.)

40. Highley, T.L. and Lutz, J.F. 1970. "Bacterial attack in water-stored bolts." *Forest Prod. J.* 20(4):43–44.

41. Hubert, E.E. 1924. "The diagnosis of decay in wood." *J. Agr. Res.* 29:523–67.

42. Hubert, E.E. 1929. "Sap stains of wood and their prevention." U.S. Dept. Com., Natl. Com. Wood Utilization. Rept. No. 10.

43. Johnson, B.R. and Gjovik, L.R. 1970. "Effect of *Trichoderma viride* and a contaminating bacterium on microstructure and permeability of loblolly pine and Douglas-fir." *Proc., Am. Wood-Preservers' Assoc.* 66:234–42.

44. Jurasek, L. 1955. "Zmeny v mikrostrukture zdrevanatele bunecene blany pri

rozkladu drevokaznymi houbami." *Biologia* (Bratislava) 10:569–79. (Translation Joint Pub. Res. Serv.: U.S. Dept. Com. FPL–653.)

45. Jurasek, L. 1958. "Mikrostruktura borove beli pri rozkladu celulosovornimi houbami." *Drevarsky Vyskum* (3):129–35. (From English summary.)

46. Juraske, L. 1964. "Zmeny v mikroskopicke strukture pri rozkladu dreva drevokaznymi houbami." *Drevarsky Vyskum* (3): 127–44. (Translation U.S. Forest Prod. Lab. FPL–618).

47. Kisser, J. and Lohwag, K. 1937. "Histochemische Untersuchungen an verholzten Zellwänden." *Mikrochemie* 23(1):51–60. (Translation U.S. Forest Prod. Lab. No. 549).

48. Knuth, D.T. 1964. "Bacteria associated with wood products and their effects on certain chemical and physical properties of wood." Ph.D. dissertation, Univ. of Wisconsin.

49. Knuth, D.T. and McCoy, E. 1962. "Bacterial deterioration of pine logs in pond storage." *Forest Prod. J.* 12:437–42.

50. Kollmann, F.F.P. and Côté, W.A. Jr. 1968. *Principles of Wood Science and Technology. I. Solid Wood.* Springer-Verlag, Berlin.

51. Konstantnaja, A.A. 1964. [Microscopic investigations on the wood of spruce and larch damaged by wood staining fungi]. *Botaniceskij Zhurnal S.S.S.R.* 49:105–109. (From For. Abstr. 25: No. 4292.)

52. Krapivina, I.G. 1960. [Destruction of the secondary layer of the cell wall by blue stain fungi]. *Lesnoi Zhurnal, Arkhangel'sk* 3(1):130–33. (Translation CSIRO No. 5329).

53. Krapivina, I.G. 1962. [Changes produced by mould fungi in wood]. *Vest. Mosk. Univ. Ser. Biol.* 17(5):47–51. (From Rev. Appl. Mycol. 43. No. 1769.)

54. Lagerberg, T., Lundberg, G. and Melin, E. 1927. "Biological and practical researches into blueing in pine and spruce." *Svenska Skogsvardsför. Tidskr.* 25:145–272; 561–739.

55. Lange, P.W. 1954. "The distribution of the components in the plant cell wall." *Svensk Papperstidning* 57:563–67.

56. Lange, P.W. 1958. "The distribution of the chemical constituents throughout the cell wall." In *Fundamentals of Papermaking Fibres.* (F. Bolam, ed.). British Paper and Board Makers' Association, England. 147–85.

57. Levi, M.P. 1965. "Decay patterns produced by *Chaetomium globosum* in beechwood fibers. A chemical and microscopic study." *Material und Organismen* 1:119–26.

58. Levi, M.P. and Preston, R.D. 1965. "A chemical and microscopic examination of the action of the soft-rot fungus *Chaetomium globosum* on beechwood (*Fagus sylv.*)." *Holzforschung* 19:183–90.

59. Levy, J.F. 1965. "The soft rot fungi: Their mode of action and significance in the degradation of wood." In *Advances in Botanical Research.* (R.D. Preston, ed.) Vol. 2. Academic Press, N.Y. 323–57.

60. Levy, J.F. 1965. "The soft rot fungi and their mode of entry into wood and woody cell walls." *Material und Organismen* 1:55–60.

61. Levy, J.F. and Stevens, M.G. 1966. "The initiation of attack by soft rot fungi in wood." *J. Inst. Wood Sci.* 16:49–55.

62. Liese, W. 1961. "Uber die natürliche Dauerhaftigkeit einheimischer und tropischer Holzarten gegenüber Moderfäulepilzen." *Mitteilungen der Deutschen Gesellschaft für Holzforschung* 48:18–28. (From English summary.)

63. Liese, W. 1963. "Tertiary wall and warty layer in wood cells." *J. Polymer Sci.* C(2):213–29.

64. Liese, W. 1963. "Neue Befunde über den Abbau des Holzes durch Pilze." *Holz-Zentralblatt* 89:505–507.

65. Liese, W. 1964. "Uber den Abbau verholzter Zellwände durch Moderfäulepilze." *Holz als Roh- und Werkstoff* 22:289–95. (Translation CSIRO No. 7294.)

66. Liese, W. 1965. "Mikromorphologische Veränderungen beim Holzabbau durch Pilze." *Material und Organismen* 1:13–26.

67. Liese, W. 1970. "Ultrastructural aspects of woody tissue disintegration." *Ann. Rev. Phytopathology* 8:231–58.

68. Liese, W. and Hartmann-Fahnenbrock. M. 1953. "Elektronenmikroskopische Untersuchungen an verblauten Kiefernholz." *Holzforschung* 7:97 102.

69. Liese, W. and Karnop, G. 1968. "Uber den Befall von Nadelholz durch Bakterien." *Holz als Roh- und Werkstoff* 26:202–208. (Translation Dept. For. Canada No. 297).

70. Liese, W. and Schmid, R. 1961. "Licht-und elekronenmikroskopische Untersuchungen über das Wachstum von Bläuepilzen in Kiefern-und Fichtenholz." *Holz als Roh- und Werkstoff* 19:329–37. [Translation Res. Inf. Service (Pergamon Press) No. 464.]

71. Liese, W. and Schmid, R. 1962. "Submicroscopical changes of cell wall structure by wood-destroying fungi." Fifth Int. Congr. for Electron Microscopy, (Philadelphia) 2:W–5.

72. Liese, W. and Schmid, R. 1962. "Elektronenmikroskopische Untersuchungen über den Abbau des Holz durch Pilze." *Angewandte Botanik* 36:291–98.

73. Liese, W. and Schmid, R. 1964. "Uber das Wachstum von Bläuepilzen durch verholzte Zellwände." *Phytopathologische Zeitschrift* 51:385–93.

74. Liese, W. and Schmid, R. 1966. "Untersuchungen über den Zellwandabbau von Nadelholz durch *Trametes pini*." *Holz als Roh- und Werkstoff* 24:454–60. (Translation CSIRO No. 8800.)

75. Lindgren, R.M. 1952. "Permeability of southern pine as affected by mold and other fungus infection." *Proc., Am. Wood-Preservers' Assoc.* 48:158–74.

76. Long, W.H. 1930. "Some microscopic characters of the rot caused by *Ganoderma Curtisii*." *Phytopathology* 20:758.

77. Lutz, J.F., Duncan, C.G. and Scheffer, T.C. 1966. "Some effects of bacterial action on rotary-cut southern pine veneer." *Forest Prod. J.* 16(8): 23–28.

78. Lutz, L. 1931. "Sur les ferments hydrolysants sécrétés par les Champignons Hyménomycètes. Dégradation des éléments constituants de la membrane cellulaire." *Bull. Soc. Chim. Biol.* 13:436–57.

79. Lutz, L. 1943. "Sur l'attaque de bois par les Hyménomycètes lignicoles. Cas du Daedalea quercina Pers." *Boissiera* 7:293–95.

80. MacDonald, W.L. and McNabb, H.S. Jr. 1970. "Fine-structural observations of the growth of *Ceratocystis ulmi* in elm xylem tissue." *Bioscience* 20(19):1060–61.

81. Meier, H. 1955. "Uber den Zellwandabbau durch Holzvermorschungspilze und die submikroscopische Struktur von Fichtentracheiden und Birkenholzfasern." *Holz als Roh- und Werkstoff* 13:323–38. (Translation Dept. For. Canada No. 92.)

82. Meier, H. 1957. "Discussion of the cell wall organization of tracheids and fibres." *Holzforschung* 11:41–46.

83. Merrill, W. 1965. "Decay of wood and wood fiberboards by common Fungi Imperfecti." *Material und Organismen* 1:69–76.

84. Merrill, W. and French, D.W. 1965. "Wood fiberboard studies. 3. Effect of common molds on the cell wall structure of the wood fibers." *Tappi* 48:653–54.

85. Necesany, V. 1957. "The nature of the so-called tertiary lamella." *Svensk Papperstidning* 60:10–16.

86. Necesany, V. 1963. "Veränderung der Zellwandstruktur bei Tannenholz (*Abies alba* Mill.) durch Pilzeinwirkung." *Holzforschung* 17:57–60. (From English summary.)

87. Necesany, V. 1965. "Einfluss der Weissfäulepilze auf die Ultrastruktur äusserer Zellwandschichten." *Material und Organismen* 1:27–39.

88. Necesany, V. and Cetlova, J. 1963. "Rozklad bunecnych blan bukoveho dreva houbou *Stereum purpureum* Pers." *Drevarsky Vyskum* (4):195–202. (From English summary.)

89. Necesany, V. and Jurasek, L. 1956. "Zmeny submikroskopicke struktury dreva, napadeneho bilou hnilobou." *Lesnicky Casopis* 2:43–52. (From German summary.)

90. Nicholas, D.D. and Thomas, R.J. 1968. "The influence of enzymes on the structure and permeability of loblolly pine." *Proc., Am. Wood-Preservers' Assoc.* 64:70–76.

91. Nobles, M.K. 1965. "Identification of cultures of wood-inhabiting hymenomycetes." *Can. J. Bot.* 43:1097–1139.

92. Nutman, F.J. 1929. "Studies of wood-destroying fungi. I. *Polyporus hispidus* (Fries)." *Ann. Appl. Biol.* 16:40–64.

93. Panshin, A.J. and deZeeuw, C. 1970. *Textbook of Wood Technology.* 3d ed. Vol. 1. McGraw-Hill Book Co. N.Y.

94. Pechmann, H. von and Schaile, O. 1950. "Uber die Anderung der dynamischen Festigkeit und der chemischen Zusammensetzung des Holzes durch den Angriff holzzerstörender Pilze." *Forstwissenschaftliches Centralblatt* 69:441–66.

95. Pomerleau, R. and Etheridge, D.E. 1961. "A bluestain in balsam fir." *Mycologia* 53:155–70.

96. Proctor, P. Jr. 1941. "Penetration of the walls of wood cells by the hyphae of wood-destroying fungi." Yale University School of Forestry Bull. No. 47.

97. Ritchie, D. 1967. "Penetration of wood cells by special extensions of *Pestalotia* hyphae." *Mycologia* 59:417–22.

98. Roelofsen, P.A. 1956. "Eine mögliche Erklärung der typischen Korrosionsfiguren der Holzfasern bei Moderfäule." *Holz als Roh- und Werkstoff* 14:208–10. (Translation CSIRO No. 5132).

99. Roff, J.W. 1964. "Hyphal characteristics of certain fungi in wood." *Mychologia* 56:799–804.

100. Sachs, I.B., Mair, V.M.G. and Kuntz, J.E. 1967. "Penetration and degradation of cell walls in oak sapwood by *Ceratocystis fagacearum.*" *Phytopathology* 57:827–28.

101. Sachs, I.B., Nair, V.M.G. and Kuntz, J.E. 1970. "Penetration and degradation of cell walls in oaks infected with *Ceratocystis fagacearum.*" *Phytopathology* 60:1399–1404.

102. Savory, J.G. 1954. "Breakdown of timber by Ascomycetes and Fungi Imperfecti." *Ann. Appl. Biol.* 41:336–47.

103. Schacht, H. 1863. "Ueber die Veränderungen durch Pilze in abgestorbenen Pflanzenzellen." *Jahrbücher für wissenschaftliche Botanik* 3:442–83.

104. Scheffer, T.C. 1936. "Progressive effects of *Polyporus versicolor* on the physical and chemical properties of red gum sapwood." USDA Tech. Bull. No. 527.

105. Scheffer, T.C. and Lindgren, R.M. 1940. "Stains of sapwood and sapwood products and their control." USDA Tech. Bull. No. 714.

106. Schmid, R. and Liese, W. 1964. "Uber die mikromorphologischen Veränderungen der Zellwandstrukturen von Buchen- und Fichtenholz beim Abbau durch *Polyporus versicolor* (L.) Fr." *Archiv für Mikrobiologie* 47:260–76. (Translation CSIRO No. 7130.)

107. Schmid, R. and Liese, W. 1965. "Elektronenmikroskopische Beobachtungen an Hyphen von Holzpilzen." *Material und Organismen* 1:251–61.

108. Schulz, G. 1964. "Versuche mit salzgetränkten Holzschwellen." *Holz als Roh- und Werkstoff* 22:57–64. (From English summary.)

109. Schulze, B. and Theden, G. 1938. "Polarisationsmikroskopische Untersuchungen über den Abbau des Werkstoffes Holz durch holzzerstörende Pilze." *Holz als Roh- und Werkstoff* 1:548–54. (From German summary.)

110. Schulze, B., Theden, G. and Vaupel, O. 1937. "Rötgen-Interferenzuntersuchungen einheimischer Holzarten im gesunden Zustand und nach Pilzangriff." *Hols als Roh- und Werkstoff* 1:75–80.

111. Sen, J. 1948. "Orientation of cellulose and its relation to decay cavities in the secondary walls of chir (*Pinus logifolia*) tracheids." *Science and Culture* (Calcutta) 14:163–64.

112. Siepmann, R. and Johnson, T.W. Jr. 1960. "Isolation and culture of fungi from wood submerged in saline and fresh waters." *J. Elisha Mitchell Sci. Soc.* 76(1):150–54.

113. Szuleta, J. 1947. "Cyto-chemiczne zmiany drewna sosnowego pod wplywem grzybow *Poria vaporaria* Fr., Poria vaillantii (de Cand.) Fr. i *Merulius lacrymans* Fr." *Acta Societatis Botanicorum Poloniae* 18:217–37. (From French summary and For. Abstr. 11. No. 359.)

114. Tamblyn, N. 1937. "Decay in timber with special reference to Jarrah (*Eucalyptus marginata* Sm.)." *Australian For.* 2(1):6–13.

115. Wardrop, A.B. and Dadswell, H.E. 1957. "Variations in the cell wall organization of tracheids and fibers." *Holzforschung* 11:33–41.

116. Waterman, A.M. and Hansbrough, J.R. 1957. "Microscopical rating of decay in Sitka spruce and its relation to toughness." *Forest Prod. J.* 7:77–84.

117. Wilcox, W.W. 1968. "Changes in wood microstructure through progressive stages of decay." U.S. Forest Serv., Res. Forest Prod. Lab. Rept. No. 70.

118. Wilcox, W.W. 1970. "Anatomical changes in wood cell walls attacked by fungi and bacteria." *Botanical Review* 36(1):1–28.

119. Wilcox, W.W. and Garcia, B.J. 1968. "Changes in wood properties at the boundary of *Polyporus amarus* decay pockets." *Wood Sci. Tech.* 2:115–27.

120. Wilhelmsen, G. 1965. "Mikromorfolgiske og biokjemiske forandringer i trevirke ved enzymatisk nedbrytning." *Norsk Skogindustri* 19:187–93. (Translation Dept. For. Canada No. 195.)

121. Willeitner, H. 1965. "Uber den Abbau von Holzspanplatten durch Moderfäulepilze." *Material und Organismen* 1:77–88.

122. Wise, L.E. and Jahn, E.C. (eds.) 1952. *Wood Chemistry.* 2d ed., Vol. 1. Reinhold Publishing Corp., N.Y.

123. Yazawa, K. 1943. [Untersuchungen ueber Zerstoerung durch Pilze und die mechanischen Eigenschaften abgestorbener Tannen- und Fichtenhoelzer]. Series 2. Rep. of the Saghalien Central Exp. Sta. (Japan) 14. (In Japanese; from German summary.)

124. Zenker, R. 1963. "Der Abbau der Zugholzlamelle durch holzzerstörende Pilze." In *Holzzerstörung durch Pilze* (H. Lyr and W. Gillwald, eds.). Int. Symp., Eberswalde. Akademie-Verlag, Berlin.

125. Zycha, H. and Brand, W. 1959. "Eine Methode zur Bestimmung des Grades der Zerstörung von Fichtenholz durch *Fomes annosus* mit Hilfe des Mikroskopes." *Phytopathologische Zeitschrift* 35:411–19. (From English summary.)

4. The Chemistry and Biochemistry of Decay

T. KENT KIRK

U.S. Forest Products Laboratory, Madison, Wisconsin

4.1 Introduction

The fungi that decompose wood do so in order to gain food and energy for growth and reproduction. They bring about changes in the high-molecular-weight polymers that make up wood cell walls, ultimately degrading them to small molecules which are ingested and serve as sources of energy and carbon. Collectively, the specific changes they cause determine the gross changes in physical properties which we associate with decay. This chapter describes some of the biochemical changes in wood caused by decay fungi. Its main purpose is to provide insight into what is happening at the molecular level during decay, and thus into what we are trying to prevent through wood preservation. A better understanding of the chemistry and biochemistry of the decay processes can lead to better protective treatments than are now used. The reader should be aware at the outset that our information is far from complete. A secondary purpose of this chapter, therefore, is to point out some of the gaps in our knowledge and thus to stimulate an interest in research to fill these deficiencies.

4.2 The Chemical Composition of Wood

4.2.1 General

In order to deal with the chemical changes caused by decay fungi, it is necessary to have in mind major aspects of the chemical composition of wood, the chemical structures of its component polymers, and the relationship of these structural polymers to one another.

Wood is made up mainly of three polymeric materials: cellulose, the hemicelluloses, and lignin. Other substances such as nitrogenous materials, pectin, starch, low-molecular-weight sugars, and minerals (Fe, Mg, Mn, etc.) also are present. In addition, a variety of extraneous materials (lignans, terpenes, polyphenols, etc.) are found in varying amounts. Pectin, starch, and low-molecular-weight carbohydrates may be especially important as initial carbon sources for the establishment of microorganisms in wood [37,60]. It has been suggested [37] that removal of these carbohydrates may be a way to prevent decay under some circumstances. Nitrogenous materials, present usually in minimal amounts in wood, are essential to the growth and activities of the wood-destroying organisms and therefore exert considerable influence on the rate of decay [21]. Wood-decay fungi require the same mineral elements as the tree for their biochemical activities (see Chapter 2 of this volume); it has been proposed that chelation or complexing of trace elements in wood may be a useful method for preventing decay [5]. Various extractive components of wood are toxic to wood-destroying microorganisms [64] (see Chapter 2) and are thus also very important in the over-all picture of the decay processes; indeed, most of the variation in decay susceptibility of various woods is due to extractive components. In this section, however, we are concerned with the structural components and will not consider the nonstructural materials further.

The relative amounts of major structural components for woods of three common angiosperms and gymnosperms are given in Table 4.1;

TABLE 4.1

Percentages of Major Components in Wood of Representative Angiosperms and Gymnosperms [74]

(values expressed as % of total weight of wood)

Component	Angiosperms			Gymnosperms		
	Betula papyrifera	Fagus grandifolia	Ulmus americana	Picea glauca	Pinus strobus	Tsuga canadensis
Cellulose	42	45	51	41	41	41
Lignin	19	22	24	27	29	33
Hemicellulose	38	29	23	31	27	23
Total*	99	96	98	99	97	97

*The difference between these totals and 100% is made up of pectin, starch, minerals, and extraneous materials.

minor components, mentioned above, make up the difference between the total percentages shown and 100 percent. Temperate-zone hardwoods generally contain 17–24 percent lignin, whereas conifers usually vary between 25 and 34 percent lignin. The cellulose content of most temperate-zone woods is between 40 and 50 percent; the hemicelluloses comprise the remainder.

In the next few sections a brief review of the chemical structures of cellulose, the most important wood hemicelluloses, and lignin are presented. Of course, space does not permit a thorough discussion of these subjects, so for more detail the reader is referred to the following references: [31] (cellulose); [74,76] (hemicelluloses); and [1,30,36] (lignin).

4.2.2 Cellulose

The chemical structure of cellulose is straightforward. It is a linear polymer of anhydro-D-glucopyranose units linked by β-(1 $\rightarrow$ 4) glycosidic bonds (Figure 4.1); each molecule of wood cellulose contains an average of about 7,000–10,000 glucose residues [34].

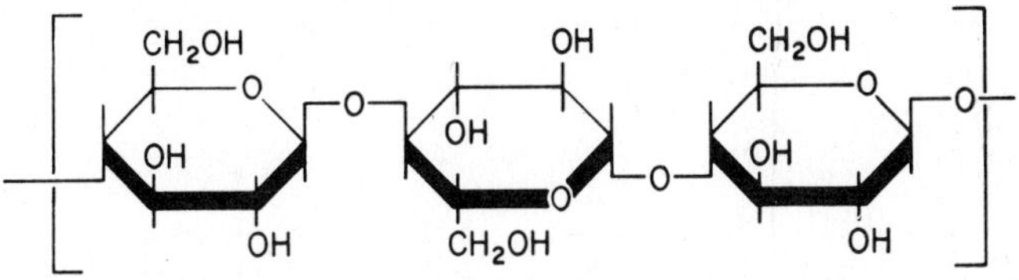

Figure 4.1. Structural formula of a 3-unit segment of cellulose. Each molecule of wood cellulose is thought to contain 7,000–10,000 such β-D-glucosyl units.

The physical structure of cellulose is less certain. In the cell walls of plants, the cellulose molecules are considered to be organized into linear bundles called elementary fibrils. Within these long elementary fibrils the molecules are bound laterally by innumerable intermolecular hydrogen bonds which in aggregate are quite strong. There is some question as to whether adjacent chains within the elementary fibrils are antiparallel (run in opposite directions), but this need not concern us here. An important point is, however, that the strong association and nearly perfect alignment of the chains gives rise to crystallinity; X-ray diffraction measurements show that wood cell-wall cellulose is about 70 percent crystalline, but it is not clear whether the noncrystalline cellulose (also called amorphous or paracrystalline) is a separate entity or just a reflection of imperfections in the crystalline lattice. The elementary fibrils, each consisting of about 40 cellulose chains (about 35 $Å^2$ in cross section), are considered by some investigators to be aggregated into flat ribbons termed microfibrils. The fibrils in the primary wall layer of mature cells are randomly oriented, but in the secondary wall layers they are oriented with a high degree of parallelism; those in the S2 layer are more nearly parallel to the long axis of the cell than those in the S1 and S2 layers.

Filling in the spaces between the microfibrils in the cell walls are the very hygroscopic hemicelluloses and the lignin. The exact nature of the association of these components with each other is not entirely clear.

This is one of the most important unknowns bearing on our understanding of the decay processes.

4.2.3 Hemicelluloses

Hemicelluloses, like cellulose, are polymers of anhydrosugar units. They are linked by glycosidic (hemiacetal) bonds; that is, they are polysaccharides. Unlike cellulose, however, a given hemicellulose molecule may include several different sugar units. Also, each hemicellulose molecule usually is branched rather than linear, and they are much lower in molecular weight.

The major hemicelluloses of wood are polymers of D-glucose, D-galactose, D-mannose, L-arabinose, D-xylose, and 4-O-methyl-D-glucuronic acid; the percentage contributions of these in hardwoods are different than in softwoods (Table 4.2).

The major hemicellulose of hardwoods (20–35 percent of the wood) is O-acetyl-4-O-methylglucuronoxylan. This is made up of a backbone of an average of about 200 xylose residues linked β-(1 → 4). The xylan polymer may be slightly branched, and is substituted at irregular intervals with 4-O-methylglucuronic acid residues. Acetyl groups are distributed along the xylan backbone also, with about 7 out of 10 xylose residues being substituted. The structure of this hemicellulose is represented schematically in Figure 4.2.

A second hemicellulose in hardwoods (3–5 percent of wood) is a glucomannan, a polymer of glucose and mannose in a ratio of 1:1 to 1:2 and

TABLE 4.2

Sugar Residues, Uronic Anhydride, and Acetyl of Woods of Representative Angiosperms and Gymnosperms [74]

(values expressed as % of total weight of wood)

Sugar Residue	Angiosperms			Gymnosperms		
	Betula papyrifera	Fagus grandifolia	Ulmus americana	Picea glauca	Pinus strobus	Tsuga canadensis
Glucose	42.6	46.2	52.4	44.7	44.8	44.2
Xylose	26.4	18.8	12.3	9.1	6.0	5.3
Mannose	1.8	2.1	2.4	11.2	11.4	11.0
Galactose	0.6	1.2	0.9	1.2	1.4	1.2
Arabinose	0.5	0.5	0.6	1.5	2.0	0.6
Uronic anhydride*	4.6	4.8	3.6	3.6	4.0	—
Acetyl	4.4	3.9	4.9	1.3	1.2	1.7

*Calculated as glucuronic acid minus H_2O.

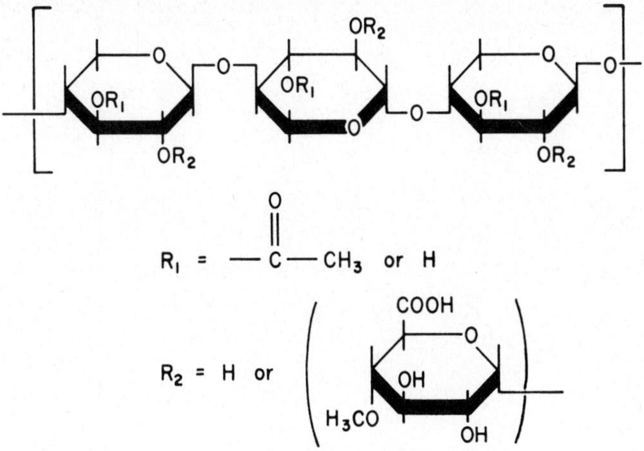

Figure 4.2. Structural formula of a 3-unit segment of a mO-acetyl-4-O-methylglucurono-xylan, the principal hemicellulose of hardwoods. Each molecule contains about 200 β-D-sylopyranosyl units.

linked β-(1 → 4). The polymer is essentially linear; neither the (DP) degree of polymerization (DP is a measure of the average number of sugar residues per molecule) nor the sequential arrangement of glucose and mannose is known for any of the glucomannans, but probably is random [74,76].

The major hemicelluloses of conifers (12–18 percent of wood) are O-acetylgalactoglucomannans. These consist of backbone polymers of β-(1 → 4)-linked glucose and mannose residues, with galactose residues and acetyl groups substituted along the backbone (Figure 4.3). The ratio of glucose to mannose is usually about 2:7, whereas the amounts of galactose relative to the glucose and mannose are much smaller and vary considerably. The backbone polymer contains at least 150 residues and may be branched [74,76].

Conifers also contain the hemicellulose arabino-4-O-methyglucuronoxylan (7–14 percent of wood), which is similar to the main hemicellulose of hardwoods described above. A backbone xylan chain is substituted not only by 4-O-methylglucuronic acid residues but also by arabinose residues; acetyl groups are absent. About one uronic acid occurs per 5–6 xylose residues, and one arabinose occurs per 8–9 xylose residues. It is not clear whether the backbone polymer is branched or what its DP is [74,76].

Both hardwoods and softwoods also contain other hemicelluloses, but they usually are not very important quantitatively [74,76] or structurally. Some of them can be extracted from wood with water, and these, like the

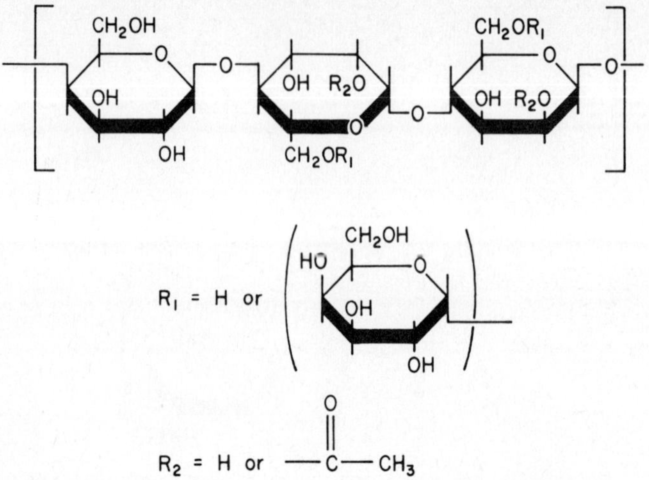

Figure 4.3. Structural formula of a 3-unit segment of an *O*-acetyl-galactoglucomannan, the principal hemicellulose of conifers. Each molecule contains at least 150 units.

low-molecular-weight sugars, the pectin, and the starch, may be important in helping decay-producing organisms get established.

It is considered most likely that the hemicelluloses are present in an amorphous state in the cell walls and, together with the lignin, surround the cellulose fibrils as a matrix, with the hemicelluloses and the lignin probably forming an interpenetrating polymer complex and being bonded covalently [59] to one another.

4.2.4 Lignin

Lignin is an amorphous, highly branched, three-dimensional polymer whose complex chemical structure has come into sharp focus only recently after many years of research. The structure is complicated and cannot be described in detail here, but it is possible to point out the main structural features in order that the reader may have a conception of what is involved in its decomposition or its alteration during wood decay. The lignin polymer is comprised of oxyphenylpropane units derived from three substituted cinnamyl alcohols: *p*-coumaryl, coniferyl, and sinapyl alcohols (Figure 4.4); their proportions differ greatly between conifers and hardwoods and among the various species of hardwoods. In a polymerization process that involves primarily radical coupling, these monomeric starting materials are combined to produce the lignin polymer. The nature of the polymerization process is such that the bonds linking the individual phenylpropane units together are of several different

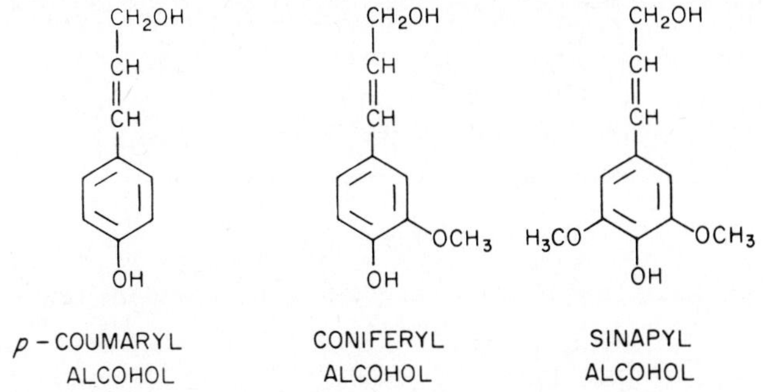

Figure 4.4. Substituted cinnamyl alcohols which are oxidatively polymerized to give lignins.

types. This, as well as the fact that three cinnamyl alcohols are involved, and that secondary reactions occur, leads to the complexity.

The most important intermonomer bond types are illustrated in Figure 4.5, which shows a hypothetical but possible portion of conifer lignin. The arylglycerol-β-arylether bonds (arrows in Figure 4.5) are the most abundant types of intermonomer linkage. An estimated 40 percent of the phenylpropane units in spruce lignin and 60 percent of those in birch lignin have such glycerol side chains bearing β-aryl substituents. Each of the other types of intermonomer bonds that are illustrated makes up a significant fraction of the total intermonomer linkages. In addition, sev-

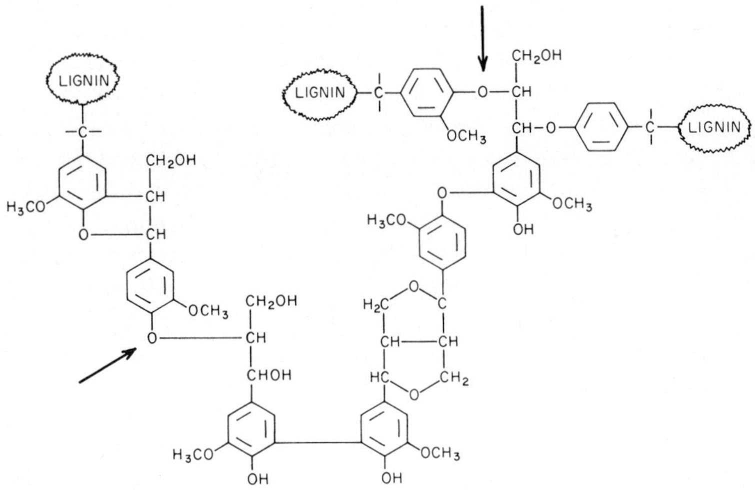

Figure 4.5. Structure of hypothetical segment of conifer lignin showing major types of intermonomer linkages.

eral other types of intermonomer linkages, which are not shown in Figure 4.5, also are known to be present in the lignin polymer.

About 70 percent of the lignin in woody plant cells is located in the secondary wall layers. The rest of the lignin is located in the very thin middle lamella regions where it is the main constituent.

4.2.5 Distribution of major structural components across the cell walls

The lignin, hemicelluloses, and cellulose are not uniformly distributed across wood cell walls. The work of Meier (summarized by Timell [74]) provides an idea of the distribution of the cellulose and hemicelluloses in wall layers, and is complemented by the recent work of Fergus *et al.* [27,28] on the distribution of lignin in wood tissues. These results, taken together, provide an approximate picture of the distribution of the major wood polymers in birch fibers and in spruce tracheids. The fibers of birch wood and the tracheids of spruce wood comprise about 81 percent [27] and about 95 percent [28] of the total tissue volumes, respectively.

In fibers of *Betula papyrifera,* the secondary wall contains 16–19 percent lignin, the middle lamella contains 34–40 percent lignin, and the cell corner regions contain 72–85 percent lignin [27]. It has been shown recently [29] that the structure of the lignin differs substantially between the secondary wall and the middle lamella–cell corner regions because different proportions of cinnamyl alcohols are involved. Cellulose makes up about 41 percent of the polysaccharides in the middle lamella–primary wall layer of *Betula verrucosa* fibers, the remainder being hemicelluloses. Cellulose makes up between 48 and 60 percent of the polysaccharides of the secondary wall and is in highest concentration in the region nearest the lumens. Hemicelluloses, by contrast, comprise 40–52 percent of the polysaccharides and are in lowest concentration nearest the lumens [74].

In *Picea mariana* tracheids, the distribution of lignin differs between latewood and earlywood. In both, the secondary walls contain about 22 percent lignin. In latewood, the middle lamella is about 60 percent lignin and the cell corners are essentially 100 percent lignin, whereas in earlywood, the middle lamella is about 50 percent lignin and the cell corners about 85 percent lignin [28]. The lignin is much more similar in structure between these morphological regions in spruce than it is in birch. About 33 percent of the polysaccharides in the middle lamella–primary wall region of tracheids of *Picea abies* is cellulose, the remainder being combined hemicelluloses. In the secondary wall, cellulose accounts for about 55–64 percent of the polysaccharides, the highest concentration being nearest the lumens, as is the case with hardwoods. Hemicelluloses comprise 36–45 percent of the polysaccharides of the secondary walls, the lowest concentration being nearest the lumens. Differences between early-wood and latewood in the distribution of the polysaccharides across cell walls are minor [74].

4.3 Progressive Gross Changes in the Chemical Composition of Wood During Decay

4.3.1 White-rot fungi

White-rot fungi derive nourishment from all the major constitutents of the wood cell walls—the cellulose, hemicelluloses, and lignin. Not sur-prisingly, various species of white-rot fungi differ in relative rates at which they remove the major components; some, such as *Polyporus berkeleyi,* remove the lignin faster than either the cellulose or the hemicelluloses, especially in early stages of decay [39,48]. Others, such as *Polyporus versicolor,* remove the three major components approximately simul-taneously [20,39,48]. Apparently only a few fungi—for example, *Fomes applanatum*—remove the carbohydrates somewhat more rapidly than the lignin [39,48]. The differences among the white-rot fungi in the relative rates of attack on the major wood components evidently reflect differences in their enzyme activities (see Section 4.4).

Figures 4.6A and 4.6B illustrate the progressive changes in the amounts of major components during decay of wood by *Polyporus versicolor* and *Lentinus nigripes.* Both fungi decompose all three major structural com-ponents, but they differ somewhat in the relative rates at which they re-move them. As mentioned earlier, greater differences in the relative rates of removal of lignin and the total carbohydrates in early stages of decay have been observed for other white-rot fungi [48]. Even with marked variation in relative rates of initial removal of the major polymers, white-rot fungi presumably can remove all the wood components. Studies of the progressive changes in the chemical composition of wood in very ad-vanced stages of decay have been made with only a few white-rot fungi.

The solubility of wood in water, 1% NaOH, and in organic solvents (decayed basis) does not change much during decay by white-rot fungi [16,17,20,62]. This indicates that the rates of production and utilization of degradation products are approximately equal. In accord with this, the polysaccharides [20,48] and lignin [50] remaining in white-rotted wood at various stages of decay are not very different in properties from these substances in sound wood. This suggests that only small parts of the polymers are attacked at any given time, and that the affected portions are completely degraded and assimilated before other parts of the poly-mers are significantly affected.

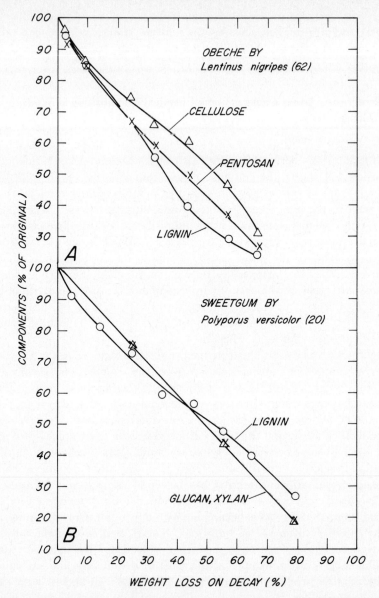

Figure 4.6. A and B: Loss of major structural components from two woods on decay by white-rot fungi. In 6B "glucan" provides a measure of cellulose. "Pentosans" (in 6A) and "xylan" (in 6B) provide a measure of the hemicelluloses.

4.3.2 Brown-rot fungi

Brown-rot fungi mainly decompose the polysaccharides in wood and usually cause only a small loss in the lignin [4,14,16,20]. Figures 4.7A and 4.7B show the progressive changes in the amounts of major wood constituents of temperate-zone woods during attack by the brown-rot fungi *Poria monticola* [20] and *Coniophora cerebella* [68]. In these cases the hemicelluloses (as indicated by "pentosans" or by xylan) and the cellulose ("glucan" in Figure 4.7A) were removed at about the same relative rates. It is conceivable that certain brown-rot fungi may preferentially remove the cellulose or one or more of the hemicelluloses.

The solubility of wood in water, and especially in 1% NaOH, increases substantially on attack by brown-rot fungi whether expressed on the basis of decayed or original wood [16,20,62]. This reflects primarily a depolymerization of the polysaccharides to low-molecular-weight, soluble molecules. This increased solubility of the wood is very evident even in early stages of brown rot. In later stages of decay, the partially degraded carbohydrate fragments are used by the fungi but the lignin becomes progressively more soluble, especially in NaOH. This gradual increase in the solubility of residual lignin reflects: (a) introduction of polar groups into the polymer, (b) freeing of the lignin from its intimate association with the carbohydrates, and perhaps (c) a fragmentation of the lignin [49]. In any event, progressively greater amounts of lignin can be dissolved out of brown-rotted wood with good lignin solvents such as dioxane-water mixtures, dimethylformamide, dimethylsulfoxide, etc. [15].

4.3.3 Soft-rot fungi

Studies of the chemical effects of soft-rot fungi have been limited to *Chaetomium globosum* on beech wood [55,63,66]. The fungus causes extensive loss in weight, removing primarily polysaccharides (Figure 4.8). Measured as a percentage of the original amounts, the cellulose is removed faster than the hemicelluloses and this is more noticeable when the latter are estimated as the alkali-soluble part of the holocellulose [55] than when they are measured as "total pentosans" [63,66]. Analysis of decayed wood for individual sugars in acid hydrolysates at various stages of decay shows that glucose and mannose are removed at a constant rate and more rapidly than other wood sugars (xylose, arabinose, galactose), which are removed at an increasing rate [54]. Although soft-rot fungi definitely deplete lignin, it is removed much more slowly than the carbohydrates [55,63,66] (Figure 4.8).

When the solubility of soft-rotted beech wood in hot water and in ethanol-benzene is expressed as a percentage of the weight of the original

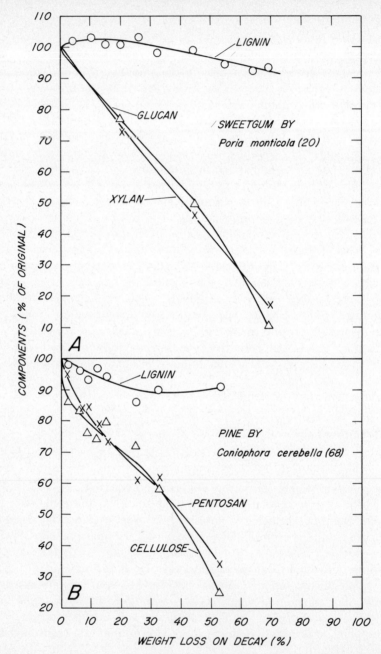

Figure 4.7. A and B: Loss of major structural components from two woods on decay by brown-rot fungi. In 7A "glucan" provides a measure of cellulose. "Xylan" (in 7A) and "pentosan" (in 7B) provide measures of hemicelluloses.

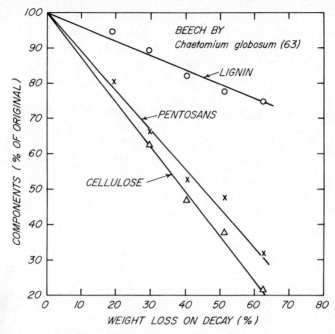

Figure 4.8. Loss of major structural components from beech wood on decay by *Chaetomium globosum*. "Pentosans" provide a measure of the hemicelluloses.

sound wood, it remains constant during decay [55]. This means that production of materials soluble in these solvents is balanced by their consumption. The solubility of the soft-rotted wood in ethanol increases during decay, even when expressed as a percentage of the original wood [66]. This is probably due to an increasing extractability of alcohol-soluble lignin. The solubility of the wood in 1% NaOH, expressed as a percentage of the sound wood, decreases during decay [55,62,66], but not as rapidly as total weight loss; thus, expressed on the basis of decayed wood, the alkali solubles increase somewhat. An increasing proportion of the alkali solubles is probably lignin [55].

4.3.4 Bacteria

We are concerned in this chapter with the fungal destruction of wood, because fungi are by far the most important causal agents. However, because of the increasing attention being paid to the effects of bacteria on wood [see, *e.g.,* 19,35,52,53], their characteristics will be mentioned briefly. Most of the damage caused by bacteria has been observed microscopically and not by chemical analysis. Microscopy reveals various corrosion patterns in cell-wall surfaces and pit membranes [52], which must involve destruction of wood polymers (see Chapter 3 of this volume). The destruction of pit membranes is reflected in an increase in permeability [19,52], probably brought about by destruction of pectic substances; pectate-depolymerizing enzymes alone have this effect [11]. Pectate lyases ("pectin transeliminases") have been isolated from *Bacillus polymyxa* [58], a bacterium which causes increased permeability of wood [35,52]. Some bacteria isolated from wood also can decompose isolated cellulose [52], but the cellulose in the lignified cell walls of intact wood seems to be resistant. Bacteria can do some damage to intact wood, but probably cause no more than slight losses in weight [52]. Virtanen [75] also found that when wood was reduced to a dust, certain thermophilic bacteria would decompose not only a considerable proportion of the cellulose but significant amounts of hemicelluloses and lignin as well. This suggests that additional work in this area would be desirable.

4.4 The Biochemistry of Wood Decay

4.4.1 The nature of enzymes [57]

Almost all biochemical reactions are catalyzed by enzymes. Most of the degradative reactions involved in the decay of wood are enzyme-catalyzed, and some of the enzymes have been partially purified and characterized.

Enzymes are proteins. Often they are associated to varying degrees with nonprotein moieties (carbohydrates, metals, coenzymes, etc.), which are important to the catalytic activity, or in imparting some desirable physical property such as structure, solubility, etc. Since they are proteins, enzymes are usually relatively large, most being considerably above molecular weight 10,000. They are very efficient catalysts, speeding reaction rates from 10^8-10^{11} times over the corresponding nonenzymatic reactions, and usually catalyzing conversion of more than 1,000 substrate molecules per enzyme molecule per minute. Another characteristic of most enzymes is their specificity—often precise—toward the substrate and the reaction catalyzed. Each enzyme catalyzes a specific reaction, but organisms have enough different types of enzymes to carry out a broad spectrum of reactions. We are mainly concerned in this chapter with the hydrolytic and oxidative reactions involved in the degradation of cellulose, the hemicelluloses, and lignin; but enzymes also catalyze the various polymerizations, transfers, isomerizations, eliminations, etc., etc., which are necessary in the intermediary metabolism of the fungi during decay.

4.4.2 The action of enzymes

To participate in a reaction, enzymes must first come in contact with the substrate molecule, then in some way enhance the rate of the conversion of substrate to product(s), and finally dissociate from the modified substrate. In many cases the enzyme must be oxidized or reduced before it can work again. The fact that the large enzyme molecules must bind to the substrate has important implications in decay, particularly in considering the initial breakdown of the insoluble polymers that comprise wood. Some enzymes are able to diffuse into the polymer matrix of wood and hydrolyze or oxidize substrate to molecules at some distance from the hyphae (see Chapter 3). Thus, the ability of these extracellular enzymes to move into the wood is important. This means that the size, shape, and distribution of the openings in the wood, the size and shape of the enzymes, the charges on the enzymes and on the wood surfaces, the amount and location of water, etc., will influence the pattern and the rate of wood decay. Structural features which influence the decay of wood are discussed in the following section.

Complete catabolism, of course, does not occur extracellularly. Once the extracellular enzymes have degraded the polymers, the low-molecular-weight solubilized molecules that are released can diffuse back to the hyphae where they are metabolized intracellularly. Some enzymes involved in the initial breakdown of wood polymers may be attached to the hyphae so that contact between the hyphae and wood cell walls is necessary; some cellulolytic enzymes are known to be bound to bacterial cell surfaces [72]. Attachment of degrading enzymes to cell surfaces of wood-destroying fungi could help account for the observed "corrosion" patterns around hyphae lying on cell-wall surfaces as seen in electron micrographs, particularly with white-rot and soft-rot fungi (see Chapter 3).

In catalyzing reactions, enzymes bind to substrates by attraction between functional groups in the enzyme and "complementary" functional groups in the substrate, e.g., the well-characterized enzyme lysozyme probably binds substrate polysaccharide by attraction between carboxyl groups in the enzyme and hydroxyl groups in the substrate [6]. Subsequent catalysis is thought to occur as a result of one or more of the following [57]: (1) orientation of the atoms of the substrate in such a way that a reaction is facilitated; (2) acid-base catalysis involving the amino acid residues near the reaction sites in the substrate; (3) so-called "covalent catalysis," in which attack on substrate by nucleophilic or electrophilic groups (or both) in the enzyme "pushes" the reaction; (4) catalysis through conformational distortion of the substrate in such a way that the subsequent reaction is facilitated because it releases an enzyme-induced conformational strain; and (5) perhaps other actions of the enzyme.

The above superficial consideration of enzymes is intended to help the reader visualize the kinds of interactions that must be involved at the molecular level during wood decay. For a more detailed presentation of enzyme action, the reader is referred to Mahler and Cordes [57].

4.4.3 Control of enzyme synthesis [57]

It is well established that most catabolic enzymes are partially induced; *i.e.,* they are not produced all of the time, but rather are synthesized when the reaction they catalyze becomes necessary to the organism. For example, cellulolytic microorganisms grown on glucose release only traces of β-(1 $\rightarrow$ 4)-glucanases because these enzymes are not needed. When grown on cellulose, however, the same organisms produce the glucanases. The reason for this regulation of enzymes synthesis is probably energy conservation, since synthesis of proteins requires substantial energy. The mechanism whereby enzyme synthesis is induced (actually it is derepressed) has received, and is still receiving, a tremendous amount of attention. This research has shown that for several catabolic pathways a "regulatory substance" (cellobiose for β-(1 $\rightarrow$ 4)-glucanases in some microorganisms) acts to derepress enzyme synthesis.

With wood-destroying fungi, the regulatory substances for synthesis of enzymes involved in the decomposition of the cellulose, the hemicelluloses, and the lignin are not known. Understanding the fine points of repression and derepression of the wood-degrading enzymes could lead to better methods for the control of wood breakdown.

4.4.4 Structural aspects of the enzymatic decomposition of individual wood polymers

We shall now consider structural factors affecting wood decomposition and then briefly treat the individual enzymes involved in wood decay or the kinds of reactions which they must catalyze. Relatively little has actually been done with the enzymes of wood-decay fungi. Thus, it is necessary to draw on information obtained for other organisms, assuming that a similar situation exists with the wood-decay fungi.

Structural factors affecting the decomposition of cellulose in wood by microorganisms have been discussed in detail by Cowling and Brown [22]. The following factors, adapted from their list, are particularly important here: (1) moisture, (2) size and diffusability of enzymes with respect to the capillary structure of the wood, (3) crystallinity of the cellulose, (4) conformation and steric rigidity of the wood polymers, (5) structural interrelationships of the wood polymer, and (6) substituent groups in the polymers. With the exception of item (3), these factors are also important in the decomposition of the hemicelluloses and lignin in wood. In addition, for the lignin and hemicelluloses another factor should be considered: namely, variation in structure. Some parts of the lignin or of the hemicelluloses—*i.e.,* certain types of bonds—may be more readily attacked by a given organism than other parts. Numerous nonstructural factors also affect the growth and activities of the wood-destroying fungi;

factors such as the availability of oxygen and mineral nutrients, hydrogen ion concentration, oxidation potential, and ionic strength in the micro-environment, the presence of toxic materials, etc., are outside the scope of this chapter (see Chapter 2). Let us now briefly consider the importance of some of the above structural factors.

4.4.4.1 Moisture in the wood

Wood will not decay unless the moisture content is above a certain critical level; this is generally about 30 percent of the oven-dry weight for temperate-zone woods and is slightly above the fiber-saturation point. Keeping the moisture content below this critical level is the most important means for preventing decay (see Chapter 2).

Water has large and important effects on wood structure; swelling of the wood polymers through hydration creates openings within the wood polymer matrix that are not present in dry wood. Diffusion of enzymes into wood to the site of action requires an enlargement of the openings through this swelling action. Water is needed also as a "solvent," *i.e.,* for creating a continuum between the organism and the substrate. It is also required, of course, as a reactant in hydrolytic reactions.

4.4.4.2 Size of enzymes and openings in wood

Gross capillaries within the water-swollen wood structure, such as cell lumina and pit apertures, are sufficiently large (2,000–10,000Å) to permit easy penetration of cellulolytic enzymes, which average 50 Å in diameter if spherical, and about 30 × 170 Å if an ellipsoidal shape is assumed [22]. Likewise, lignin-degrading enzymes and hemicellulases, even in the un-likely event that they are found to be considerably larger than the average cellulases, will also be able to penetrate the gross capillaries. Thus, degradation of the wood polymers at the surfaces of gross capillaries is not restricted by accessibility problems. However, most of the wood is not exposed as gross capillary surface, and decay is not limited to such surfaces [22]. A larger total surface area in wood is exposed as so-called "cell-wall capillaries," but the size of these capillaries in water-swollen wood is too small (average about 10 Å) to permit penetration by known enzymes. It must be assumed on this basis, then, that entry of enzymes into cell-wall capillaries requires an enlargement of these openings.

4.4.4.3 Crystallinity of cellulose

The importance of cellulose crystallinity to its enzymatic hydrolysis is considered in connection with cellulolytic enzymes in Section 4.4.5 and is discussed in some detail by Cowling and Brown [22].

4.4.4.4 Conformation and steric rigidity of wood polymers

It is likely that enzyme attack on the wood polymers is hampered not only by inaccessibility but also by unfavorable steric rigidity and unfavorable conformation caused by close molecular association of the polymers in the wood. This is certainly likely for crystalline cellulose in which the glucose units are held in a rigid orientation that apparently is not favorable for attack by enzymes. But it is also probable that considerable portions of the lignin and hemicellulose polymers also are sterically oriented in such a way or held in such a conformation that enzymes cannot bind to the appropriate sites. Degradation thus would be expected to depend on the disruption of the protective associations among the polymers. For this reason, as well as the accessibility problem, it is not anticipated that any component (that is, lignin, cellulose, or the hemicelluloses) can be completely removed enzymatically without alteration or partial removal of another component. This seems to be the case. Brown-rot fungi and soft-rot fungi alter lignin as they remove polysaccharides, and certain white-rot fungi that preferentially remove lignin always remove some of the carbohydrates as well.

4.4.4.5 Structural interrelationships of the wood polymers

Intact, untreated wood is resistant to degradation by polysaccharidases which can rapidly degrade isolated wood polysaccharides. Similarly, organisms such as *Myrothecium verucaria* and *Trichoderma viride,* as well as many other fungi and bacteria, which are virulently cellulolytic, are unable to significantly affect the cellulose in wood. The reason for this is the structural interrelationship of the polysaccharides with the lignin in wood. If the lignin is even partially removed by chemical or biological means, or its relationship to the polysaccharides modified sufficiently, as with treatment with NaOH, the polysaccharides become much more susceptible to the enzymes that can degrade them.

As has been mentioned previously, the molecular association of the lignin with the cellulose and hemicelluloses in wood is not entirely clear. Evidence points, however, to the following picture: the lignin and hemicellulose form a three-dimensional, interpenetrating matrix that surrounds the cellulose microfibrils, the lignin and hemicellulose being bonded to each other via covalent linkages. If this is correct, it seems likely that wood-destroying fungi may have to alter the lignin before they can decompose the cellulose. In accordance with this, it is found that wood-decay fungi causing all three types of decay alter the lignin, even though they do not all metabolize it. It should be emphasized at this point, however, that further research is needed to really elucidate this point.

4.4.4.6 Presence of substituent groups

Because contact between substrate and enzyme is necessary for catalysis, and because most enzymes (especially the polysaccharidases) are very substrate specific, almost any synthetic modification of the substrate will prevent effective contact of the enzymes at the site of modification on the substrate polymer. Thus, substitution, such as acetylation or cyanoethylation of polysaccharides, decreases their susceptibility to enzymatic hydrolysis. Wood-decaying organisms have evolved with the capacity to accommodate the naturally occurring substituent groups found in the hemicelluloses and lignin, although it may be expected that the organisms vary in ability to cope with the substituents. Natural substituents include galactose, arabinose, acetyl groups, 4-O-methylglucuronic acid residues and branches in hemicelluloses, esters of aromatic acids (p-hydroxybenzoic acid, vanillic acid, ferulic acid, etc.), as well as covalent linkages between the carbohydrates and lignin.

Because of the large number of hydroxyl groups in cellulose, hemicelluloses, and lignin, it is possible chemically to introduce large amounts of many types of substituents into wood. With cellulose, almost any group introduced onto a sufficiently high proportion of the glucose residues (*i.e.,* a high enough degree of substitution) will thwart enzyme attack. The same undoubtedly is true for hemicelluloses, and may be true for lignin as well. It is known that wood can be protected from decay fungi by acetylation, cyanoethylation, and other treatments which do not alter other properties seriously [5,33]. Acetylation of wood to an acetyl content of only 10–12 percent severely retards decay [33]; at an acetyl content of 12 percent, about 22 percent of the hydroxyls in spruce wood are covered, and it seems likely that these are the most accessible ones, and therefore mainly in the lignin and the hemicelluloses. Since acetylation causes a decrease in the hygroscopicity of wood, it is not clear whether decay resistance is due to a hindering of enzyme action or to disruption of necessary water relations; the latter may be greatly affected by modification of hemicelluloses. Many derivatives of cotton have been studied in a search for agents to impart luster, improved dye acceptance, fire retardance, stretching properties, wrinkle resistance, rot resistance, etc. Relatively few derivatives have been made of wood, and most of the ones studied have been with a primary interest in dimensional stabilization [65]. Protection from decay through the attachment of derivative groups may be easier to achieve, and should be considered further.

168   T. KENT KIRK

4.4.5 Cellulose decomposition

4.4.5.1 General

Cellulose is degraded by microorganisms through enzymatic hydrolysis of intermonomer bonds in the chains. At least three different types of enzymes apparently are involved: a C_1 component, the β-(1 → 4) glucanases, and the β-glucosidases. These have collectively been termed the "cellulase complex" [42]. The decomposition of crystalline cellulose by this complex has been viewed as in Figure 4.9.

Crystalline areas in cellulose are not attacked by the isolated hydrolytic enzymes [the β-(1 → 4) glucanases] of some organisms unless they are first acted on by C_1. The C_1 of *Trichoderma viride* has been found to be a glycoprotein with a molecular weight of about 57,000; it has little detectable effect on crystalline or noncrystalline cellulose. When mixed with a β-(1 → 4) glucanase, which in itself is without effect on crystalline cellulose, however, the two enzymes act synergistically to cause efficient depolymerization [69]. Just what C_1 does to crystalline cellulose has not been clarified; apparently it can cause local disruption of the highly crystalline structure of the cellulose so that the β-(1 → 4) glucanases can hydrolyze the chains [69].

Wood-destroying fungi can decompose the crystalline cellulose in wood, but it is not clear whether they require a separate C_1 factor. Enzyme preparations from several wood-destroying fungi have been found to be essentially ineffective against "native celluloses," but to depolymerize modified cellulose preparations [32,40,44]. Some evidence that the white-rot fungus *Chrysosporium lignorum,* which has been classified as a white-rotting Basidiomycete [12], does produce a C_1 factor was obtained by Eriksson and Rzedowski [26]. However, Ahlgren and Eriksson [2] reported that a partially purified β-(1 → 4) glucanase from the white-rot fungus *Stereum sanguinolentum* was effective against native cotton, and

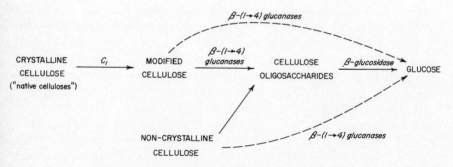

Figure 4.9. Action of the cellulase complex on cellulose.

thus that no C_1 was necessary. King [43] found that culture filtrates of *Coniophora cerebella* would rapidly degrade the cellulose in never-dried chlorite holocellulose from spruce, but neither cotton nor α-cellulose prepared from the spruce holocellulose were significantly affected. (Holocellulose includes both cellulose and the hemicelluloses; α-cellulose is holocellulose from which most of the hemicelluloses have been extracted.) King suggested that cotton and other "native" cellulose preparations may not be appropriate substrates for studying cellulases of wood-destroying fungi.

The β-(1 $\rightarrow$ 4) glucanases frequently have been termed "C_X" enzymes. Most of those described for wood-destroying fungi catalyze the hydrolysis of the cellulose chains at random points along the length of the molecule, and thus cause a rapid decrease in the average DP. Conversely, some C_X types of enzymes act on high-molecular-weight cellulose to catalyze hydrolysis of one glucose unit at a time from the end of the chain [6,61]; in that way, they effect a gradual decrease in DP. This latter type of C_X is related in action to β-glucosidases, which are enzymes that act on short-chain cellulose fragments by taking glucose residue off one by one from the nonreducing end of the chains.

Intracellular cellulolytic enzymes that cleave cellulose oligosaccharides by phosphorolysis have been described in certain anaerobic bacteria of the genus *Clostridium* [42]. Whether wood-decay fungi or other microorganisms also employ such enzymes is not known.

Present knowledge concerning the cellulases of wood-destroying fungi has been summarized recently [40]. So far, no general distinctions have been found between the cellulases of the three types of wood-destroying fungi; it was thought [8,20] that such differences might exist and might help explain the differences in mode of attack of wood. Investigations indicate that β-(1 $\rightarrow$ 4) glucanases of all the wood-destroying fungi are, in general, smaller enzymes than the corresponding β-glucosidases [25] and that the former vary considerably in molecular weight (from about 11,000 to about 50,000). A really small β-(1 $\rightarrow$ 4) glucanase—in fact, the smallest enzyme known—has been described from the cotton destroyer *Myrothecium verucaria;* its molecular weight is around 5,000 [70].

4.4.5.2 White-rot fungi

White-rot fungi cause a gradual decrease in cellulose DP as decay proceeds [20,48]. This indicates that the bulk of the cellulose in wood is intact at any stage of decay, either because glucose residues are removed from the ends of the chains or because attack is restricted to a small percentage of the total cellulose chains at any time, or both [20]. The latter explanation probably is correct, since all the glucanases investigated to date apparently act to deploymerize the cellulose molecules randomly. Evidently, the segments of cellulose which are released during decay are consumed by white-rot fungi about as rapidly as they are produced; *i.e.,* there is a close coordination between breakdown and utilization [20]. As a consequence of this mode of attack, oligosaccharides soluble in water or in 1% NaOH do not accumulate in white-rotted wood. Furthermore, the degree of crystallinity of the cellulose remaining in wood which has been decayed by white-rot fungi is very similar to that in the original wood [20].

4.4.5.3 Brown-rot fungi

The most striking change that occurs in the brown-rot type of decay, occurring at weight losses between 1 and 10 percent, is a large decrease in the average DP of the cellulose. This has been shown directly for sweet-gum and spruce woods on attack by *Poria monticola* and *Lenzites trabea* [20, also Cowling, personal communication], and is surely a general phenomenon since it is in accord with the characteristically rapid loss in strength [17] that would be difficult to explain in any other way. This rapid decrease in cellulose chain length implies that the catalyst that facilitates the depolymerization readily gains access to the cellulose chains. How this can occur with enzymes, which are thought to be much too large, presents a real enigma. It has been suggested [20] that perhaps cellulose-depolymerizing enzymes of brown-rot fungi are very small and able thoroughly to penetrate the wood structure. As pointed out above, however, the cellulases so far studied for brown-rot fungi do not appear to differ significantly from those of the white- or soft-rot fungi [40]. Recently it has been suggested that the initial rapid loss in DP may really be nonenzymatic [22]. Another suggestion has been that a "precellulolytic system" of unknown nature may be involved [7].

DP measurements of sweetgum holocellulose during decay by *Poria monticola* indicate that the initial loss in DP results in formation of chains of an average DP of about 200 [20]. This, and the rapid initial and subsequently much slower rate of decrease in DP during brown-rot are analogous with the effects of acid.

Isolated β-(1 $\rightarrow$ 4) glucanases from the brown-rot fungi *Polyporus schweinitzii* [41] and *Coniophora cerebella* [43] were relatively inactive against native cotton fibers. This suggested that a C_1 component is essential for brown rot. However, as mentioned above, King [44] found that the cellulose in never-dried holocellulose from spruce was rapidly degraded on incubation with culture filtrates of *C. cerebella*.

4.4.5.4 Soft-rot fungi

During attack of beech wood by *Chaetomium globosum,* there is an initial increase of about 10 percent in the average DP of the holocellulose, followed by a gradual decrease. This pattern indicates that this fungus initially removes the lowest molecular weight holocellulose components and then gradually attacks the remaining longer chains. This mode of attack thus seems to differ from that of white-rot fungi, and certainly from that of brown-rot fungi.

Bailey *et al.* [40] have recently studied a β-(1 $\rightarrow$ 4) glucanase from *Chaetomium globosum,* and found it to hydrolyze bonds within the cellulose chain, causing a rapid loss in DP. It was relatively inactive against native cellulose.

4.4.6 Hemicellulose decomposition

4.4.6.1 General

Hemicelluloses, like cellulose and starch, are biologically degraded through cleavage of the chemical bonds between the sugar residues. Enzymes which catalyze hydrolysis of xylans and mannans have been demonstrated in a large number of microorganisms, including the wood-destroying fungi. In addition, enzymes analogous to β-glucosidases, *i.e.,* "β-xylosidases" and "β-mannosidases," which act on low-molecular-weight oligosaccharides—and which thus are different from the β-(1 $\rightarrow$ 4) xylanases and β-(1 $\rightarrow$ 4) mannanases—have been isolated from wood-destroying fungi as well as from other microorganisms [25]. At least some of the enzymes involved in the depolymerization of xylans and mannans, therefore, seem to be analogous to those that depolymerize cellulosic substrates (excluding crystalline cellulose, which may require in addition the C_1 factor). The xylans and mannans used to assay the xylanases and mannanases have usually been linear homopolymers and thus structurally analogous to cellulose.

But wood hemicelluloses differ from cellulose in having branches, in being composed of more than one sugar unit, and in having substituent groups. These structural features complicate their depolymerization, and suggest that several different enzymes must be involved. Few of the details of the enzymatic hydrolysis of wood hemicelluloses have been elucidated, however, and we can only speculate by analogy with other enzyme systems.

Enzymes involved in polysaccharide hydrolysis usually are specific for substrate as well as for bond types; in fact, the polysaccharidases probably are among the most substrate-specific enzymes known [3]. As a case in point, the hydrolysis of glycogen by enzymes requires one enzyme for the α-(1 → 4) glycosidic bonds and a separate enzyme for the branch linkages, which are α-(1 → 6) glycosidic bonds. Even more indicative of the specificity of polysaccharidases is the fact that glucanases active on β-(1 → 4) glycosidic bonds have no effect on the α-(1 → 4) bonds of glycogen. From the known specificity of polysaccharidases, it is to be expected that branch points in wood hemicelluloses require different enzymes for hydrolysis than are involved in hydrolysis of the unsubstituted portions of the backbone polymers. It is also likely that hydrolysis of linear glucomannans requires more than one enzyme. The β-(1 → 4) mannose–glucose bonds probably will not be affected by glucanases that hydrolyze β-(1 → 4) glucose–glucose bonds [6], and perhaps not even by some mannanases that hydrolyze β-(1 → 4) mannose–mannose bonds.

The effect of substituent groups—*i.e.,* acetyl groups and arabinose, galactose, 4-*O*-methylglucuronic acid units—on enzymatic hydrolysis of wood hemicelluloses has not been examined specifically. Because of the high degree of specificity of polysaccharidases, it is likely that substituents will be found to hinder hydrolysis of the backbone polymer and must first be removed by separate enzymes. Limited data supports this. A xylanase in a commercial "pectinase" was unable to attack certain bonds in a birch 4-*O*-methylglucuronoxylan in the vicinity of the 4-*O*-methylglucuronosyl substituents [73]. The enzymes involved in removal of these substituent groups have not been studied, although their effects have been observed. A commercial hemicellulase mixture, acting on what was probably a 4-*O*-methylglucuronoxylan, released 4-*O*-methylglucuronic acid residues, showing that the enzyme mixture evidently contained a component with the capacity to hydrolyze the α-(1 → 2) bond linking the uronic acid to the xylan backbone (see Timell [73]). Similarly, an extracellular enzyme from a rumen bacterium removed arabinose substituents from a grass arabinoxylan. Removal of the arabinose was necessary before the xylan could be hydrolyzed by xylanases, which also were secreted by the organisms [7].

The above discussion makes it evident that a considerable amount of further research is needed to understand in detail how fungi degrade wood hemicelluloses. Future research may disclose that wood-destroying microorganisms employ polysaccharide-depolymerizing enzymes in addition to hydrolases. Possibilities are: (a) phosphorylases, which are involved in starch and cellulose metabolism in certain microorganisms [42]; and (b) lyases, which are important in pectate depolymerization (pectate lyase) in a number of phytopathogenic bacteria and fungi [10]. Although hemicellulose lyases should be considered, it is possible that this type of depolymerizing reaction, which is an elimination, requires the carboxyl

groups, or esterified carboxyl groups, in the 6-position as in the galactu-
ronic acid residues of pectates; the carboxyl groups probably facilitate
the elimination reaction by rendering the hydrogen atom on C-5 more
acidic.

4.4.6.2 White-rot fungi

Different white-rot fungi remove the individual hemicellulose sugars
from wood at different rates [48]. This evidently reflects differences in
levels of activity of the individual hemicellulose-degrading enzymes involved, and suggests that the molecular distribution of the hemicelluloses
in the wood does not alone determine the rates of their removal.

β-(1 $\rightarrow$ 4) xylanase, β-(1 $\rightarrow$ 4) mannanase, β-(1 $\rightarrow$ 4) xylosidase,
and β-(1 $\rightarrow$ 4) mannosidase activities have been demonstrated in culture
filtrates of the white-rot fungi *Fomes annosus, Stereum sanguinolentum,*
and *Chrysosporium lignorum* [2]. The enzymes of the latter organism
were partially characterized physically, but their substrate specificities—
including their activities against wood hemicelluloses—were not studied.
The glycosidases (oligosaccharide-cleaving enzymes) were found to be
smaller than the corresponding glycanases (polysaccharide-cleaving enzymes) [2]. Lyr [56] had earlier demonstrated xylan-depolymerizing activity in culture filtrates of several white-rot fungi.

4.4.6.3 Brown-rot fungi

It was mentioned above that Cowling [20] observed a rapid loss in cellulose DP in early stages of decay of sweetgum by *Poria monticola.* DP was
determined from measurements of the viscosities of holocellulose solutions. Even though the holocellulose includes the hemicelluloses as well
as the cellulose, it cannot be concluded that hemicelluloses were also
depolymerized. (It is evident that such a large drop in DP would have to
involve cellulose depolymerization.) Seifert [67] demonstrated rather
constant, low levels of xylobiose, xylotetraose, mannobiose, mannotriose,
and arabinobiose in beech wood during decay by the brown-rot fungus
Coniophora cerebella. This indicates that assimilable fragments are
formed from the hemicelluloses at a constant rate, probably in response
to needs of the fungus. The finding of small amounts of fragments of very
low DP does not mean that some extensive depolymerization of oligosaccharides of larger DP does not accompany the initial loss in cellulose
DP. Thus, it is not clear at the moment whether the hemicelluloses are
rapidly depolymerized along with the cellulose.

Lyr [56] demonstrated xylanase activity in culture filtrates of several
brown-rot fungi, and recently both xylan- and mannan-depolymerizing

enzymes have been demonstrated in culture filtrates of the brown-rot fungi *Coniophora cerebella* [43,45] and *Polyporus schweinitzii* [40]. Culture filtrates of *C. cerebella* produced oligosaccharides when incubated with either a spruce glucomannan or a spruce xylan [43,45]. In further studies [46], β-(1 → 4) xylanase and β-(1 → 4) xylosidase were resolved and partially purified from culture filtrates obtained by culturing the organism on a 4-*O*-methylglucuronoxylan of aspen. The xylosidase degraded xylo-oligosaccharides, producing xylose, and exhibited weak activity against the intact 4-*O*-methylglucuronoxylan polymer. The β-(1 → 4) xylanase depolymerized the latter, producing neutral oligosaccharides (mainly xylobiose, -triose, -tetraose, and -pentaose), plus a series of acidic oligosaccharides and some residual polymeric material that was resistant to the enzyme. It was suggested that the acid substituents protected the backbone xylan from the xylanase, so that oligosaccharides containing the uronic acid residues were formed. Of special interest is the notation by the investigators [45,46] that *Coniophora cerebella* evidently did not produce an extracellular enzyme which would remove the uronic acid groups.

4.4.6.4 Soft-rot fungi

Sorensen [71] studied the xylanase produced by *Chaetomium globosum* grown on wheat straw xylan. The xylanase-containing protein from the culture filtrate converted the xylan primarily to xylose. As with culture filtrates of *C. cerebella*, a uronic acid substituent in the xylan was not freed on incubation with the enzyme preparation. When grown on a mannan, *C. globosum* produced a mannanase which released reducing sugar from the mannan, but this enzyme was not studied further.

Xylan- and mannan-depolymerizing enzymes were demonstrated recently in *C. globosum* by Keilich *et al.* [41], and the enzymes were resolved and partially purified. The purified mannanase depolymerized a pine glucomannan and a pine galactoglucomannan, as well as a mannan homopolymer, whereas a purified xylanase depolymerized an arabino-4-*O*-methylglucuronoxylan from pine, as well as a xylan homopolymer [41]. Assays were based on viscosity changes, which reflect primarily a decrease in DP, and revealed little about which linkages were hydrolyzed and which were resistant.

4.4.7 Lignin degradation

4.4.7.1 General

(For a recent treatment of the effects of wood-destroying fungi on lignin, see reference [47].)

As we have seen (Section 4.3), both white-rot fungi and soft-rot fungi cause depletion of lignin, whereas brown-rot fungi cause only limited changes in structure and only a small depletion. Apparently there is no relationship between the lignin content of woods and their susceptibility to decay by any of the three types of decay fungi, but this is a difficult thing to evaluate experimentally and has not been studied per se. Those fungi which are most active against lignin, the white-rot fungi and soft-rot fungi, seem generally to prefer hardwoods. In this respect, the fact that hardwoods contain less lignin than conifers and that the lignin differs structurally from that of conifers may be significant. Brown-rot fungi seem to attack coniferous wood preferentially.

4.4.7.2 White-rot fungi

White-rot fungi readily decompose and metabolize lignin, but the enzymatic mechanism by which they do this is not known. Evidently, in some way the polymer is broken down into small fragments by extra-cellular enzymes and the fragments are ingested by the hyphae and further metabolized. Perhaps the biggest unknown at the present time is how the fragments are released from the polymer; *i.e.,* whether the benzene rings are cleaved while still in the polymer or whether fragments containing aromatic rings are released, ingested, and metabolized intracellularly. Perhaps some of both types of changes occur; *i.e.,* some of the easily released portions containing aromatic rings are freed and then ingested, whereas other more resistant structures are degraded while still bound in the polymer and released subsequently as aliphatic products of ring cleavage. All detailed studies of microbial catabolism of aromatic substances have been with nonpolymeric compounds of low molecular weight [23,24].

Benzene rings are decomposed aerobically in nature by the catalytic action of enzymes known as oxygenases, which act on rings substituted with two hydroxyl groups either *ortho* or *para* to each other [23,24]. The benzene rings of lignin are already substituted with oxygen, but these are mainly in ether linkages and not in hydroxyl groups. The hydroxyl groups required for ring cleavage must therefore be formed by ether cleavage reactions, including demethylation of methoxyl groups, and/or by direct hydroxylation of the rings. Direct hydroxylation by enzymes requires molecular oxygen [23], as does demethylation of aromatic methoxyl groups [18]. Cleavage of appropriately hydroxylate aromatic rings also requires molecular oxygen [23]. Thus, the key reactions involved in the breakdown of the aromatic rings of lignin by white-rot fungi undoubtedly are oxidative and require molecular oxygen. As has been mentioned, the specific structural changes that the lignin polymer undergoes during its metabolism by white-rot fungi are not known. The few changes in functional groups and in physical properties that have been shown to occur are in accord with an oxidative breakdown, but provide relatively little definitive information about specific structural changes [47].

As with the monosaccharides and oligosaccharides formed by degradation of polysaccharides, lignin degradation products do not accumulate during white rot; evidently the fungi use the fragments as they are released. This lack of accumulation of partial decomposition products is reflected in an absence of significant quantities of extractable materials—even materials extractable with good lignin solvents, such as methyl cellosolve and 1% NaOH [16,20,62]. Similarly, at any stage of wood decay the amount of altered lignin polymer may be small—the fungi confining their attack to a limited part of the lignin at any given time [50].

4.4.7.3 Brown-rot fungi

Even though brown-rot fungi cannot metabolize lignin in wood, they do alter its structure as they decompose the wood polysaccharides [47]. Specific changes they cause in the polymer include: (1) demethylation of methoxyl groups, leaving phenolic hydroxyl groups [49]; (2) formation of carboxyl groups; and (3), with at least one fungus [51], limited hydroxylation of aromatic rings. The lignin in the rotted wood is also darkened by fungal attack, possibly as a result of oxidation of some O-diphenol structures formed on demethylation of rings bearing free phenolic hydroxyl groups. Some indirect evidence has been obtained that brown-rot fungi may cause a certain amount of depolymerization of the lignin [49]. It is possible that this limited degradation of lignin, especially depolymerization if it occurs, is necessary before the polysaccharides can be broken down completely.

4.4.7.4 Soft-rot fungi

Chaetomium globosum has been shown to cause depletion of the lignin in beech wood (Figure 4.8) [55,63,66]. The lignin remaining in the decayed wood was shown to be deficient in methoxyl and to be more acid-soluble than the lignin in the sound wood [55]. Thus, this soft-rot fungus can bring about at least some degradation of lignin, but, as with the white-rot fungi, it is not known what specific sequential changes are involved. Other soft-rot fungi have not been studied.

4.5 Conclusions

1. White-rot fungi degrade and metabolize all the structural polymers in wood—the cellulose, the hemicelluloses, and the lignin. The components remaining in wood at any stage of decay are relatively intact; there is no rapid loss in DP of the total cellulose as with brown-rot fungi.

2. Brown-rot fungi depolymerize and metabolize the cellulose and hemicelluloses. They also alter the lignin. Thus, brown rot involves progressive removal of carbohydrates, leaving degraded lignin behind. Rapid loss in DP of the total cellulose characterizes brown-rot attack; this is effected by an extracellular, highly diffusible catalyst that has not been characterized (nonenzymatic?).

3. The effects of the soft-rot fungus *Chaetomium globosum* on the gross composition of the wood are similar to those of white-rot fungi, except that the lignin is much less severely attacked. Other soft-rot fungi have not been studied.

4. Cellulose and hemicellulose depolymerization occurs by splitting apart the monomeric units. The enzymes from white-, brown-, and soft-rot fungi depolymerize isolated polysaccharide molecules hydrolytically and usually in an apparently random manner, producing oligosaccharides and causing rapid depolymerization.

5. The mechanism of lignin degradation is not completely understood, but is probably largely oxidative. It is not likely to involve simple splitting apart of the monomeric phenylpropane units. The nature of the fragments released from the lignin polymer by white-rot and soft-rot fungi and the specific reactions involved are not known.

6. The intimate association of the lignin with the polysaccharides apparently makes wood resistant to decomposition by both enzymes and whole organisms that can decompose the isolated wood polysaccharides. Thus, decomposition of wood by all wood-decay fungi probably involves a concerted degradation of all components, and this may be the key to their unique ability to decay wood.

7. Much remains to be learned about the chemistry and biochemistry of wood decay, knowledge about lignin and hemicellulose degradation being especially meager.

REFERENCES

1. Adler, E. 1968. "The chemical construction of lignin." *Svenska Kem. Tidskr.* 80:279–90. (In Swedish.)
2. Ahlgren, E. and Eriksson, K.E. 1967. "Characterization of cellulases and related enzymes by isoelectric focusing, gel filtration and zone electrophoresis. II. Studies

on *Stererium sanguinolentum, Fomes annosus* and *Chrysosporium lignorum* enzymes."
Acta Chem. Scand. 21:1193–1200.

3. Albersheim, P., Jones, T.M. and English, P.D. 1969. "Biochemistry of the cell wall in relation to infective processes." *Ann. Rev. Phytopathol.* 7:171–194.

4. Apenitis, A., Erdtman, H. and Leopold, B. 1951. "Studies on lignin. V. The decay of spruce wood by brown-rotting fungi." *Svenska Kem. Tidskr.* 63:195–207.

5. Baechler, R.H. 1959. "Improving wood's durability through chemical modification." *Forest Prod. J.* 9:166–171.

6. Barras, D.R., Moore, A.E. and Stone, B.A. 1969. "Enzyme-substrate relationships among β-glucan hydrolases." In *Cellulases and Their Applications* (G.J. Hajny and E.T. Reese, eds.). 105–138. Am. Chem. Soc. Press, Washington, D.C.

7. Bailey, R.W. and Gaillard, B.D.E. 1965. "Carbohydrases of the rumen ciliate *Epidinium caudatum* (Crawley). Hydrolysis of plant hemicellulose fractions and β-linked glucose polymers." *Biochem. J.* 95:758–766.

8. Bailey, P.J., Liese, W. and Rösch, R. 1968. "Some aspects of cellulose degradation in lignified cell walls." *Biodeterioration of Materials.* Proc. 1st Internat. Symp., Southampton. Elsevier, Amsterdam, Netherlands. 546–57.

9. Bailey, P.J., Liese, W., Rösch, R., Keilich, G. and Afting, E.G. 1969. "Cellulase (β-1, 4-glucan 4-glucanohydrolase) from the wood-degrading fungus *Polyporus schweinitzii* Fr." *Biochem. Biophys. Acta* 185:381–91.

10. Bateman, D.F. and Millar, R.L. 1966. "Pectic enzymes in tissue degradation." *Ann. Rev. Phytopathol.* 4:119–46.

11. Bauch, J., Liese, W. and Berndt, H. 1970. "Biological investigations for the improvement of the permeability of softwoods." *Holzforschung* 24:199–205.

12. Bergman, O. and Nilsson, T. 1967. "On the outside storage of aspen chips at Hörnefors sulfite mill." Swedish Royal College of Forestry Res. Note No. 55. p. 60.

13. Brauns, F.E. and Brauns, D.A. 1960. *The Chemistry of Lignin.* Supplement Volume. Academic Press, N.Y. 157–65.

14. Bray, M.W. and Andrews, T.M. 1924. "Chemical changes of groundwood during decay." *Ind. Eng. Chem.* 16:137–39.

15. Brown, W., Cowling, E.B., and Falkehag, S.I. 1968. "Molecular size distributions of lignins liberated enzymatically from wood." *Svensky Papperstidning* 71:811–21.

16. Campbell, W.G. 1952. "The biological decomposition of wood." In *Wood Chemistry* (L.E. Wise and E.C. Jahn, eds.). Reinhold, N.Y. 1061–1116.

17. Cartwright, K. St. G. and Findlay, W.P.K. 1946. *Decay of Timber and Its Prevention.* H.M. Stationery Office.

18. Cartwright, N.J. and Smith, A.R.W. 1967. "Bacterial attack on ethers. An enzyme system demethylating vanillic acid." *Biochem. J.* 102:826–41.

19. Courtois, H. 1966. "Uber den zellwandabban durch Bacterien im Nadelholz." *Holzforschung* 20:148–54.

20. Cowling, E.B. 1961. "Comparative biochemistry of the decay of sweetgum sapwood by white-rot and brown-rot fungi." USDA Tech. Bull. No. 1258.

21. Cowling, E.B. 1970. "Nitrogen in forest trees and its role in wood deterioration." *Acta Universitatis Upsaliensis 164.*

22. Cowling, E.B. and Brown, W. 1969. "Structural features of cellulosic materials in relation to enzymatic hydrolysis." In *Cellulases and Their Applications* (G.J. Hajny and E.T. Reese, eds.). Am. Chem. Soc. Press, Washington, D.C. 152–87.

23. Dagley, S. 1967. "The microbial metabolism of phenolics." In *Soil Biochemistry* (A.D. McLaren and G. Peterson, eds.). Marcel Dekker, New York. 287–317.

24. Dagley, S. 1971. "Catabolism of aromatic compounds by micro-organisms." *Adv. Microbial Metab.* 6:1–46.

25. Eriksson, K.E. 1967. "Studies on cellulolytic and related enzymes." *Svenska Kem. Tidskr.* 79:660–78.
26. Eriksson, K.E. and Rzedowski, W. 1969. "Extracellular enzyme system utilized by the fungus *Chrysosporium lignorum* for the breakdown of cellulose. II. Separation and characterization of three cellulase peaks." *Arch. Biochem. Biophys.* 129:689–95.
27. Fergus, B.J. and Goring, D.A.I. 1970. "The distribution of lignin in birch wood as determined by ultraviolet microscopy." *Holzforschung* 24:118–24.
28. Fergus, B.J., Procter, A.R., Scott, J.A.N. and Goring, D.A.I. 1969. "The distribution of lignin in sprucewood as determined by ultraviolet microscopy." *Wood Sci. Tech.* 3:117–38.
29. Fergus, B.J. and Goring, D.A.I. 1970. "The location of guaiacyl and syringyl lignins in birch xylem tissue." *Holzforschung* 24:113–17.
30. Freudenberg, K. 1968. "The constitution and biosynthesis of lignin." In *Constitution and Biosynthesis of Lignin* (A.C. Neish and K. Freudenberg, eds.). Springer-Verlag, N.Y. 47–122.
31. Frey-Wyssling, A. 1969. "The ultrasctructure and biogenesis of native cellulose." *Fortschritte Chem. org. Naturst.* 27:1–30.
32. Gascoigne, J.A. and Gascoigne, M.M. 1960. *Biological Degradation of Cellulose.* Butterworths, London.
33. Goldstein, I., Jeroski, E.B., Lund, A.E., Nielson, J.F. and Weaver, J.W. 1961. "Acetylation of wood in lumber thickness." *Forest Prod. J.* 11:363–70.
34. Goring, D.A.I. and Timell, T. 1962. "Molecular weight of native celluloses." *Tappi* 45:454–60.
35. Greaves, H. 1970. "The effect of some wood-inhabiting bacteria on the permeability characteristics and microscopic features of Eucalyptus regnans and Pinus radiata sapwood and heartwood." *Holzforschung* 24:6–14.
36. Harkin, J.M. 1967. "Lignin—a natural polymeric product of phenol oxidation." In *Oxidative Coupling of Phenols* (A.R. Battersby and A.I. Taylor, eds.). Marcel Dekker, N.Y. 243–321.
37. Hulme, M.A. and Shields, J.K. 1970. "Biological control of decay fungi in wood by competition for non-structural carbohydrates." *Nature* 227:300–301.
38. Immergut, E.H. 1963. "Cellulose." In *The Chemistry of Wood* (B.L. Browning, ed.). Interscience, N.Y. 103–90.
39. Kawase, K. 1962. "Chemical components of wood decayed under natural conditions and their properties." *J. Fac. Agr.,* Hokkaido Univ. 52:186–245.
40. Keilich, G., Bailey, P. and Liese, W. 1970. "Enzymatic degradation of cellulose, cellulose derivatives and hemicelluloses in relation to the fungal decay of wood." *Wood Sci. Tech.* 4:273–83.
41. Keilich, G., Bailey, P.J., Afting, E.G. and Liese, W. 1969. "Cellulase (β-1,4-glucan 4-glucanohydrolase) from the wood-degrading fungus *Polyporus schweinitzii* Fr. II. Characterization." *Biochim. Biophys. Acta* 185:392–401.
42. King, K.W. and Vessal, M.I. 1969. "Enzymes of the cellulase complex." In *Cellulases and Their Application* (G.J. Hajny and E.T. Reese, eds.). Am. Chem. Soc. Press, Washington, D.C. 7–25.
43. King, N.J. 1966. "The extracellular enzymes of *Coniophora cerebella*." *Biochem. J.* 100:784–92.
44. King, N.J. 1968. "Degradation of holocellulose by an enzyme preparation from a wood-destroying fungus." *Nature* 218:1173–74.
45. King, N.J. 1968. "The degradation of wood cell wall components by the extracellular enzymes of *Coniophora cerebella*." In *Biodeterioration of Materials,* Proc. 1st Internat. Symp., Southampton. Elsevier, Amsterdam, Netherlands. 558–64.

180

T. KENT KIRK

46. King, N.J. and Fuller, D.B. 1968. "The xylanase system of *Coniophora cerebella*." *Biochem. J.* 108:571–76.
47. Kirk, T.K. 1971. "Effects of microorganisms on lignin." *Ann. Rev. Phytopathol.* 9:185–210.
48. Kirk, T.K. Unpublished.
49. Kirk, T.K. and Adler, E. 1970. "Methoxyl-deficient structural elements in lignin of sweetgum decayed by a brown-rot fungus." *Acta Chem. Scand.* 24:3379–90.
50. Kirk, T.K. and Lundquist, K. 1970. "Comparison of sound and white-rotted sapwood of sweetgum with respect to properties of the lignin and composition of extractives." *Svensky Papperstidning* 73:294–306.
51. Kirk, T.K., Larsson, S. and Miksche, G.E. 1970. "Aromatic hydroxylation resulting from attack of lignin by a brown-rot fungus." *Acta Chem. Scand.* 24:1470–72.
52. Knuth, D.T. and McCoy, E. 1962. "Bacterial deterioration of pine logs in pond storage." *Forest Prod. J.* 12:437–42.
53. Liese, W. 1971. "The action of fungi and bacteria during wood deterioration." *Intern. Pest Control* 13:20–24.
54. Liese, W. and Karnop, G. 1968. "Uber den Befall von Nadelholz durch Bakterien." *Holzals Roh-und Werkstoff* 26:202–208.
55. Levi, M.P. and Preston, R.D. 1965. "A chemical and microscopic examination of the action of the soft-rot fungus *Chaetomium globosum* on beechwood (*Fagus sylv.*)." *Holzforschung* 19:183–90.
56. Lyr, H. 1960. "Die Bildung von Ektoenzymen durch holzzerstorende und holzbenohnende Pilze auf vershiedenen Nabroboden. V. Ein komplexes Medium ak C-Quelle." *Archiv für Mikrobiologie* 35:258–78.
57. Mahler, H.R. and Cordes, E.H. 1966. *Biological Chemistry.* Harper & Row, N.Y.
58. Nagel, C.W. and Wilson, T.M. 1970. "Pectic acid lyases of *Bacillus polymyxa*." *Appl. Microbiol.* 20:374–83.
59. Pearl, I.A. 1967. *The Chemistry of Lignin.* Marcel Dekker, N.Y.
60. Peterson, C.A. and Cowling, E.B. 1964. "Decay resistance of extractive-free coniferous woods to white-rot fungi." *Phytopathology* 54:542–47.
61. Reese, E.T. 1969. "Estimation of exo-β-1$\rightarrow$4-glucanase in crude cellulase solutions." In *Cellulases and Their Application* (G.J. Hajny and E.T. Reese, eds.). Am. Chem. Soc. Press, Washington, D.C. 26–33.
62. Savard, J. and André, A.M. 1956. "Etude Chimique de l'attaque d'un *Triplochitor sclerozylon* par *Poria* sp. et par *Lentinus nigripes*." Centre Technique Forestier Tropical, Nogent-sur-Marne, France. Publ. No. 10.
63. Savory, J.G. and Pinion, L.C. 1958. "Chemical aspects of decay of beech wood by *Chaetomium globosum*." *Holzforschung* 12:99–103.
64. Scheffer, T.C. and Cowling, E.B. 1966. "Natural resistance of wood to microbial deterioration." *Ann. Rev. Phytopathol.* 4:147–70.
65. Seborg, R.M., Tarkow, H. and Stamm, A.J. 1962. "Modified woods." U.S. Forest Serv., Forest Prod. Lab. Rept. No. 2192.
66. Seifert, K. 1966. "Die chemische Veränderung der Bucherholz-Zellwand durch Moderfäule (*Chaetomium globosum* Kunze)." *Holz als Roh-und Werkstoff* 24:185–89.
67. Seifert, K. 1962. "Die chemische Veränderung der Holzzellwand unter dem Einfluss pflanzlicher und tierischer Schändlinge." *Holzforschung* 16:102–13.
68. Seifert, K. 1968. "Zur systematik der Holzfäulen, ihre chemischen und physikalischen Kennzeichen." *Holz als Roh-und Werkstoff* 26:208–15.
69. Selby, K. 1969. "The purification and properties of the C-component of the cellulase complex." In *Cellulases and Their Applications* (G.J. Hajny and E.T. Reese, eds.). Am. Chem. Soc. Press, Washington, D.C. 34–52.

70. Selby, K. and Maitland, C.C. 1967. "The cellulase of *Trichoderma viride*. Separation of the components involved in the solubilization of cotton." *Biochem. J.* 104:716–24.

71. Sorensen, H. 1952. "On the specificity and products of action of xylanse from *Chaetomium globosum* Kunze." *Physiol. Plant.* 5:183–98.

72. Suzuki, H., Yamane, K. and Nisizawa, K. 1969. "Extracellular and cell-bound cellulase components of bacteria." In *Cellulases and Their Applications* (G.J. Hajny and E.T. Reese, eds.) Am. Chem. Soc. Press, Washington, D.C. 60–82.

73. Timell, T. 1962. "Enzymatic hydrolysis of a 4-*O*-methylglucuronoxylan from the wood of white birch (*Betula popyrifera* Marsh)." *Svensky Papperstidning* 65:435–47.

74. Timell, T. 1967. "Recent progress in the chemistry of wood hemicelluloses." *Wood Sci. Tech.* 1:45–70.

75. Virtanen, A.I. and Hukki, J. 1946. "Thermophilic fermentation of wood." *Suom. Kemistilehti* 19:4–13.

76. Whistler, R.L. and Richards, E.L. 1970. "Hemicelluloses." In *The Carbohydrates* (W. Pigman, D. Horton and A. Herp, eds.). Academic Press, N.Y. 447–69.

5. Control Methods

MICHAEL P. LEVI
School of Forest Resources
North Carolina State University, Raleigh, North Carolina

5.1 Introduction

Millions of dollars are lost annually worldwide because of the biodeterioration of wood products by microorganisms. A large proportion of this money could be saved by the correct selection of available control methods and wood species which would prevent this biodeterioration. Certain species of timber are naturally resistant to attack because they contain toxic heartwood extractives. These timbers perform well in service without the use of control methods. Unfortunately, natural durability is variable within and between trees of the same species, and naturally durable timbers are becoming scarcer and more expensive. Consequently, it is now generally more economical to use properly protected nondurable timber than naturally durable timber.

Bacteria, wood-staining and mold fungi, and wood-destroying fungi (brown-, white-, and soft-rot fungi) all affect the quality of nondurable timber. The need to use control methods against these organisms depends upon the deterioration caused by the respective groups.

Bacteria have little effect on wood quality other than to increase the permeability of sapwood. This is beneficial in the case of impermeable timbers such as spruce [71], and bacterial infection may become a standard method of pretreatment for poles and posts [41]. However, bacterial attack can also be detrimental, causing highly absorbent zones in permeable timbers. Such an effect is particularly troublesome in millwork. Attempts have been made to control attack with bactericides [43], but these methods have not been widely adopted commercially. The best control method is to avoid storage of felled timber in ponds or under water sprays, which provide conditions favorable for bacterial attack. This, however, is not feasible in many areas of the world. It seems unlikely that chemical methods will gain widespread acceptance, because the problems

183

caused by bacterial attack are not sufficiently serious to warrant the cost of such methods. No further consideration therefore will be given to the prevention of bacterial attack in wood.

Wood-staining fungi have little effect on the strength of wood, but can drastically reduce its commercial value because of the discoloration they cause in sapwood. Their growth is particularly rapid in warm, humid conditions, where the use of chemical treatment to prevent attack is essential if serious economic losses are to be avoided. In colder, less humid climates, attack can be prevented by careful stacking and rapid drying of wood. When drying cannot be accomplished for some time after felling, staining can be prevented by storage of logs under water.

Wood-destroying fungi present the greatest hazard to the economic use of wood. The importance of controlling them has been recognized since man's earliest times. Noah coated his ark with pitch in order to keep it dry and thus prevent decay. By the middle of the eighteenth century it was known that copper sulphate stopped decay [20], and 50 years later Chapman [24] illustrated the interest in the use of chemical control methods when he complained that "almost every chemical principle or compound of any plausibility has been suggested in the course of the last five years and submitted either to the admiralty or navy boards; but the multiplicity and contradiction of opinions formed nearly an inextricable labyrinth." Thus, over 100 years ago, before Hartig had discovered that decay was caused by fungi [53], it was known that decay could be controlled either by keeping wood dry or by treating it with certain chemicals.

The two major control methods for the protection of wood in service are still prevention of the entry of moisture into wood by the use of proper construction techniques and water-impermeable barriers, and treatment of wood with chemicals toxic to wood-destroying fungi. The former method is widely used in low-hazard environments; for example, internal building timbers in temperate zones. The latter method is used in medium- and high-hazard environments; for example, ground-contact timbers and marine timbers.

A major portion of this chapter is concerned with the types of chemicals used to control fungi, their modes of action, and the tolerance of some fungi to certain of these chemicals. Consideration will not be given to the intricacies of formulation or to methods of applying preservatives, since these will be dealt with in Chapters 1, 2, and 3 of Volume II. Recommendations for specific preservative retentions depend entirely upon the end-use for the wood. Such recommendations can be found in various national standards and are beyond the scope of this chapter.

The other control methods discussed are moisture control, biological control, and alteration or removal of wood constituents. Of these, only the first is a widely used method at the present time. The other methods may assume growing importance in the future. The final part of this chapter considers some of these possible future control methods as well as the areas where research is needed.

The control of deterioration of wood composite materials such as plywood and particleboard, of chip piles, and of wood pulp is assuming growing importance as the production of these materials increases. Consideration of such control methods, however, will be limited to those which are similar to the methods used for the protection of solid wood.

5.2 Addition of Fungicides

The first requirement for a fungicide to be used in wood preservation is the ability to prevent attack of wood by wood-destroying, or wood-staining and mold fungi. Fungicides prevent attack by affecting fungi so that they cannot digest wood. An alternative form of chemical treatment involves modification of wood so that it cannot be digested by fungi. Protection of this type will be discussed in Section 5.3.

A fungicide can affect a fungus by killing hyphae and spores with which it comes in contact, in which case its action is fungicidal. Alternatively, it can inhibit growth of fungi, but not kill them; its action is then called fungistatic. Frequently, the action will change from fungistatic to fungicidal as the concentration of the fungicide is increased. In practice, no distinction is drawn between these two modes of action. Methods of evaluating wood preservatives study the effect of the fungus on the treated timber, not the direct effect of the preservative on the fungus. The smallest amount of preservative required to just prevent weight loss or strength loss of treated blocks of wood exposed to fungi in the laboratory, or under field conditions, is determined (see Chapter 6). This amount gives what is called the threshold or toxic concentration. Various weathering procedures can be applied to treated blocks before exposure to the fungi in the laboratory, and the threshold concentrations which are obtained may be used as a guide to the effectiveness and permanence of the preservative.

When threshold concentrations for a fungicide have been determined against the important fungi which are likely to occur in the environment where the preservative is to be used, the cost–effectiveness of the product can be compared with that of established preservatives. If the cost–effectiveness is similar to or lower than that of products in use, then several other requirements must be met before the fungicide can be introduced onto the market. These basic requirements are:

1. Low toxicity to animals at the concentrations recommended for use in timber.

2. Permanence in the conditions where it is to be used.

3. Little or no effect on the strength properties of timber.

4. For certain end-uses, little or no effect on materials coming in contact with treated timber, *e.g.,* paints, adhesives, metal fastenings, and plastics.

5. Good penetration properties in the formulation in which it is used.

6. Ready availability.

Many thousands of chemicals have been examined for use as fungicides by industrial and government laboratories. About 280 chemicals were being marketed for use in plant disease control in 1964 [83]. Only about 18 of these were being used commercially for the treatment of timber products because the others failed to meet the rigorous requirements for a fungicide to be used successfully in wood preservation.

Several references are available, listing the compounds that have found favor as wood preservatives [10,62,111], but only those important at the present time will be discussed in detail. Results demonstrating the effectiveness of the various compounds discussed can be found in the *Proceedings* of the American Wood-Preservers' Association; the *Record* of the British Wood Preserving Association; and in the field-test reports issued by Forest Products Research Laboratory, Princes Risborough; USDA Forest Products Laboratory, Madison; and many other national forestry laboratories.

5.2.1 Types of fungicide

Two basic types of fungicide exist—oilborne and waterborne—which are distinguished by the solvent used to introduce the toxicant into the timber. Oilborne preservatives can be further divided into distillates of coal tar, or creosotes, which can be diluted with petroleum oils or undistilled coal tar, and solutions of oil-soluble fungicides in organic solvents (usually petroleum oils).

5.2.1.1 Oilborne fungicides

Creosote. The use of creosote for the protection of timber was first patented in 1838 by Bethell, and since that time it has remained the most important and the most widely used wood preservative. It contains numerous active components which render it effective against almost all types of wood-destroying and wood-inhabiting fungi, although a few organisms are tolerant to it (see Section 5.2.3).

It has been used successfully for the protection of poles, posts, and sawn timber in all types of environment where fungi occur. The restrictions on its application are where odorless, uncolored, or paintable timber is required.

As is shown in Chapter 1 of Volume II, the constituents of creosote can be grouped into three main classes: tar acids, including phenols, cresols, xylenols and naphthols; tar bases, including pyridines, quinolines, and acridines; hydrocarbons, including benzene, toluene, xylene, naphthalene, acenaphthene, phenanthrene, anthracene, and fluorene. High-temperature creosotes generally contain a higher proportion of aromatic hydrocarbons and a lower proportion of aliphatic hydrocarbons and tar acids than low-temperature creosotes.

Tar acids, tar bases, and hydrocarbons all contain a wide range of fungicidal constituents. Schulze and Becker [96] investigated the toxicity of whole creosote, 15 distillate fractions boiling between 120°C and 360°C, the distillation residues, and numerous individual components of creosote to the wood-destroying fungi *Coniophora cerebella, Poria vaporaria,* and *Lentinus lepideus.* They found that different distillate fractions varied widely in their toxicity to the fungi, those boiling between 180–240°C being the most active. Among the individual compounds which exhibited greatest toxicity in the fractions in which they occurred were thionaphthene, 2-naphthol, 2-methylnaphthalene, and isoquinoline.

There is conflicting evidence on the relative contributions made to fungicidal activity by the various components of creosote. These conflicts are probably due to the use of different types of creosote. It has been shown that tar acids and bases do not contribute greatly to the toxicity of high-temperature creosotes [15,17,89]. In low-temperature creosotes, however, tar acids are essential [8,16,33,37]. Bland's conclusion [16], that consideration of the toxicity of a creosote and of various fractions and compounds shows that constituents do not act independently of each other, is a most powerful argument for studying creosote as a whole rather than as a combination of dozens of different compounds.

Pentachlorophenol. Polychlorinated phenols were first used in wood preservation in the late 1920s. The commercial introduction of pentachlorophenol in the United States followed a few years later. Since that time, it has become established as the most widely used single oil-soluble fungicide in wood preservation.

Penta and its water-soluble sodium salt are toxic to wood-destroying fungi, stain fungi, and molds. They are used to prevent attack of logs in the forest, unseasoned timber at the sawmill, and seasoned timber in service as poles, railway ties, building timbers, etc.

The permanence, and hence effectiveness, of penta is largely dependent upon the solvent system and treatment method used to apply the preservative. Numerous papers have been written on the importance of the choice of solvent [*e.g.,* 11,54,66,84]. The evidence now available suggests that when penta is deposited in the wood in the crystalline state, or is kept in solution in a nonvolatile oil, it maintains its effectiveness over many years. When the compound is applied in a relatively volatile oil, however, it migrates to the surface of the timber where some is lost with the solvent by evaporation.

Tetra- and tri-chlorophenol and chloro-2-phenyl phenol are other chlorinated phenols that have been used as wood preservatives. Their physical properties make them less useful than pentachlorophenol. In order to reduce the irritant properties of penta and increase its permanence, several derivatives have been developed. Three of these are copper pentachlorophenate, dehydroabietylamine-pentachlorophenate (Fumgamin or Rosin amine D pentachlorophenate), and pentachlorophenyl laurate. These compounds have been used successfully as textile preservatives, but little information has been published on their use as wood preservatives. The recommendations that they can be successfully used at the same concentration as pentachlorophenol have yet to be justified in the literature.

Tributyltin oxide. In the 1950s it was shown that some organotin compounds possess fungicidal properties. Extensive tests have shown that when cost, permanence, and mammalian toxicity are all considered, tributyltin oxide is the most effective of the organotins for wood preservation. The compound is toxic to a wide range of wood-destroying fungi. It is used mainly for the protection of building timbers in Europe. It is easier to use than pentachlorophenol since it is readily soluble in petroleum solvents, does not require co-solvents or anti-blooming agents, and is less toxic and irritating. The role of tributyltin oxide as a wood preservative has been reviewed by Hof [57].

Copper naphthenate. Naphthenic acids which have been neutralized with alkali react with a number of metal salts to form naphthenates. Copper naphthenate is the most important such compound in wood preservation. It was first recommended for timber protection in 1889 and was introduced commercially in Denmark in 1911. Its use spread until after the Second World War when it partially replaced creosote, which was then in short supply. However, as creosote supplies increased again, copper naphthenate has been used mainly for the dip or brush treatment of millwork, horticultural timbers, and boat timbers. It is toxic to a wide range of wood-destroying fungi and, because of its low water solubility and low vapor pressure, it has good permanence in timber. It is normally applied in solutions containing from 1–3 percent copper metal, and colors timber green.

Zinc naphthenate has occasionally been used where the green color of copper naphthenate is objectionable, but as the zinc compound is much less toxic than the copper salt, its use is not common.

Copper-8-quinolinolate. This chemical is the copper chelate of 8-hydroxyquinoline. It is considerably more expensive than copper naphthenate, but is more effective against a wide range of wood-destroying fungi, including copper-tolerant organisms. It has a very low toxicity to humans, as well as being odorless. These properties have led to its acceptance for speciality uses such as food containers. In 1970 it was the only wood preservative permitted by the U.S. Food and Drug Administration for the treatment of timber in direct contact with food.

5.2.1.2 Waterborne fungicides

Various metal salts used either alone or in combination with each other and with fluorine-, arsenic-, or boron-containing compounds have found favor as wood preservatives. Horsfall [58] arranged the metals in the following order of descending fungitoxicity: silver > mercury > copper > cadmium > chromium > nickel > lead > cobalt > zinc > iron > calcium.

Of these metals, mercury, copper, chromium, lead, and zinc have been used in commercial wood preservatives, but copper and chromium, and to a lesser extent zinc, are the only ones still used widely. The others have not become established because of low cost–effectiveness or high human toxicity.

The first waterborne wood preservatives contained only one toxic component; for example, fluorine, copper, or zinc. Except in the case of boron, these have now been superseded by multisalt preservatives.

Borax and boric acid. Taken separately, borax and boric acid have quite low solubilities in water. When used together, their solubilities increase considerably, and this mixture is used in Scandinavia, Australia, and New Zealand for the diffusion treatment of green timber and for vacuum–pressure treatment of seasoned timber. The borax–boric acid mixture is effective against a wide range of wood-destroying fungi [22] but, because of its relatively high solubility in water, it can be readily leached from timber. Thus, the treatment is recommended only for timber out of ground contact. Considerable efforts have been devoted to making boron more permanent in timber, but these have not yet been successful.

Acid copper chromate. Acid copper chromate is a mixture of copper sulphate and sodium dichromate which was patented in 1928. The dichromate serves two purposes. It reduces the corrosiveness of copper sulphate and it precipitates the soluble copper as insoluble copper chromate so that when timber has been dried after treatment, the preservative will not leach out in wet conditions. This was an important step forward in the development of waterborne preservatives.

Acid copper chromates applied by vacuum–pressure processes have been used successfully for the protection of poles, posts, and sawn lumber in both high- and low-hazard environments. The main weakness of the preservative is its susceptibility to copper-tolerant fungi, and some failures have been noted in service because of attack by these fungi.

Copper-chromium-arsenate. After the introduction of the acid copper chromate, the next major step in the development of highly fixed water- borne preservatives was taken in 1933 when Kamesan patented a mixture of copper sulphate, arsenic pentoxide, and potassium dichromate [65]. Copper, chromium, and arsenic used in the form of salts or oxides, and in varying proportions, have now become established as the most widely used multisalt preservatives. The general properties and uses of these formulations have been discussed by Wallace [115], and field-test data are available to show that they are effective against a broad spectrum of wood-destroying organisms. Copper-chromium-arsenates are generally applied by vacuum–pressure impregnation, and these salts protect poles, posts, and sawn timber products in all environments where wood-destroy- ing fungi occur. These preservatives have also been used for the protec- tion of particleboard and plywood.

The presence of hexavalent chromium in the preservative causes the precipitation of a large proportion of the copper and arsenic when the preservative solution comes in contact with wood. This precipitation gives the high degree of permanence for which these preservatives are noted. Copper is the main fungicidal component, but arsenic is important in preventing attack by copper-tolerant fungi. Generally, if fungi are tolerant to copper, they are susceptible to arsenic and vice versa [69].

Ammoniacal copper arsenite. Another preservative that utilizes the fungicidal properties of copper and arsenic is a solution of copper hydrox- ide and arsenic trioxide in ammonium hydroxide. This solution is applied by vacuum–pressure to dry timber. When the timber dries after treat- ment, ammonia evaporates, and copper arsenite is precipitated in the wood. The ammoniacal solvent makes this preservative more difficult to handle than the other waterborne preservatives, and it is more susceptible to leaching than copper-chromium-arsenates. However, ammoniacal cop- per arsenite is being used in increasing amounts because it is toxic to a wide range of wood-destroying fungi.

Copper-chromium-fluoride and copper-chromium-boron. These preserva- tives contain a toxic component which remains soluble after impregnation into wood (fluoride and boron, respectively), which is claimed to give improved penetration in impermeable timbers. However, this advantage can be offset by the loss of the soluble components in wet conditions. Both these preservatives have performed well as fungicides under severe exposure conditions over a short period, but tests have not been conducted for sufficient time to determine their long-term effectiveness [47].

Fluoride-chromium-arsenate-dinitrophenols. Multisalt preservatives containing fluoride, chromium, arsenate, and phenol, which were developed at the beginning of this century, have been widely used for the protection of timber out of ground contact, *e.g.,* house timbers. They have also been used for the short-term protection of ground-contact timbers, but they are not sufficiently insoluble when in the wood to give long-term protection. Their use has decreased with the increased availability of highly fixed copper containing multisalt preservatives.

Other water-soluble fluoride-containing preservatives have also been used, particularly in Germany, the most important of these being magnesium silicofluoride and sodium fluoride.

5.2.2 Mode of action of fungicides

Considerable effort has been devoted to determining the mode of action of fungicides in recent years to try to improve their effectiveness. Studies have concentrated on organic fungicides used in agriculture, and a comprehensive review of present knowledge was edited by Torgeson [108,109]. More recent reviews include those by Lukens [73] and Sisler [100], while Horsfall's *Principles of Fungicidal Action* [58] remains the standard treatise on the subject.

The general mechanisms of action of fungicides will now be discussed, followed by an outline of the mode of action of the more important wood preservatives.

5.2.2.1 General mechanisms of action of fungicides

Wood-destroying fungi decay timber by the secretion of extracellular enzymes acting either at the surface of hyphae or some distance from them. These enzymes depolymerize the carbohydrates and, in some cases, the lignin components of the wood to smaller molecules which can be metabolized further by intracellular enzymes of the fungi (see Chapters 3 and 4 of this volume). Thus, white-rot fungi can destroy almost 100 percent of the mass of timber, and brown-rot and soft-rot fungi can destroy more than 60 percent.

Fungicides kill or inhibit the growth of fungi. In the case of wood-destroying fungi, this can be achieved in two ways. First, the fungicides can disrupt cellular organization of fungi so that normal intracellular metabolic processes cannot occur, and the fungi die or their growth is inhibited. Second, the fungicides can inhibit the production of, or inactivate, extracellular enzymes so that in the absence of an alternative food source the fungi die [46].

The existence of these two types of action partly explains the need to use wood as a substrate when determining the effectiveness of a fungicide as a timber preservative. If soluble substrates such as malt-agar are used, the extracellular enzymes responsible for the depolymerization of wood components will not be required, and a fungicide which acts primarily against these enzymes will not be found effective against the test fungus. When timber is used as substrate, however, the fungicide will kill or inhibit the growth of the fungus.

Another important reason for using wood as substrate for the evaluation of potential preservatives is to take into account any effects wood may have on the solubility or chemical form of the preservative.

Wood-staining and mold fungi metabolize the contents of wood cells, not the walls, and the role of extracellular enzymes is less important than for wood-destroying fungi. To be effective against stain and mold fungi, therefore, a fungicide must disrupt cellular organization. This distinction may explain why several fungicides which protect timber against wood-destroying fungi are not very effective against stain and mold fungi.

The first requirement for fungicidal action is that the fungicide be present at the site, where it can prevent fungal attack of the timber. When properly applied, wood preservatives cover the external surfaces of treated timber. Consequently, hyphae or spores encountering a piece of treated timber will automatically come in contact with the fungicide. If the fungicide affects extracellular enzymes, then it will be present at the site of action. If the fungicide acts by disrupting cellular organization, then it must penetrate the hyphae or spores before it can act.

Hyphae and spores are surrounded by a semipermeable double membrane composed of layers of protein and lipid. This membrane limits the rate of movement of metabolites and toxicants into and out of the living fungal cells. A fungicide will effectively prevent attack if it either increases or decreases the permeability of this membrane so that normal metabolic processes are upset. If the fungicide passes the membrane without affecting it, the fungus can be killed or its growth inhibited if the toxicant disrupts fungal metabolism by, for example, denaturing proteins or inhibiting enzymes.

The majority of wood preservatives are water-insoluble, whereas wood-destroying and wood-inhabiting fungi grow only in the presence of moisture. This immediately raises the problem of mobilization of preservatives from the timber to the site of action in the fungal cell. Many hypotheses have been put forward to explain how chemicals of very low water solubility can inhibit or kill fungi. Prevost [87] suggested that fungi could accumulate the fungicide (in this case, copper) from the environment until a toxic amount was present in the fungus. This accumulation theory, however, does not explain the rapid action of many insoluble fungicides. It was then suggested [13,106] that fungal metabolites could mobilize the fungicide, an idea that has now received much experimental support, particularly with insoluble copper fungicides [69,82,114]. In 1899 Overton [86] developed the lipoid theory of cell permeability which stated that movement of a substance into and out of a cell is determined by the coefficient of distribution between the lipoid membranes and aqueous cytoplasm. There is still considerable dispute about the validity of this hypothesis [85], but it is likely that it partially explains how some fungicides work.

As techniques for localizing the position of fungicides within cells are improved, and ways are found for distinguishing between primary and secondary effects of fungicides on fungal organization, then knowledge of the mode of action of fungicides will increase. In the meantime, much of the information available is only preliminary and many basic questions remain to be answered, as will be demonstrated in the discussion of the mode of action of wood preservatives which follows.

5.2.2.2 Mode of action of some wood preservatives

Creosote. Numerous studies of the toxicity of creosotes have been published. A few of these consider the relative toxicities of the various components of creosote [*e.g.,* 15,16,96]. To the author's knowledge, however, no work has been done on the mobilization of creosote or its components by wood-destroying fungi or on its penetration into, and effect on, fungal cells.

The components of creosote come from three main groups: mononuclear and polynuclear aromatic phenols (tar acids), heterocyclic nitrogen compounds (tar bases), and aliphatic and aromatic hydrocarbons. Organic sulphur compounds are also frequently present in small amounts. Some research has been carried out on the mode of action of representative compounds from these groups against non-wood-destroying fungi, and the results of these experiments will be outlined.

Phenolic compounds have been used as antiseptics since the middle of the last century, but their use in plant protection has been limited because of their great phytotoxicity. However, this toxicity does not limit their use in wood preservatives, and they form an important fungicidal component of creosote. Phenols are general biocides, effective against many types of microorganisms. Their fungicidal action is probably due to combination with wall membranes or to penetration of undissociated, lipid-soluble chemicals into fungal cells where they react with essential metabolites—*e.g.,* phenols denature proteins, probably by reaction of the acid group with basic groups in the protein [28]. The primary sites of action of these chemicals, however, have not been established.

Heterocyclic nitrogen compounds are essential for life. They occur in nucleic acids, coenzymes, and vitamins. Thus, the introduction of synthetic heterocyclic nitrogen compounds can interfere with normal metabolic processes, such as growth and membrane transport. However, little is known about the mode of action of the types of nitrogen compounds that occur in creosote, other than that they are general metabolic suppressants. Some work has been published on the effect of acridines suggesting that in bacteria they act on the membrane [1], but this work has not been extended to fungi.

Most unsubstituted aliphatic and aromatic hydrocarbons have very low fungicidal activity, although several such compounds can retard fungal growth. Acenaphthene, fluorene, and phenanthrene influence nuclear division in hyphae of *Sclerotinia fructicola* [59], and acenaphthene retards the growth of *Fomes annosus* in nutrient medium [14]. This effect may be due to attachment of the acenaphthene nucleus to proteins [27].

Although numerous fungicidal compounds are present in creosote, some of its activity is probably due to the physical protection given to treated timber. Thus, hydrophobic components of creosote retard the entry of moisture into timber, and hence inhibit the growth of fungi. The importance of the contribution made by this type of action will, however, be very difficult to determine.

Pentachlorophenol. Generally, the toxicity of phenols can be increased by increasing halogenation. Chlorine and bromine are usually superior in this respect to fluorine [45]. The highly substituted phenols are phytotoxic but, as with creosote, this does not prevent their use in wood preservatives. Pentachlorophenol acts as a fungicide by uncoupling oxidative phosphorylation [76]. Thus, it must be transported through the fungal cell wall before it becomes effective. Phosphate metabolism in the cell is altered so that sugar phosphates and nucleic acids decompose to inorganic phosphate and phosphorus compounds, some of which are lost from the cell. Uncoupling leads to an increased consumption of oxygen as the cell tries to produce the phosphorylated compounds needed for continued growth, and cell death ensues.

No studies on mobilization of penta by fungi have been reported, although much work has been published on the volatility and movement of penta exposed to natural and accelerated weathering conditions. The important effect of solvent systems on volatility and movement was discussed earlier.

Tributyltin oxide. There are two hypotheses for the action of tributyltin oxide as a wood preservative. The first of these suggests that the compound acts as a fungicide by inhibiting oxidative phosphorylation. This effect has been demonstrated in the mitochondria of animal tissues [4,103], but has yet to be demonstrated in fungi. No studies have been published on the mobilization and uptake of tributyltin oxide by wood-destroying fungi.

The second hypothesis suggests that tributyltin oxide prevents attack of timber by reacting with cellulose so that it cannot be metabolized by the extracellular enzymes of the wood-destroying fungi [95]. In other words, the compound is acting on the timber, not the fungus. No experimental evidence has been presented in support of this hypothesis. It seems likely that although tributyltin oxide may react with the carbohydrate components of wood, this reaction is relatively weak and the compound is released to act as a conventional fungicide. The answer to this problem, however, will be found only when it has been determined whether tin accumulates within the hyphae of wood-destroying fungi or remains localized in, or on, the wood cell walls.

Copper naphthenate. Both the copper ion and the naphthenic acid portions of this compound contribute to its fungicidal effectiveness [79]. The role of the latter is demonstrated by the fact that with copper oleate-treated textiles, copper-resistant fungi can utilize the oleic acid, remove the copper, and leave the textiles unprotected; however, with copper naphthenate-treated textiles, the naphthenic acid prevents growth of the fungi so that copper is not removed. Copper naphthenate is soluble in lipids, and this may assist fungicidal action [42]. Mobilization of copper naphthenate by wood-destroying fungi has not been studied, although many of these fungi discolor copper naphthenate-treated timber before causing decay. This suggests that the compound is readily dissociated or absorbed by hyphae.

The mode of action of naphthenic acids is not known, but the action of copper—particularly its effect on the germination of spores—has been examined extensively. Most heavy metals, including copper, can form complexes with ligands containing sulphur, nitrogen, or oxygen as electron donors. Thus, copper can react chemically with most of the essential compounds in the cell. The reactions which actually occur depend upon the accessibility of the cell constituents to the metal toxicant. After exposure for a few minutes, the effect of copper is fungistatic. The copper does not penetrate into the cell. For longer exposures, the copper penetrates into the cells and acts fungicidally. Reaction with ligands of the cell surface results in interference with membrane function. This can take several forms, such as inhibition of the production of extracellular enzymes or an effect on transport of nutrients and toxicants into and out of the cells. Once copper has entered the cell, it binds with protein, thus inhibiting enzyme action. If sufficient quantities of copper are available, the fungus is killed by nonspecific denaturation of protein and enzymes [101].

Copper-8-quinolinolate. 8-hydroxyquinoline (oxine) has been used as a disinfectant and antiseptic since 1895 [3]. It consists of two fused, 6-membered rings, one a phenol and the other a pyridine. Copper-8-quinolinolate is more toxic than either copper or 8-hydroxyquinoline alone [2,18]. Experiments on the mode of action of this compound have been reviewed by Lukens [74]. It is suggested that copper-8-quinolinolate, which is lipid-soluble, permeates cellular membranes, and then dissociates to the half-chelate [2], which may then act by inserting copper at metal-binding sites on proteins and enzymes [118], or other cellular constituents [64] where other metals normally function. Alternatively, the 8-hydroxyquinoline can compete with coenzymes for metal-binding sites on enzymes. In both cases, the fungicide effectively blocks the normal metabolic processes of living cells and either inhibits growth or kills the fungus.

Acid copper chromate, copper-chromium-arsenate, and ammoniacal copper arsenite. These three important wood preservatives are grouped together because they are all highly fixed in the wood and rely on copper as the main fungicidal component. Thus, their modes of action are probably similar. They are neither lipid-soluble nor water-soluble, so the first problem that must be solved in explaining their mode of action is that of mobilization to the site of action. As discussed with copper naphthenate, copper can act either extracellularly—on the fungal cell membrane—or intracellularly. If action is extracellular, the fixed copper containing preservatives will be effective, provided they can bind with enzymes to inhibit their action. For the other types of action, some form of mobilization must occur.

The mobilization and uptake of a copper-chromium-arsenate preservative by wood-destroying fungi has been studied by Levi [69] and Chou et al. [26], these papers being two of the few published detailed studies of the action of a wood preservative in timber.

Levi [69] showed that culture filtrates obtained from five wood-destroying fungi growing on glucose media were all able to solubilize the preservative components from copper-chromium-arsenate treated sawdust. The solubilization of arsenic and chromium increased as the pH of the culture filtrate decreased, but there was no clear relationship between pH and copper solubilization.

Chou et al. [26] confirmed that a similar phenomenon occurs when timber which has been treated with copper-chromium-arsenate is exposed directly to attack by wood-destroying fungi. The fungi studied were *Poria vaillantii, Poria monticola, Coniophora cerebella, Lentinus lepideus,* and *Lenzites trabea. Pinus sylvestris* veneers, which had been treated with different concentrations of copper-chromium-arsenate, were exposed to fungal attack for four weeks and the timber weight losses at the end of this period were noted. The veneers were then ground and extracted with cold water. The pH and titratable acid content of the water extracts were found, and the loss of copper, chromium, and arsenic from the veneers was calculated. The pH of the water extract from untreated timber decreased as decay proceeded, while the change in pH of the treated wood depended on the decay fungus and preservative concentration. With the *Poria* sp., the drop in pH of the water extracts from timber treated with the lower concentrations of copper-chromium-arsenate was similar to or greater than for untreated wood. In all other cases, there was a rise in the pH during exposure to the fungus. Acids were produced in treated and untreated veneers by all the fungi except *L. lepideus,* even when no decay occurred. Analysis of the veneers after exposure to the fungi showed that the fungi had solubilized one or more of the components of the copper-chromium-arsenate from the treated veneers, which were both sound and decayed. The amount of copper solubilized from veneers treated with a 0.5 percent solution of copper-chromium-arsenate ranged from 0 percent for *L. lepideus* to 50 percent for *L. trabea;* of chromium, from 0 percent for *C. cerebella* to 40 percent for *P. vaillantii;* and of arsenic, from 0 percent for *L. lepideus* to 50 percent for *P. vaillantii.* There was no obvious relationship between the solubilization of the three elements, and the mechanism of solubilization was not established. However, copper-chromium-arsenates are soluble in acid, and since brown-rot fungi produce large amounts of organic acid, this would seem to be an obvious mechanism. On the other hand, *C. cerebella,* which produces the most acid of the above fungi during decay, was found to be one of the weakest solubilizing fungi. It would appear, therefore, that something more than acid production is involved in mobilization of the copper-chromium-arsenate. Possible alternative solubilizing or complexing agents include amino-acids and their derivatives [80,114]. The mechanism of solubilization will almost certainly depend on the decay fungus and the concentration of preservative. However, this work did demonstrate that water-insoluble copper-chromium-arsenates are solubilized by wood-destroying fungi. The next stage in the work was to determine whether the preservative entered the fungi.

The combined electron miscroscope microanalyzer was used to study the location of copper, chromium, and arsenic in treated veneers exposed to attack by *P. monticola*. In conjunction with normal transmission electron microscopy, this instrument allows elemental analysis of spots as small as 0.1 micron in thin-sectioned material. Copper and chromium were found to be completely removed from some wood cell walls adjacent to fungal hyphae, confirming the results of chemical analysis of decayed veneers. Also, copper, chromium, and arsenic were all present in the fungal hyphae. There were considerable variations in the quantities and ratios of the elements in each cell, but average figures were approximately 1% w/w for each element. This suggests strongly that mobilization followed by adsorption into the cells is the way in which the copper-chromium-arsenate acts.

Electron-microscopic examination of hyphae of *P. monticola* and *P. vaillantii* growing in treated and untreated timber [26] showed that the copper-chromium-arsenate caused progressive changes in cell structure which were not noted in the hyphae of untreated wood. There was a decrease in the density of ribosomes and other cell organelles such as endoplasmic reticula and mitochondria. This was followed by plasmolysis, coagulation of cytoplasm with disappearance of organelles, and finally by cell lysis.

From this work, Chou *et al.* [26] suggested that copper-chromium-arsenates are first solubilized by wood-destroying fungi, then the preservative penetrates the fungus cell and acts as a fungistat or fungicide by reacting with essential cell constituents. The actual toxicants were not determined, but probably consist of various complexes of copper, chromium, and arsenic.

The observation that there is no clarification of microfibrils around bore holes in treated wood exposed to *P. vaillantii,* whereas there is clarification in untreated wood, suggests that extracellular enzyme inhibition may also play a part in the mode of action of the preservative [26].

Other waterborne preservatives. Boron compounds and fluorides are nonspecific general toxicants but, to the author's knowledge, no work has been published on their mode of action. When these compounds are used in conjunction with copper-containing preservatives, it is probable that they complement the copper component rather than combine with it as does arsenic. The mode of action of zinc is similar to that of copper, but less effective.

5.2.3 Tolerance to fungicides

The initial stage in evaluating a potential wood preservative is to determine its fungicidal activity against pure cultures of several wood-destroying fungi. The threshold concentrations so obtained for a fungicide generally vary widely with the species, and also the strain, of the attacking fungus [29,30,38,48,92,93,117]. Tolerant species or strains are those which require considerably more toxicant to prevent attack than the other test fungi. Their practical importance depends on the frequency with which they occur in nature, and also on whether they exhibit the same degree of tolerance under field conditions as they do in laboratory tests. Tolerance in the laboratory is not always equal to tolerance in the field because the laboratory test generally provides optimum conditions for the fungus and therefore a more severe test for the fungicide [69].

The remainder of this section will consider some of the more important species of tolerant fungi, their practical importance, and some mechanisms of tolerance.

5.2.3.1 Preservative-tolerant fungi and their practical importance

The list of fungi which have been shown to be tolerant to one or more preservatives in laboratory tests is extensive. Table 5.1 shows wood-destroying fungi known to be tolerant to the more important wood-preservative components. The strains of fungi have not been included because in most cases the species can be regarded as generally tolerant. In any test work, however, it is essential to note the strain of fungus used, as this will often govern the degree of preservative tolerance.

Generally, as the number of toxic components in a preservative increases, the number of tolerant fungal species decreases. The reason for this is that the various components inhibit or kill fungi in different ways. Therefore, a fungus must possess mechanisms of tolerance to each toxicant in a multicomponent preservative if it is to be tolerant to the preservative. Thus, very few fungi are tolerant to creosote, a mixture of several hundred chemicals. Similarly, multisalt waterborne preservatives such as copper-chromium-arsenates are more effective than copper or copper-chromates.

The frequency with which the fungi listed in Table 5.1 attack untreated wood in different environments is quite variable. *Lentinus lepideus, Lenzites trabea, Poria radiculosa, Poria xantha,* and *Poria monticola* all cause considerable decay in poles, posts, and ties in ground contact [40,44,94]. *Poria vaillantii, Coniophora cerebella,* and *Poria cocos* also cause decay in timbers in ground contact [40].

Timber in boats, automobiles, and other transportation items is often attacked by *L. trabea, P. monticola, Polystictus versicolor, P. xantha,* and *Daedalea quercina* [40]. Finally, building timbers are most frequently attacked by *L. trabea, Poria incrassata, P. vaillantii, P. xantha,* and *C. cerebella* [23,40,99].

TABLE 5.1

Fungal Species Tolerant to the More Important Wood-Preservative Constituents

Preservative	Fungus	Reference
Creosote	Lentinus lepideus	29,117
	Polystictus tulipiferae	29
	Poria radiculosa	60
Pentachlorophenol	Fomes applanatus	38
	Fomes subroseus	29
	Lenzites trabea	117
	Polystictus tulipiferae	29
	Polystictus versicolor	21
Copper naphthenate	Fomes subroseus	38
	Polystictus tulipiferae	29
	Poria cocus	116
	Poria incrassata	29,38
	Poria monticola	117
	Poria vaillantii	38
	Poria xantha	56
Tributyltin oxide	Polystictus versicolor	95
Copper-8-quinolinolate	Polystictus adustus	29
	Polystictus tulipiferae	29
	Poria xantha	29
Copper or acid copper chromate	Coniophora cerebella (puteana)	7,21
	Daedalea quercina	29
	Polystictus tulipiferae	29
	Poria incrassata	29
	Poria monticola	29
	Poria vaillantii	29
Arsenate	Lenzites trabea	7
	Poria vaillantii	30
Copper-chromium-arsenate	Poria incrassata	31
	Poria vaillantii	30
Zinc or chromated zinc chloride	Coniophora cerebella (puteana)	23
	Daedalea quercina	29
	Fomes subroseus	29
	Lenzites trabea	93
	Polystictus tulipiferae	29
	Poria incrassata	29
	Poria monticola	29
	Poria vaillantii	30
Fluoride	Lenzites trabea	92
Fluor-chromium-arsenate-dinitrophenol	Fomes subroseus	29
	Lenzites trabea	29

The widespread occurrence of many of these tolerant species has led to the withdrawal of some preservatives and the requirement for relatively high loadings of others. Sufficient creosote must be used to control *L. lepideus* and *P. radiculosa,* although considerably smaller quantities would control other wood-destroying fungi. Failure to do this has led to the failure of many poles and posts [40,60]. Similarly high, and consequently uneconomic, loadings of copper, zinc, and their chromated salts must be used to prevent fungal attack of timber in ground contact by tolerant *Poria* sp., *L. trabea,* and *C. cerebella.* However, the situation is different with the copper-chrome-arsenates. Although fungi which are tolerant to these preservatives in the laboratory occur frequently in untreated timber in service, retentions of preservative below levels needed for complete protection of wood in laboratory tests will give excellent protection to wood in service [31].   This is because the conditions in laboratory tests are highly favorable to the fungi [69] as there is a large external food source and only a small amount of preservative in relation to the amount of fungus. In service, however, this situation is normally reversed as there is a small external food source and a large amount of preservative in relation to the amount of fungus. Unnecessarily high retentions of other preservatives are probably used as a result of laboratory tolerance tests, particularly in wood out of ground contact, but more work must be undertaken to prove whether less preservative would give adequate protection.

It can be seen that although many fungi are tolerant to preservatives in laboratory tests, the practical significance of this tolerance is highly variable. The frequency with which the tolerant fungus occurs in nature is of prime importance. Other critical factors are the cost of a preservative, which determines whether a sufficient quantity can be economically introduced into wood to control a tolerant fungus, and also the tolerance of the fungus in actual service compared with its tolerance in laboratory tests. Each of these variables must be evaluated before the significance of tolerant fungi can be determined.

5.2.3.2 Mechanisms of preservative tolerance

Many mechanisms can account for the differences in tolerance of fungi to toxicants. Ashida [6] listed the following theoretically possible factors, which were based on suggestions by Davis [34].

1. Formation of, or increase in, activity of metabolic pathways bypassing the inhibited reaction.

2. Increased production of a metabolite which inactivates the fungicide, possibly by binding with it.

3. Increased production of the enzyme inhibited by the fungicide.

4. Decreased requirement for a product of the inhibited metabolic system.

5. Formation of an altered enzyme, with decreased affinity for the fungicide or with increased relative affinity for the substrate as compared with the fungicide.

6. Increased destruction of the fungicide.

7. Decreased permeability of the cell (or of subcellular structures) to the fungicide.

Little work has been published on the mechanism of tolerance of wood-destroying fungi to wood preservatives, but there is evidence for the operation of some of these mechanisms.

Lyr [75] suggested that fungal oxidases such as laccase, tyrosinase, and peroxidase may be responsible for the tolerance of some wood-destroying fungi to dinitrophenol and pentachlorophenol. The oxidases detoxify the phenols by oxidation. This work was carried out with extracts from fungi. It has not yet been demonstrated that this form of detoxification occurs in treated wood. Such a mechanism would be an example of increased destruction of the fungicide by tolerant fungi.

In experiments with *Coniophora puteana,* it was shown that a considerable portion of pentachlorophenol was removed by the fungus from treated pine blocks exposed for 52 days [110]. These blocks, however, did not contain a toxic loading of the preservative, and the fate of the penta was not determined.

Increased production of metabolites which inactivate the fungicide may explain copper tolerance in wood-destroying fungi [63,69,88,116]. A reduction of the pH of the substrate is closely associated with copper tolerance. It has been suggested that low pH's prevent copper from chelating with amino acids so that enzymes are not deactivated and fungal growth is not stopped [58]. Alternatively, extracellular precipitation of copper as metabolically inert copper oxalate [88] or copper sulfide [69] may account for tolerance in some fungi. It is probable that both of these mechanisms have a part to play in the tolerance of fungi to copper.

Extracellular precipitation of copper by tolerant fungi does not occur when copper is applied in copper-chromium-arsenate preservatives [26]. In this case, copper, chromium, and arsenic are absorbed by the fungal hyphae. The form and distribution of the elements, however, have not yet been identified.

Before more definite conclusions can be drawn on the mechanisms of tolerance in wood-destroying fungi, further work on the mode of action of fungicides is necessary. Only then will it be possible to ascribe tolerance mechanisms to the various types listed by Ashida [6].

Another phenomenon which may be very important in explaining decay of treated wood in the field is preservative detoxification by non-wood-destroying fungi and bacteria. *Coprinus micaceus* and *Fusarium oxysporium* are regularly associated in the decay of birch and poplar fence posts treated with fluor-chrome-arsenate-dinitrophenol preservative, although only the former fungus decays wood [77]. Toxicity tests on the preservative and its components showed that *Coprinus* is more readily killed than *Fusarium*. Thus, it was suggested that *Fusarium* is able to decrease the toxicity of the preservative and facilitate attack by *Coprinus*. Later work showed that *Fusarium* reduced dinitrophenol to less toxic compounds [78].

Mixed microorganisms found on creosoted piles in sea water have been shown to metabolize creosote, particularly the naphthalene and phenanthrene components [36]. The bacterium *Pseudomonas creosotensis,* isolated from a similar source, is able to utilize the neutral fractions of creosote [36]. The regular occurrence of the fungus *Hormodendrum resinae* in creosoted timber suggests that it too is able to metabolize creosote [39]. However, no experiments have been carried out successfully to determine the decrease in toxicity of creosote to wood-destroying fungi after exposure of the wood to these wood-inhabiting fungi and bacteria.

Duncan and Deverall [39] exposed wood which had been treated with either ammoniacal copper arsenite, fluor-chrome-arsenate-dinitrophenol, creosote, or pentachlorophenol first to a non-wood-destroying fungus and then to a wood-destroying fungus. In several cases, exposure to a non-wood-destroying fungus predisposed the preservative-treated blocks to attack by the wood-destroying fungus. Losses of pentachlorophenol and of arsenic from fluor-chrome-arsenate-dinitrophenol treated wood were noted after the first exposure period. Some of the conclusions of this work have been contested [68], but it certainly demonstrated that wood preservatives can be affected by fungi without any decay occurring. Further proof of this was obtained by Unligil [110], who showed that *Trichoderma viride* can remove large quantities of penta from treated wood without causing decay.

Wood-destroying fungi also can affect a preservative without causing any decay. Water-leaching of copper-chromium-arsenate treated blocks after exposure to *Lenzites trabea* made them susceptible to decay by *Lenzites* on reexposure, whereas leached blocks not preexposed to Lenzites were not decayed [32]. This is due to the solubilizing effect of *Lenzites* on the preservative components which can be removed by water-leaching after exposure to the fungus [26,69].

However, the importance of these detoxification mechanisms in the field is not known as yet. Similarly, virtually nothing is known about the role of organism synergism and inhibition in determining preservative effectiveness in complex environments such as the soil. These are areas where much valuable research could be initiated.

5.3 Alteration or Removal of Wood Constituents

The addition of toxicants to timber is not the only chemical method available for controlling attack by wood-destroying and wood-inhabiting fungi. An alternate, although at the moment generally more expensive, method is treatment of timber with chemical which either alter the wood structure so that it cannot be utilized as food by the fungus, or which remove wood constituents essential for fungal growth. Although most of the work on wood modification has been aimed at increasing the dimensional stability of wood, the greatly increased awareness of the importance of environmental pollution with toxic chemicals makes wood modification an attractive method for preservation.

Thiamine is a minor constituent of wood which is essential for the growth of most wood-destroying Basidiomycetes. Removal of thiamine from wood, first described by Baechler [9], is probably the most practicable of the wood modification methods now available from a commercial point of view. It is recommended only for wood to be used out of ground contact.

Destruction of thiamine can be achieved by heating wood which has been made alkaline. Pressure treatment with aqueous ammonia [9,55], sodium hydroxide [55], or ammonia gas [55] followed by heating at approximately 100°C for one to two hours have all been used successfully in the laboratory.

Test panels treated with aqueous ammonia and then heated have been exposed out of ground contact for eight years, and at the end of that period were sound, whereas untreated panels were severely decayed [49]. Panels placed in ground contact, however, were rapidly decayed, as would be expected because the fungi had an external source of thiamine.

Recent work by Highley [55] suggests that thiamine destruction may not be the only reason for the resistance of alkali-treated wood to decay. Addition of thiamine to alkali-treated blocks before exposure to decay fungi did not always lead to the expected decay susceptibility. It is possible that at least some of the decay resistance in treated blocks is due to modification of the major components of the wood, or to the formation of toxicants in the wood. Further work will be required, therefore, to extablish that dethiaminization is the protective mechanism operative in the alkaline treatment of wood at elevated temperatures. Even if this is not the case, the process remains an attractive one for the protection of wood out of ground contact—particularly if it can be carried out economically with ammonia gas, which would penetrate many species impermeable to liquid preservatives.

Baechler [9] has also suggested that deactivation of some of the essential trace elements which occur in wood could also be used to control fungal attack of wood out of ground contact. The addition of several chelating compounds has been investigated [107]. The only one to give protection against *Poria monticola* and *Polystictus versicolor* at low concentrations was dimethylglyoxime. No field tests using this approach have been reported, and it is unlikely that such a control method could have wide application because of the difficulty of excluding trace elements from treated timber.

Esterification of the hydroxyl groups in cellulose to make them inaccessible to cellulose enzymes has been used successfully to protect cotton from attack by fungi, and similar methods have been tried with wood. The addition of side groups to the cellulose prevents contact between the cellulase enzyme and the wood substrate, thus preventing breakdown. Acetylation of wood with acetic anhydride in an inert solvent gives protection against decay fungi with no decrease in the impact strength of the wood [51], but the high cost of this process has prevented its general use.

Cyanoethylation of wood with acrylonitrile and ammonia is another method that has been used to protect small wood samples [9]. However, this form of treatment has not been fully developed because it leads to a decrease in the strength of treated wood, and protection is highly dependent on the reaction conditions.

Numerous other studies have been published on the modification of wood cellulose to impart decay resistance and dimension stability, but these have all been either more expensive or less successful than acetylation.

Another wood-modification process that is claimed to prevent attack by wood-destroying fungi is bromination [70]. This method involves treatment of wood with a bromide solution and chlorine in the presence of catalysts. Liberated bromine is said to react with lignin to yield durable, nonflammable wood. To date, this process has not been developed commercially.

5.4 Moisture Control

In order to decay wood, fungi require air and water. Control of the environment so that wood is always kept either dry or waterlogged (so that air is excluded) represents the simplest available form of control method for preventing decay. Keeping wood dry also represents the oldest control method known to man. In practice, wood with a moisture content below 20 percent will not decay (the moisture content of wood exposed only to atmospheric water vapor normally ranges from 8 to 15 percent), and wood immersed in, or sprayed with water will decay only very slowly. The practical application of these principles will now be discussed.

5.4.1 Wet storage of wood before conversion

Ponding—the storage of logs under water—has been practiced for many years in several countries around the world. The success of this method in preventing attack of wood by stain and decay fungi has led to the development of continuous water spraying for use in areas where ponding is not practicable [52,67]. Experiments in the United States with birch logs showed that veneer quality was unaffected after a 2-year storage of the logs under water or 6 months under continuous water spray [52]. Longer storage periods were not investigated.

Similar storage practices have been adopted with great success by pulp and paper mills [25,81,113], particularly in the southern part of the United States where losses due to fungal attack can be very severe. Storage of pine roundwood in water or under continuous spray prevented a significant loss of wood density, pulp yield, pulp strength, and tall-oil and turpentine production over a 12-month storage period [25, 113]. Considerable reductions in all of these properties would occur in dry storage over a similar time period.

The results of water spraying in wood-chip piles are less certain. In one experiment, little or no difference was noted between a conventional dry chip pile of gum and one wetted during construction and sprinkled with water during the storage period [19]. It is doubtful, however, whether the pile was properly wetted. In another study, wetting a pile of southern pine chips during construction impeded reduction in tear strength, but effects on byproducts loss were not evaluated [102]. Finally, Djerf and Volkman [35] have shown that water spraying of chip piles may be economically advantageous for periods of a month or less, but over longer periods no advantage over dry storage is obtained. Further research on the variables involved in spray protection of chip piles is required before this method can be adopted commercially.

5.4.2 Construction methods

Wood is an excellent construction material because of its strength, insulating properties, aesthetic appeal, and the ease with which it can be fabricated. Its major drawback, however, is that it can be attacked by fungi and insects when it becomes moist. Thus, builders, many hundreds of years ago, began to use naturally durable timbers in house building and also learned to keep wood separated from the earth and as dry as possible. In Europe, stone foundations were frequently used to raise wooden structural timbers above the soil, and in the United States houses were built a foot or more above the ground to allow good ventilation beneath the flooring timbers. These simple precautions, together with the use of roof overhangs which channeled water away from the house, were suffi-cient to almost completely prevent decay of wood. Many wood houses which were built several centuries ago are still in excellent condition.

In recent years, the supply of naturally durable wood for house building has almost disappeared, and the fashion in house design in some countries has changed considerably. In the United States, most houses now contain wood close to the ground on solid foundations instead of on piers. Heat-ing and cooling systems in houses have also become more sophisticated and efficient so that the risk of condensation on wood in houses has greatly increased, particularly when moisture barriers are installed in-correctly. Consequently, some of the wood used in houses must be pressure treated with preservative if decay is to be avoided. This applies to all wood in direct soil contact and also to structural timbers in con-tact with concrete slabs or foundations which are in contact with soil.

The remainder of the wood in houses can be protected without recourse to chemical control by the correct application of two rules. Failure to obey these rules, however, can lead to rapid attack of wood and, for this reason, many people advocate—with some justification—preservative treatment of virtually all wood used in construction.

In using wood as a building material, the first essential is to use prop-erly seasoned, undecayed wood. When wood is placed in a building, it should have a moisture content below 20 percent. Properly air- or kiln-dried wood will meet this requirement. If it is impractical to keep wood dry after it is seasoned and before it is placed in a building, a super-ficial treatment with a water repellent and/or preservative should be given to provide short-term protection.

Once wood has been installed in the house, the second essential is to keep it dry. Woodwork close to the ground should be protected from condensed water that has evaporated from the soil by ensuring that the building site is well drained. Vapor-resistant covers (4-mil polyethylene) can be placed under concrete slab floors and on the soil under basement-less houses to reduce the risk of decay due to moisture movement from the soil. There should be sufficient vents in foundation walls, roof eaves, and roof gables to prevent moist air from accumulating in crawl spaces and attics. The diffusion of water from the soil through the foundations into wood sills can be prevented by the insertion of moisture barriers under-neath the sills. Cold-water pipes should be insulated so that water will not condense on them and moisten wood in walls or floors. [5].

External woodwork can be partially protected by overhanging roofs and the proper use of flashing. Window units can be protected by careful maintainance of paintwork and putty, although pretreatment with a water-repellent preservative is a much surer method of preventing decay in these structures. Large doors should be built to shed water, and accumulation of water at the base of doors should be avoided by grading the thresholds. Leaks should be avoided in gutters and roofs, around showers, bathtubs, sinks, washing machines, and finally in any water pipes. If these, for the most part, elementary rules of construction are followed, wood will give many years of service with a minimum amount of maintainence. However, in the absence of any preservative treatment, this maintainence must be continual. Vents must be kept clear, paint films on joinery must be kept intact, and any leaks in gutters or pipe work must be rapidly repaired. The financial savings made by taking these few precautions will be well worth the effort involved, and the oldest and cheapest control methods in wood preservation will continue to be successful.

5.4.3 Water repellents, plastics, and resins

Control of decay by the physical exclusion of water from wood has received much attention. Conventional water repellents based on waxes and resins or stearates reduce the rate at which liquid water enters wood and have no effect on the movement of water vapor. Thus, they have only a marginal effect in preventing decay in wood exposed to moisture for long periods. Wooden boxes treated with water repellent alone and exposed to severe decay conditons in the southern United States had a service life of 7.3 years, compared with 5 years for untreated boxes [112]. Water repellents can, however, provide useful protection for wood exposed to intermittent wetting or to wetting for only a short period, *e.g.,* during construction. Plastic coatings have been used successfully in the absence of any fungicide to prevent decay and to reduce maintainance costs for millwork. This form of treatment, however, is of limited use and is susceptible to mechanical damage. An alternative and more expensive method of applying plastics is to introduce monomers into the wood and polymerize them *in situ* to give a plastic sheet in the wood. Various plastics will prevent decay [12], but the cost of such treatments prohibits their general use.

Impregnation of wood with cell-wall-penetrating phenol-formaldehyde resins followed by drying and heat curing prevents decay by reducing the amount of water that can be absorbed to below the level required for fungal attack [104,105]. Cross linking wood with formaldehyde prevents decay in the same way [105]. However, as in the case of impregnation with plastics, the cost of treatment limits the use of these processes to high-cost speciality items.

5.5 Biological Control

The idea of using one organism to control attack by another organism is not new in the biological sciences. In fact, it has become a practical reality in the control of some insect pests which attack such diverse plants as cucumber and sugar cane. However, the development of fungal control methods for the prevention of decay in wood has not been successful to date.

Several workers have found that *Trichoderma* sp. inhibit the growth of wood-destroying fungi [50,72,98]. In one series of experiments [97], freshly cut ends of birch logs, 4 feet in length, were sprayed with a spore suspension of *Trichoderma viride* and two weeks later sprayed with a spore and mycelial suspension of *Polyporus adustus*. The logs were then stored from May until late November and, at the end of this period, fungal isolations were attempted. *Trichoderma viride* almost completely prevented colonization by the wood-destroying fungus. Bolts sprayed only with *Polyporus adustus* yielded many isolates of that fungus, and control bolts sprayed with water yielded a variety of wood-destroying and wood-staining fungi. Earlier experiments by the same author [98] gave less successful control, and in some bolts unidentified Basidiomycetes had caused attack in *Trichoderma*-sprayed bolts.

It has been suggested that *Trichoderma* inhibits the attack of wood-destroying fungi by removing some structural carbohydrates from the wood which are necessary for rapid colonization and initiation of decay by wood-destroying fungi. The mechanism does not appear to involve antibiotic production [61].

An alternative form of biological control involving antibiotic production has been developed by Ricard *et al.* [90,91]. Incipient decay in Douglas-fir poles caused by *Poria carbonica* was controlled by artificial inoculation with *Scytalidium* sp., FY strain. A dependable inoculant was found to be essential; other strains of the same species of fungus were found to be ineffective. Although the method has not yet been fully developed and tested, the results do show promise for the eventual goal of developing biological control of rot in poles in service.

If dependable inoculation techniques can be developed with non-wood-destroying fungi which inhibit growth of all wood-destroying fungi likely to attack the protected wood, then biological control will be a valuable tool in wood preservation, particularly as it does not involve the use of any toxic chemicals. Inoculum dependability linked with broad spectrum activity has yet to be demonstrated in service tests, however.

5.6 The Future

This chapter has demonstrated that by the correct selection of control method and timber species, deterioration of timber because of the action of wood-destroying and wood-inhabiting fungi can be virtually eliminated. The fact that vast amounts of timber are decayed or discolored shows that in the immediate future, the first requirement in wood preservation is education of timber producers and users so that they will ask for, and use, the appropriate control methods. The usage of timber and timber products must increase in the future because, unlike most other construction materials, timber can be regenerated. However, as long as the layman associates timber with twisted and swollen millwork and decayed porches and floors, this increase in usage will be jeopardized.

Along with education, there is also a need for further research into control methods. Considerable effort is now being devoted to the production of composite wood materials such as plywood, particleboard, and wood–plastic combinations. The methods for controlling the attack of wood-destroying and wood-inhabiting fungi in these materials are generally the same as those used for protecting solid timber. While many of these methods are quite suitable for wood composite materials, more emphasis could be placed on research into control methods designed specifically for wood composites—the development of effective fungicidal glue line additives is one such method.

The fungicidal chemicals available commercially for wood preservation are relatively cheap and highly effective when correctly selected for the end-use of the timber. However, doubts have been cast about continued use of many of these chemicals because of possible decreased availability in the future and, in some cases, because of high mammalian toxicity. Thus, the search is continuing for new chemicals which can be used as wood preservatives. It is most likely that future wood preservatives will be based on oil-soluble fungicides of low mammalian toxicity and possibly a limited spectrum of activity, so that two or more fungicides will be used in a single preservative. New formulations, however, are unlikely to displace the present range of preservatives for at least 10 years. In the meantime, more research is required on the mode of action of the presently available preservatives so that their limitations can be more fully understood and possibly overcome. Also, more work is required on the distribution and economic importance of tolerant and nontolerant wood-destroying and wood-inhabiting fungi in different environments.

Possibly the greatest step that remains to be taken in timber products protection is the development of a commercially feasible wood-modification process in the gaseous or vapor phase. Such a process would free for treatment many commerical timber species that are impermeable to conventional treatments. It should be remembered, however, that this requirement has been recognized for many years, and the quest for such a process may be similar to the alchemists' search for a method for changing base metals into gold. Pending this breakthrough, further development of liquid-phase wood-modification techniques may yield promising results.

Finally, treatment of the living tree has always seemed an attractive method of preserving timber, particularly to the layman. Little research has been carried out on this type of treatment, partly because of the cost and also because of the lack of control that can be exercised. With the recent development of relatively cheap systemic fungicides, further research into this type of treatment may be warranted. Both short-term protection against wood-inhabiting fungi and longer term protection against wood-destroying fungi would be desirable end-points for such research.

REFERENCES

1. Albert, A. 1951. *Selective Toxicity with Special Reference to Chemotherapy*. Methuen, London.
2. Albert, A., Gibson, M.I. and Rubbo, S.D. 1953. "The influence of chemical constitution on antibacterial activity. VI. The bacterial action of 8-hydroxyquinoline (oxine)." *Brit. J. Exptl. Pathol.* 34:119–30.
3. Albert, A., Rubbo, S.D., Goldacre, R.J. and Balfour, B.G. 1947. "Influence of chemical constitution on antibacterial activity. III. A study of 8-hydroxyquinoline (oxine) and related compounds." *Brit. J. Exptl. Pathol.* 28:69–87.
4. Aldridge, W.N. 1958. "The biochemistry of organotin compounds: Trialkyltins and oxidative phosphorylation." *Biochem. J.* 69:367–76.
5. Anonymous. 1969. "Wood decay in houses, how to prevent and control it." USDA Home and Garden Bull. No. 73.
6. Ashida, J. 1965. "Adaptation of fungi to metal toxicants." *Phytopathol. Rev.* 3:153–74.
7. Baechler, R.H. 1941. "Resistance to leaching and decay protection of various precipitates formed in wood by double diffusion." *Proc., Am. Wood-Preservers' Assoc.* 37:23–31.
8. Baechler, R.H. 1953. "Toxicity of various fractions of low temperature coal-tar creosote." *Proc., Am. Wood-Preservers' Assoc.* 49:12–17.
9. Baechler, R. H. 1959. "Improving wood's durability through chemical modification." *Forest Prod. J.* 9:166–71.
10. Baechler, R.H. 1967. "Application and use of fungicides in wood preservation." In *Fungicides*, Vol. I. (D.C. Torgeson, ed.). Academic Press, New York and London. 425–461.
11. Baechler, R.H. and Roth, H.G. 1962. "Effect of petroleum carrier on rate of loss of pentachlorophenol from treated stakes." *Forest Prod. J.* 12:187–90.
12. Barnes, H.M. and Choong, E.T. 1968. "Decay resistance of selected wood-plastic combinations." Louisiana State Univ. Wood Utilization Note No. 8.
13. Barth, M. 1896. *Die Blattfallkrankheit der Reben und ihre Bekampfung.* 4th ed. Gebweiler.
14. Bateman, E. and Henningsen, C. 1923. "Theory on the mechanism of protection of wood by preservatives. IV. Experiments with hydrocarbons." *Proc., Am. Wood-Preservers' Assoc.* 19:136–45.
15. Bateman, E. and Henningsen, C. 1925. "Theory on the mechanism of the protection of wood by preservatives: Toxic principles of creosote." *Proc., Am. Wood-Preservers' Assoc.* 21:22–28.

16. Bland, D.E. 1942. "A study of the toxicity of Australian vertical retort creosote oils to *Lentinus lepideus, Polystictus versicolor*, and Madison 517." *J. Coun. Sci. Ind. Res. Aust.* 15:135–46.

17. Blew, J.O. Jr. 1964. "Comparison of wood preservatives in stake tests. (1964 Progress Report)." U.S. Forest Serv., Forest Prod. Lab. Res. Note FPL–02.

18. Block, S.S. 1956. "Examination of the activity of 8-quinolinol to fungi." *J. Appl. Microbiol.* 4:183–86.

19. Bois, P.J., Flick, R.A. and Gilmer, W.B. 1962. "A study of outside storage of hardwood pulp chips in the southeast." *Tappi,* 45:609–18.

20. Boulton, S.B. 1844. "The antiseptic treatment of timber." *Proc. Inst. Civil Eng.* 78:12–74.

21. British Standards Institution. 1961. "Method of test for the toxicity of wood preservatives to fungi." British Standard 838.

22. Carr, D.R. 1959. "The effectiveness of boron as a wood preservative." *Timber Technol.* 67(2242):335, 337–38.

23. Cartwright, K. St. G. and Findlay, W.P.K. 1958. *Decay of Timber and Its Prevention.* H.M. Stationery Office, London.

24. Chapman, W. 1817. *Treatise on the Preservation of Timber.* London.

25. Chesley, K.G., Hair, J.C. and Swartz, J.N. 1956. "Underwater storage of southern pine pulpwood." *Tappi* 39(9):609–14.

26. Chou, C. K., Levi, M.P. and Preston, R.D. 1972. (In press.)

27. Clarke, J.G. and Edwards, W.G.H. 1962. "Acenaphthene derivatives and c-mitosis." *Nature* 193:1072–73.

28. Corden, M.E. 1969. "Aromatic compounds." In *Fungicides,* Vol. 2 (D.C. Torgeson, ed.). Academic Press, New York and London. 477–529.

29. Cowling, E.B. 1957. "The relative preservative tolerances of 18 wood-destroying fungi." *Forest Prod. J.* 7:355–59.

30. Da Costa, E.W.B. 1959. "Abnormal resistance of *Poria vaillantii* strains to copper-chrome-arsenate wood preservatives." *Nature* 183:910–11.

31. Da Costa, E.W.B. and Kerruish, R.M. 1964. "Tolerance of *Poria* sp. to copper based wood preservatives." *Forest Prod. J.* 14:106–12.

32. Da Costa, E.W.B. and Osborne, L.D. 1968. "Laboratory evaluations of wood preservatives. II. Effect of timber substrate on the performance of a copper-chrome-arsenic preservative." *Holzforschung* 22:81–88.

33. Da Costa, E.W.B., Johanson, R. and Osborne, L.D. 1969. "Laboratory evaluation of wood preservatives. III. Effectiveness of Australian vertical retort creosotes against decay in relation to phenolic content." *Holzforschung* 23:99–107.

34. Davis, B.D. 1957. "Physiological mechanisms responsible for drug resistance." In *Drug Resistance in Microorganisms* (G.E.W. Wolstenholme and C.M. O'Connor, eds.). Churchill, London.

35. Djerf, A.C. and Volkman, D.A. 1969. "Experiences with water spray wood storage." *Tappi* 52:1861–64.

36. Drisko, R.W. and O'Niell, T.B. 1966. "Microbiological metabolism of creosote." *Forest Prod. J.* 16(7):31–34.

37. Duncan, C.G. 1952. "Evaluating wood preservatives by soil block tests. 5 Lignite-tar and oil-tar creosotes." *Proc., Am. Wood-Preservers' Assoc.* 48:99–104.

38. Duncan, C.G. 1958. "Studies of the methodology of soil block testing." U.S. Forest Serv., Forest Prod. Lab. Rept. No. 2114.

39. Duncan, C.G. and Deverall, F.J. 1964. "Degradation of wood preservatives by fungi." *J. Appl. Microbiol.* 12(1):57–62.

40. Duncan, C.G. and Lombard, F.F. 1965. "Fungi associated with principal decays in wood products in the United States." U.S. Forest Serv., Forest Prod. Lab. Rept. No. WO–4.

41. Dunleavy, J.A. and McQuire, A.J. 1970. "The effect of water storage on the cell structure of Sitka spruce (*Picea sitchensis*) with reference to its permeability and preservation." *J. Inst. Wood Sci.* 5(2)26:20–28.

42. Durkee, A.B. 1958. "Fungitoxicity of some substituted pyridines and quinolines related to 8-quinolinol (oxine)." *J. Agr. Food Chem.* 6:194–96.

43. Ellwood, E.L. and Ecklund, B.A. 1959. "Bacterial attack of pine logs in pond storage." *Forest Prod. J.,* 9:283–92.

44. Eslyn, W.E. 1970. "Utility pole decay. II. Basidiomycetes associated with decay in poles." *Wood Sci. Tech.* 4(2):97–103.

45. Finger, G.C., Reed, F.H. and Tehon, L.R. 1955. "Aromatic fluorine compounds as fungicides." Illinois State Geol. Surv. Circ. No. 199. 1–15. (*Chemical Abstracts* 50:9312. 1956.

46. Finholt, R.W., Weeks, M. and Hathaway, C. 1952. "New theory on wood preservation." *Ind. Eng. Chem.* 44:101–105.

47. Fougerouse, M. 1970. "Field tests, in different climates, of some wood preservatives." Third Report. Note Tech. Centre Technique Forestier Tropical No. 6–3.

48. Gersonde, M. 1958. "Uber die Giftempfindlichkeit verschiedener Stamme holzzerstorender Pilze." *Holz als Roh- und Werkstoff* 16(6):221–26.

49. Gjovik, L.R. and Baechler, R.H. 1968. "Field tests on wood dethiaminized for protection against decay." *Forest Prod. J.* 18(1):25–27.

50. Glaser, T., Tarocinski, E. and Bauza, J. 1959. "Study of the interaction of *D. brunneo-tingens* and the most important fungi accompanying it in the coffee brown discoloration of pine sawlogs." *Prace Inst. Tech. Drewna* 6(2):45–58. (*Forestry Abstracts* 22:5156. 1961.)

51. Goldstein, I.S., Jeroski, E.B., Lund, A.E., Wilson, J.F. and Weaver, J.W. 1961. "Acetylation of wood in lumber thickness." *Forest Prod. J.* 11:363–70.

52. Hansbrough, J.R. 1953. "Storage of northern hardwood logs and bolts." *Forest Prod. J.* 3(3):33–35,92.

53. Hartig, R. 1874. *Wichtige Krank heiten der Waldbaume.* Springer-Verlag, Berlin.

54. Hatfield, I. and Sakornbut, S.S. 1955. "Relationship of oil carriers to utility of pentachlorophenol." *Forest Prod. J.* 5:361–63.

55. Highley, T.L. 1970. "Decay resistance of four wood species treated to destroy thiamine." *Phytopathology* 60:1660–61.

56. Hirt, R.R. 1949. "An isolate of *Poria xantha* on media containing copper." *Phytopathology* 39:31–36.

57. Hof, T. 1969. "Review of literature concerning the evaluation of organotin compounds for the preservative treatment of wood." *J. Inst. Wood. Sci.* 4(5)23:19–28.

58. Horsfall, J.G. 1956. *Principles of Fungicidal Action.* Chronica Botanica, Waltham, Mass.

59. Horsfall, J.G. and Rich, S. 1953. "Differential action of compounds in spore germination and hyphal growth." *Phytopathology* 43:476.

60. Hudson, M.S. 1952. "*Poria radiculosa,* a creosote tolerant organism." *Forest Prod. J.* 2(2):73–74.

61. Hulme, M.A. and Shields, J.K. 1970. "Biological control of decay fungi in wood by competition for nonstructural carbohydrates." *Nature* 227(5255):300–301.

62. Hunt, G.M. and Garratt, G.A. 1967. *Wood Preservation.* 3d ed. McGraw-Hill Book Co., N.Y.

63. Ishii, Y. and Kawamura, H. 1967. "Transformation of copper salt by wood-decaying fungi." *J. Soc. Materials Sci. Japan* 16(168):741–45.

64. Jones, O.T.G. 1963. "The inhibition of bacteriochlorophyll biosynthesis in *Rhodopseudomonas spheroidu* by 8-hydroxyquinoline." *Biochem. J.* 88:335–43.

65. Kamesan, S. 1933. British patent 404,855.

66. Kelso, W.C., Behr, E.A. and Hill, R.E. 1955. "Pentachlorophenol gradients in pressure-treated wood under exposure to weather." *Forest Prod. J.* 5:369–77.

67. Lane, P.H. and Scheffer, T.C. 1960. "Water sprays protect hardwood logs from stain and decay." *Forest Prod. J.* 10:277–82.

68. Leutritz, J. 1965. "Biodegradability of pentachlorophenol as a possible source of depletion from treated wood." *Forest Prod. J.* 15:269–72.

69. Levi, M.P. 1969. "The mechanism of action of copper-chrome-arsenate preservatives against wood-destroying fungi." *Record, British Wood Preserving Assoc.* 113–27.

70. Lewin, M. 1964. U.S. patent 3,150,919.

71. Liese, W. and Karnop, G. 1968. "Attack on softwood by bacteria." *Holz als Roh- und Werkstoff* 26(6):202–208.

72. Lindgren, R.M. and Harvey, G.M. 1952. "Decay control and increased permeability in Southern pine sprayed with sodium fluoride solutions." *Forest Prod. J.* 2:250–56.

73. Lukens, R.J. 1968. "Fungitoxic action of non-metallic organic fungicides." In *Biodeterioration of Materials, Microbiological and Allied Aspects* (A.H. Walters and J.J. Elphick, eds.). Elsevier, Amsterdam, London, and New York. 486–97.

74. Lukens, R.J. 1969. "Heterocyclic nitrogen compounds." In *Fungicides,* Vol. 2 (D.C. Torgeson, ed.). Academic Press, New York and London. 395–445.

75. Lyr, H. 1962. "Detoxification of heartwood toxins and chlorophenols by higher fungi." *Nature* (London) 195:289–90.

76. Lyr, H. and Ziegler, H. 1959. "Die Wirkung von Pentachlorophenol auf den Stoffwechsel hoherer Pilze." *Phytopathol. Z.* 35:146–62.

77. Madhosingh, C. 1961(a). "Tolerance of some fungi to a water-soluble preservative and its components." *Forest Prod. J.* 11:20–22.

78. Madhosingh, C. 1961(b). "The metabolic detoxification of 2.4 dinitrophenol by *Fusarium oxysporium.*" *Can. J. Microbiol.* 7:553–67.

79. Marsh, P.B., Greathouse, G.A., Bollenbacher, K. and Butler, M.L. 1944. "Copper soaps as rotproofing agents on fabrics." *Ind. Eng. Chem.* 36:176–81.

80. Marten, E.A. and Leach, J.G. 1944. "Some factors influencing the solubility of cuprous oxide in relation to its toxicity as a fungicide." *Phytopathology* 34:459–70.

81. Mason, R.R., Muhonen, J.M., and Swartz, J.N. 1963. "Water sprayed storage of Southern pine pulpwood." *Tappi* 46:233–40.

82. McCallan, S.E.A. and Wilcoxon, F. 1936. "The action of fungus spores on bordeaux mixture." Contrib. *Boyce Thompson Inst.* 8:151–65.

83. McGrath, H. 1964. "Chemicals-plant disease control." *Agr. Chem.* 19(7):18–22; (8)22–27; (9):28–37.

84. Meyer, F.J. and Gooch, R. M. 1956. "The effect of oil carriers on the performance of treated wood." *Forest Prod. J.* 6:117–21.

85. Miller, L.P. 1969. "Mechanisms for reaching the site of action." In *Fungicides,* Vol. 2 (D.C. Torgeson, ed.). Academic Press, New York and London. 1–59.

86. Overton, E. 1899. "Uber die algemeinen osmotischen Eigenschaften der Zellen ihre vermutlichen Ursachen und ihre Bedeutung fur Physiologie." *Vierteljahresschr. Naturforsch. Kes.* (Zuerich) 44:88–135.

87. Prevost, P. 1807. "Memoire sur la cause immediate de la carie ou charbon des bles,

et de plusieurs autres maladies des plantes, et sur les preservatifs de la carie."
Bernard, Paris. (English translation by G.W. Keitt, *Phytopathol. Classics* 6:1–95,
1939).

88. Rabanus, A. 1939. "Uber die Saure Produktion von Pilzen und deren Einfluss auf die
    Wirkung von Holzchutzmitteln." *Mitt. Dtsch. Forstver.* 23:77–89.

89. Rhodes, F.H. and Erickson, I. 1933. "Efficiencies of tar oil components as preserva-
    tives for timber." *Ind. Eng. Chem.* 25:989–91.

90. Ricard, J.L. and Bollen, W.B. 1968. "Inhibition of *Poria carbonica* by *Scytalidium* sp.,
    an imperfect fungus isolated from Douglas fir poles." *Can. J. Bot.* 46(5):643–47.

91. Ricard, J.L., Wilson, M.M. and Bollen, W.B. 1969. "Biological control of decay in
    Douglas fir poles." *Forest Prod. J.* 19(8):41–45.

92. Richards, C.A. 1924. "The comparative resistance of 17 species of wood-destroying
    fungi to sodium fluoride." *Proc., Am. Wood-Preservers' Assoc.* 20:37–44.

93. Richards, C.A. 1925. "The comparative resistance of 18 species of wood-destroying
    fungi to zinc chloride." *Proc., Am. Wood-Preservers' Assoc.* 21:18–22.

94. Richards, C.A. 1938. "Defects in cross ties caused by fungi." *Cross Tie Bull.*
    19(3):3–6,8,10–31.

95. Richardson, B.A. 1968. "Action mechanism of some organometallic preservatives."
    In *Biodeterioration of Materials, Microbiological and Allied Aspects* (A.H. Walters and
    J.J. Elphick, eds.). Elsevier, Amsterdam, London, and New York. 498–505.

96. Schulze, B. and Becker, G. 1948. "Untersuchungen uber die pilzwidrige und insekten-
    totende Wirkung yon Fraktionen und Einzelstoffen des Steinkohlenteerols."
    Holzforschung 2:97–127.

97. Shields, J.K. 1968. "Role of *Trichoderma viride* in reducing storage decay of birch
    logs." *Bi-m Res. Notes Dep. For. Can.* 24(1):9–10.

98. Shields, J.K., and Atwell, E.A. 1963. "Effect of a mold *Trichoderma viride* on decay
    of birch by four storage-rot fungi." *Forest Prod. J.* 13:262–65.

99. Silverborg, S.B. 1953. "Fungi associated with decay of wooden buildings in New
    York State." *Phytopathology* 43:20–22.

100. Sisler, H.D. 1969. "Effect of fungicides on protein and nucleic acid synthesis." *Ann.
     Rev. Phytopathol.* 311–30.

101. Somers, E. 1963. "The uptake of copper by fungal spores." *Ann. Appl. Biol.*
     51:425–37.

102. Somsen, R.A. 1962. "Outside storage of southern pine chips." *Tappi* 45(8):623–28.

103. Sone, N. and Hagihara, B. 1964. "Inhibitory action of trialkyltin compounds on
     oxidative phosphorylation in mitochondria." *J. Biochem.* (Tokyo) 56:151–56.

104. Stamm, A.J. 1946. "Modified Woods." *Proc., Am. Wood-Preservers' Assoc.*
     42:150–67.

105. Stamm, A.J. and Baechler, R.H. 1960. "Decay resistance and dimensional stability
     of five modified woods." *Forest Prod. J.* 10:22–26.

106. Swingle, W.T. 1896. "Bordeaux mixture: its chemistry, physical properties, and toxic
     effects on fungi and algae." USDA Div. Vegetable Physiol. Pathol. Bull. 9:1–37.

107. Thompson, W.S. 1964. "Response of two wood decay fungi to metal binding com-
     pounds." Louisiana State Univ. Wood Utilization Note No. 3. Louisiana School of
     Forestry.

108. Torgeson, D.C., ed. 1967. *Fungicides,* Vol. 1. Academic Press, New York and London.

109. Torgeson, D.C., ed. 1969. *Fungicides,* Vol 2. Academic Press, New York and London.

110. Unligil, H.H. 1968. "Depletion of pentachlorophenol by fungi." *Forest Prod. J.*
     18(2):45–50.

111. Van Groenou, H.B., Rischen, H.W.C. and Van Der Berge, J. 1951. *Wood Preservation During the Last 50 Years.* A.W. Sijthoff's Uitgeversmaatschappij N.V. Leiden, Netherlands.

112. Verrall, A.F. and Sheffer, T.C. 1969. "Preservative treatments for protecting wood boxes." U.S. Forest Serv. Forest Prod. Lab. Rept. No. 106.

113. Volkman, D. 1966. "Water spray storage of Southern pine pulpwood." *Tappi* 49:48A–53A.

114. Wain, R.L. and Wilkinson, E.H. 1943. "Studies upon the copper fungicides. VI. The solution of copper from bordeaux and burgundy mixtures." *Ann. Appl. Biol.* 30:379–91.

115. Wallace, E.M. 1968. "The copper-chrome-arsenate preservatives and their use in modern wood preservation." *Proc., Am. Wood-Preservers' Assoc.* 60:50–56.

116. Young, G.Y. 1961. "Copper tolerance in some wood-rotting fungi." U.S. Forest Serv., Forest Prod. Lab. Rept. No. 2223.

117. Zabel, R.A. 1954. "Variations in preservative tolerance of wood-destroying fungi." *Forest Prod. J.* 4:166–69.

118. Zentmyer, G.A., Rich, S. and Horsfall, J.G. 1960. "Reversal of fungitoxicity of 8-quinolinol by amino acids and other chelators." *Phytopathology* 50:421–24.

6. Decay Test Methods

ELDON A. BEHR

Department of Forestry
Michigan State University, East Lansing, Michigan

6.1 The Goals in Testing

There are a variety of reasons why wood preservatives are subjected to tests in which resistance of the wood or wood-based material is evaluated. These involve development of new preservatives, comparison of existing preservatives, study of permanence or natural durability, evaluation of altered formulations, and quality control. Doubtless, other aims could be added.

Tests have been developed over a period of years for obtaining information on which to base meaningful decisions. Much testing is done to save time and money in answering the question: Is this chemical or mixture a potential wood preservative? Some organizations such as the National Woodwork Manufacturer's Association require decay tests before approving a preservative for millwork. The Preservatives Committee of the American Wood-Preservers' Association expects substantial test information of several kinds before it will consider a new preservative for adoption as a standard. Large-scale users of preserved wood look for assurance from tests that their purchasing agents can use as a guide. Then, of course, there are governmental and industrial laboratories which use testing as a means of understanding how wood preservatives function and how their performance can be predicted.

Ultimately, what should be sought is a laboratory test or tests that would allow one to predict that the preservative tested would perform satisfactorily in the field. No field tests would be needed. The time and money saved would be substantial. Probably the greatest hindrance to the discovery and acceptance of new wood preservatives is the time required at present to bring one to the marketplace.

6.2 Laboratory Tests

According to Colley [15], laboratory testing of wood preservatives has been carried on in the United States for at least 60 years and equally as long in Europe.

Laboratory testing for decay, or inhibition of decay, was more appealing than field testing for a variety of reasons. It seemed a logical place to start, offered the potential of a faster answer, and could be conducted in a laboratory equipped with but a few pieces of apparatus. Also, it seemed more scientific. To this day, anyone interested in evaluation of chemicals as wood preservatives generally starts with some form of laboratory decay test.

Decay testing, of course, is only one facet of the investigation of a chemical or mixture for its worth as a preservative. Recalling the generally stated requirements of a wood preservative—besides toxicity to fungi, permanence, inertness to wood, penetration, harmlessness to man and animal, and cleanliness—one can readily see that decay testing is only the beginning. These additional tests are only touched on here, but this does not mean they are unimportant.

Permanence is of maximum importance for a wood preservative, for without resistance to leaching by water and low volatility it simply would not remain in the wood long enough in outside exposure to be worthwhile. The weathering portion of laboratory tests, discussed in the next section, bears on this property.

Penetration of a liquid preservative into wood is necessary to its use, and separate tests are employed for nonpressure and pressure methods of treatment. Verrall [63] determines penetration on 1 × 1- or 1 × 2-inch pieces of wood 3–10 inches long by applying an impervious coating on all surfaces except one and immersing the block with the uncoated edge down. Radial, tangential, and longitudinal measurements are made. The block is allowed to dry one or more weeks to minimize liquid spread, split, and penetration measured. Penetration in earlywood and latewood is reported separately. Details are given in NWMA [47]. Penetration for pressure-treated wood is measured on end-coated 2 × 4's after sawing lengthwise and crosswise.

With increasing concern of the public for the environment and protection of users of pesticides, manufacturers must be informed of toxicological properties. A frequently used value in industrial toxicology is the LD_{50}. This is the milligrams of chemical per kilogram of body weight which will kill half of a group of experimental animals. The Federal Government classifies pesticides as to their hazardous nature by LD_{50} values.

6.2.1 Screening tests

There is probably no generally accepted definition of screening, but it is used here to designate those tests which separate compounds or mixtures that have potential as wood preservatives from those that do not. It separates the possible from the impossible, but does not tell the experimenter much more than this. These tests do have a place in the over-all evaluation picture because they are usually fast and relatively inexpensive to conduct.

Until the early 1940s, the agar-plate toxicity test as described by Schmitz [51] was the test most widely used in the United States for all toximetric evaluations of potential wood preservatives in the laboratory. It is still used as a starter in spite of its shortcomings.

Briefly, the agar-plate toxicity test is described as follows. The chemical or mixture is dissolved in alcohol or acetone and placed in a sealed, thin glass bulb. A range of weights is used so that a series of concentrations of the chemical will result when it is introduced into a weighed amount of malt-agar in a flask. After steam sterilization of the flasks of agar, the bulbs are surface-sterilized, dropped into the agar, broken, and then the contents are dispersed by shaking. After being poured into a sterile petri dish and allowed to harden, a square of growing fungus culture is placed in the center of the petri dish and examined for growth over a period of two weeks. If the inoculum is prevented from growing while in contact with the culture medium containing the test chemical, but resumes growth when in contact with malt-agar, it is considered to be only *inhibited*. On the other hand, if no growth develops on either petri dish, or when transferred, the fungus is considered dead. Then the toxic values are reported —as inhibition point or killing point—as percent by weight of the malt-agar. The total time involved in conducting such a test is about 3–4 weeks, depending on the inherent growth rate of the fungus.

The main objection to the malt-agar toxicity test is that the substrate is not wood. As some critics have pointed out, who cares about protecting malt-agar? Nevertheless, the test has been used widely and it is the only test used for fungal toxicity of many chemicals reported in the literature. The spread between toxicity values for this and other tests is evident in Table 6.1. Thus, if a certain chemical is reputed to have a high toxicity (low percentage) toward wood-destroying fungi, the prospective user had better ask: by what test?

Another test described by Toole [59,60] could also be used for screening. Cubes of wood 1.9 cm on a side are treated with various levels of a chemical and are then placed on an actively growing culture of a decay fungus. Other cubes of wood cut adjacent to the impregnated cubes are held in a

TABLE 6.1

Comparison of Inhibition and Killing Points for Various Wood-Destroying Fungi Grown
on Wood Blocks or Malt-Agar Treated with Inorganic Salts

| Fungus | Substrate | Preservative Salt % by Weight of Substrate | | | |
| | | Sodium Fluoride | | Zinc Chloride | |
		Inhibition	Killing	Inhibition	Killing
Lentinus lepideus	Southern pine*	0.26	0.41	1.00	1.3
Lentinus lepideus	Malt-agar	0.10	0.15	0.05	0.075
Lenzites trabea	Southern pine	0.50	0.59	1.00	2.09
Lenzites trabea	Malt-agar	0.30	>0.30	0.15	0.45
Polyporus versicolor	Oak[†]	2.10	3.50	0.80	1.77
Polyporus versicolor	Malt-agar	0.10	0.15	0.30	0.35

*Where a wood is shown as the substrate, the numbers appearing in "Inhibition" and "Killing" are the range in threshold values reported in the literature. Southern pine is assumed to weigh 32 lbs/cu ft for these values, which were originally reported in pounds of chemical/cu ft. Baechler and Roth [6].

[†]Oak is taken as 40 pounds per cubic foot. The Malt-agar values are from Richards [50].

sterile bottle at a moisture content above the fiber-saturation point. In 2–4 weeks, all are tested in radial compression and the modulus of elasticity, stress at the proportional limit, and stress at 5 percent compressive strain are determined. The level of chemical at the point of minimum reduction is taken to be the protective concentration in the wood. This can be compared to values found when using standard preservatives. A disadvantage of this test is that another variable—strength of wood—is added to the test.

If rapidity is important in screening, then the test proposed by Levi [41] should be considered. He treats pieces of *Pinus sylvestris* or *Fagus sylvatica* veneer measuring 0.15 × 1.5 × 4 cm and places these on growing cultures of fungus on malt-agar. In 3–6 weeks, depending on the species of fungus, the weight loss is measured and the toxic limit determined. Both a brown rotter and white rotter should be used in screening tests, especially if softwoods and hardwoods are employed. In this test, the toxic limits can be as much as three times as great as in other tests using wood blocks because of the greater surface area–volume ratio. This is a concrete example of how toxic limits are dependent upon sample size.

6.2.2 Threshold tests

The definition of "threshold," as given in standard M10–63 of the American Wood-Preservers' Association or D1413–61 of the American

Society for Testing and Materials, is: "the minimum amount of preservative that is effective in preventing decay, under the conditions of the test, by a particular fungus." Thus, if blocks are impregnated with a series of retentions of preservative and tested immediately after evaporation of the solvent of the preservative mixture, the threshold will be one of the retentions calculated from the impregnation data. If some weathering or exposure conditions are applied to the treated blocks before they are subjected to a decay fungus, the threshold will be the impregnation retention but will usually be larger because some preservative is volatilized or leached. Unfortunately, all too many workers in this field have taken a loose interpretation of the definition; therefore, it behooves the reader to pay close attention to what an author means when he uses the term "threshold."

The object of this type of test is to find the threshold for a fungus and wood combination. This information is useful in comparing effectiveness of preservatives and, to some extent, predicting how well the preservative will perform in service. With so much expected of a test there has naturally been a great deal of experimentation to make such tests more reliable and of shorter duration. Colley [15], Hartley [30], Duncan [21], and Smith [52], among others, summarize and delve into a good deal of this methodology.

In Europe, an agar-block test is used and specified in British Standard 838 and German Standard DIN 52176. A typical test is shown in Figure 6.1. Basically, the test fungus is grown on sterile malt-agar in a Kolle flask until the medium is well covered with mycelium. Then a sterile glass support rod is placed on the fungus mat, and both a block of wood treated with the preservative under test and an untreated block are set on the support rod so that the blocks do not touch the malt-agar but the fungus is able to reach the blocks. In some tests, three blocks are placed in each flask. The blocks are $1.5 \times 2.5 \times 5$ cm, with the 5-cm dimension being parallel to the grain of the wood. Since a graded series of retentions of the preservative is used, there will be some blocks that are attacked and others that are not if a wide enough range is employed. Degree of attack is measured by the difference in ovendry weight before exposure to the fungus and the ovendry weight after 3–4 months on the culture. Visual examination is a supplement to the weight-loss percentages. In such a test there will be some retention (usually given in Kg per cubic meter) where the block will not lose weight, or above which the weight loss will be nearly constant. This is considered to be the upper toxic limit. The lower toxic limit for the preservative-fungus-wood combination is the next retention where the wood loses weight and shows visible evidence of decay.

There have been many workers willing and able to evaluate this stan-

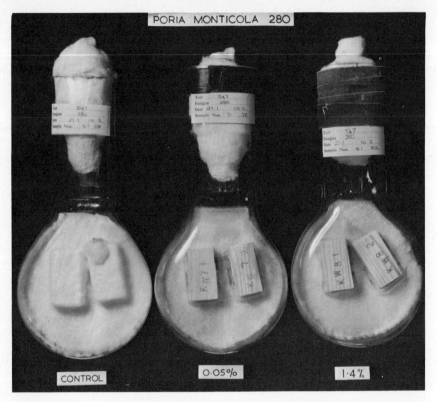

Figure 6.1. B.S. 838 malt-agar (Kolle flask) test with control and treated samples on mat of *Poria monticola*. (Courtesy International Research Group on Wood Preservation)

dard method and modify it to improve it; for example, Alliot [1] preferred smaller blocks—0.5 × 1 × 3 cm—that would fit into a test tube, as did Theden and Starfinger [58], who used 0.4 × 0.7 × 5 cm pieces of wood. This approach aims at shortening the test and lessening the cost of equipment. Unfortunately, the toxic limits are usually raised by such tactics— which may be undesirable, depending on how one thinks. Kolle flasks are expensive, so it is natural that a less costly culture chamber should be sought. (Just why the adherents of the Kolle flask have not tried a square 8-ounce screw-cap bottle is unclear. It would accept the blocks used now and would only be 5 percent of the cost.)

Besides decreasing the sample size, the other approach to amending the European agar-block test is to substitute a more sensitive measure of decay than weight loss. Trendelenburg [61] used change in impact bending strength, whereas Göhre [27] relied on change in static bending strength. Mateus [43] describes a method which measures change in deflection of a piece of wood before and after exposure to a fungus culture. Test pieces 0.5 × 0.5 × 8 cm are tested right in the petri dish by using a thin plastic sheet as a cover. Where wood is attacked, there is as much as a 40 percent increase in deflection in 2 weeks' exposure to the fungus. However, in wood treated to a little less than threshold, about 9 weeks are required for significant increase in deflection.

One method of increasing attack in the agar-block test while using the larger samples is to place a feeder strip on a glass rod over the growing culture and then place the test piece on this after the feeder strip is well rotted. Behr [9] found a much increased rate of respiration by this alteration, in comparison with tests where no feeder strip was used.

In North America and Australia the soil-block test as outlined in AWPA Standard M10-63 or ASTM Standard D1413-61 is most widely used by research and development people in wood preservation. It is much like the previously described agar-block test, except that soil is used as the substrate for growing the fungus. Blocks are generally of southern pine in $\frac{3}{4}$-inch (1.9 cm) cubes, and are weighed before and after 12 weeks' exposure to the fungus culture. They are either oven dried before and after the test, or brought to the same constant conditions of temperature and relative humidity. Figure 6.2 shows the arrangement of soil, feeder strip, and block. After sterilization of the soil and feeder strip, a square of malt-agar with an actively growing culture of the test fungus is placed on it. In 2 or 3 weeks, depending on the species of fungus, the mycelium will have covered the feeder strip. The sterilized test blocks are then inserted in the jars. Either 1 or 2 blocks can be used per jar. After 12 weeks the blocks are removed and the weight loss is determined. The threshold is either given as a range of retentions or as a single value.

Standards AWPA M10 and ASTM D1413 include a weathering procedure to aid in evaluation of the permanence of the preservative under test. It consists of a series of heating periods in a water bath, followed by static leaching in distilled water. The weathering procedure was adopted after a long period of development, starting with outdoor exposure. Nevertheless, it has certain shortcomings, some of which are pointed out by Da Costa and Osborne [19]. They find that the forced-air oven gives more consistent results at 50°C than the weathering box called for by the standard methods. The main bone of contention regarding the weathering procedure is that ASTM D1413 is not severe enough for creosote to parallel what happens in field exposure. Objectors say that soil-block tests do not have to show a threshold that is the same as that found in poles or stakes just starting to rot. They seem to feel that if creosote shows a higher threshold in the soil-block test, it is somehow weakened in reputation. These arguments can be heard at almost any meeting of the Preservatives

Figure 6.2. ASTM-AWPA soil-block test. Blocks with increasing retentions of creosote (left to right) exposed to *Lenzites trabea*, Madison 617. (Courtesy U.S. Forest Products Laboratory)

Committee of the AWPA. Since pentachlorophenol and waterborne treatments are not as sensitive to the weathering tests, they are not usually involved.

The soil-block method is also a target for criticism, but efforts are being made to improve it or to offer alternatives. There are inherent errors in any method that involves moisture changes in wood. In spite of impressive-looking tables and graphs, equilibrium moisture content in wood is still not an exact value for any given set of conditions. Thus, if we can get away from weight loss as a method of detecting preservative action, we should improve the reliability of the test.

Some of the means of detecting fungus attack already described for the agar-block test could be used for the soil-block test as well. In addition, Brown [14] finds thresholds in about 25 days by measuring decrease in tensile strength on thin wood specimens subjected to decay fungi. Specimen preparation is critical. Toughness, impact bending, static bending, and elasticity are all sensitive to fungus attack on wood and have been suggested as possible measurement criteria. The species of fungus and nature of its attack affect the rate of strength loss. Brown rots usually cause a more rapid loss than white rots.

A number of workers—Behr [9], Halabisky and Ifju [29], and Smith [54]—are investigating respirometry as a means of evaluating wood preservatives. These methods are based on the simplified reaction shown below:

Wood + Oxygen → Carbon dioxide + Water + Other gases and solids

Smith measures carbon dioxide evolution with a gas chromatograph, while the others use a respirometer to measure oxygen consumption. Again, this kind of evaluation is more sensitive than weight loss and requires less time.

With the myriad number of methods on the books for laboratory assessment of wood preservatives, no one has yet compared all of them objectively and designated one method as the best. Perhaps it cannot be done. There may be more than one method needed to satisfy all conditions. However, for a method to gain headway, it is almost mandatory that it have the sanction of an official agency such as ASTM or the British Standards Institution.

Regardless of the means for evaluation in tests using a wood specimen, there are certain truths that should be considered concerning fungus and wood. First, the choice of fungus or fungi for the test is important. As Findlay [24] so ably points out, the desired characteristics of fungi for such tests are:

1. Ability to cause rapid decay in the species of wood used.

2. High degree of tolerance or resistance to toxicants.

3. Preferably of economic importance.

4. Easily cultivated and not unduly sensitive to slight variations in environmental conditions.

For many years a fungus thought to be *Fomes annosus* was the only one used in many tests at the U.S. Forest Products Laboratory, but thinking has changed and *Poria monticola, Lenzites trabea,* and *Lentinus lepideus* are now used extensively in evaluating softwoods impregnated with various kinds of chemicals and wood preservatives in the United States. For hardwoods, *Polyporus versicolor* is included.

Second, the tolerance of a fungus varies with the wood preservative or chemical class being tested. To substantiate this, the reader is referred to Chapter 5 of this volume and to Table 6.2, which contains data provided

TABLE 6.2

Preservative Thresholds Found by the Agar-Block Method Using Impregnated Blocks of Ponderosa Pine Sapwood

Fungus	Mean Threshold Pounds Per Cubic Foot		
	Penta-chloro-phenol	Coal-Tar Creosote	Acid Copper Chromate
Lentinus lepideus	0.03	3.08	0.019
Poria monticola	0.06	0.85	0.36
Lenzites trabea	0.039	1.47	0.23
Poria incrassata	0.075	<0.20	0.36
Fomes subroseus	0.24	0.20	0.36

by Cowling [18]. Cowling's tests were agar-block, and the thresholds do not agree with those found by the soil-block method in every case, but the variation in tolerance is clearly shown. *Lentinus lepideus* is found to be much more tolerant of creosote than *Poria monticola,* but it is more tolerant to acid copper chromate than *Lentinus lepideus.*

Third, the *strain* of fungus influences the degree of wood attack. For example, Van Groenou *et al.* [62] report percentage weight losses in agar-block tests running for three months using various strains of *Coniophora cerebella* as follows: standard strain, 25 percent; strain 266, 20 percent; strain 173/1, 15 percent; and strain 178 C, 46 percent. Accordingly, just any old culture of one of the fungi that meets Findlay's criteria is unacceptable if the results are to be compared to those where standard recognized strains were used. For this reason, most workers use cultures of recognized virulence in destruction of wood. In the United States, these are maintained at the Forest Products Laboratory, Madison, Wisconsin, and are assigned a number—for example, *Lenzites trabea* (M617). Canada maintains cultures of these and other fungi at both Eastern (Ottawa) and Western (Vancouver) Forest Products Laboratories.

Fourth, the species of wood influences the threshold for a preservative–fungus combination. In the monumental work of Duncan [21], this difference in thresholds resulting from use of various woods is brought out, as shown in Table 6.3. Here it can readily be seen that thresholds—for

TABLE 6.3

Thresholds as Found on Various Sapwoods in the Soil-Block Test

Fungus	Preservative	Threshold, Pounds Per Cubic Foot			
		Wood			
		Southern Pine	Red Pine	Ponderosa Pine	Sweet-gum
Lentinus lepideus	CREO	3.5	4.5	6.0	1.9
Lenzites trabea	CREO*	2.4	—	—	0.8
Lenzites trabea	PCP[†]	0.135	0.135	0.2	0.175
Polyporus versicolor	PCP	0.05	—	—	0.28
Poria monticola	CZC[‡]	0.53	—	—	0.5

*Creosote.
[†]Pentachlorophenol.
[‡]Chromated zinc chloride.

creosote, even on different kinds of pine—can vary almost twofold when subjected to attack of *Lentinus lepideus*. The differences are even more pronounced when a white-rot fungus, *Polyporus versicolor,* is the test organism on southern pine and sweetgum treated with pentachlorophenol.

Da Costa and Osborne [19] have also found that the kind of wood used for test blocks has an influence on the weathering aspect of the test. Various kinds of creosote are lost more rapidly from one wood than another, as is shown in Table 6.4.

As a summary of the dependence of threshold or toxic limits on the variables just discussed, the following factors by which the threshold or toxic limit can change are offered: (1) species of fungus, 40 times; (2) strain of fungus, 10 times; (3) size and shape of specimen, 4 times; (4) species of wood, 2 times; and (5) kind of test, at least 20 times.

One objection raised by Schmitz [51] to laboratory toxic-limit tests that involve adding a preservative to a wood block is that even distribution of

TABLE 6.4

Effect of Wood Species on Loss of Creosotes by Weathering and on Threshold for *Lentinus lepideus*

	Creosote		Pinus radiata		Eucalyptus regnans		Eucalyptus maculata
Code	Phenols, % vol/wt	0–315°C Distillate, %	Weathering Loss, %	Threshold pcf	Weathering Loss, %	Threshold pcf	Weathering Loss, %
E	18.6	58.0	45	4.5	42	<2	52
I	8.2	78.6	69	7.7	69	—	74
G	24.1	90.6	71	4.5	67	<2	—

preservative in the test blocks is hard to achieve. Some tests by Smith and Cockroft [55] have shown him to be correct in at least one instance. These workers at the Forest Products Research Laboratory, Princes Risborough, felt that the concentration of preservative in the B.S. 838 test (5 × 2.5 × 1.5-cm blocks) might not be uniform, and analysis of layers of blocks proved them correct. When blocks of this size are treated with benzene–copper naphthenate mixtures, there is a much higher concentration of toxicant toward the outside of the blocks than in the center after the benzene evaporates. They found that the blocks could be frozen shortly after treating and then placed in a freeze-drying apparatus to sublimate the benzene. This left an essentially level concentration gradient. The leveling of the concentration gradient is most noticeable from the end-grain toward the center, where air drying produced a concentration twice that of the block average. This finding may also be important to users of the $\frac{3}{4}$-inch block. At present we may be trusting to luck. Some of the results coming from the soil-block test which are hard to explain may be a result of testing a surface retention that is not the same as the calculated retention so confidently used.

As a parting consideration of threshold testing, the thoughts of Horsfall [31] should be mulled over. This renowned scientist has the knack of seeing the whole picture in an analytical way. He says that thresholds are artificial. They do not exist in nature. In his words, "... [there] are those who hold that natural processes have thresholds, that point which separates action from no action. In case of fungicidal action there is no point that separates killing a fungus from not killing a fungus.... This static concept of thresholds has delayed seriously the progress of biological science."

Perhaps this explains why no completely satisfactory threshold test has been devised.

6.2.3 Tests for non-Basidiomycete wood-destroying fungi

The substantial work of Duncan and Lombard [23] lists hundreds of examinations of wood decayed by Basidiomycetes. All of the fungi commonly used in the tests described to date are also Basidiomycetes. However, since about 1944 scientists have recognized that wood is attacked by Ascomycetes, Fungi Imperfecti, and even bacteria. Sap stains were known, of course, but their activity is usually on the cell contents and not destructive to the wood. The name "soft rot" has been applied to this group of fungi in England, and it is denoted *Moderfäulepilzen* in Germany.

Because of their different requirements for growth, such fungi cannot be handled by the same test procedures as Basidiomycetes. Although soft rots can grow at lower and higher wood-moisture contents, their rate of attack is much slower. As a rule, they attack hardwoods more rapidly than softwoods. Some of the tests use a nutrient agar or soil as a substrate for growing the fungus [22]. In Europe, blocks are sometimes buried in soil or in soil mixed with vermiculite [34]. Test methods are still undergoing development, but are likely to gain in importance because soft rots may ultimately prove to be the fungi that cause the destruction of wood in contact with soil.

6.3 Field Tests for Solid Wood

It is generally agreed that laboratory tests alone are not sufficient for putting the stamp of approval on a chemical or mixture as a wood preservative. Thus, the next step in evaluation beyond the laboratory is to field test the preservative after it is impregnated into wood. Since an accelerated test is desired, some form of wood is exposed outdoors in supposedly near-ideal conditions for decay fungi and nonideal for wood. Tests of this kind are conducted throughout the world, including such unlikely places as northern Sweden, although such a test would hardly be accelerated. Gibson [26] gives a list of 32 different tests from 10 different countries, and doubtless there are others not so well known.

6.3.1 Soil contact exposures

Experience has proved that wood in contact with the soil decays much faster than when not in or on the ground. This is the case because of higher equilibrium moisture content in the wood in contact with moist soil, a better possibility of leaching, and plenty of microorganisms to inoculate the wood or cause degradation of the preservative. In the United States, where more extensive field testing is conducted than in any other country, the types of ground-contact tests include specimens ranging in size from $\frac{3}{4}$-inch stakes to full-size railroad cross ties and utility poles. As might be guessed, the Forest Products Laboratory (Madison) has a preeminent part in this type of testing, although several universities, state laboratories, utilities, and railroads also have test plots or lines.

6.3.1.1 Stakes

The philosophy of testing preservatives by impregnating them into stakes is that the contributing effects of wood, preservative, weather, and fungus flora are all interacting as they would on treated wood in commercial use. The main differences are that the stakes expose a larger surface per volume, thus accelerating preservative loss, and they are supposed to be completely and uniformly penetrated. The word "supposed" is the qualifier. Supporters of the $\frac{3}{4}$-inch-square cross-section stake maintain that there is a better chance of uniform treatment than there is with a 2 × 4-inch stake. There is some evidence to indicate that they are correct.

A standard method of conducting stake tests has been promulgated as ASTM D–1758 or AWPA M–7. Stakes of either clear sapwood or heartwood, but not mixed, are $\frac{3}{4}$ × $\frac{3}{4}$ inches and at least 18 inches long. The nominal 2 × 4 stake has also been included in the standards, but there is sentiment for its removal. In the original version of stake testing with $\frac{3}{4}$-inch stakes, a stick about 38 inches long was treated, sawed in half, and a center piece cut out for analysis, leaving two 18-inch stakes for test plots. Twenty replicates of each retention level are specified. A narrow weight-selection class is generally maintained for the stakes in order to keep the retention levels in a group of replicates within a narrow range. It is the usual practice to treat twice as many stakes as are needed and then discard, or use in a secondary test plot, all those falling outside the preselected retention range.

The stakes are treated by the full-cell method without final vacuum, using toluene as a diluent for oil-type (creosote) or oilborne (pentachlorophenol) preservatives and water for waterborne preservatives. Receptiveness of the wood to treatment and the concentration of active ingredients in the solution determines the retention. A range of retentions is used so that some stakes will be attacked and some protected over a few years. If the retentions used are too high, the test takes too much time; if too low, no protective effect is found. As an example for a creosote or related mixture, stakes would be treated to the following levels of retention: 6, 7, 8, 9, 10, and 11 pounds per cubic foot.

After the stakes are treated, they are piled so that air can flow over the stakes to remove organic solvent or placed in a kiln or oven to remove water. When essentially all of the solvent has been removed, the stakes are ready for insertion in the test ground. They can be randomized, or the plot divided into 10 blocks and all stakes placed according to the units digit. For example, stakes 1, 11, 21, 31, etc., would go into one section of the plot.

Inspection is usually made once a year. However, the 20 or more untreated control stakes are first examined for decay to determine the elapsed time from installation to first examination. If there is little or no decay in the controls, there is not much to be gained in examination of the treated stakes.

Inspection and evaluation of the amount of decay is largely visual. The standards allow pressing the underground portion with the thumbnail but no "probing, picking, and gouging of the wood." In many of the test plots, subterranean termites also attack the stakes, and it is often difficult to separate termite and decay damage. A number is assigned to each decay and termite grade. The latter is considered in Chapter 8. The decay grades are: 10 = Sound, 9 = Trace of Decay, 7 = Moderate Decay, 4 = Heavy Decay, 0 = Failure due to Decay. The ratings per level for each treatment are averaged and the results compared to those from other levels and preservatives to arrive at decisions. Stakes that have failed are sometimes used to identify the fungus causing attack. Further discussion of evaluation of the results is taken up in Section 6.5.

As far as the size of the stake is concerned, opinion seems to be divided into two camps; one, headed by the Forest Products Laboratory (Madison), favors 2 × 4's, while the other, initiated at Bell Telephone Laboratories, favors the $\frac{3}{4}$-inch square stake. The main drawback to the 2 × 4 stake is that it has a relatively large cross section and just takes too long to decay, thus distorting the aim of an accelerated test, according to Colley [17]. This slowing down of decay due to use of 2 × 4's is evident in results reported for creosote in the annual report of stake tests published by the Forest Products Laboratory and authored by Blew and Davidson [12]. Forty percent of the $\frac{3}{4}$-inch-square stakes treated with 8 pounds of creosote per cubic foot have been destroyed by decay and 50 percent by termites. On the other hand, only 30 percent of the 2 × 4 stakes have been removed, although treated with 7.8 pounds per cubic foot of the same creosote and exposed in the same test plot.

Another point concerning 2 × 4 stakes that is often overlooked is that in soil contact, the life expectancy of wood is directly proportional to its *thickness* and not its cross-sectional area. Thus, the same results could be expected with a 2 × 2 as a 2 × 4. This relationship was discovered by Purslow [48] when testing linden, English oak, Scots pine, and western redcedar.

Another question that arises in connection with stake tests is: Should full-cell or empty-cell pressure treatment be used? If it is agreed that a $\frac{3}{4}$-inch-stake test is an evaluation of the *preservative* and not the *preservative treatment,* then full-cell treatment is more appropriate. Leutritz [39], in a review of 30 years of test-plot evaluations for the Bell Telephone Companies, found that full-cell treatments using toluene dilutions of creosote gave more consistent results than empty cell–no dilution treatments.

Colley [16] urged test-plot experimenters to make up composite test-plot specimens of $\frac{3}{4}$ × $2\frac{1}{2}$ × 32–42 inch wood pieces of varying retention levels. The pieces are placed in the soil as a unit, one in contact with the other with edges exposed to the soil. In the same test plot, indicator stakes of a retention near the suspected level of marginal protection are scattered. The latter are inspected before any of the layered stakes to let the worker know when to inspect these. The advantages claimed for such a test are that all levels of retention are exposed in one spot, the ground–stake environment is not disturbed until the stakes have been exposed for a considerable period, and there are enough extra stakes for strength tests and isolation of decay fungi. As logical as this test seems, no one has undertaken it.

Klem [36] has even advocated laying test stakes on the soil surface instead of inserting them in the ground. Using this method, he finds as fast a decay rate as when stakes are inserted to half their length. However, it is doubtful that this would occur in places with a drier climate than Norway.

Rennerfelt [49] used a test where the stakes were subjected to a field bending test to give fracture when 80 percent of its original bending strength has been lost. In an attempt to avoid visual ratings, Amemya [2] found a correlation between compressive strength or Brinell hardness and visual grades. Birkner [13] has proposed a standard method for field tests which is reminiscent of American test standards except that empty-cell treatment is advocated, and like his countryman, Rennerfelt, assigns a visual rating of 0 (for sound) up to 100 (for failure).

Possible means of promoting the speed-up of stake tests should be considered. Smith [52] suggests that: (1) stake size be kept small, (2) retentions be held to low levels to allow early decay but still give longer life than controls, (3) exposures be in decay-promoting soils and climates, and (4) deterioration be measured by a sensitive method capable of numerical evaluation. One of the weaknesses of presently accepted stake-test methods is the assignment of rating values by visual means. This can lead to the situation where, for example, two stakes are each given a 70 rating, but one can be lightly attacked and the other well attacked. This lack of precision casts doubt on the use of statistics in analyzing the results. However, in spite of these shortcomings, the test has been used with some success over a period of years. Remarkably enough, if three experienced inspectors rate the same stakes, they will arrive at means which will be within a few percent of each other.

One of the obstacles to rating the strength of the stakes, as Rennerfelt and Amemya suggested, is that moisture content affects the strength of wood. Attempting to use a moisture content less than fiber saturation is fraught with difficulties. At an annual inspection, the stakes would have to be removed and placed in a controlled-humidity room to bring them all to the same moisture content at which they were tested before insertion in the test plot. This is time-consuming, and could adversely affect the fungus mycelium already in the stakes. Even if all stakes were tested at moisture contents above the fiber-saturation point, there would be problems that are not readily solved.

Smith [52,53] has offered a method for evaluating decay on stakes such as 2 × 4's that could revolutionize stake testing. The rate of decay is estimated on treated stakes by scraping off the rotted wood, exposing sound wood in small spots. A micrometer device is used to measure the depth of decay. (Of course, a period of years of exposure are necessary before enough superficial decay develops to allow a reading.) The rate of decay is then estimated and predictions can be made on length of life of the particular stakes, or other sizes for that matter.

Another important consideration in stake testing is the test ground. Standard methods instruct the practitioner to "select an area of fertile, level land of uniform soil character that is moist but well drained.... The presence of wood destroying fungi...shall be proved by observation or experience and checked by exposure of suitable small specimens of untreated wood." These are lofty and worthy goals but hardly met by some of the plots in use by well-recognized authority, simply because logistics and economics also have to be considered.

Each area of land, otherwise suitable for a test plot, has a different fungus flora from others. It is time-consuming and perhaps not even possible to evaluate it for its decay potential before selection as a test plot. One reason this is not as easy as it appears is that the rate of decay of untreated wood is not necessarily an indication of the rate of deterioration of treated wood in the same site [52]. Thus, to be on the safe side, it is best to have more than one test plot. Some plots have been in use long enough—exposed to a great variety of preservatives—so that their potentials are known and can be compared to other plots. In such a case perhaps one plot will do; but in testing a radically new toxicant, it is best to expose the stakes in more than one plot.

Table 6.5, adopted from Smith's [52] work, indicates how the rate of decay varies in his plots at Thetford and Princes Risborough, England. Also note that the difference in rate of decay varies between plots, depending on the species of wood and type of pressure treatment. This shows why one plot may not be enough. Blew and Davidson [12] likewise find

TABLE 6.5

Rate of Decay of Pressure-Creosoted Wood in Different Test Plots
in 0.001 Inch Per Year [52]

Wood	Test-Plot Location Kind of Treatment	Princes Risborough		Thetford	
		Full-Cell	Empty-Cell	Full-Cell	Empty-Cell
Beech		1.5	5	1	3.5
Scots pine		0.2	2	0	0.3

that area of exposure makes a difference. For example, the average life of 2 × 4 southern pine stakes pressure treated with an average of 0.3 lb/cu ft of FCAP preservative is 6.4 years in the Panama Canal Zone; 13.7 years in Bogalusa, Louisiana; 15.4 years in Eastport, Florida; 18 years in Saucier, Mississippi; and 16.5 years in Madison, Wisconsin. Termites caused some of the damage in all but the Madison plot, however.

6.3.1.2 Posts, poles, and large rectangular timbers

If a firm is trying to develop a new preservative, it will usually treat some posts, poles, and crossties with it after favorable results with stakes. The Preservatives Committee of the American Wood-Preservers' Association expects results from tests on such commercial-size units before it will consider the preservative for inclusion in its book of standards.

The AWPA has a standard method for post evaluation, M8, while ASTM D2278 is another. It should be noted here that AWPA and ASTM standards are not static. They are subject to periodic scrutiny; therefore, both laboratory and field tests can change. Although there are differences in AWPA and ASTM stake and post tests, the prevailing mood of the members of both committees, many of whom are the same, is to bring them into conformance.

When the development of a potential preservative reaches the point that it is worth the expense of this type of test, the producer is looking for more than just resistance to decay or termites. He is also seeking information on penetration and its effect on the treated unit and the physical effect of the preservative on the wood in use, such as the tendency to increase or decrease checking, any hardening or softening effects, etc.

Inspection of such large units as posts or poles is sometimes an arduous task, and time-consuming as well. In the ASTM standard, three alternative inspection procedures are allowed: (1) posts can be withdrawn from the ground, usually by a chain and jack; (2) soil can be shoveled away and the below-ground portion examined; and (3) a post can be pushed firmly on opposite sides to cause failure if the post is weakened through advanced decay. At the same time, the aboveground portion is also examined for decay, checking, bleeding, or any other abnormal condition.

The post test is terminated when the average life has been reached, usually when 60 percent of the specimens have failed.

Although push inspection is fast, it tells very little about the below-ground condition of the posts until failure. Perhaps this is all that is wanted from such units—the useful life. If, however, prefailure condition can be used to predict useful life, the over-all time of testing can be reduced. Walters [65] recommends that a uniform load be applied for the push test and tells how to do it. However, posts vary in diameter in spite of our best intentions, so a 100-pound pull on a weaker species or small-diameter post does not give the same effect as on a stronger species or thicker post.

The Bell Telephone Laboratories have conducted extensive tests on pole sections in test plots maintained at Gulfport, Mississippi, and Orange Park, Florida. Lumsden [42] describes the test method and gives interesting histories of the performance of various preservatives. And that is the trouble with testing full-cross-section poles. Although some valuable information is derived, much of it is history. By the time the information is available, conditions have changed and the information cannot be applied. This plot, however, has revealed useful facts about the effect of retention and penetration on permanence of the treated wood.

Although thousands of railroad ties have been in test in the United States and Canada, most of these would be considered as service tests because they are under actual use.

6.3.1.3 Service tests

A service test is usually the confirming effort needed to give a preservative respectability; that is, to have it accepted by industry and as a standard of ASTM or AWPA.

The American Wood-Preservers' Association publishes much of the information on service tests. There is a bit of bending of the definition of service test as far as posts are concerned, because many of these included in reports of the Post Service Records Committee [5] are installed in test plots. Nevertheless, such records are an excellent reference if information on life expectancy of a certain species-preservative-locale combination is desired. The 1966 *Proceedings* of the AWPA include 1,246 service records —that ought to be enough for anyone. Until 1966 the Utilization and Service Record Committees of the AWPA compiled records on poles, ties, posts, piles, and other treated wood. Page 44 of the 1966 *Proceedings* has an index to service records from 1949 to 1966. Blew [10] gives directions for service tests on posts, but some of the specifics refer to plot tests.

One main difference between service tests and plot tests is that commercially treated wood with all its variability is used in service tests, whereas test plots include the most carefully treated specimens. Thus, a service test will include the treating plant and possibly the operator as variables of the type that can be expected.

With the advent of better methods of chemical analysis, commercially treated wood in service tests can be analyzed for retention of preservative during the course of the test in order to obtain information on rate of depletion under service conditions.

Care is needed in the use of service records. This is especially true in using old records to predict present-day performance. For example, the sapwood was narrower on much of the old-growth southern pine pole stock, resulting in a higher retention in the sapwood compared to that in the wide sapwood found on pole stock today. Another thing to consider is the range in retention in the items in the service test. Unfortunately, this is often ignored or omitted from published information, possibly because it was unknown or not provided.

The Rural Electrification Administration has embarked on a continuing study of the poles of its borrowers on 120 electric distribution systems throughout the United States. This useful information can be found in Kulp's report [37] and that of AWPA Committee U–4 [5]. Findings from these extensive service tests never would have resulted from laboratory or, possibly, controlled plot tests. For example, lodgepole pine poles treated from 1949 through 1953 had a high rate of decay failure because steam conditioning was used before treatment. After these poles were placed in line, further drying resulted in deep checks extending into untreated heartwood. Those lodgepole pine poles that were air dried before treatment had a relatively low failure rate due to decay.

Groundline preservative treatment of poles is practiced extensively on utilities' lines. Service-test information on such structures is largely in the files of the pole owners or the applicator, but a report on service tests of electric line poles by Lancaster [38] and one by Behr [8] on historic restorations are available.

Service-test information on treated wood used in docks, buildings, bridges, and the like can also be found in AWPA U-Committee reports, as well as in papers such as that by Gurd and Paterson [28]. There are extensive service tests of cross ties in the railroad tracks of the United States and Canada. Reports can be found in publications of the American Railway Engineering Association and the *Cross Tie Bulletin*. A paper by Blew [11] summarizes results on test tracks of the Milwaukee Railroad in the vicinity of Madison, Wisconsin. Service tests of crossties bring out very well the causes of failure other than decay and the effect of the rail hardware in the over-all preservative picture.

6.3.2 Aboveground exposures

Only recently have those concerned with wood decay and preservation research given much-needed attention to field tests for wood to be used away from soil contact. It was apparently assumed that accelerated tests, even though largely consisting of some type of exposure involving soil, would do for both. There would not be much dispute over the worth of a preservative for use aboveground if it had been thoroughly tested in soil contact. However, aboveground uses may not require, or even permit, some preservatives that do well in soil contact. There are not many who would treat residential millwork with creosote. Thus, a preservative for use on such an item does not need to withstand the rigors of soil contact and its attendant microbiological breeding ground. A potential preservative for use away from the soil should not be relegated to oblivion because it does not give a good account in a stake test. To cite a related case, pentachlorophenol fails in a marine environment but this is no reason to exclude it from use on land.

6.3.2.1 Post and rail dimension tests

E. E. Hubert [33] pioneered the testing and application of preservatives for aboveground use in the United States. A. F. Verrall [63] has almost singlehandedly originated the test methods presently used. Pressure-treated wood is not used in aboveground application to the same extent as it is for poles, posts, crossties, etc. Accordingly, most of the testing is done on non-pressure-treated wood, which may or may not be completely penetrated.

After trials with many different types of specimens, Verrall adopted the post-and-rail unit shown in Figures 6.3 and 6.4. It has a high decay hazard and is easily constructed. Such test units also need to be made to allow ready inspection. Verrall [63] used a visual rating scheme of 6 grades as follows: 0 = no obvious decay, 20 = discoloration suggesting that decay had started, 40 = obvious decay but in a confined area, 60 = general decay but still serviceable, 80 = advanced decay that requires replacement, 100 = failure. Unfortunately, ratings 20, 40, and 60 can take place without external evidence; consequently, most conclusions should be based on 80 and 100 ratings. At 5-, 10-, and 15-year intervals, 20 percent of the samples are removed and ripped lengthwise to reveal internal decay. Average life is considered to be the number of years of exposure at which 60 percent of the samples were 80 or 100. These tests can be used for predicting life expectancy of wood used in exterior of buildings, and results have been used as the basis for Federal Housing Authority Minimum Property Standards.

Verrall also used various demonstration units such as steps, ammunition boxes, shutters, and large or small porch-flooring units for tests, but states that it is difficult to match wood in such large units. They are intended for special studies and not for general testing. Zabel and Moore

Figure 6.3. Post-rail test units at Harrison Experiment Forest. (Courtesy U.S. Dept. Agr. Forest Service)

Figure 6.4. Post-rail test units cut lengthwise to reveal interior.   Piece A, treated and sound; piece B, untreated with decayed interior.   (Courtesy T. Scheffer, Oregon State University, School of Forestry)

[67] measured effectiveness of different oil-soluble preservatives by nailing boards, treated with the test preservative, to the edge of treated 2 × 4's resting on the soil. A visual rating scale and reaction to a 150-pound load were used for inspection. Gersonde and Becker [25] also tested flooring units 50 × 85 cm made of alternate strips of treated and untreated wood. These were not exposed outside like the others, but in a dark cellar at 90 percent relative humidity. The supporting beams were inoculated with wood-decay fungi.

6.3.2.2 Service tests

Almost any residence with ponderosa pine sash, erected since about 1950, would serve as a test unit because nearly all such items have been treated with a water-repellent wood preservative. Unfortunately, few records are available. Some of the same statements made for service tests for preserved wood used in soil contact will also hold here. Verrall [64] describes many tests and observations made on buildings with treated parts. All of his work was with non-pressure-treated wood.

On the other hand, Walters and Peterson [66] used buildings on the University of Illinois campus to study behavior of pressure-treated millwork. In this case, only the moisture content and paintability were monitored, since the buildings were demolished before decay could occur. Reports of U-Committees of the AWPA and the paper by Gurd and Paterson [28] also include service records of preserved wood in aboveground use.

One of the chief benefits of these service tests is that they give ammunition to the sales department because the advantage of preserved wood in structures is so visual. Another revelation is that pressure-treated wood is not necessary for all outdoor exposures of wood.

6.4 Tests of Processed and Converted Wood

In addition to wood, preservatives are applied to hardboard, insulation board, plywood, and particleboard. The future for these panel products is bright, so methods for their preservation should grow in importance. The standard laboratory tests have been used in evaluation in Europe and in North America. For example, Huber [32] used the soil-block test in evaluation of sodium pentachlorophenate on hardboard and particleboard. More imagination is needed in developing field tests for these panel goods, mainly because they are not used interchangeably with lumber in all cases. For example, these sheets are rarely used in soil contact for permanent installation; therefore, why use a stake test? It would seem that field tests more in keeping with intended use are needed.

Behr [7] exposed treated 4 × 12-inch insulation-board samples made of three pieces of board wired together. These were set on the soil with $\frac{1}{4}$-inch sapwood pine slats separating the boards and placed inside a wooden box with a lattice cover so they would be slightly wetted by rain. Interpretation of results was difficult. Merrill and French [44] also devised a laboratory test for evaluation of preservatives in insulation board. The load necessary to pull a nail head through the board is the criterion of strength loss due to decay. Prior to evaluation on the universal testing machine, the 2.5 × 2.5-inch pieces of board are placed in a soil culture. Using *Lenzites trabea*, they found a 50 percent reduction in resistance to nail-head pull-through when weight loss was 12–15 percent. Moisture-content effects on strength have to be carefully controlled. Since Fungi Imperfecti have been found by Merrill, French, and Hossfeld [46] to rot insulation board in the field, laboratory cultures favorable to their growth are used instead of those for Basidiomycetes that decay solid wood.

Service tests are unwieldy because of the size of the sheets (usually 4 × 8 feet) and the measures needed for examination. Many of these products that are subject to decay and need preservation are used as sheathing, floor underlayment, or roof or wall insulation. As such, examination almost requires demolishing the building—hardly a convenient approach. Merrill and French [45] reported on a service test of roof insulation that was infected with one of the Fungi Imperfecti, but other reports are scarce.

6.5 Evaluation of Test Results and Interpretation

Almost no one believes that results from the laboratory testing of chemicals can be used to select new wood preservatives without field tests. However, researchers will keep trying to do so. It is a worthy aim. Some believe we can go back one step and eliminate threshold tests on creosote. Snoke [56] felt that the threshold could be calculated from the amount of creosote distilling below 355°C that remains in the blocks after weathering. However, he acknowledged that he was not sure the same relation would hold in stakes.

It is doubtful that laboratory-derived thresholds can be transposed directly to the field, even though it is frequently stated that the pentachlorophenol threshold of 0.15 lb/cu ft is valid in the field as well. This is a coincidence, because in the laboratory there is only one species of fungus while in the field there are many, or possibly one different from that used in the laboratory. Also, a culture jar is not the same as soil contact. Reproducible relations between field and laboratory lend confidence toward correlation, but coincidence of one set of values does not.

Some aspects of evaluation have already been considered during the discussion of each test method and will not be repeated here. Field tests give the most trouble, possibly because of the conflicting demands upon the tests. The Forest Products Laboratory, as indicated in yearly issues of Report 1761 or Research Note FPL-02, seems unwilling to draw conclusions until some of the stakes have been destroyed, while Colley [17] proposes faster action and uses intermediate conditions and their rate of attainment by plotting index of condition versus retention.

One of the weak spots in correlation of laboratory thresholds with stake evaluation is the existence of retention gradients. The importance of this has already been indicated for laboratory tests. As far as can be determined, there is no published information of retention gradients in $\frac{3}{4}$-inch stakes, full-cell treated with toxicants diluted with toluene, which had been tested shortly after the toluene has evaporated. Some data indicate it is probably flat as it is for LPG treatments. Empty-cell treatments for $\frac{3}{4}$-inch stakes (Davies and Henry [20]) and for 2 × 4's (Kelso, Behr, and Hill [35]) have gradients. Because of these gradients, one does not always know the retention of that part of a stake that shows rot unless chemical analyses are made of all layers before and after removal. Even then there can be unanswered questions. This lack of recognition of the existence and importance of preservative gradients places much of the past test-plot work in the category of "limited reliability." The surprising thing is that correlation of laboratory and field tests have been as good as they have.

The time during an experiment at which to make decisions in regard to performance is important because if it is delayed too long, differences are masked and time is lost. One way to ease the decision-making process is to include a "standard" preservative and compare the results with it to those in the experimental stakes.

Colley [17] and Stasse [57] have tried to get the weathering of creosote in the soil-block tests to parallel what happens in stakes. Reasonable correlation has been found by Stasse between these two tests, even with the weathering procedure that was then current. (One point in all of this that is sometimes wrongly stressed is that the test stakes indicate the number of years that wood treated commercially will last. This notion should be dispelled.) Stasse [57] believes that the lower boiling fraction of creosote should be evaporated from the stakes by a heat treatment prior to exposure to speed up time to significant decay. These recommendations are worthy of consideration for creosote, but there is still the problem of what to do with new and untried chemicals offered as wood preservatives. As Smith [52] indicates, if a new preservative passes laboratory toxicity tests with high marks, showing resistance to many fungi and other wood destroyers, and meets volatility, leaching, and other requirements, it is usually a safe bet that it will perform well commercially. However, if it shows some weaknesses, it may or may not show up well in service. It is about like studying past performances of race horses in the *Daily Racing Form*. Some are standouts and they are the favorites in the betting, but some that do not look quite so good prove to be winners. The soil-block threshold, a weathering procedure and its effect, the physical and chemical properties of the preservative, and the results of stake tests are all the "past performances." Their interpretation differs among workers, but the differences are gradually disappearing. Thus, we still cannot always predict future performance—we have to wait until the race is over to see who won.

ACKNOWLEDGMENT

Research for part of this chapter was sponsored by the Michigan Agricultural Experimental Station and is published as Journal Article No. 5793.

REFERENCES

1. Alliot, H. 1945. "Methode d'essais des produits anticryptogamiques." Bull. Tech. Inst. Nat. Bois. No. 1.
2. Amemya, S. 1963. "Stake test in Asakawa Experiment Forest 1: Methods for estimation of decay on stakes." Bull. For. Exp. Sta. Meguro, Tokyo, No. 150. 143–56.
3. ASTM 1961. "Standard method of testing wood preservatives by laboratory soil-block cultures." D1413 Am. Soc. for Testing and Materials, Philadelphia.
4. AWPA 1963. "Standard method of testing wood preservatives by laboratory soil-block cultures." M10 63 Am. Wood-Preservers' Assoc., Washington, D.C.
5. AWPA 1966. "Reports of utilization and service records committees." Proc., Am. Wood-Preservers' Assoc. 62:43–131.
6. Baechler, R.H. and Roth, H.G. 1956. "Laboratory leaching and decay tests on pine and oak blocks treated with several preservative salts." Proc., Am. Wood-Preservers' Assoc. 52:24–33.
7. Behr, E.A. 1948. "Preservation of fiber insulating board with chlorinated phenols." The Paper Industry and Paper World 30:930–35.
8. Behr, E.A. 1970. "Effectiveness of ground line wood preservative treatments for park structures." Michigan Agr. Exp. Sta. Res. Rept. No. 112.
9. Behr, E.A. 1972. "Development of respirometry as a method for evaluating wood preservatives." Forest Prod. J. 22:26–31.
10. Blew, J.O. 1955. "Service tests on posts as a means of evaluating wood preservatives and methods of treatment." U.S. Forest Serv., Forest Prod. Lab. Rept. No. 1726.
11. Blew, J.O. 1963. "A half century of service testing cross ties." Proc., Am. Wood-Preservers' Assoc. 59:138–46.
12. Blew, J.O. and Davidson, H.L. 1969. "Comparison of wood preservatives in stake tests." U.S. Forest Serv., Forest Prod. Lab Rept. No. 02.
13. Birkner, L. 1969. "Suggested standard method for field tests with wooden stakes." Material und Organismen 4(1):1–6.
14. Brown, F.L. 1963. "Tensile strength test for comparative evaluation of wood preservatives." Forest Prod. J. 8:405–12.
15. Colley, Reginald H. 1953. "The evaluation of wood preservatives." Bell Telephone System Tech. Pub. Monograph No. 2118. American Telephone and Telegraph Co., N.Y.
16. Colley, R.H. 1955. "A weathered laminated stake test technique for evaluation of wood preservatives." Forest Prod. J. 5:272–76.
17. Colley, R.H. 1970. "The practical meaning of preservative evaluation tests." Proc., Am. Wood-Preservers' Assoc. 66:16–37.
18. Cowling, E.B. 1957. "The relative preservative tolerances of 18 wood destroying fungi." Forest Prod. J. 7:355–59.
19. Da Costa, E.W.B. and Osborne, L.D. 1969. "Laboratory evaluations of wood preservatives. IV. Effect of experimental variables in testing creosotes against decay fungi." Holzforschung 23:206–12.
20. Davies, D.L. and Henry, W.T. 1965. "Preservative distribution as found in field exposure stakes and its potential effect on performance." Proc., Am. Wood-Preservers' Assoc. 61:72–80.
21. Duncan, C.G. 1958. "Studies of the methodology of soil-block testing." U.S. Forest Serv., Forest Prod. Lab. Rept. No. 2114.
22. Duncan, C.G. 1965. "Determining resistance to soft rot fungi." U.S. Forest Serv., Forest Prod. Lab. Rept. No. 48.

23. Duncan, C.G. and Lombard, F.F. 1965. "Fungi associated with principal decays in wood products in the United States." U.S. Forest Serv., Forest Prod. Lab. Rept. No. WO-4.
24. Findlay, W.P.K. 1935. "A standard laboratory test for wood preservatives." *British Wood Preserving Assoc. J.* 5:89–93.
25. Gersonde, M. and Becker, G. 1958. "Prüfung von Holzschutz mitteln für den Hochbau auf Wirksamkeit gegen Pilze an praxisgemässen Holzproben (Schwamkeller Versuche)." *Holz als Roh- und Werkstoff* 16:346–57.
26. Gibson, E.J. 1966. "The role of laboratory testing in the evaluation of wood preservatives." Supplement to Wood (London). 10–15
27. Göhre, K. 1955. "Holzschutzmittelkurzprüfung mit Hilfe der statischen Biegefestigkeit." *Arch. Forstw.* 4:293–301.
28. Gurd, J.M. and Paterson, A.L. 1963. "The utilization of treated wood in unusual modern types of construction." *Proc., Am. Wood-Preservers' Assoc.* 59:84–91.
29. Halabisky, Donald D. and Ifju, G. 1968. "Use of respirometry for fast and accurate evaluation of wood preservatives." *Proc., Am. Wood-Preservers' Assoc.* 64:215–23.
30. Hartley, C. 1958. "Evaluation of wood decay in experimental work." U.S. Forest Serv., Forest Prod. Lab. Rept. No. 2119.
31. Horsfall, J.G. 1956. *Principles of Fungicidal Action.* Chronica Botanica, Waltham, Mass.
32. Huber, H.A. 1958. "Preservation of particle board." *Forest Prod. J.* 8:356–60.
33. Hubert, E.E. 1938. "The preservative treatment of millwork." *Ind. Eng. Chem.* 30:1241–50.
34. Kaune, P. 1967. "Beitrag zur Laboratoriums prüfung mit Möderfäulepilzen." *Material und Organismen* 2:229–38.
35. Kelso, W. Jr., Behr, E.A. and Hill. R.E. 1955. "Pentachlorophenol gradients in pressure treated wood under exposure to weather." *Forest Prod. J.* 5:369–77.
36. Klem, G.G. 1957. "Ny metode for utsetting av prover pa impregnerings felter." *Norsk Skogbr.* 3:75–76.
37. Kulp, J.W. 1962. "Service life of poles in REA-financed electric systems (Third Report)." U.S. Forest Serv., Forest Prod. Lab. Report No. 2240.
38. Lancaster, E.L. 1963. "Inspection spots 700 dangerous poles: prompts ground-line treatment plan." *Elec. World* 160(17):50–51, 170.
39. Leutritz, J. Jr. 1964. "Three decades of evaluation of wood preservatives in stakes in outdoor test plots." *Proc., Am. Wood-Preservers' Assoc.* 60:130–144.
40. Levi, M.P. 1969. "The mechanism of action of copper-chrome-arsenate preservatives against wood-destroying fungi." *Record, British Wood Preserving Assoc.* 113–27.
41. Levi, M.P. 1969. "A rapid test for evaluating the fungicidal activity of potential wood preservatives." *J. Inst. Wood Sci.* 4(5):45–50.
42. Lumsden, G.Q. 1964. "Evaluation of wood preservatives in poles and posts at the Gulfport test plot." *Proc., Am. Wood-Preservers' Assoc.* 60:45–60.
43. Mateus, T.J.E. 1957. "A mechanical test for studying wood preservatives." *Record, British Wood Preserving Assoc.* 137–70.
44. Merrill, W. and French, D.W. 1964. "A nailhead pull-through method to determine the effects of fungi on strength." *Tappi* 47:449–51.
45. Merrill, W. and French, D.W. 1966. "Decay in wood and wood fiber products by *Sporotrichum pruinosum*." *Mycologia* 58:592–96.
46. Merrill, W., French, D.W. and Hossfeld, R. 1965. "Effects of common molds on physical and chemical properties of wood fiberboard." *Tappi* 48:470–74.
47. NWMA 1963. "Water-repellent preservative seal of approval program for millwork." Natl. Woodwork Mfrs. Assn., Chicago, Ill.

48. Purslow, D.F. 1962. "The effect of specimen size on the life of timber in contact with the ground." *Wood* (London) 27:99–100.

49. Rennerfelt, Erik. 1963. "A comparison between Swedish field tests and laboratory experiments with some wood preservatives." *Proc., Am. Wood-Preservers' Assoc.* 59:19–27.

50. Richards, C.A. 1925. "The comparative resistance of 18 species of wood destroying fungi to zinc chloride." *Proc., Am. Wood-Preservers' Assoc.* 21:18–22.

51. Schmitz, H. 1930. "A suggested toximetric method for wood preservatives." *Ind. Eng. Chem.*, Anal. Ed. 2:361–63.

52. Smith, D.N. 1965. "The evaluation of wood preservatives." *Record, British Wood Preserving Assoc.* 123–49.

53. Smith, D.N. 1969. "Field trials on coal-tar creosote and CCA preservatives. Results from a new method of assessment." *Holzforschung* 23:185–92.

54. Smith, R.S. 1969. "Wood preservative toxicity evaluation using wood weight loss and fungal respiration methods." *Wood Sci.* 2(1):44–53.

55. Smith, D.N. and Cockcroft, R. 1961. "A method of obtaining uniform distribution of wood preservatives in toxicity test blocks." *Nature* 189(4759):163–64.

56. Snoke, Lloyd R. 1954. "Observations on a possible method of predicting soil-block bioassay thresholds by distillation characteristics of weathered creosotes." *Forest Prod. J.* 4:111–14.

57. Stasse, Hans. 1968. "1958 Cooperative Creosote Project. V. Field tests with stakes and posts: Laboratory Evaluation Tests." *Proc., Am. Wood-Preservers' Assoc.* 64:17–36.

58. Theden, G. and Starfinger, K. 1952. "Versuche mit einem abgewandelten Laboratoriumsverfahren zur Kurzfristigen Prüfung der pilzwidrigen Wirksamkeit von Holzschutz mitteln." *Holzforschung* 6:105–10.

59. Toole, E.R. 1969. "Effect of decay on crushing strength." *Forest Prod. J.* 19:36–37.

60. Toole, E.R. 1971. "Evaluation of wood preservatives using crushing strength." *Phytopathology* 61:182–85.

61. Trendelenburg, R. 1940. "Uber die abkurzung der Zeitdauer von Pilzversuchen an Holz mit Hilfe der Schlagbieg prufüng." *Holz als Roh- und Werkstoff* 3:397–407.

62. Van Groenou, H.B., Rischen, H.W.L. and Van Den Berge, J. 1962. "Wood preservation during the last 50 years." A.W. Sijthoff's Uitgerversmaatschappij N.V., Leiden, Netherlands.

63. Verrall, A.F. 1965. "Preserving wood by brush, dip and short-soak methods." USDA Tech. Bull. No. 1334.

64. Verrall, A.F. 1966. "Building decay associated with rain seepage." USDA Tech. Bull. No. 1356.

65. Walters, C.S. 1954. "A uniform service test for fence posts." *J. Forestry* 52:527.

66. Walters, C.S. and Peterson, K.R. 1964. "Exposure test of painted, pressure treated millwork." *Forest Prod. J.* 14:87–94.

67. Zabel, R. and Moore, R.A. 1958. "Relative effectiveness of several oil-soluble wood preservatives." *Forest Prod. J.* 8:258–63.

7. Degradation and Protection of Wood from Marine Organisms

HARRY HOCHMAN

Naval Civil Engineering Laboratory
Port Hueneme, California

7.1 Introduction

Animals that attack wood in a marine environment, known collectively as marine borers, are widely distributed throughout the world and are especially destructive in warm-water regions. Throughout the 2,000-year recorded history of the destructive activities of these animals, little was achieved in their control until recently. Efforts to arrive at effective borer control were approached empirically during most of this time and one of the earliest to recognize the futility of this approach was Stephen Hale [9] who, in 1743, stated that it "might prove of very great service to shipping" to have "a short account drawn up and published of the principal methods that are now in use or that have from time to time been proposed and tried for preventing the planks and timbers of ships being eaten by worms."

Although the preservation of wood in a marine environment today is chiefly concerned with fixed structures, the preservation of wooden ships was of greater importance in the past. More ships were probably lost as a result of the ravages of borers than were lost by poor seamanship.

The empirical approach did result in the discovery of creosote as a wood preservative. Creosote is an effective preservative in cold-water harbors but has failed to provide an acceptable service life in tropical harbors. Because tropical and warm-water harbors have become important only recently, the inability of creosote to protect wood in those harbors was discounted. The creosote producers always placed the blame on the treater—never on the creosote. Either he used a poor grade of creosote, or he diluted his creosote with petroleum, or he did a poor job of impregnating. More recently, we have learned that this was not so. Creosote failed in warm-water harbors because it is not an effective preservative in those harbors. Creosote-treated wood also failed due to poor construction practices.

7.1.1 Scope and economic aspects

Although many methods have been employed to combat their destructive activities, marine boring organisms cause an estimated $50 million in damage each year to waterfront structures along the coasts of the United States. In addition to these costs is the inconvenience that occurs when piers are removed from service during the reconstruction period.

The rate at which untreated timbers can be destroyed by marine boring organisms is illustrated by a situation that occurred in Hawaii and was reported by Dr. C. H. Edmondson of the Bernice P. Bishop Museum [12].

In the process of laying an outfall sewer off Sand Island in Hawaii, a long trestle was constructed of untreated Douglas-fir from which the heavy equipment required to handle the huge concrete pipe was to operate. Danger from marine borers was realized, but since the project was to be completed in 8 months, the construction company considered the use of treated structural timbers an unnecessary expense. In 70 days sections of the trestle collapsed, plunging a number of pieces of heavy equipment, including diesel engines, into the sea. The equipment was recovered, but valuable time was lost in removing what was left of the trestle and completing the job from barges.

Harbor engineers will be presented with similar decisions in the future and similar, although hopefully less dramatic, results can be expected. This pessimism is based on the speed with which changes in the harbor environment are taking place as harbor clean-up campaigns progress. Borer infestation occurs as soon as a sufficient oxygen supply develops. Harbor engineers who have developed a complacent attitude toward their wooden structures because they have had few or no borer problems for many years may be surprised by the sudden onslaught and rapid destruction of wood by these animals.

7.1.2 Characteristics of infested wood

Wood that has been attacked by marine borers may or may not show visible damage. *Limnoria,* or "gribble," burrow just below the surface of the wood and produce a lacework that is readily observable. As the action of the waves in the intertidal zone removes the thin covering of the *Limnoria* burrows, the animals burrow deeper into the wood in a pile, producing an ever-decreasing diameter and the familiar "hourglass" shape. The teredinids, or shipworms, enter through a tiny hole on the surface and bore into the wood as they grow. They can destroy the interior of a pile without any essential show of surface damage. Sudden failures of piers are the work of these animals.

7.1.3 Naturally resistant wood

All wood species tested for resistance to marine boring organisms have been damaged to some extent. Most native American wood species used for marine piling are readily attacked by marine borers [7]. There are a few woods, however, that have gained reputations for borer resistance. Among these are the South and Central American woods, Greenheart and Angelique, and the Australian *Syncarpia laurifolia* or turpentine wood.

Although resistant woods may withstand borer attack for long periods of time in some harbors, they are readily attacked in others. For example, Greenheart piles rated as being in good condition after 80 years in the harbor of Liverpool, England, were attacked in 4 years at Salem, England, and failed in Java and India in 5–10 years [1,6].

In addition to the variable resistance to marine borers offered by resistant woods in various harbors, the same species of wood grown in different soils may differ considerably in both composition and resistance. Turpentine wood, *Syncarpia laurifolia,* is used extensively as a pile timber in Australia. In exposure tests in Honolulu Harbor, Australian-grown turpentine wood was lightly attacked by *Teredo* and showed moderate superficial action by *Limnoria* after four years [13]. Blocks of the same species grown in Hawaii were often badly damaged in five months. Chemical analysis showed the Australian-grown wood to contain up to 1.25 percent silica; the maximum silica content of Hawaiian grown wood was 0.17 percent. The averages of a number of samples were 0.59 and 0.091 percent, respectively.

Some correlation seems to exist between the silica content of wood and its resistance to marine borers. Woods with a high silica content, with few exceptions, are more resistant than woods of low silica content [12,24]. To test the effects of increasing the silica content of wood, southern pine blocks were impregnated with silica in the author's laboratory. The borer resistance was increased. Untreated blocks were destroyed in 3–6 months while panels impregnated to a high silica content were only lightly damaged after two years. Unfortunately, although the resistance to wood borers had increased, the resultant product appeared to be suitable for rock-boring pholads and the panels were severely damaged by these animals.

Some resistant woods such as Greenheart and *Lignum vitae* do not have a high silica content. Their resistance has often been attributed to their alkaloid content [22,23]; a number of bis-benzylisoquinoline alkaloids have been isolated from Greenheart and identified in the author's laboratory [16].

It should be noted, however, that in no case have woods of high silica content been low in borer resistance, although a few woods of low silica content may be resistant because of their alkaloid content or for other reasons.

It can be seen from the preceding discussion that naturally resistant woods can be used for waterfront structures in some harbors, but the number of harbors in which they can be used without preliminary investigation is comparatively small.

7.2 Marine Borer Groups

The term "marine borer" generally has been used to include those marine invertebrates which bore into and consequently damage timber and other solid objects in salt water. Here, the definition will be restricted to those marine invertebrates which attack wooden structures.

The animal organisms responsible for the biological deterioration of wooden marine structures are members of two main groups [17]. The first group is composed of animals from the phylum Mollusca. In their larval stages, they are oyster- or clamlike in appearance and metamorphose into wormlike animals as they bore into wood. Members of this phylum are responsible for the rapid destruction of timbers exposed in a marine environment. The particular genera involved are the *Teredo* and *Bankia* of the family Teredinidae, and the pholads *Martesia* and *Xylophaga*.

The second group of animals are of the phylum Crustacea and are comprised mainly of species of the genus *Limnoria* and, in some harbors, of the genus *Sphaeroma*. The *Limnoria* are like sow-bugs in appearance and are about $\frac{1}{8}$ inch long. The *Sphaeroma* are about $\frac{3}{8}$ inch long and look like white pill bugs. They generally burrow just beneath the surface of the wood and their activities are readily observable on surface inspection.

7.2.1 Molluscan borers

The molluscan or teredine borers begin their existence as free-swimming larvae (Figure 7.1). The two *Teredo* species, *Teredo navalis* and *Teredo diegensis,* found on the west coast of the continental United States, are bisexual. Fertilization and development of the larvae occurs within the body of the animal, and the mature larvae are ejected into the sea through the excurrent siphon of the animal. At this stage the larvae of *Teredo diegensis,* the only species identified at Port Hueneme, are about 250 microns (0.01 inch) in diameter, and they must attack wood within 48 hours or they lose their ability to bore successfully into wood. The larvae

Figure 7.1. *Teredo* larvae, average diameter 250 microns.

crawl on the surface of the wood by means of an amoeboid projection called the foot, apparently in search of a suitable spot to bore into the wood. When that spot has been found, the foot is used to clean away all debris and boring begins.

Four significant changes now take place: (1) a serated projection develops at a 90-degree angle to the original shell hemisphere; (2) siphons develop which permit the animal to pump seawater through its body; (3) the clear chitin shell of the larva starts to calcify; and (4) the animal begins to elongate (Figure 7.2), with the shell or boring end proceeding into the wood and the siphon end remaining at the original site of penetration. Once an animal has bored into wood, its life cycle is completed in that piece of wood.

The only *Bankia* species of any significance on the west coast of the United States is *Bankia setacea* (Figure 7.3). Like all other members of this genus, and in contrast to some species of *Teredo,* adult animals eject sperm and eggs into the sea where fertilization takes place. Swimming immature larvae develop within a few hours, but it is about a month before they attack wood. After wood is attacked, the *Bankia* larvae metamorphose in a manner similar to those of the *Teredo.*

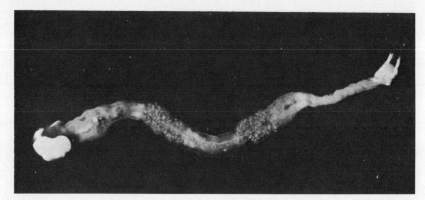

Figure 7.2. Adult *Teredo*, up to 6 inches in length. "Granules" within the body are larvae.

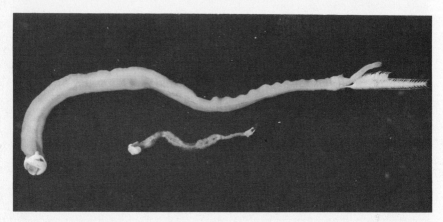

Figure 7.3. Adult *Bankia* and *Teredo*. *Bankia* in Hueneme harbor grow to a length of 12–14 inches in 1 year.

Pholads are molluscan borers that are important only in warm-water harbors. Like the teredinids, they begin their existence as free-swimming larvae and, after they attack a piece of wood, complete their life cycle within that piece of wood. Unlike the teredinids, they retain their bivalve structure and develop a clamlike appearance as they grow. As a result, they produce wider but shorter holes than do the teredine borers.

Pholads of the genus *Martesia* are active in the waters off Hawaii and other Pacific islands, but have not been reported in harbors of the western United States. They have been reported in East Coast harbors from South Carolina southward, but assume economic importance from Florida southward.

One of the most surprising recent findings is the discovery of wood-boring organisms in the deep ocean. Pholads of the genus *Xylophaga* have been captured in large numbers in test boards in both Atlantic and Pacific waters [10,30,31]. The Atlantic Ocean site was in the Tongue of the Ocean, Bahama Islands, at a depth of 5,762 feet. The Pacific Ocean sites were near San Miguel Island, about 75–80 nautical miles southwest of Port Hueneme, California, at water depths of 2,500–6,800 feet (Figure 7.4).

The large number of *Xylophaga* larvae found at all test sites suggests that these animals normally burrow into the mud in the ocean bottom. Larval settlement on wood samples was heaviest within 1–2 feet above the mud line and decreased rapidly so that there was only an occasional one 6 feet or more above the mud line.

7.2.2 Crustacean borers

The crustacean borers resemble a sow bug in appearance. The most common wood borers of this class are members of the genus *Limnoria*. The bodies of these animals are from $\frac{1}{8}$–$\frac{1}{4}$ inch in length and about one-third as wide. Their seven pairs of legs end in sharp, hooked claws which enable the animals to cling to wood and move freely on its surface. They burrow just below the surface of the wood and form a series of tunnels.

Figure 7.4. *Xylophaga* species removed from pine panel after 2 years at 6,000 feet off the coast of southern California.

Menzies [26] found that at a low population density there are only two animals in each tunnel, one male and one female, with the female in the blind end of the tunnel.

The female carries the eggs in a brood pouch on the underside of the body between the two rows of legs. The number of eggs in a single brood is seldom less than 6 or more than 17. When hatched, the young differ only in size from the adult and are ready to bore at once. They begin to bore near the parent so that *Limnoria* infestation generally spreads from a focal point. Heavily infested wood may contain 300–400 animals (of all ages) per square inch.

The three *Limnoria* species found along the west coast of North America [26,27,28,29] and two along the East Coast [44] are shown in Figure 7.5. The largest species, *Limnoria lignorum,* is found from Alaskan waters as far south as Point Arena, California, and in the colder waters of the East Coast as far south as Port of New York. Between Point Arena and Port Hueneme or Los Angeles, California, the predominant *Limnoria* species is *Limnoria quadripunctata.* From Port Hueneme or Los Angeles harbors southward and in the warmer waters of the East Coast, the smallest *Limnoria* species, *Limnoria tripunctata* [27,28,29], predominates.

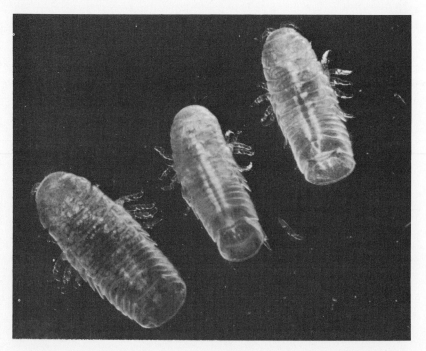

Figure 7.5. *Limnoria* species. Left to right: *lignorum, tripunctata, quadripunctata.*

The relationship between *Limnoria* species and water temperature has been pointed out by Menzies [26]. *Limnoria lignorum* requires cold water, *Limnoria tripunctata* requires water of an intermediate temperature.

7.2.3 Borer damage and temperature

The exaggerated effect of comparatively small changes in water temperature on the *Limnoria* populations was demonstrated in Port Hueneme harbor in the years 1956–1958 [18], during which a limited study was made of their migration habits. Monthly counts were made of animals that had migrated to collection boards. In 1956 two-thirds of the migrating animals were *Limnoria quadripunctata*. In 1958 the ratio of *Limnoria quadripunctata* to *Limnoria tripunctata* had changed to 1:10, a twentyfold increase in the proportion of the latter species. Interestingly, the number of *Limnoria quadripunctata* remained the same while the number of *Limnoria tripunctata* had increased 20 times. The temperature change responsible for this tremendous change in populations of *Limnoria* species was only 3.3°F—from 57.8°F in 1956 to 61.1°F in 1958. Additional studies have recently been reported that relate *Limnoria* populations with water temperatures [14,22].

In addition to the average harbor temperature, the duration of the extremes of annual fluctuation may be significant. Thus, Ryabchikov and Nikolayeva [38] demonstrated the tremendous influence not only of temperature level but also of temperature duration on the settlement of *Teredo navalis* larvae. There was minimal larval settlement at 20–21°C. Mass settlement occurred at temperatures of 24–27°C. If a mean temperature of 24°C persisted for one month, settling was slight. If it persisted for two months, settlement intensity increased sixfold. If, however, it persisted for three months, settlement intensity increased twenty-seven fold. Peak settlement occured at the end of the period of optimum temperature.

Harada [15] used the change in burrow volume as a measure of the growth rate of *Bankia bipalmulata* in the Formosan Strait. He found that a change in temperature from the 17.2–17.5°C range to the 26.1–28.1°C range resulted in an almost logarithmic change in the monthly growth rate from 0.2 cc per animal per month to 13.5 cc per animal per month. The latter growth rate could not be maintained, and in two months at this temperature range the volume per animal had increased to only 14.5 cc.

The inescapable conclusion is that a small change in harbor temperature can have an inordinately large effect on the biological activity in that harbor.

Two other variables which influence the biological activity in a harbor, but which have not been thoroughly studied, are salinity and oxygen concentration. These are not independent variables and their effects are influenced by temperature. The higher the temperature, the greater is their influence. Thus, *Limnoria* will live longer under conditions of low salinity (such as one-half that of seawater) at 5°C than at 25°C. One borer species, *Teredo healdi,* has even adapted to essentially fresh water. This organism is found both in the brackish water of Lake Maracaibo in Venezuela and the essentially fresh water of Miraflores Lake in the Panama Canal. Wakeman [46] has also shown that *Limnoria* require at least 2.0 ppm of oxygen to survive. No similar data is available on the oxygen requirements of teredinids.

Salinity and oxygen concentration are important because they can change rapidly in river estuaries, where most wooden structures are located. The distance that borer infestation will proceed up-river will depend upon the volume of water coming down the river, and therefore with seasonal and annual rainfall in the river basin. Such an event is dramatically reported in the Final Report of the San Francisco Marine Piling Committee, which describes in detail the disastrous effects of a decreased water flow in the Sacramento River. Similarly, as pollution abatement steps are taken, formerly polluted waters are becoming sufficiently oxygenated to support borer populations.

In the latter stages of *Limnoria* attack, the *Limnoria* is frequently associated with another amphipod, a member of the genus *Chelura.* At one time these animals (Figure 7.6) were considered to be wood borers because they were often present in large numbers on wood undergoing rapid surface deterioration. Careful experiments have shown, however, that *Chelura* merely browse on wood and in the absence of *Limnoria* would cause little wood destruction. The results of *Chelura* browsing on a test panel in the laboratory are shown in Figure 7.7 and can readily be differentiated from the burrowing done by *Limnoria* (Figure 7.8) on a similar panel. Barnard [3] states that "*Chelura* has never been found in nature without the concurrent presence of *Limnoria.*" Kühne [25] suggests that a symbiotic relationship exists between these animals. *Limnoria* feed on wood and *Chelura* feed on the *Limnoria* feces, thus keeping the burrow clean. *Chelura* also increase the size of the *Limnoria* burrow by their browsing action. The cleansing and enlarging of the *Limnoria* burrow also permits better water circulation to increase the supply of oxygen to the *Limnoria* and permits them to burrow deeper into the wood.

The largest crustacean known to damage wood is the *Sphaeroma,* (Figure 7.9). While their burrows are much larger than those of *Limnoria,* the animals themselves are not as numerous nor as destructive. They are reported to exist along the Pacific Coast as far north as Alaska and have been found in test boards outside San Francisco Bay. They appear to prefer very soft wood, and do not constitute a serious economic problem in United States waters. *Sphaeroma* have caused serious problems in

Figure 7.6. *Chelura terebans* (dorsal view), with ventral view of *Limnoria* species.

Australian waters and are numerous in some parts of the harbor in San Juan, Puerto Rico.

7.2.4 Visual evidence of borer damage

Examination of the surface of a cleaned, laminated 4 × 4 × 12-inch southern pine block, made up of $\frac{1}{4}$-inch lamina, shows comparatively little borer damage as a result of its eight months' exposure in Hueneme harbor (Figure 7.10). Figure 7.11 is a magnified view of *Limnoria* in their burrows just below the surface of untreated wood.

Close examination of the block while it is still in the seawater (Figure

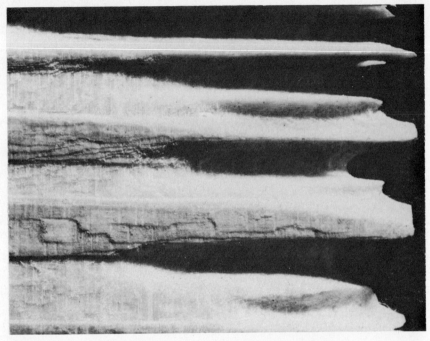

Figure 7.7. Results of *Chelura* browsing on a pine panel.

7.12) shows the siphons of the teredine borers projecting from the surface. This is the only evidence of the presence of the shipworm type of borer that is visible on surface inspection of the block. Even these, however, may not be seen unless the block has been cleaned to remove fouling organisms.

Sawing the block into two parts (Figure 7.13), or separating the lamina (Figure 7.14), shows the severe structural damage which the shipworms have caused. The larger holes are caused by *Bankia setacea,* which, in Hueneme harbor, can grow to a length of 10–12 inches in 8 months. The smaller holes are caused by *Teredo diegensis,* which seldom grow to lengths of more than 5 or 6 inches in Hueneme harbor.

7.3 Testing Experimental Preservatives

A good discussion of the various tests and test methods which have been performed in the past is covered in a summary by Behr and Vind [8]. After reviewing this summary, it is readily apparent that a standard test procedure is nonexistent. Consequently, it is difficult—if not impossible— to directly compare results of the various tests.

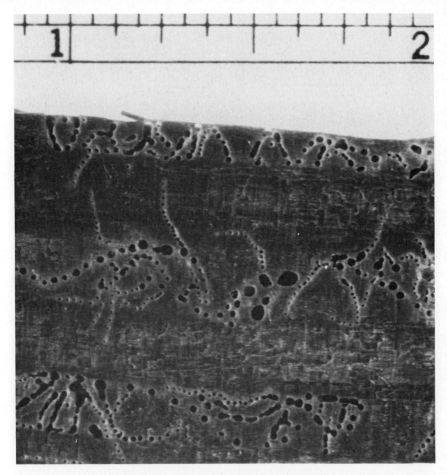

Figure 7.8. *Limnoria* burrows in a pine panel.

In general, three basic types of tests have been utilized in studying the degradation of wood by marine borers [8]. A brief description of these test methods is presented below.

Experimental wood treatments are customarily evaluated by exposing wooden panels impregnated with solutions of the test chemical in a harbor. The test specimens vary in size and shape from $\frac{3}{4}$-inch cubes to full-size piles. The duration of the tests is frequently a matter of years, and the analysis of the test results is made by persons who did not initiate the tests. Under these circumstances, one might expect the testing programs to be well designed and carefully planned. The contrary is true, and experimental piles being tested for marine-borer resistance have been driven

Figure 7.9. *Sphaeroma* species from San Juan, Puerto Rico.

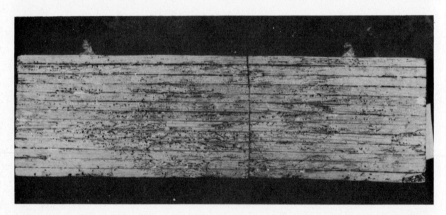

Figure 7.10. Surface attack on laminated pine block after 8 months in Port Hueneme harbor.

on dry land and in a river estuary! As a result, valid deductions are difficult to obtain, the same materials are repeatedly retested, and specifications are sometimes based on insufficient data.

For a test program to produce valid results, it must be designed for the specific information that is sought. A municipal harbor engineer is interested in maintaining structures in a single locality. A company which

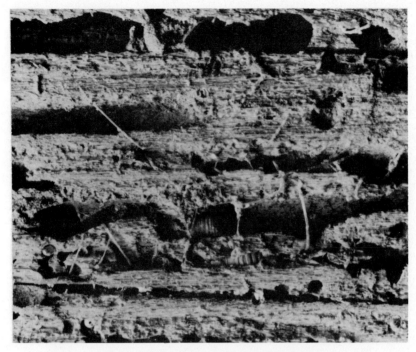

Figure 7.11. Limnoria in burrows in pine block.

is seeking a market for a chemical will be solely interested in the effectiveness of that chemical. A worldwide user of treated wood, such as the U.S. Navy, is interested in getting the maximum possible service life under a wide variety of harbor conditions. Each goal will require a different test program.

Factors to be considered in devising a test program are as follows:

1. Test specimens must be exposed in a biologically active environment. One cannot test for resistance to marine borers at test sites where there are no borers. Nor should the panels be exposed where the borer hazard is minimal; rather, the exposure should be at sites where the number, kinds, and appetites of the borers are at a maximum.

2. Untreated panels are useful in determining the numbers and species of borer populations and the suitability of the test site, but are of no value as controls in the evaluation of preservative treatments. At an active test site, borers will destroy untreated wood in a short time—less than one year. An effective treatment must protect wood for many years. Controls, therefore, must serve two functions. They provide an integrated record of the severity of the bioenvironment and compare the resistance to biodeterioration of the experimental treatment with that of a reference

Figure 7.12. End-surface of a laminated pine block, with *Teredo* (small) and *Bankia* (large) siphons extending into the surrounding water.

treatment. The best control or reference treatment is one with which there has been a considerable amount of experience—that is, the standard preservative treatment, creosote.

3. The test facility should be in an area that is protected from physical damage by storm or by the curious. A marine-borer test program, by its nature, must expose test specimens for long periods of time. It is disheartening as well as wasteful to have years of exposure data nullified by an unusual storm or by vandalism.

4. Proper statistical design is one of the most important factors in a successful test program. Replication is important in the testing of uniform materials. Its importance is magnified in a material as nonuniform

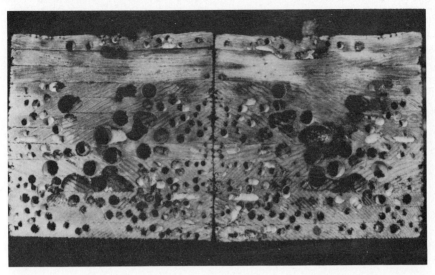

Figure 7.13. Sawed laminated block. Large holes caused by *Bankia*, smaller holes by *Teredo*.

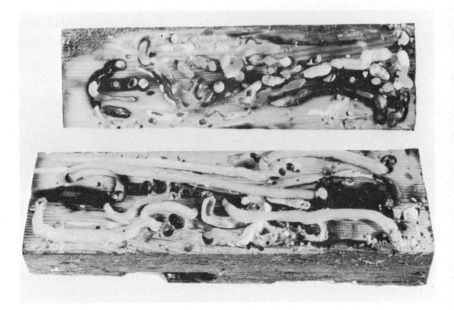

Figure 7.14. Separated lamina. Large animals are *Bankia*, smaller ones are *Teredo*.

as wood. Statisticians have estimated that if test piles are used, 7 piles per treatment will differentiate between 2 treatments. Differentiation is seldom sufficient. A larger number of replicates is required to determine how much better one treatment is than another. In a panel-testing program, at least 10 replicates are recommended for each experimental treatment.

5. The length of exposure should not be predetermined. Instead, exposures should be continued until the specimens have been severely damaged and are supporting active colonies of borers. In the poorer treatments, borer damage becomes progressively more severe with time after initial attack. In the better treatments, it is not uncommon for some test panels within a test group to show early initial attack but little or no progress with further exposure. Some panels within the group may even remain free from attack during their entire period of exposure. This is possible because initial attack normally refers to attack by *Limnoria*. Teredinid or pholad attack normally cannot be noted until it has progressed sufficiently to weaken the panel. As a result, panels within a test group may show initial *Limnoria* attack or remain free from *Limnoria* attack during their entire exposure and still be destroyed by teredinidae or pholads.

The fallacy of accepting short-term exposure data as sufficient was embarrassingly demonstrated several years ago. Treatment with copper formate was recommended for wood to be exposed in a marine environment after about two years of exposure at an eastern harbor. Exposures in western and Pacific island harbors for the same length of time revealed the inadequacy of this treatment.

It should be noted that no specific recommendations are given for the size of the test specimen, species of wood, method of treatment, etc. These parameters should be chosen to suit the goals of the test program. Only when test programs are to be compared quantitatively must there be uniformity.

A second test method, which is basically a screening test, is performed by exposing small treated blocks to marine borers maintained in suitable containers in the laboratory. Generally, the water is static, but in a recent test the water was circulated and aerated [35]. The advantage of this type of test is that controlled exposure conditions, reproducibility, and accelerated results are attained. The principle disadvantage is that additional field tests must be carried out before the results can be applied to commercial operations.

The third test method, which has been developed in recent years, is the Toxicity Screening Test [21,42,43]. In this test, the marine borers are placed in salt-water solutions which contain varying amounts of chemicals. These chemicals are then rated by determining the time required to kill the marine borers. This test makes it possible to screen a large number of chemicals in a short period of time and has led to the development of several new preservative systems for marine exposure. The details and results of this test are covered in Section 7.4.3.

7.4 Historical Control Methods

Since man first recognized the shipworm problem, many remedies have been tried. The earliest means of combating borers probably consisted of anchoring ships upstream from river estuaries. In addition to killing any shipworms that were in the wooden hulls, this procedure also caused fouling organisms to drop off of the sides and bottoms of the vessels. As ships traveled farther and farther from shore and were away from their harbors for longer periods of time, other procedures were inaugurated.   These included such practices as applying brews and concoctions of many kinds, as well as metal sheathing and scupper nailing—*i.e.,* driving closely spaced flathead nails over the entire surface that is to be exposed to borers. Some of these methods have persisted for many years. Fisherman in Iran, for example, still bring their fishing vessels out of the water periodically and apply a concoction prepared from local berries to the entire hull.

7.4.1 Control factors

The most satisfactory method which has been developed for the preservation of wood in a marine environment is creosoting. In some harbors —especially the cold-water harbors—creosoted timbers have lasted 30 years and more. In warmer harbors, however, creosoted pilings, just like some of the naturally resistant woods, do not last longer than 10–15 years. More recently, the practice of incorporating coal tar into creosote has given protection for longer periods of time in some harbors.

The incidence of early failure of creosoted timbers coincides to a considerable extent with the presence of *Limnoria tripunctata*. These animals apparently can live in the presence of high concentrations of creosote, as seen in Figure 7.15. As they erode the creosoted surface, the lightly treated or untreated portions of the structure are exposed. The structure now can be attacked by the shipworm type of organisms, and is destroyed in a relatively short period of time. Any new treatment should, therefore, be aimed primarily at *Limnoria tripunctata*.

7.4.2 Creosote

Impregnation with creosote has been used for many years as a means of protecting wood from marine boring organisms. Creosote did protect wood in those areas where it was originally used. As the use of creosoted

Figure 7.15. Section of creosoted pile after 17 years in Port Hueneme harbor. Note the complete *Limnoria* attack on the part that was always above the mud line and the partial attack where the mud line shifted.

wood spread, environments were found where it had a very short service life. Instead of accepting the conclusion that creosote might not be the proper preservative for this environment, wood preservers rationalized away these facts in a number of ways. From this mass of rationalization a pattern of both fact and fiction eventually evolved [18].

The pattern assumes that: (1) the service life of creosoted wood in a marine environment is governed entirely by the quality and quantity of creosote that is used; (2) creosote is an ideal preservative because it is a liquid and can migrate in the wood; (3) it can replenish, by the "reservoir effect," the toxic materials that are leached away from the surface of a pile; (4) all that is necessary to protect wood is to maintain a certain minimum threshold amount of creosote in the wood at all times; (5) creosote losses are caused entirely by leaching of creosote from the wood by seawater and therefore the greater the quantity of creosote that is impregnated into the wood, the longer will be the service life of that wood; (6) any method that will decrease the rate of loss of creosote by leaching will also increase the service life of wood.

Although there is some truth to these assumptions, with time the original idea became altered or was extrapolated beyond all reasonable limits. Thus, the term "reservoir effect" as used today differs radically from that described by Bateman [4,5]. Bateman considered creosote to be composed of two groups of compounds. One group was sufficiently soluble in water to render it toxic and the other group was water-insoluble and therefore nontoxic. The nontoxic or "barren oil" fraction acted as a reservoir for the toxic fraction and automatically fed the latter fraction into the surrounding water to maintain a toxic condition. Today, the reservoir theory is used to describe the migration of creosote from the interior of a pile to its surface as that surface becomes depleted by leaching or other mechanisms.

The assumption most frequently encountered was that the greater the amount of creosote that was impregnated into the wood, the longer would be the service life of that piece of wood. Losses of creosote with time were assumed to be due entirely to the leaching action of seawater, and it was supposed that the wood would remain immune from borer attack so long as a minimum quantity—a threshold amount—of creosote was still left in the wood. This assumption would be correct if leaching were the only mechanism by which creosote loses its effectiveness. There are, however, three processes which occur when creosoted wood is placed in a marine environment—and leaching may be the least important one.

Everyone who has watched creosoted piling being driven through water is acquainted with the oil slick that appears around the pile and persists for a long period of time. Sweeney [40] and, later, Stasse [39] showed that this oil slick is a result of the mechanical expulsion of creosote as the

wood fibers swell during their hydration; 30–40 percent of the creosote
originally impregnated into the wood may be lost by this process.   The
60–70 percent left in the pile would still be an effective preservative if
mechanical expulsion were not followed by leaching and by bacterial
alteration [11,32] to a less toxic material.   These latter processes are
slower, and their rate is highly dependent upon the water temperature.
Bacteria that metabolize creosote have been isolated from all harbors that
were examined and, interestingly, creosote constituents that are toxic to
marine borers are more readily metabolized than are the nontoxic
components.

7.4.3 Search for new preservatives

The failure of creosote to protect wood in warm-water harbors for more
than a short time has prompted a search for new and better preservatives.
The empirical approach was used with little success until a systematic
study was undertaken by the U.S. Navy at the Naval Civil Engineering
Laboratory (NCEL) in Port Hueneme, California.

The common method of testing and comparing wood preservatives is
to impregnate wooden panels with a solution of the test chemical and expose the experimentally treated and control panels to borer attack in
harbors with known borer activity.   Those chemicals that protected wood
better than creosote would become potentially useful treatments.   There
are so many thousands of chemicals available that testing them all in this
manner was impractical.   A search was therefore instituted to find a
method of reducing this number to practical proportions and the Toxicity
Screening Test was developed [21,42,43].

The Toxicity Screening Test was based on the assumption that to act
as a wood preservative a chemical must be toxic to the borer when ingested.   Further, the toxicity must be at least as great as that of creosote
to merit further investigation.

In principle, toxicity alone may not be necessary for a chemical to be a
good wood preservative.   Other factors such as substrate hardness and
repellency might also operate to achieve the same objective.   The measure
of hardness becomes less attractive when one realizes that marine wood-
boring organisms have bored into objects as soft as kelp and as hard as
ironwood.   Repellency cannot be used to differentiate between chemicals
because there is no means presently available to test this property in an
aqueous medium.

The test animals used in the Toxicity Screening Test were adult *Limnoria tripunctata* and *Teredo diegensis* larvae [43].   The *Limnoria* were obtained from a heavily infested section of creosoted piling that had been
removed from a pier in Hueneme harbor.   When *Limnoria* were needed,

a few square inches of pile surface were removed, brought into the laboratory, covered with a towel soaked in seawater and placed in a refrigerator. (After a few hours the *Limnoria* leave their burrows and crawl on the surface, from which they can be easily removed to a holding dish of seawater.) After several days the healthy vigorous animals were removed for use in the Toxicity Test and the others were discarded. Hundreds of animals could be obtained from each square inch of pile surface and generally all were *Limnoria tripunctata*. There were occasional pockets of *quadripunctata*.

To obtain *Teredo* larvae, 4 × 4 × 12-inch southern pine blocks were suspended in Hueneme harbor for 6–8 months to insure a heavy infestation with *Teredo diegensis*. The blocks were removed from the harbor, scraped free of fouling and placed in glass aquaria provided with running filtered seawater and a system for permitting the overflow to pass through a fine-mesh stainless steel or plastic screen. The *Teredo* larvae were collected on this screen, suspended in clean seawater and transferred to test dishes by pipetting.

In the preliminary screening, solutions or suspensions were prepared containing 100 ppm of test chemical. Ten milliliters of solution or suspension was placed in a petri dish and either 10 vigorous *Limnoria tripunctata* or about 50 swimming *Teredo diegensis* larvae were added to each dish. Chemicals that did not kill at least half of the *Limnoria* in 200 hours or all of the *Teredo* larvae in 72 hours were considered to have too little toxicity to warrant further consideration. The chemicals that warranted further consideration were retested at a lower chemical concentration. Chemicals toxic to the test animals were found among all chemical groups except the saturated hydrocarbons.

The most prominent finding was the evidence that chemical compounds that are toxic to one borer genus generally are relatively nontoxic to the other borer genus. Chemicals that are most toxic to *Limnoria* include those that interfere with sulfhydryl enzyme activity, exhibit parasympathomimetic activity by cholinesterase inhibition, and block the activity of inositol, a member of the vitamin B complex. *Teredo* larvae, on the other hand, are especially sensitive to sympathomimetic agents and glycolytic enzyme inhibitors. Although the teredinid, *Bankia,* and the pholad, *Martesia,* were not included in the screening program, their closer relationship to *Teredo* might lead one to predict that they will be controlled by agents toxic to *Teredo*. To some extent this is so, although higher concentrations of chemicals are required to poison these animals.

It must also be borne in mind that the reported mechanisms by which an agent exerts its toxicity are generally based on studies of terrestrial animals and of enzymes isolated from these animals. An agent that operates by one mechanism on terrestrial animals may operate by a different mechanism on marine invertebrates. Also, chemical compounds may be capable of more than one type of pharmacological activity. When one type of activity is dominant, the other may not be exhibited until the first is suppressed. Thus, the organophosphates are generally reported to be cholinesterase inhibitors and are toxic to both *Limnoria* and *Teredo* larvae. They are especially toxic to the latter animal. Eserine or physostigmine is a specific cholinesterase inhibitor and is very toxic to *Limnoria*. *Teredo* larvae appear to thrive in the presence of this alkaloid. The organophosphates must, therefore, exert their toxicity on the *Teredo* larvae by some mechanisms not associated with cholinesterase inhibition or the eserine must be unable to penetrate the larval membrane. The latter possibility appears to be unlikely, and a nonparasympathomimetic mechanism must be required for *Teredo* toxicity. Indeed, extensive investigations of the organophosphates have shown that anticholinesterase activity is associated primarily with aliphatic phosphates and that the aryl esters operate by a different and as yet ill-defined mechanism.

7.4.4 New preservatives

The finding in the Toxicity Screening Test that chemical compounds that are toxic to one borer genus are generally little toxic or even nontoxic to the other borer genus suggests that no single chemical will be able to preserve wood adequately and that a combination of chemicals must be used. This approach was tested in a Harbor Screening Test [20] and found to be valid. Southern pine and Douglas-fir sapwood panels ($\frac{1}{4} \times 1\frac{5}{8} \times 6$ inches) were impregnated with solutions of individual chemicals and combinations of chemicals and exposed at Port Hueneme and Pearl Harbor. Combinations of chemicals that were toxic to both test species were more effective wood preservatives than individual chemicals.

There were basically three types of combination treatments: (1) treatment with a solution of a compound toxic to *Limnoria* in creosote; (2) treatment with a solution in an inert solvent of a combination of a chemical toxic to *Limnoria* and one toxic to *Teredo;* (3) double treatment with a combination of chemicals as in (2), but which are not soluble in the same solvent and must be impregnated separately—for example, metal salts and creosote [19].

These combinations did indeed produce preservative treatments that are superior to creosote or creosote–coal tar solution alone. Specific examples of the effectiveness of combination treatments are given in Tables 7.1 and 7.2. In Table 7.1, creosote effectiveness is compared with that of its solutions of chemical compounds that are toxic to either *Limnoria* or to teredinids. Panels treated to retentions of 15 lbs/cu ft of chlorinated hy-

TABLE 7.1

Preservative Values of Creosote Solutions in Pearl Harbor

Additive	Retentions (lb/cu ft)		Time to Destruction (months)	Major Attacking Organism*	Factor of Improvement
	Additive	Creosote			
None	0	15.0	11	L	—
Chlordane	1.56	15.6	32	M	2.9
Dieldrin	0.28	14.2	32	M	2.9
Endrin	0.13	13.4	73	M	6.6
Toxaphene	0.15	14.8	42	L & M	3.8
Malachite green	0.81	16.2	16	L	1.4
Tributyltin oxide	0.30	14.5	49	L	4.4
Cu naphthenate	0.64	13.2	70	M	6.3

*L = *Limnoria.*
M = *Martesia.*
T = Teridinid.

TABLE 7.2

Preservative Values of Chemical Combinations in Pearl Harbor

Treating Solution	Retentions (lb/cu ft)	Total Exposure (months)	Major Attacking Animal*	Factor of Improvement
Creosote	35.0	32	L	—
Copper naphthenate	0.45	63	M	2.0
Tributyltin salt	0.25	50	L	1.6
Copper naphthenate	0.75 }	102	L	3.2
Tributyltin salt	0.25			
Dieldrin	0.15	8	T & M	0.25
Tributyltin salt	0.25	50	L	1.6
Dieldrin	0.25 }	97	0†	3.0
Tributyltin salt	0.25			
Toxaphene	0.25	10‡	T & M	0.3
Tributyltin salt	0.25	50	L	1.6
Toxaphene	0.26 }	105	0†	3.3
Tributyltin salt	0.26			
Endrin	0.16	8	T & M	0.25
Malachite green	0.29	3	L	0.10
Endrin	0.75 }	35	M	1.0
Malachite green	0.44			

*L = *Limnoria;* M = *Martesia;* T = Teridinid.
†Unattacked panels were removed from test because of erosion in the periodic scraping.
‡Estimated.

drocarbon are heavily attacked by *Limnoria* and teredinids, respectively, in 8–11 months in Pearl Harbor. When similar retentions of chlorinated hydrocarbons and creosote in combination are used, longevity is increased to as much as 73 months. In most harbors in the continental United States, the increased longevity would have been more dramatic because *Martesia,* the major animal attacking these combinations, is either absent or present only in small numbers. Malachite green—which has only a slight toxic effect on, but is effective against, teredinids—had very little effect as a creosote additive.

It should be noted that high-temperature creosote was used in establishing Table 7.1. Richards [34] had shown that creosotes produced by different manufacturing processes had different preservative abilities. The most effective creosotes were those produced at high temperatures, such as in coke ovens.

The apparent improvement resulting from the addition of tributyltin oxide or copper naphthenate to creosote must be qualified, because either of these compounds alone will produce a similar longevity. One might therefore say that the addition of creosote to either of these compounds did not improve their effectiveness. Although tributyltin oxide is more toxic to *Limnoria* than is creosote, its primary effectiveness is against the teredinids. As a result, tributyltin oxide treatment alone or in combination with creosote, when it is attacked, is attacked by *Limnoria.* Copper salts, on the other hand, are primarily effective against *Limnoria* and less effective against teredinids. Neither copper naphthenate alone or in combination with creosote is effective against *Martesia,* and both kinds of treatment will fail when this animal is present. In the absence of *Martesia,* failure is due primarily to teredinid action.

In Table 7.2, the wood-preservative ability of chemical compounds, singly and in combination, are compared with that of creosote. Combinations that contain one component toxic to *Limnoria* and a second component toxic to *Teredo* are always more effective than either component alone. Combinations that are at least three times as effective as creosote can be readily formulated. Some of these combinations have been impregnated into 16–20-foot piles which were driven in Pearl Harbor between 1963 and 1966. Differentiation between treatments should become apparent within the next few years.

7.4.5 Physical barriers

One method used to halt the deteriorating effect of an environment is to remove the object from that environment. This can be done for marine piling by the use of barrier systems. The most common barrier in the past has been encasement in concrete, but sheet metal and plastic have become more popular as their economic advantage over concrete increases.

Sheet-metal and plastic barriers are normally installed after a pile has lost 10–15 percent of its cross-sectional area by the action of marine boring organisms, but is still able to bear its design load. The application of the barrier arrests further deterioration and the wrapped pile will maintain its bearing capacity indefinitely. Concrete barriers can not only maintain bearing capacity but, by the proper use of reinforcing steel, can increase the bearing capacity of a pile. The concrete barrier, therefore, can be applied after almost any amount of pile deterioration, but at a much higher cost than that for the metal or plastic wrap.

Wakeman and Whiteneck [46] investigated several barrier systems and adopted Pile-Gard® [33], a system using flexible polyvinylchloride (PVC) sheet in thicknesses of 0.030 inch, as a standard pile-maintenance procedure in the Port of Los Angeles. Roe [36,37] compares the costs of several barrier systems and shows flexible PVC to be the lowest cost system. Roe also points out that in the several hundred thousand lineal feet of flexible PVC barriers that has been installed in the past 10 years, there have been no reported failures.

REFERENCES

1. Attwood, W.G. and Johnson, A.A. 1924. "Marine structures, their deterioration and preservation." National Research Council, Washington, D.C.
2. Barger, G. 1922. "Deterioration of structures in sea water." Second (Interim) Report of the Committee of Civil Engineers, London.
3. Barnard, J.L. 1951. "Role of Chelura in the destruction of marine timbers." Report of the Marine Borer Conference, U.S. Naval Civil Eng. Res. and Evaluation Lab., Port Hueneme, Calif., Section P. May 10–12.
4. Bateman, E. 1920. "A theory on the mechanism of the protection of wood by preservatives." Proc., Am. Wood-Preservers' Assoc. 16:251.
5. Bateman, E. 1921. "A theory on the mechanism of the protection of wood by preservatives." Proc. Am. Wood-Preservers' Assoc. 17:506–14.
6. Beach Erosion Board Technical Memorandum No. 66. 1955. "Factors affecting the economic life of timbers in coastal structures."
7. Beckman, C., Menzies, R.J. and Wakeman, C.M. 1957. "Biological aspects of attack on creosoted wood by Limnoria." Corrosion 13:162t.
8. Behr, E.A. and Vind, H.P. 1962. "A summary of tests for screening wood preservatives for marine use." Proc., Am. Wood-Preservers' Assoc. 58:156–64.
9. Clapp, W.F. and Kenk, R. 1963. "Marine borers, an annotated bibliography." Office of Naval Research, Washington, D.C. p. v.
10. DePalma, J.R. 1962. "Marine fouling and boring organisms in the Tongue of the Ocean, Bahamas—Exposure II." Unpublished. U.S. Naval Oceanographic Office, Washington, D.C., Rept. No. 0-64-62.
11. Drisko, R.W. and O'Neill, T.B. 1966. "Microbiological metabolism of creosote." Forest Prod. J. 16:31–34.

12. Edmondson, C.H. 1951. "Observations on marine borers in the Central Pacific area." Report of the Marine Borer Conference, U.S. Naval Civil Eng. Res. and Evaluation Lab., Port Hueneme, Calif., Section D.

13. Edmondson, C.H. 1955. "Resistance of woods to marine borers in Hawaiian waters." Bull. No. 217, Bernice P. Bishop Museum, Honolulu, Hawaii.

14. Eltringham, S.K. 1965. "Environmental factors influencing the settlement, activity and reproduction of the wood-boring Isopod Limnoria." *Material und Organismen* 1:465–78.

15. Harada, I. 1958. "Über das Wachstum der Terediniden an der Kusten Formosanas." In *Protection of Wooden Ships from Boring Damage* (Y.K. Okada, ed.). Japan Association for the Advancement of Science, Tokyo, Japan. 95–97.

16. Hearst, P.J. 1963. "Greenheart alkaloids." U.S. Naval Civil Eng. Lab. Tech. Rept. R–224, Port Hueneme, Calif.

17. Hochman, H. 1959. "Deterioration of wood by marine boring organisms." *Corrosion* 15:45t–48t.

18. Hochman, H. 1967. "Creosoted wood in a marine environment—A summary report." *Proc., Am. Wood-Preservers' Assoc.* 63:138–50.

19. Hochman, H. 1970. "Tailoring a wood treatment for the marine environment." *Proc., Am. Wood-Preservers' Assoc.* 66:38–42.

20. Hochman, H. and Roe, T. Jr. 1959–1969. "Harbor screening tests of marine borer inhibitors—I to IX." U.S. Naval Civil Eng. Lab. Tech. Repts. R–027 (1959), R–077 (1960), R–147 (1961), R–184 (1962), R–236 (1963), R–301 (1964), R–380 (1965), R–544 (1967), R–639 (1969). Port Hueneme, Calif.

21. Hochman, H. and Vind, H.P. 1966. "Screening of chemical toxicity to marine borers—Final report." U.S. Naval Civil Eng. Lab. Tech. Rept. R–426, Port Hueneme, Calif.

22. Hockley, A.R. 1965. "Population changes in Limnoria in relation to temperature." *Material und Organismen* 1:457–64.

23. Iterson, G. van, Jr. 1934. "The significance of the anatomy of wood for the preservation of marine structures against the shipworm (Teredo)." *Proceedings of the Fifth Pacific Science Congress,* Canada.

24. Iterson, G. van and Söhngen, N.L. 1911. "Rapport over onderzoekingen omtrent geconstateerde aantasting van het zoogenaamde manbarklak." *De Ingenieur* 26:231–32.

25. Kühne, H. von. 1965. "Uber bezeichungen zwischen Teredo, Limnoria und Chelura." *Material und Organismen* 1:447–56.

26. Menzies, R.J. 1951. "The phylogony, systematics, distribution and natural history of Limnoria." Ph.D. dissertation, Univ. of Southern California.

27. Menzies, R.J. 1951. "A new species of Limnoria (Crustacea: Isopoda) from Southern California." Southern California Academy of Sciences, Vol. L, May–Aug. Part 2.

28. Menzies, R.J. 1957. "The marine borer family Limnoriidae (Crustacea, Isopada)." Bull. Marine Science Gulf and Caribbean 7(2):101–200.

29. Menzies, R.J. and Turner, R. 1957. "The distribution and importance of marine borers in the United States." ASTM Special Tech. Pub. 200:3–21.

30. Muraoka, J.S. 1964. "Deep ocean biodeterioration of materials. I. Four months at 5640 feet." U.S. Naval Civil Eng. Lab. Tech. Rept. R–329, Port Hueneme, Calif.

31. Muraoka, J.S. 1965. "Deep ocean boring mollusc." *Bioscience* 15(3):191.

32. O'Neill, T.B., Drisko, R.W. and Hochman, H. 1961. "Pseudomonas creosotensis sp. n., a creosote-tolerant marine bacterium." *Appl. Microbiol.* 9:472–4.

33. Pile-Gard®. A process developed by Marine Barriers, Inc., Avalon, Calif., and patented under U.S. patent nos. 3,027,610 and 3,103,103.

34. Richards, A.P. 1957. "Cooperative creosote program, final report on marine test panels." *Proc., Am. Wood-Preservers' Assoc.* 53:117–30.

35. Richards, B.R. 1971. "A laboratory method for screening assays of treated wood samples exposed to *Limnoria tripunctata.*" *Proc., Am. Wood-Preservers' Assoc.* 67:144–47.

36. Roe, T. Jr. 1964. "Barrier systems for in-place wooden piling." U.S. Naval Civil Eng. Lab. Tech. Note N–581, Port Hueneme, Calif.

37. Roe, T. Jr. 1964. "New barrier systems studied to lengthen life of wood piling." *Navy Civil Engineer* 5(9):12–13.

38. Ryabchikov, P.I. and Nikolayeava, G.G. 1963. "Settlement of the larvae of the marine borer *Teredo navalis* L. (Mollusca, Teredinidae) and the temperature of the water in Gelendzhikskaya bukhta of the Black Sea." *Marine Fouling and Borers*, I.V. Starostin, ed., U.S. Naval Oceanographic Office, Translation No. 221. Washington, D.C. 1965 (TT 65–62932; AD 619257). Translation of the Transactions of Akademiya Nauk. USSR, Institute Okcanologii Trudy 70:185,179–65,256.

39. Stasse, H.L. 1959. "Cooperative creosote program, post-mortem studies of marine panels." *Proc., Am. Wood-Preservers' Assoc.* 55:176–81.

40. Sweeney, T.R., Price, T.R. and Saunders, R.A. 1956. "Marine borer control. V. Studies on the leaching of creosote from wood." Naval Res. Lab. Rept. No. 4822. Washington, D.C.

41. Turner, R.D. 1965. "Some results of deep water testing." Annual Reports for 1965 of the American Macological Union. 9–11.

42. Vind, H.P. and Hochman, H. 1959. "Standard toxicity evaluation of chemicals poisonous to the marine borer." ASTM Special Tech. Pub. 275:11–21.

43. Vind, H.P. and Hochman, H. 1960. "Toxicity of chemicals to marine borers." U.S. Naval Civil Eng. Lab. Tech. Rept. R–048. Port Hueneme, Calif.

44. Wallour, D.B. 1959. Compiler of 13th progress report on marine borer activity in test boards operated during 1959. William F. Clapp Laboratories Rept. No. 11466, Duxbury, Mass.

45. Wakeman, C.M. Personal communication.

46. Wakeman, C.M. and Whiteneck, L.L. 1959. "Extending service life of wood piles in sea water." Symposium on Treated Wood for Marine Use. American Society for Testing and Materials Special Tech. Pub. 275:36–49.

8. The Degradation of Wood by Insects

ROBERT N. COULSON
Texas A & M University, College Station, Texas

ANDERS E. LUND
Texas Forest Products Laboratory, Lufkin, Texas

8.1 Introduction

The class Insecta is a large and diverse group of organisms which has successfully invaded both terrestrial and aquatic habitats. Insects form the greatest single category of consumers within the animal kingdom and, as a result, are man's most serious competitors for food and fiber. It is not surprising, then, to find insects to be important in the degradation of wood and wood products.

The intent of this chapter is to present representatives of the important wood-destroying insects, with descriptions of the types of damage characteristic of the various groups. It is far beyond the scope of this writing to consider in detail all insects which are important in the degradation of wood, and emphasis has been placed upon representative families within the orders Coleoptera, Hymenoptera, and Isoptera. More detailed information regarding the important species involved in wood degradation can be obtained from the references cited at the end of the chapter, or by direct examination of primary source material in entomological journals.

8.2 Systematic Classification of Wood-Destroying Insects

Generally, the class Insecta is subdivided taxonomically into 26 orders of which the following 6 contain species which are often important wood-destroying insects: Isoptera (termites), Hemiptera (bugs), Coleoptera (beetles), Lepidoptera (moths and butterflies), Diptera (flies), and Hymenoptera (bees, wasps, and ants).

Oftentimes, however, instead of categorizing the destructive insects by their taxonomic affinities, the type of damage caused or the physiological state of the host tree when attacked is used as a basis for classification. The terms honeycombing, grub holes, pitch pockets, pith flecks, birdseye, powderposting, and pin-holing, are all used to describe the activities and effects of the various types of wood-destroying insects.

Certain of the wood-destroying insects are found attacking living trees, while others prefer dying, recently felled, or even seasoned wood. The degree of damage caused is also quite variable, and ranges from degrading caused by staining of wood to actual destruction of wood fiber.

Most of the economically important wood-destroying insects occur in the Coleoptera, Hymenoptera, and Isoptera orders. Within each order, a number of families and many species are of noteworthy significance. The important familes, along with the common name of the destructive agent and the type of damage attributed to each, are contained in Tables 8.1, 8.2, and 8.3.

8.2.1 Coleoptera (beetles)

The order Coleoptera is the largest in the class Insecta and contains about 40 percent of all described species, or approximately 350,000. Of the 110 families within the order, 9 are important in the degradation of wood.

TABLE 8.1

Families of Coleoptera Causing Wood Destruction

Family	Common Name	Type of Injury
Anobiidae	Powderpost beetles	Powderposting
Bostrichidae	Powderpost beetles	Powderposting
Brentidae	Timber worms	Pin holes
Buprestidae	Flat-headed borers	Grub holes, powderposting
Cerambycidae	Round-headed borers	Grub holes, powderposting, black check
Lyctidae	Powderpost beetles	Powderposting
Lymexylidae	Timber worms	Pin holes
Platypodidae	Ambrosia beetles	Pin holes
Scolytidae	Ambrosia beetles	Pin holes

TABLE 8.2

Families of Hymenoptera Causing Wood Destruction

Family	Common Name	Type of Injury
Formicidae	Ants	Honeycombing
Siricidae	Wood wasps & horntails	Grub holes
Xyelidae	Wood wasps	Grub holes

TABLE 8.3

Families of Isoptera Causing Wood Destruction

Family & Form	Common Name	Type of Injury
Rhinotermitidae, lower	Subterranean termites	Honeycombing in damp wood
Kalotermitidae, lower	Drywood termites	Honeycombing in dry wood
Termitidae, higher	Subterranean, mound builders, or arboreal nest termites	Honeycombing in almost any kind of cellulosic material, living or dead.
Termopsidae, lower	Dampwood termites	Honeycombing in damp wood
Mastotermitidae, lower	A single living termite species	Honeycombing in damp and dry wood
Hodotermitidae	Harvester termites	Vegetation only

The Coleoptera are characterized by having two pairs of wings: the first pair are thickened and termed elytra, and the second pair are membranous. The metamorphosis is complete, and the mouth parts are well developed and of the chewing variety.

8.2.1.1 Cerambycidae

The family Cerambycidae is one of the largest in the order Coleoptera, and contains approximately 1,200 species dispersed through 300 genera in the United States. Adults in the family are characterized by having antennae usually longer than half the body length of the insect, tarsi which are five-segmented (although superficially appearing to be four-segmented), and emarginated compound eyes. The adults are often referred to as "longhorn beetles," owing to the characteristically long antennae (Figure 8.1). The larvae are commonly described as "round-headed wood borers," presumably because of the circular appearance of the emergence holes made by the insects.

The greatest number of representatives of wood-destroying species within a single family occurs in the Cerambycidae, and these attack both deciduous broad-leaved trees and conifers.

Living trees are attacked by some species, but the tree rarely dies as a result. Freshly felled or killed timber is also attacked, as is dry and seasoned wood.

The galleries excavated by Cerambycidae larvae are oval in shape and wind irregularly through the inner bark and/or wood (Figure 8.2). The size of the gallery is quite variable and is dependent on the size of the insect. Galleries 1–2 inches in diameter are produced by some of the larger species. Some species remove frass and borings from the galleries while

Figure 8.1. *Saperda Calcarata* (Coleoptera:Cerambycidae). (Photograph by Mark W. Houseweart)

others keep granular and/or fibrous borings, either loosely or tightly packed, within their galleries.

Several examples of economically important species of cerambicids representing the different types of damage and different states of host condition attacked are presented in Table 8.4

8.2.1.2 Buprestidae (metallic wood-boring beetles)

The Buprestidae, like the Cerambycidae, constitute one of the larger families within the Coleoptera, and in the United States there are approximately 38 genera which contain a total of 662 species.

Adults in the family are characteristically metallic-colored and hard-bodied, with strongly deflexed heads and a transverse metasternal suture. (Figure 8.3).

The adults are commonly called "metallic wood borers," which name derives from the coloration of the insect. The larvae are referred to as "flat-headed wood borers" because of the large and flattened prothorax,

Figure 8.2. Damage to black locust caused by the locust borer *Megacyllene robiniae* (Coleoptera:Cerambycidae). (Photograph by Mark W. Houseweart)

which appears to form the head of the insect. The larvae are the only injurious stage.

Dying or felled trees are most often attacked; however, there are species which attack living trees, including both deciduous broad-leaved trees and conifers.

The galleries excavated by the Buprestidae, although not suitable for species recognition, are characteristic in that they are always tightly packed with fine borings, which—with their more oval-to-flattened appearance—serves to separate them from the galleries produced by some powderpost beetles.

There are several common species of buprestids which are associated with wood degradation. The western cedar borer, *Trochykele blondeli* Mars., attacks living western redcedar as well as several other hosts, including sequoia and juniper, thereby reducing the value of certain wood products such as shingles and siding.

The golden buprestid, *Buprestis aurulenta* Linn., is another common species which attacks conifers. Damage is typical of buprestids and living and recently felled trees—and even dry, seasoned wood—are attacked.

TABLE 8.4

Common Cerambycidae Important in the Degradation of Wood

Insect	Common Name	Host Condition	Host Type	Damage Type
Goes spp.		Living trees	Deciduous broad-leaved trees (oaks & hickories)	Trunk & branch borers
Megacyllen robiniae (Frost.)	Locust borer	Living trees	Black locust	Grub holes, honey-combing
Saperda calcarata (Say)	Aspen borer	Living trees	Aspen	Boring in main bole
Plectrodera scalator (F.)	Cottonwood borer	Living trees	Cottonwood	Boring in main bole
Monochamus spp.	Sawyers	Dying or freshly felled trees	Conifers	Inner bark and wood
Ergates spiculatus Lec.	Ponderosa borer	Recently felled, dead or decaying	Douglas-fir, pines	Boring in main bole
Hylotropes bajulus (L.)	Old house borer	Dried wood	Conifers	Powderposting

Figure 8.3. *Buprestis lineata* (Coleoptera:Buprestidae). (Photograph by Mark W. House-weart)

8.2.1.3 Powderpost beetles, pin-hole borers, and timber worms

The remaining families of wood-destroying insects within the Cole-optera can conveniently be separated into three groups, based upon type of damage, as follows: (1) powderpost beetles (Lyctidae, Bostrichidae, Anobiidae); (2) pin-hole borers (Scolytidae, Platypodidae); and (3) timber worms (Brentidae, Lymexylidae).

8.2.1.3.1 Powerpost beetles: Lyctidae, Bostrichidae, Anobiidae

The powderpost beetles constitute one of the most economically important groups of wood-destroying insects and are overshadowed in significance only by the termites. In contrast to the Cerambycidae and Buprestidae, seasoned wood is generally preferred.

Lyctidae. The family Lyctidae is small and is represented by only 19 species in the United States. The genus *Lyctus* contains the most important wood-degrading species and the common name for the group, "*Lyctus* powderpost beetles," derives from the importance of the species within the group. *Lyctus* beetles are characterized by, and can be distinguished from, other powderpost beetles by their exposed head, which is narrowed behind the eyes; by the two-segmented antennal club, and a subdepressed body.

Lyctus beetles are extremely serious pests of dry, seasoned wood and often are associated with the sapwood of broad-leaved deciduous trees. (Heartwood is immune to their attack.) *Lyctus* beetles derive nourishment primarily from the starch and reserve food materials stored in the parenchyma of the rays. Oaks, hickories, poplars, and ash are the trees most often attacked by these beetles.

The larvae bore small tunnels approximately $\frac{1}{16}$ inch in diameter (Figure 8.4), and the repeated attack by the insect reduces the wood to a fine, flourlike powder. The galleries produced by this feeding contain the powdery borings, and the tell-tale powder commonly accumulates around infested wood. Common representatives of the genus *Lyctus* in the United States are *L. planicollis* Lec. and *L. parallelopipedus* (Melsh.).

Bostrichidae. The family Bostrichidae is represented by 31 genera, which contain a total of 62 species in North America. The beetles in this family characteristically are elongate and somewhat cylindrical, with the head being inserted into the prothorax and usually deflexed downward and barely visible from above. The antennal club is three- or four-segmented.

The principal hosts of bostrichid beetles are deciduous broad-leaved trees; however, some conifers are also attacked. Damage is of the type caused by *Lyctus.*

One of the most common representatives of the family is the "red-shouldered hickory borer," *Xylobiops basilare* (Say), which is capable of attacking freshly cut and partially seasoned wood of a number of hardwood species in the East. *Polycaon stouti* (Lec.) is a western species which

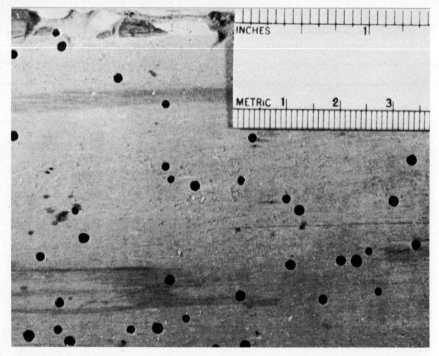

Figure 8.4. Damage to pine caused by *Lyctus* sp. powderpost beetles. (Photograph by Mark W. Houseweart)

also attacks a variety of hardwoods, and is an economically serious pest associated with plywood manufacture.

Anobiidae. The last family of powderpost beetle, Anobiidae, is represented by 250 species and 50 genera in the United States. The adults of the Anobiidae possess contractile legs and a strongly deflexed head, which is often covered by the pronotum. These characteristics separate the Anobiidae from the lyctids and bostricids.

The common name for the entire family, "death-watch beetles," derives from the ticking sound which the insects produce by striking their vertex against the anterior margin of the pronotum, associated in folklore with rapid passage of time as a forewarning of death.

The damage caused by the anobiid powderpost beetles is similar to that caused by the *Lyctus* beetles, with old seasoned wood being utilized. However, both coniferous and hardwood species are susceptible and heartwood, as well as sapwood, is attacked.

The "furniture beetle," *Anobium punctatum* Deg., is a common, economically important, and widely distributed species which attacks both hardwood and pines and is capable of developing in both seasoned and freshly felled timber.

The "death-watch beetle," *Xestobium rufovillosum* (De Geer) is another very common and cosmopolitan representative of the Anobiidae. The insect prefers well-seasoned wood, particularly oaks, walnut, and elm, but several other hosts are suitable.

8.2.1.3.2 Pin-hole borers

Two families are important pin-hole borers, Scolytidae and Platy-podidae. The destructive insects in the group are also termed "ambrosia beetles," and are of much less economic importance than the powderpost beetles in terms of actual destruction of wood fiber. They are significant in that they degrade wood through staining. Interestingly, the demand for exotic paneling containing stains and insect galleries has substantially increased the value of some host species.

Scolytidae. The family Scolytidae contains many of the most economically significant forest insect pests. In the United States there are 76 genera and 566 species. The taxonomic state of this important group of insects is poorly defined.

Adults characteristically are cylindrical in shape, brown to black in coloration, and range in size from $\frac{1}{32}$–$\frac{3}{8}$ inch in length. The antennae are geniculate and possess a distinct club.

There are two common names for the family—"bark beetles" and "ambrosia beetles"—and the latter designation contains the representatives important as pin-hole borers.

The ambrosia beetles are so named because they cultivate and feed upon fungi which they introduce into their galleries. They derive little or no nourishment from the wood itself.

Damage to host trees is wrought by adult beetles, which bore into recently felled logs and, less commonly, into standing green trees. The galleries are usually excavated across the grain of the wood and are kept clean of boring dust. The walls of the gallery, however, become stained from the implanted fungus, and this staining results in degradation of the value of the wood products produced from the wood. Generally, the boring by ambrosia beetles is not extensive enough to weaken structurally the lumber produced from infested trees.

Both hardwoods and conifers are attacked and the type of gallery and degree of damage caused varies, depending on the type of attacking insect.

The "Columbian timber beetle," *Corthylus columbianus* Hopk., is a common ambrosia beetle in the eastern United States, where it attacks a

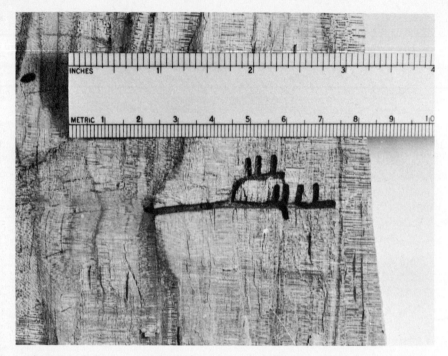

Figure 8.5. Gallery excavated in soft maple by the Columbian timber beetle, *Corthylus columbianus* (Coleoptera:Scolytidae). (Photograph by Mark W. Houseweart)

variety of hosts including soft maples, sycamore, white oak, and others. Figures 8.5 and 8.6 illustrate damage caused by this insect.

Platypodidae. The second family of ambrosia beetles, Platypodidae is represented by only one genus, *Platypus,* and seven species in the United States. Platypodid beetles are elongate and cylindrical, with declivous elytra, and elongate first tarsal segments.

Damage by these insects is typical of that described for the scolytid pin-hole borers. The borings produced by *Platypus* spp. are characteristically fibrous, in contrast to the more granular borings of other species.

Platypus flavicornis (F) is a common pin-hole borer in the southern United States, and is often associated with pine trees attacked by the southern pine beetle, *Dendroctonus frontalis* Zimm. Figure 8.7 illustrates typical damage to loblolly pine by *P. flavicornis.*

8.2.1.3.3 Timber worms

Two familes of Coleoptera—Brentidae and Lymexylidae—form the class of wood borers known as timber worms. Both families are very small, and only a few species are of substantial economic importance.

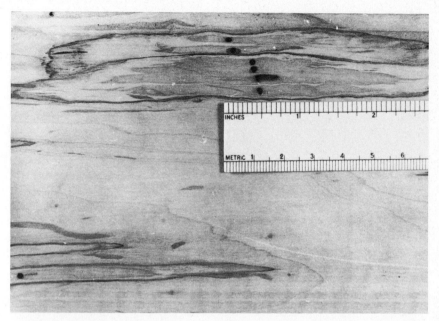

Figure 8.6. Staining and pin-holing in soft maple caused by Columbian timber beetle, *Corthylus columbianus* (Coleoptera:Scolytidae). (Photograph by Mark W. Houseweart)

Brentidae. The Brentidae are very closely related taxonomically to the Curculionidae and are commonly designated "straight-snouted weevils." The family is distinguishable from true weevils by their elongated bodies and long, straight, prognathous beaks.

Damage is effected only by the larvae, which produce pin holes similar to those of the ambrosia beetles. (Size of holes is not a true indicator of the insect responsible, however, as the holes made by any one species will vary in size.) Galleries are kept clean of borings and are not normally stained.

Several hardwood species are suitable hosts, including weakened or wounded living trees and freshly felled trees and logs. Oaks, beech, and poplar are often attacked.

The "oak timber worm," *Arrhenodes minuta* (Drury), is the only common species in the United States and is principally a pest of white oak in the East. White oak, which is used almost exclusively in the manufacture of barrel-stave bolts, is often rendered unusable because of boring by this insect. (Wooden barrels are still extensively used today in the manufacture and storage of bourbon whiskey.) The Columbian timber beetle, mentioned above, is also an important pest of white oak.

Lymexylonidae. The family Lymexylonidae, or "ship-timber beetles," contains only two genera and five species native to the United States. The

Figure 8.7. Gallery excavated in loblolly pine by the pin-hole borer, *Platypus flavicornis* (Coleoptera:Platypodidae). (Photograph by Mark W. Houseweart)

adults are long and slender, with serrate antennae and large, four-jointed maxillary palpi.

The most noteworthy species in the family is the "chestnut timber worm," *Melittomma sericeum* (Harr.) which is responsible for the worm holes in chestnut.

The description of damage caused by the Brentidae also applies to the Lymexylidae.

8.2.2 Hymenoptera

Hymenoptera—the third largest order in the Insecta, with approximately 103,000 described species—are characterized by having two pairs of membranous wings, chewing or chewing-sucking mouth parts, usually a well-developed ovipositor, and a complete metamorphosis. Of the 71 families which occur in the United States, most are beneficial to man and only 3 are of importance in the degradation of wood: Formicidae (ants), Xylocopidae (carpenter bees), and Siricidae (horntails and wood wasps).

8.2.2.1 Formicidae

The family Formicidae is very common and widespread. The adults are easily recognized by their antennae, which are usually elbowed with the first segment very long, and the characteristic form of the pedicel of the abdomen, which is one- or two-segmented and nodiform. All ants are social insects and each colony usually contains three castes: queens, males, and workers.

The ants which are of importance in the degradation of wood belong to the subfamily Formicinae and the genus *Componotus,* and are known as "carpenter ants" (Figure 8.8).

Carpenter ants are cosmopolitan in distribution and attack a great variety of tree species. All types of wood are subject to their attack, but soft moist wood is preferred.

Damage is wrought by adult ants, which do not utilize the wood as food, but, rather, for the making of a cavity in which to live. Galleries are large and smooth-sided and never contain borings.

Figure 8.8. Carpenter ant, *Camponotus* sp. (Hymenoptera:Formicidae) (Photograph by Mark W. Houseweart)

Eastern white cedar is frequently attacked, and the most serious damage is usually confined to the butt section of the tree.

The most common and destructive species of carpenter ants is *Componotus herculeanus pennsylvanicus* (De Geer), which occurs throughout the United States. Figure 8.9 illustrates typical damage caused by this insect.

Figure 8.9. Damage to pine timber caused by carpenter ants, *Camponotus* sp. (Hymenoptera:Formicidae). (Photograph by Mark W. Houseweart)

8.2.2.2 Xylocopidae

The family Xylocopidae, which contains the large and small carpenter bees, is often considered to be the subfamily of Apidae, Xylocopidae.

The small carpenter bees, *Ceratina* spp., superficially resemble bees of the family Halictidae. They are not important wood destroyers, as their activity is confined to boring in the pith of stems of various bushes.

The large carpenter bees, *Xylocopa* spp., closely resemble the bumblebee, *Bombus americanorum* (Fab.), but can be distinguished by the near-absence of setae on the dorsum of the abdomen and by the shape of the second submarginal cell in the wings, which is triangular.

Most tree species are suitable hosts and dry, seasoned wood of the softer species such as pines, cedars, and redwood are preferred.

The galleries excavated by carpenter bees are constructed with the grain of the wood, after initial entry, and are of considerable size, about $\frac{3}{8}-\frac{9}{16}$ inch in diameter and 5–18 inches in length. The galleries are divided into compartments which serve as brood-development chambers. The cross walls which divide the individual chambers are constructed from macerated wood by adult bees, and provide an easily recognizable characteristic of carpenter-bee activity.

Two species of large carpenter bees are common in the United States: *X. orpifex* Smith and *X. virginica* (Drury).

8.2.2.3 Siricidae

The Siricidae, or "horntails," are characterized by having the abdomen broadly joined to the thorax and a large spearlike plate on the last abdominal tergete, which in the female encases the ovipositor. Horntails are usually metallic in color, and are often dark brown or black with yellow and orange markings (Figure 8.10). Horntails attack a variety of hosts,

Figure 8.10. *Sirex* sp. wood wasp (Hymenoptera:Siricidae). (Photograph by Mark H. Houseweart)

Figure 8.11. Drywood termite (*Kalotermes minor*) colony. The letters identify the various members as follows: A, Alate; N, Nymph; S, Soldier. (Courtesy Neil A. Maclean Co., Inc. Copyright 1969. Photograph by Stennett Heaton.)

including both hard- and softwood species, but most injury is reported to Pinaceae conifers, with a majority of the damage occuring to unseasoned or moist wood. A distinct preference is shown toward fire-damaged trees.

Females deposit eggs deep within the wood, and the ensuing larval stages are responsible for the damage wrought. The larvae are xylophagous, and construct tunnels with almost perfectly circular holes. Wood borings are tightly packed to the rear of the tunnel in back of the insect.

There are several species of horntails which occur in the United States, the most destructive occurring in the genera *Tremex* and *Sirex*.

8.2.3 Isoptera (termites)

The Isoptera are social insects with a well-developed caste system. Representatives of the group are characterized by the possession of two pairs of equal-size membranous wings (in the winged forms), chewing mouth parts, and simple metamorphosis. The abdomen is broadly joined to the thorax, which characteristic serves to separate the group from ants.

There are generally considered to be 6 families (Table 8.3) included among the order Isoptera (Figure 8.11), with about 1,800 species.

For simplicity, three developmental castes of termites can be recognized.

(1) *Adults*. If winged, the wings are membranous, varying in color from transparent to a light brown and ordinarily about twice as long as the insect body. The adult size ranges from approximately 0.25 inch to 0.75 inch. Color ranges from black for the primary reproductive adult to a creamy white for others.

(2) *Worker*. In many species a worker caste may not be obvious but, if present, the worker can be identified by a somewhat enlarged head and chitinized head and thorax with an off-white body. The size of the worker is generally smaller than the adult. This caste is the one most often seen when infested wood is broken open, and most wood destruction is attributed to the worker caste.

(3) *Soldier*. This caste is easily recognized by the greatly enlarged head and mandibles, which are heavily chitnized. In certain species a well-developed horn-like projection appears on the head. A viscous fluid is expelled from this structure when the soldier is disturbed. The soldier is often larger than the worker.

8.2.3.1 General biology

Termites are social insects and therefore exist in quite well-defined colonies under crowded conditions (positively thigmotaxic). The size of these colonies may vary from a few thousand individuals to some with millions of insects. Most species are crytobiotic. They require high moisture and carbon dioxide levels, and shun the light (negatively phototaxic); thus, termites are commonly found in subterranean situations.

Termites exist worldwide, and may be found between latitudes 50° north and 50° south. Due to shipping of wood products, however, it seems reasonable to conclude that the spread of these insects will continue.

Figure 8.12. Protozoa from the intestine of the drywood termite, *Kalotermes minor*. (Courtesy Neil A. Maclean Co., Inc. Copyright 1969. Photograph by Stennett Heaton.)

8.2.3.2 Feeding

This discussion is limited to only those termites which attack wood, excluding, for example, the harvester termites.

A convenient division of termite types is based on the presence or absence of protozoan intestinal symbionts. All lower forms of termites harbor protozoa, which are essential in the digestion of cellulose (Figure 8.12). Cellulose is the major portion of wood that is utilized by these insects, with little or no digestion of lignin—consequently, without protozoa most lower forms of termites will die.

Higher forms of termites—family Termididae (Table 8.3)—which comprise 75 percent of the total termite species, are devoid of protozoa; thus, the presence of the cellulase enzyme is indicated. It is not yet known whether the termite itself secretes this enzyme or if the termites' intestinal bacteria produce it.

8.2.3.3 Colony development

A typical subterranean termite, *Reticulitermes flavipes* (Kollar), establishes its colonies in one of two ways. In a parent colony, a number of nymphs molt into sexual reproductives with compound eyes, wings, and a black color. Under certain environmental conditions, temperature and moisture probably being the most influential, these reproductives swarm from the colony. After swarming, one male and one female pair up and establish a new colony. Colony growth is slow for the first four to five years.

A second type of establishment occurs through the accidental walling off or separation of a subgroup of termites from the original colony. Functioning reproductives will then develop in this subgroup and a new colony is formed. The transportation of infested lumber products—provided sufficient moisture is available—can also accomplish the establishment of colonies in new areas. This species must, of course, maintain contact with a high level of moisture—normally, the moisture available in the ground.

In contrast, the typical drywood termite, *e.g., Kalotermes* spp., requires much less available moisture, as its name indicates. Sufficient moisture for colony establishment and growth of this species is present in wood, provided there is minimum moisture content of about 5–6 percent.

8.2.3.4 Damage

Figures 8.13 and 8.14 show damage typical of that attributed to subterranean termites. It will be noted that subterraneans normally attack

Figure 8.13. Damage caused by *Coptotermes formosanus* Shiraki. (Photograph by Mark W. Houseweart)

the less dense section of wood; thus, the earlywood portion of the annual growth increment in wood is preferred. However, once the earlywood is depleted they will readily feed on the latewood.

The termite tears off small particles of wood with its mandibles (Figures 8.15 and 8.16), and these small pieces are then ingested and ground into finer particles in the termite's crop. The particles then pass into the hind gut where cellulolytic enzymes from protozoa, bacteria, etc., reduce the cellulose portion of the particle to nutrients. Excreta is high in lignin content.

8.3 Termite Test Methods

8.3.1 Standardized laboratory test methods

The development of laboratory test methods using termites has progressed rapidly in the last 10 years, and there are now standardized methods for screening the effectiveness of chemicals in preventing attack on cellulosic materials. Similar methods have been accepted by both AWPA and ASTM.

Figure 8.14. Damage caused to southern yellow pine by *Reticulitermes flavipes* (Isoptera:Rhinotermitidae) (frass removed). (Photograph by Mark W. Houseweart)

Essential equipment for these test methods consists of containers, sand, and water. Termites and cellulosic material are introduced into the prepared containers, and the various tests conducted.

8.3.2 Standardized field-test methods

There are no separate field-test methods for termites, as insect and decay resistance are usually studied simultaneously in field tests.

Standardized methods for field testing are detailed in Chapter 6 of this volume.

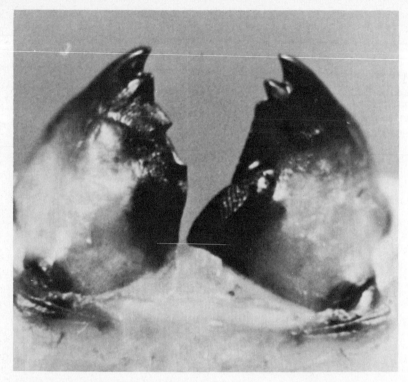

Figure 8.15. Mandible structure of the drywood termite, *Kalotermes minor.* (Courtesy Neil A. Maclean Co. Inc. Copyright 1969. Photograph by Stennett Heaton.)

8.4 Insect Control Methods

Methods and procedures used to prevent loss or damage to wood and wood products have been subjected to serious scrutiny during recent years, largely because of the public attention focused on the harmful effects resulting from long-term dependence on the use of insecticides.

There are three different circumstances in which insects exert a significant impact on wood destined for use in the manufacture of wood products and on wood already fabricated into a product. Different problems characterize control effects within each category.

The first control problem is associated with trees which are destined for harvest and which have already been attacked. Control of damage or degradation in this case is primarily a responsibility of forest management, and the specific techniques range from insecticide application to silvicultural techniques—determined in large part by the intended use and/or value of the wood. The large-scale production of plywood and the

Figure 8.16. Front view of the head and mandibles of the drywood termite, *Kalotermes minor*. The termite is tearing off a small piece of wood. Note how the wood surface is torn up from previous termite activity. (Courtesy Neil A. Maclean Co. Inc. Copyright 1969. Photograph by Stennett Heaton.)

exploitation of stained wood for use as exotic paneling are examples of methods of wood utilization which circumvent the possibly more difficult problem of curtailing insect damage prior to wood-product manufacture.

The second problem of insect control is associated with damage caused after the manufacture of the wood product. Procedures for curtailing damage are almost completely dependent upon the use of insecticides. Although considerable research effort is being expended on developing better procedures of insect control, undoubtedly use of insecticides will continue to be the main method of curtailing damage in this category for some time—though perhaps curtailed somewhat by the more rigorous constraints in the form of licensing which have been placed on individuals involved in pest control application. The use of insecticides for specific application have also been more seriously considered in recent years. Only certain insecticides administered by defined techniques can be used for individual species of insects.

The third type of control problem is associated with prevention of insect damage to wood which has been processed for use as a specific product. There are a number of specific prophylactic processes which have been developed by wood product scientists which are outlined in detail below.

8.4.1 Isoptera

8.4.1.1 Effectiveness of various chemicals

Effective resistance to the termite attack of wood can be imparted by employing AWPA-approved preservatives using recommended treating practices. Approved preservatives include creosote, pentachlorophenol, and waterborne chemicals. There is considerable variation among the types of preservatives, however, and this is clearly shown in a recent study [1] which compared several of the standard preservatives in ground-contact situations. A summary of this study is shown in Table 8.5.

Based on Table 8.5, at equivalent retentions, the waterborne salt preservatives can be ranked in accordance with relative effectiveness as follows: ACA > CCA > FCAP > ACC > CZC. The general ranking for the oilborne preservatives would be as follows: Coal-tar creosote > copper naphthenate > penta. With regard to the waterborne preservatives, it should be pointed out that the same relationship may not hold for aboveground exposure, since the degree of fixation varies with the preservative. Hence, leaching may be a significant factor in these tests.

Another interesting observation in Table 8.5 is that there is considerable variation in the effectiveness of the preservatives when different wood

TABLE 8.5

Summary of Quality Index Ratings for Termite Attack on Stakes Treated with Different Preservatives After 100 Months' Exposure in the Ground [1]

Preservative	Species	Retention (PCF)	Rating*	Retention (PCF)	Rating*	Retention (PCF)	Rating*
Coal-tar creosote	Oak	4.6	97.5	8.7	100.0	16.4	100.0
	Fir	5.3	100.0	8.1	100.0	16.4	100.0
	Pine	4.3	90.0	7.6	97.5	15.9	100.0
Chromated zinc	Oak	0.51	20.0	0.99	42.5	1.99	50.0
chloride (CZC)	Fir	0.51	45.0	0.94	50.0	2.00	57.5
	Pine	0.50	10.0	1.00	35.0	2.04	52.5
Tanalith (FCAP)	Oak	0.30	12.5	0.53	42.5	0.98	87.5
	Fir	0.27	47.5	0.53	65.0	1.08	77.5
	Pine	0.25	0.0	0.50	52.5	0.99	65.0
5% Penta solution	Oak	4.3	62.5	8.00	92.5	15.1	100.0
	Fir	4.3	50.0	8.50	67.5	14.5	100.0
	Pine	4.6	50.0	7.80	60.0	15.8	95.0
Copper	Oak	4.3	67.5	8.00	95.0	12.2	100.0
naphthenate	Fir	4.2	60.0	9.20	97.5	16.8	100.0
	Pine	4.4	55.5	8.50	82.5	16.8	100.0
Acid copper	Oak	0.62	57.5	1.00	87.5	1.98	92.5
chromate	Fir	0.55	50.0	1.17	82.5	2.13	95.0
(ACC)	Pine	0.51	40.0	1.00	62.5	2.07	82.5
Ammoniacal	Oak	0.29	92.5	0.51	97.5	1.00	100.0
copper arsenite	Fir	0.25	95.0	0.49	100.0	0.75	100.0
(ACA)	Pine	0.20	75.0	0.39	97.5	0.79	100.0
Chromated	Oak	0.43	37.5	0.75	70.0	1.51	97.5
copper arsenate	Fir	0.44	67.5	0.86	85.0	1.48	100.0
(CCA)	Pine	0.38	55.0	0.74	65.0	1.50	87.5

*A rating of 100 indicates no attack; a rating of 0 indicates complete destruction.

species are used. The reason for this variation is not known, but certainly must be considered in test programs.

Since the waterborne preservatives are mixtures of various chemicals, it is of interest to evaluate the comparative effectiveness of the various components. Based on studies reported in the literature [6,9,10,15,21,23], these chemicals can be approximately ranked according to comparative effectiveness as follows: As > Cu > Zn > F > Cr. In general, arsenic compounds are extremely effective and copper compounds are fairly effective. Unless extremely high retentions are used, Zn, F, and Cr compounds show very little effectiveness against termites.

A recent study by Tynes [27] is summarized in Table 8.6, and shows that

TABLE 8.6

Average Degree of Damage to Pine Boards by Subterranean
Termites in Aboveground Test After 8 Years' Exposure
and in Soil-Burial Test After 4 Years' Exposure [27]

Formulation	Average Degree of Attack*	
	Aboveground	Soil Burial
5% Penta	2.5	4.4
5% Penta + 1% aldrin	0.9	0.5
5% Penta + 2% chlordane	1.1	0.3
5% Penta + 1% dieldrin	0.3	0.4
5% Penta + 1% heptachlor	0.4	0.4
2% Copper naphthenate	0.9	1.8
2% Copper naphthenate + 1% dieldrin	0.2	0.3
2% Chlordane	1.3	—
1% Dieldrin	0.9	0.5
Control	4.3	5.0

*A rating of 0 indicates no attack; a rating of 5 indicates complete destruction.

the effectiveness of penta can be increased considerably by adding chlorinated hydrocarbons such as aldrin, chlordane, dieldrin, and heptachlor. These chlorinated hydrocarbons appear to be effective chemicals against wood-destroying insects. It is anticipated that their use in wood preservation will expand in the future.

8.4.1.2 Mode of action of preservatives

Wood preservatives are generally recognized as stomach poisons; however, compounds such as aldrin and dieldrin are known as contact insecticides. Because of the more rapid relative action of contact insecticides, additional study of this type of compound should be encouraged.

8.4.1.3 Tubing over treated wood

Lund and Dreher [18] have reported that termites can build tubes over wood treated with standard preservatives. Hence, wood treated with standard preservatives will not provide a barrier to prevent entry of termites into structures.

Recent work by Beal [5], however, indicates that the addition of aldrin, dieldrin, chlordane, and heptachlor to penta or Wolman solutions prior to treatment will effectively control tubing by termites. Based on this study, it would appear that repellent action can be incorporated into standard-preservative-treated wood by the use of certain additives.

8.4.1.4 Natural resistance of various wood species

Presumably because of extractive content, and hardness, some species of wood are more resistant to termite attack than others. Some idea of this variation can be seen in Tables 8.7 and 8.8 [20,26]. It is apparent

TABLE 8.7

Comparative Termite Resistance of the Heartwood of Several Wood Species When Exposed to Subterranean Termites (*Coptotermes* sp.) in Laboratory Tests [20]*

Wood	Av. Wt. Loss, %
Toona (*Toona* sp.)	3.4
Ohia (*Metrosideros collina*)	3.8
Mahogany (*Swietenia* sp.)	18.1
Robusta (*Eucalyptus robusta*)	23.2
Redwood (*Sequoia sempervirens*)	23.3
Cedar (*Thuja plicata*)	26.2
Douglas-fir (*Pseudotsuga menziesii*)	97.2
Koa (*Acacia koa*)	100.0

*Test method was similar to Standard AWPA Test except that a large container was used so that all species could be included in in a single container.

that species such as redwood, cedar, and baldcypress are less susceptible to attack than pine, fir, etc. Nevertheless, by sustained attack termites can do considerable damage to these so-called resistant species.

A worldwide list of termite-resistant commercial timbers has been compiled by Harris [12].

8.5 Future Research Needs

Preliminary studies [16,17] of a fragmentary nature have shown that the use of attractant–insecticide and attractant–pathogen combinations may become effective termiticides when added to wood. Additional effort toward this development should be encouraged. Specific actions of pathogens can range from those of the cell-protoplasm precipitators to nerve-synapse stimulators which cause insect death through hyperactivity. Additional actions can be attributed to septicemia (massive infection).

The use of biological controls requires major research effort for a number of reasons, since they may be safer in the environment, easier to apply, and more versatile.

TABLE 8.8

Comparative Amount of Wood Eaten When
Samples Were Exposed to Termites in a
Sand Substrate [26]

Wood	Wood Eaten (mg)
Redwood	78
Baldcypress	103
White oak	231
Black walnut	249
Douglas-fir	258
Western larch	313
Sugar maple	314
Ponderosa pine	348
Black cherry	368
Loblolly pine	399
Slash pine	411

REFERENCES

1. Anonymous. 1966. "Termite control investigation inspection of specimens after 100 months exposure." Am. Assoc. of Railroads Rept. No. ER–66.
2. Anonymous. 1969. *Insect-Pest Management and Control.* Vol. 3, *Principles of Plant and Animal Pest Control.* National Academy of Sciences, Pub. 1965, Washington, D.C.
3. Anderson, R. F. 1960. *Forest and Shade Tree Entomology.* John Wiley & Sons, Inc., N.Y.
4. Arnett, R.H. 1968. *The Beetles of the United States.* American Entomol. Inst., Ann Arbor, Mich.
5. Beal, R.H. 1969. "Treating pine lumber with insecticide and preservative prevents tubing by subterranean termites." *J. Economic Ent.* 62:757–58.
6. Blew, J.O. 1957. "An international termite exposure test—Twenty-third and final report." *Proc., Am. Wood-Preserves' Assoc.* 53:225–34.
7. Borror, D.J. and DeLong, D.M. 1964. *An Introduction to the Study of Insects.* Holt, Rinehart and Winston, N.Y.
8. Findlay, W.P.K. 1967. *Timber Pests and Diseases.* Pergamon Press, N.Y.
9. Gay, F.J. and Wetherly, A.H. 1958. "Laboratory studies of termite resistance. I. The anti-termite value of some chlorinated naphthalenes and phenols." Div. of Ent. Tech. Paper No. 2. Commonwealth Sci. and Ind. Res. Organization, Melbourne, Australia.
10. Gay, F.J., Harrow, K.M. and Wetherly, A.H. 1958. "Laboratory studies of termite resistance. III. A comparative study of the anti-termite value of boric acid, zinc chloride and 'Tanalith U.'" Div. of Ent. Tech. Paper No. 4. Commonwealth Sci. and Ind. Res. Organization, Melbourne, Australia.
11. Graham, K. 1963. *Concepts of Forest Entomology.* Reinhold Publishing Corp., N.Y.
12. Harris, W.V. 1961. *Termites: Their Recognition and Control.* Longmans, Green and Co., Ltd., London.
13. Kilgore, W.W. and Doutt, R.L. 1967. *Pest Control.* Academic Press, N.Y.

14. Krishna, K. and Weesner, F.M., eds. 1969. *Biology of Termites.* Vols. 1 and 2. Academic Press, N.Y.

15. Lund, A.E. 1958. "The relationship of subterranean termite attack to varying retentions of water-borne preservatives." *Proc., Am. Wood-Preservers' Assoc.* 54:44–53.

16. Lund, A.E. 1969. "Termite attractants and repellents." In *B.W.P.A. Termite Symposium.* British Wood Preserving Association, London. 107–15.

17. Lund, A.E. 1971. "Microbial control of termites." In *Microbial Control of Insects and Mites* (H.D. Burgess and N.W. Hussey, eds.). Academic Press, London, 385–86.

18. Lund, A.E., and Dreher, W.A. 1968. "Field test evaluates termite tubing on wood treated with preservatives." *Pest Control* 5:74–77.

19. Mallis, A. 1960. *Handbook of Pest Control.* 3d ed. MacNair-Dorland Co., N.Y.

20. Nicholas, D. and Skolman, R. 1971. "Termite resistance of several woods used in Hawaii." Unpublished report.

21. Nicholas, D.D., Johnson, B.R. and Weldon, D. 1972. "Evaluation of the AWPA termite laboratory test method." *Proc., Am. Wood-Preservers' Assoc.* In press.

22. Rabb, R.L. and Buthrie, F.E. 1970. *Concepts of Pest Management.* North Carolina State Univ. Press. Raleigh, N.C.

23. Randall, M., Herms, W.B. and Doody, T.C. 1934. "The toxicity of chemicals to termites." In *Termites and Termite Control* (C.A. Kofoid, ed.). Univ. of California Press, Berkeley, Calif. 368–84.

24. Ratcliffe, F.N., Gay, F.J. and Greaves, T. 1952. *Australian Termites. The Biology, Recognition, and Economic Importance of the Common Species.* CSIRO, Melbourne.

25. Skaife, S.H. 1955. *Dwellers in Darkness.* Longmans, Green and Co., Ltd., London.

26. Smythe, R.V. and Carter, F.L. 1969. "Feeding responses to sound wood by the eastern subterranean termite, *Reticulitermes flavipes.*" *Ann. Ent. Soc. Amer.* 62(2):335–37.

27. Tynes, J.D. 1969. "Evaluation of combination of insecticides and standard wood preservatives in preventing damage to wood by termites." U.S. Forest Serv. Rept. FS-S02201–7.103.

9. Degradation and Protection of Wood from Thermal Attack

IRVING S. GOLDSTEIN

Texas A & M University, College Station, Texas*

9.1 Introduction

The thermal degradation of wood has been familiar since man first discovered fire. For most of this time it has been a positive process, providing both heat and light. We still enjoy our fireplaces and campfires. Until recently, the controlled thermal degradation of wood by pyrolysis and distillation was used as a source of chemicals, and by carbonization to charcoal has provided fuel.

However, in the industrially developed areas of the world, fossil materials such as coal, oil, and natural gas—and now nuclear energy—have replaced wood in its early role of supplying heat and light. Chemicals are also more conveniently obtained from fossil fuels. Although we may eventually return to our renewable resource—wood—as a raw material for chemicals, current economics favors petroleum. Chemicals from wood and charcoal production will not be covered in this review.

Under these circumstances, the thermal degradation of wood remains only a negative process destructive of life and property, and increasing attention has been given to its prevention. In 1970 fire killed approximately 12,200 people in the U.S. and destroyed a record $2.7 billion worth of property [83].

Recent studies have clarified the mechanisms involved in the thermal degradation of wood and provided plausible theories for the action of fire retardants (essentially all empirically discovered) in preventing or minimizing this degradation. It is noteworthy that despite the hundreds of technical articles and patents which have been devoted to improving the fire resistance of wood, and despite our current understanding of the phe-

---

*Presently Professor of Wood and Paper Science and Head of the Department, School of Forest Resources, North Carolina State University, Raleigh, North Carolina.

307

nomena involved, present commercial practice still relies on certain inorganic salts such as ammonium phosphates, ammonium sulfate, borax,
and zinc chloride, which have been recognized as fire retardants for as
long as a century and a half. Ammonium phosphate and borax were
recommended for flameproofing cellulosic fabrics by Gay-Lussac [37] in
1821, and ammonium phosphate and ammonium sulfate were patented as
fire retardants for wood by Schuler [106] in 1893.

Even though they suffer from various disadvantages, these salts continue to be used because they are effective and inexpensive. As the desirability of fire-retardant-treated wood has been recognized by more
building codes and insurance companies, its use has been increasing. In
recent years, the annual level has reached almost 20 million pounds of
salts [39]—equivalent to about 75 million board feet of lumber at a retention of 3 pounds per cubic foot.

9.2 The Effect of Heat on Wood

The application during the past decade of sensitive instrumentation to
the study of the behavior of wood on heating has provided a good understanding of the processes involved in the thermal degradation of wood.
Five methods of analysis have been credited by Eickner [28] with affording
new insights. These are static and dynamic thermogravimetric analysis,
differential thermal analysis, heat of combustion measurements, and determination of identity and quantity of the degradation products.

In thermogravimetric analysis (TGA), the loss in weight of a specimen
is measured as it occurs, either at a constant temperature in static studies
or as a function of a programmed increase in temperature in dynamic
studies. Differential thermal analysis (DTA) measures the temperature of
the specimen in relation to the temperature to which it is subjected. This
is usually done dynamically, using a programmed increase in temperature.
Reactions occurring in or on the heated wood which give off heat are
called "exothermal," and are indicated by a specimen temperature which
is greater than that to which the wood was subjected. Reactions occurring
in the heated wood which absorb heat are called "endothermal," and are
indicated by a specimen temperature lower than that to which the wood
was subjected. A review of the literature on thermal degradation of wood,
with special emphasis on TGA and DTA, has been prepared by Beall and
Eickner [9].

9.2.1 Low-temperature processes (below 200°C)

For the purpose of this discussion, low-temperature processes are arbi-
trarily defined as those occurring below 200°C. Decomposition of the

wood components is slow although steady, and sound wood will not ordinarily ignite below 200°C.

As wood is heated above room temperature, the first effect is endothermal as the water adsorbed by the hygroscopic wood components is driven off. This endotherm continues past 200°C [5], well above the boiling point of water (100°C), because some of the water is tightly bound and some water is being formed by decomposition of carbohydrates. The strength of the wood is increased by the drying below 100°C, but prolonged exposure to temperatures above 100°C causes losses in strength.

The initial decomposition temperature of wood components was determined by Ramiah and Goring [95] by dilatometric measurement of the evolved gases. The hemicelluloses birch xylan and pine glucomannan showed initial decomposition at 117°C and 127°C. Spruce lignin preparations decomposed at 130°C and 145°C, while various cellulose samples showed decomposition temperatures of 156–170°C.

Although slow, the decomposition is not negligible. Beech sawdust heated at 160°C for 28 days retained only 20 percent of its cellulose. Lignin content after 14 days was only 2.3 percent, and 37 percent of the pentosan was lost in only 2 days [72]. Carbohydrates showed high losses in only 2 days at 80–130°C.

MacLean [77] reported an average loss in weight for 11 species of wood of 2.7 percent in 1 year at 93°C, 26.8 percent in 470 days at 121°C, 14.8 percent in 400 hours at 149°C, and 21.4 percent in 102 hours at 167°C. Charring of the surface was pronounced, even at 93°C. Yellow birch and basswood were more severely affected than softwoods, in agreement with their higher content of susceptible pentosans.

The gases evolved during this slow, low-temperature pyrolysis are not flammable. Water vapor and carbon dioxide predominate, with lesser amounts of carbon monoxide and traces of organic acids being present.

9.2.2 High-temperature processes (above 200°C)

The phenomena associated with thermal degradation above 200°C, such as rapid pyrolysis, combustion, glowing, and smoke, are considered high-temperature processes.

9.2.2.1 Pyrolysis

As heating is continued in the absence of air or in nitrogen above 200°C, the rate of decomposition increases but still remains relatively slow. The main products of slow decomposition remain water, carbon dioxide, and carbon monoxide [120].

Thermogravimetric analysis of beech wood in vacuum showed rapid weight losses at 260°C, 280°C, and 330°C. Differential thermal analysis studies showed that the pyrolysis peaks at 260°C and 330°C were exotherms. For spruce, the corresponding rapid pyrolysis temperatures were found to be 280°C and 330°C, while for Scots pine, the exotherms were at 270°C and 340°C [53]. Peschek [91] had reported the exothermal decomposition of wood at 260–290°C, using relatively primitive equipment. The agreement is excellent. Kollman [68] has observed that the temperature of exothermal decomposition is lower for hardwoods than for softwoods because the hardwoods contain more heat-sensitive pentosans.

Tang [112] has reported that for ponderosa pine, the higher exotherm at 335°C has the maximum decomposition rate and the pyrolysis is essentially finished at 360°C.

There is less agreement among different investigators on the decomposition behavior of the separate wood components. This may result from the different chemical composition of hemicelluloses and lignins prepared by different methods, and the variations in hemicellulose content, crystallinity, and degree of polymerization of the cellulose preparations. Arseneau [5] has stated that thermal effects in wood can be related directly to thermal effects in one or more of the separated components except for a probable displacement of temperature for lignin.

In contrast to the thermal stability order of hemicelluloses < lignin < cellulose indicated by the initial decomposition temperature data of Ramiah and Goring [95], there appears to be a change in the order at higher temperatures with hemicelluloses < cellulose < lignin. For Kudo and Yoshida [71], hemicellulose decomposed at 200–250°C, cellulose decomposed violently at 280°C ending at 300–350°C, and lignin decomposed most vigorously at 300–350°C ending at 400–450°C. Sandermann and Augustin [103] found hemicellulose to suffer exothermal decomposition at about 200°C, cellulose began to decompose exothermally at 290°C with the maximum rate at 315°C, and lignin showed a small exotherm at 300°C with a maximum at 425°C. Ramiah [94] reported TGA maxima of 260°C for potassium xylan, 280°C for regenerated cellulose, 345°C for Avicel microcrystalline cellulose, 295°C for periodate lignin, and 375°C for Klason lignin.

With the onset of rapid pyrolysis, flammable gases are evolved such as carbon monoxide, methane, formaldehyde, formic and acetic acids, and methanol. Included are highly flammable tars containing furfural and other furan derivatives from the decomposition of pentosans, levoglucosan (1,6-anhydro-beta-D-glucopyranose) from the decomposition of the cellulose, and aromatic fragments such as phenols, xylenols, guaiacols, cresols, and catechols from the decomposition of the lignin [17]. The residue becomes charcoal, with carbonization becoming complete at 400–500°C and the crystalline structure of graphite developing [105].

9.2.2.2 Combustion

In the presence of air or oxygen, the flammable gases and tars evolved during rapid pyrolysis of the wood can further react with the oxygen in the process we call burning, adding their heat of combustion to the over-all degradation process and changing it significantly from pyrolysis alone. Kollmann [68] has noted that the beginning of the exothermal reaction on heating wood depends on the composition of the surrounding atmosphere. The temperature at which exotherm sets in decreases with increasing pro-portions of oxygen, and the heating duration necessary to reach this temperature also decreases.

While Kollmann's observations may relate to the experimental temper-ature to which the wood is subjected rather than the true temperature of the decomposing wood, the effect of the oxygen is obvious. The pyrolytic thermal degradation, which is self-sustaining only under special heat-conserving conditions, is transformed into combustion—which is all too often so self-sustaining that it becomes uncontrollable and destructive.

Ignition of the flammable gases occurs as the temperature increases and the ratio of gases to oxygen reaches an appropriate value. The minimum ignition temperature is affected by the temperature of the surrounding air, the exotherm associated with the pyrolytic decomposition, and the rate of air flow or ventilation. The flash temperature at which ignition occurs from an external heat source such as a flame is lower than the self-ignition temperature in the absence of an ignition source. Continuation of burning depends on the transfer of sufficient heat from the flame to the wood to maintain the supply of flammable gases [54].

The shape of the wood has a profound effect on the rate and self-sus-taining nature of the combustion. Burning is a surface phenomenon, so surface–volume ratios are important. Rapid evolution of pyrolysis gases prevents diffusion of oxygen to the charcoal formed at the wood surface. Flaming occurs in the gas phase often at a considerable distance from the wood. As the charcoal layer builds up, it may insulate the underlying wood from the heat in the flame, first delaying and finally preventing at-tainment of the exothermal pyrolysis temperature. Without a continuing source of flammable gases, the burning stops—even though the charcoal itself has a lower spontaneous ignition temperature than the other pyroly-sis products [17].

The surface nature of burning and the insulating effect of charcoal are the reasons why heavy timber construction has a high degree of fire re-sistance without any treatment. This is why it is difficult to keep a single log burning in a fireplace.

The rapid pyrolysis of the wood enhanced by the heat of combustion tends to produce less charcoal and a greater volume of more flammable tars and gases than does slow pyrolysis, which tends to produce more charcoal and a smaller volume of less flammable gases. Combustion in turn of the greater volume of more flammable materials reinforces the rapid pyrolysis and the self-sustaining cycle is complete.

Tang and Neill [114] have assigned different effects in the burning of wood to its components. Their work shows that the cellulose fraction contributes most of the flaming combustion, while the lignin fraction supports most of the glowing combustion.

9.2.2.3 Glowing

Glowing is the light emitted by the residual solid charcoal when heated to incandescence by flameless combustion, a process independent of the flaming combustion of the gaseous and liquid phases. The combination of solid carbon with oxygen to form carbon dioxide is believed to occur in two steps [75].

The first reaction takes place at the surface between carbon and oxygen:

$$C + \tfrac{1}{2}O_2 = CO + 26.43 \text{ kcal/mole}$$

The carbon monoxide formed can then react further in the gas phase with much greater liberation of heat to form the final combustion product, carbon dioxide:

$$CO + \tfrac{1}{2}O_2 = CO_2 + 67.96 \text{ kcal/mole}$$

The total heat evolved in glowing is sufficient to maintain the carbon at the surface at 600–700°C or dark red heat. Glowing is often self-sustaining, and will continue until the charcoal is completely consumed.

9.2.2.4 Smoke

If combustion of wood were complete, the only products other than heat and light would be carbon dioxide and water—which are colorless gases at combustion temperatures. Complete combustion is difficult to attain even under controlled conditions, so the burning of wood is usually associated with more or less smoke—the solid and liquid particles from partial combustion suspended in the combustion gases.

Very little difference between species of wood in smoke yield and little smoke is observed on flaming exposure. On nonflaming exposure to radiant heat, more smoke is evolved, with the smoke level dependent on the level of irradiation. At low levels of irradiation, spruce, larch, redwood, and red oak gave less smoke than southern pine, sugar maple, and red lauan. At high levels, birch, sugar maple, red oak, and white oak yielded less smoke than redcedar, Douglas-fir, redwood, and red lauan [15]. Smoldering woods yield denser smokes than burning woods [36].

9.3 Mechanisms for Reducing Thermal Degradation

Analysis of the processes involved in the thermal degradation of wood, as described in Section 9.2, shows the following sequence of steps leading to rapid sustained degradation by combustion:

1. Wood is heated to its decomposition point.
2. Wood decomposes to flammable gases.
3. Flame is propagated by flammable gases.

Interference with one or more of these steps can prevent or retard combustion. The best fire retardants probably act in more than one manner; some possibly affect all three steps.

It is axiomatic that if the wood does not become hot enough to decompose, degradation will not take place. This principle underlies the use of insulating coatings for the protection of wood from thermal degradation, and the fire resistance of heavy timbers large enough to form an insulating layer of charcoal when exposed to fire.

Early theories on the mechanism of action of fire-retardant chemicals [17] postulated interference with step 1 by the formation of insulating coatings, glazes, or foams; by increasing the thermal conductivity of the wood to cause rapid dissipation of applied heat; and by the absorption of enough heat to prevent decomposition of the wood, by chemical or physical changes in the fire-retardant chemical such as change of state, loss of water by hydration, or endothermal decomposition.

While these thermal effects may contribute to the over-all efficiency of fire-retardant chemicals, they are probably minor compared to the interference with steps 2 and 3 by the chemical action of the retardants. These more recent theories are discussed below in the sections on pyrolysis and combustion.

9.3.1 Low-temperature processes (below 200°C)

The need for the reduction of the low-temperature (below 200°C) thermal degradation of wood, when recognized, is generally met by insulation of either the wood or the heat source. Chemical modification of the cellulose by etherification or esterification can increase its thermal stability in this range, but these reactions are not commercially applied to wood. Substitution of the hydroxyl groups probably decreases both the dehydration and oxidation of the cellulose.

Cyanoethylated paper has improved heat resistance and retains its strength in transformer oil at 175°C [49], while cyanoethylated fabrics withstand prolonged heating at 150–160°C without significant loss of mechanical strength [100]. Cellulose acetate has been used in commercial ironing-board covers because of its thermal stability.

9.3.2 High-temperature processes (above 200°C)

The high-temperature (above 200°C) thermal degradation processes of pyrolysis, combustion, and glowing are chemical reactions. Consequently, they are subject to inhibition or modification by suitable chemicals acting by various mechanisms.

9.3.2.1 Pyrolysis

Although he did not deduce the correct mechanism, Gillet [40] was among the first to report the different course pyrolysis of wood takes in the presence of fire-retardant chemicals. He observed that the impregnated salts increased the rate of carbonization, with the most rapid decomposition being produced by those generally considered to be the best fire-retardant agents. The evolved gases were noted to be nonflammable. Tamaru [111] observed decreased gas formation during thermal decomposition of wood treated with various chemicals.

Metz [80] recognized that chemical changes in the decomposition of treated wood are of great importance. Wood treated with acid or alkaline compounds was found to be more or less charred after 15 minutes at 200°C, while neutral salts caused no decomposition at that temperature and had hardly any protective value. In a later paper [81], Metz theorized that effective fire-retardant compounds cause a premature carbonization of wood, thus producing an insulating layer on the surface.

Richardson [98] provided the mechanism for this most important fire-retardant effect by relating the increased yield of charcoal obtained from wood treated with salts, which reduce combustibility to dehydration of the cellulose and yield more fixed carbon and less combustible volatile matter. Koritnig [69] showed that at comparatively low temperatures, substances which give a pronounced acid reaction in aqueous solution or decompose to form an inorganic acid caused carbonization of the wood. Alkaline substances, or chemicals forming alkali on decomposition, required higher temperatures for carbonization.

Scanning electron microscope studies of pyrolyzed Douglas-fir cell walls indicated no structural differences between untreated wood and wood treated with a mixture of zinc chloride and sodium dichromate. However, in the presence of a mixture of urea, monoammonium phosphate, and glucose, the cell walls appeared to undergo plastic flow which might interfere with the liberation of pyrolysis gases [67].

Detailed mechanisms for the modified pyrolysis reactions leading to increased amounts of charcoal by dehydration of the cellulose were given by Schuyten, Weaver, and Reid [107]. They applied modern concepts of catalytic dehydration of alcohols through carbonium ions generated by Lewis acids (electron acceptors) or carbanions generated by Lewis bases (electron donors) to the polyhydric alcohol cellulose.   This generalized concept of acids and bases is far broader than one merely of compounds which dissociate to hydrogen or hydroxyl ions.   Furthermore, the fire-retardant compound used does not need to be a Lewis acid or base itself, but only needs to form such an acid or base at a temperature below the normal rapid decomposition point of untreated wood.

Evidence has recently been presented for the occurrence of free radical processes during the degradation of cellulose in the presence of inorganic fire retardants [6]. The mechanism proposed assigns the free radical signals to the later stages of the elimination of water.

Many quantitative studies of the modified pyrolysis of wood in the presence of fire-retardant compounds have been carried out by means of calorimetry (heat of combustion), thermogravimetric analysis (TGA), and differential thermal analysis (DTA) [14,18,19,73,96,112,113,114].

The char formation during pyrolysis is greatly increased by these chemicals.   Some lower the threshold temperature for pyrolysis while others do not.   Good fire retardants decrease the temperature at which active pyrolysis ends.   The increased char formation occurs at the expense of volatile flammable tars.   The cellulose is preferentially converted to carbon and water rather than through the normal decomposition to levoglucosan.   Flammability is reduced because of a lower total quantity of tar, dilution of the tar with water vapor, and formation of an insulating layer of charcoal. The heat of combustion of the volatiles is markedly reduced.

Browne [17] speculated that effective fire retardants must have the hydrophilic properties that lead to solubility in water since the highly effective inorganic fire retardants are all soluble in water. Insoluble salts deposited by double treatments are not comparable in effectiveness. However, there is evidence that one of the necessary conditions which is really being met is that the fire retardant be intimately associated with the wood at the molecular level. Impregnation with water-soluble salts and drying accomplishes this, while double-treatment reactions may cause precipitation of large particles which are ineffective.

McCarthy [78] observed that borax did not reduce the flaming characteristics of sawdust when mixed with it as a dry powder, but borax was effective when applied from solution. In the treatment of cellulosic materials with an aqueous suspension of insoluble fire-retardant resin particles, it was found that less than acceptable flameproofing properties resulted when the particle size exceeded 50 micrometers [42].

9.3.2.2 Combustion

Several of the theories of fire-retardant action [17] relate to the combustion or flame-propagation step in the process.   The coating theory previously cited as an insulating barrier has also offered the possibility that oxygen is prevented from coming in contact with the wood surface. Since the actual flaming combustion is a gas-phase process, the coating theory is probably not applicable.

Another theory first proposed by Gay-Lussac [37] is that noncombustible gases formed by decomposition of the fire retardant dilute the combustible gases liberated in pyrolysis sufficiently to make the mixture nonflammable. Possible diluting gases include water, carbon dioxide, ammonia, sulfur dioxide, and hydrogen chloride. It has been argued that even such salts as borax, with 10 molecules of water of crystallization, could not have a significant diluting effect. However, when combined with such factors resulting from the modified pyrolysis reaction as reduced flammable-tar evolution and increased water from cellulose dehydration, the net effect is a large decrease in flammable-tar concentration. The gas-dilution effect probably plays an important part in the over-all fire-retardant mechanism even if the decomposition of the fire-retardant chemical is not the chief source.

A final inhibitory mechanism believed to take place in the gas-phase combustion is the breaking of the free radical chain reactions normally operative in combustion. This is accomplished by the combination of the reactive flame propagating radical fragments with halogen radicals to form more stable, less reactive intermediates which do not undergo chain reactions.

The inhibitory effect of halogens and hydrogen halides on combustion has been widely studied, especially in plastics [54]. The diffusion flames resulting from combustion of solid substrates are much more complex and less well understood than premixed flames which have been studied comparatively extensively. Synergism between halogen compounds and free radical generators such as peroxides in reducing flammability supports the theory of radical chain-reaction inhibition. The efficiency of halogens increases in the order $F < Cl < Br$. Halogen radicals are not necessarily the only chain stoppers—merely those most studied.

9.3.2.3 Glowing

Prevention of access of oxygen to the wood surface by a melted or glazed coating could be an effective mechanism for inhibiting the combustion of solid charcoal, even if an unlikely mechanism for inhibiting flaming combustion. However, more subtle interference with the two-step flameless combustion described in Section 9.2.2.3 is indicated from studies of glow retardants. In fact, the gas-phase nature of the second-step reaction of carbon monoxide with oxygen may be questioned, since it is inhibited by materials present in the solid phase which presumably do not act at a distance. The oxidation of carbon monoxide may very well take place catalytically at the charcoal surface.

Support for a two-step process is provided by the change in composition of the gaseous products in the presence of glow retardants. Char from untreated cotton cellulose yielded a ratio of CO/CO_2 of 0.1 compared to a ratio of 4 when a phosphate salt was present [87]. The marked increase in CO at the expense of CO_2 greatly reduces the heat liberated, since most heat is derived from the second reaction of CO with oxygen. This reduction in heat available allows the substrate to cool below the temperature at which the first reaction of carbon with oxygen takes place, thus terminating the glowing combustion.

It is apparent that the presence of glow retardants inhibits the reaction of CO with oxygen. The stimulation of glowing in the presence of salts of chromium, manganese, cobalt, copper, and iron may, conversely, result from catalytic promotion of the reaction of carbon monoxide and oxygen or, alternatively, catalytic promotion of the first reaction of carbon with oxygen to form carbon monoxide more rapidly.

The exact mechanism by which glow retardants effect the inhibition of carbon monoxide oxidation is not known. Suggestions have included alteration of heat of activation, interference with regenerative cycles involving carbon, carbon monoxide, and carbon dioxide, and adsorption on active sites on the charcoal to lower its reactivity.

Although many chemicals have been found to be effective against flaming, only systems containing phosphorus or boron in forms capable of forming phosphoric or boric acids during pyrolysis are effective glow retardants.

9.3.2.4 Smoke

Since smoke is the product of incomplete combustion, it should not be surprising that reductions in flaming brought about by fire-retardant treatments are often accompanied by increases in smoke [30]. However, smoke generation is dependent on many other factors such as air access, rate and type of heating, moisture content, etc. These are not under control in unplanned fires in buildings, in contrast to power plants and waste burners where combustion conditions may be manipulated to minimize smoke.

While dense smoke from inhibited decomposition of fire-retardant-treated wood is undesirable, it is limited in extent by the absence of flame spread. Consequently, the total smoke generated will be less than in a general conflagration, even if locally concentrated. Smoke abatement by complete combustion is antithetical to fire-retardant treatment. Smoke abatement by minimizing evolution of liquid and solid particles can be accomplished with some degree of success by selection of the nature and amount of chemical treatment for the species of wood involved.

9.4 Measurement of Fire-Retardant Properties

During the evolution of present concepts of the mechanisms for fire-retardant action and the continued search for new and improved fire-retardant treatments, the methods of testing fire performance have undergone both proliferation and standardization. The difficulty of controlling in a single test all the factors governing combustion, such as geometry, ventilation, and duration and degree of heating, has been one cause of test proliferation. Another has been the need to obtain information on different aspects of fire performance. Fortunately, a manageable number of tests has been given preferred status in the United States by adoption and standardization by the American Society for Testing and Materials [1].

These tests range from small-scale methods suitable for laboratory screening through larger scale procedures still useful in research and development work to actual performance tests used for rating and classification of assemblies. Another classification of test methods has been according to resistance to flame spread or resistance to penetration of fire. The empirical observations made relate to loss in weight, spread of flame, increase in temperature, and loss of function expressed as a value relative to untreated wood on the one hand and a nonflammable material on the other, or expressed as duration of resistance.

9.4.1 Laboratory screening tests

Two small-scale test methods, the fire-tube test and the crib test, measure the extent of combustion by weight loss after exposure to a standard source of heat. These tests relate to the properties of treated wood as such, rather than to the performance of a fabrication used as an element of construction.

9.4.1.1 Fire-tube test

The fire-tube test [1a] was developed at the U.S. Forest Products Laboratory about 1928, and has provided most of the reported information on the behavior of treated wood in burning. The specimen, $\frac{3}{8} \times \frac{3}{4}$ inch in cross section and 40 inches long, is suspended in a perforated sheet-metal tube from one arm of a balance beam. A standard flame from a Bunsen burner is applied to the lower end of the sample for 4 minutes and then removed. Untreated wood will allow the flame to spread up the tube, consuming the specimen. Loss of weight during the test may be followed by watching the balance pointer.

In contrast to untreated specimens, which exhibit weight losses of 80–90 percent and maximum temperatures at the top of the chimneylike tube of 700–800°C, effectively treated specimens cease burning as soon as the igniting flame is withdrawn and exhibit weight losses of 15–20 percent and maximum temperatures of only 200°C. Duration of glowing can also be observed in this test.

9.4.1.2 Crib test

The crib test [1f] was developed at Columbia University about 1900. It uses 24 specimens, $\frac{1}{2} \times \frac{1}{2}$ inch in cross section and 3 inches long, arranged in a wire frame in 12 tiers of 2 pieces each placed 1 inch apart, with the alternate tiers at right angles. After application of a standard Meker burner flame below the center of the resultant crib for 3 minutes, the igniting flame is removed.

The weight loss from combustion is determined, and duration of glowing and flaming are observed. This test also measures relative combustibility rather than absolute performance. Well-treated specimens show weight losses of less than 30 percent.

9.4.2. Development tests

Larger scale tests still suitable for research and development work measure flame spread. Two frequently used methods are the tunnel tests and the radiant-panel test.

9.4.2.1 Surface flammability using radiant heat

The radiant-panel test [1g] was devised at the National Bureau of Standards [50]. The sample, which is 18 inches long by 6 inches wide, is inclined at an angle to a vertical radiant ceramic heat source. A pilot light ensures ignition at the top, which is closer to the heat source. The rate of flame spread downward on the specimen and the rate of heat liberation as determined by a thermocouple in the stack are used in the calculation of a flame-spread index. Smoke is also measured.

9.4.2.2 Surface flammability using tunnel furnaces

The 8-foot tunnel test [1i] was developed at the U.S. Forest Products Laboratory to provide reduced specimen size and reduced testing costs compared to the large-tunnel test (Section 9.4.3.1). The small-tunnel test is more applicable to research and development work, and is correlatable with the large-tunnel test. Unlike the larger scale test, it is not used as a basis for ratings for building-code purposes.

The test specimen, $13\frac{3}{4}$ inches wide by 8 feet long, is laid on an angle-iron frame tilted 30° from the horizontal. The tunnel itself is sloped at a 6° angle to allow natural convection of air and avoid the need for draft control. Ignition of the specimen is by gas flames 1 inch from its end.

Flame spread is expressed as an index relative to a rate for red oak of 100 and for asbestos board of 0. Treated wood will show a flame-spread index of less than 25. Stack temperature is used to determine a fuel contribution index, and smoke density is also measured and converted to an index based on red oak and asbestos.

A 2-foot tunnel test developed by the Monsanto Company is also used for screening purposes before proceeding to the large 25-foot tunnel test, and is useful since it requires less material than the 8-foot tunnel.

9.4.3 Full-scale performance tests

Several tests using large specimens have been developed for evaluating the full-scale performance of materials and assemblies. The results of these tests are used to rate fire-retardant-treated wood for conformance to building codes and insurance requirements.

9.4.3.1 Surface burning characteristics

This test is the original tunnel test developed by Underwriters' Laboratories [1b] after which the 8-foot tunnel test was modeled. It uses a test panel 20 inches wide and 25 feet long, ignited at one end by standardized gas flames. Index values are based on the performance of red oak (100) and asbestos (0).

The test determines the comparative burning characteristics of the material being tested by evaluating the flame spread over its surface, fuel contributed by its combustion, and the density of the smoke developed when the material is exposed to a test fire. It provides a basis on which the surface burning characteristics of different materials may be compared.

The test is used to register performance, provide flame-spread classifications, and allow the rating and labeling of treated wood. This is a very widely used flame-spread test for building-code purposes. Classes of interior finish have been established such as A = Flame spread 0–25, B = Flame spread 25–75, C = Flame spread 75–200, etc. For different construction areas such as exits, access to exits, etc., and different types of buildings such as residential, mercantile, institutional, etc., a building code will require that the materials used conform to more or less stringent flame-spread performance as rated by this test. The more sensitive areas in terms of fire safety require Class A ratings, while some spaces in sparsely occupied buildings might be allowed to use materials with ratings of C or higher.

9.4.3.2 Roof coverings

In these tests [1c] sections of roof decking are evaluated for their fire-retardant characteristics against fire originating outside the building on which they are to be installed. Three different tests are applied: (1) intermittent exposure, (2) spread of flame, and (3) burning brands. The latter involves the affixation of pieces of untreated wood to the treated roof and their ignition to provide continued contact with flaming wood.

9.4.3.3 Building construction materials

This test [1d] is applicable to assemblies of structural materials for buildings, including bearing and other walls and partitions, columns, girders, beams, slabs, and composite slab and beam assemblies for floors and roofs. The assembly is exposed to a standard fire of controlled extent and severity which follows a time–temperature curve yielding 1000°F at 5 minutes, 1700°F at 1 hour, 2000°F at 4 hours, and 2300°F at 8 hours or over. Results are reported in terms of the number of hours elapsing before the first critical point in the behavior of the assembly is observed.

9.4.3.4 Door assemblies

Using the same standard time–temperature curve as that in Section 9.4.3.3, the resistance of door assemblies to fire is determined [1e] and rated in terms of hours of fire resistance.

9.4.3.5 Window assemblies

Similar to that mentioned in Section 9.4.3.4 but designed for window assemblies, this test [1h] does not use as great a heat intensity. The standard time–temperature curve advances from 1000°F at 5 minutes to 1638°F at 45 minutes.

9.4.4 Miscellaneous fire tests

Many other tests have been used to evaluate fire retardance, with almost every investigator making a contribution in this area and different standard tests being adopted in different countries. In addition to the tests measuring flame spread, weight loss, or structural integrity, special tests have been devised for restricted aspects of over-all fire performance. Examples of these are fuel contribution and smoke.

9.4.4.1 Fuel contribution

Fuel contribution is usually estimated in fire tests from the temperature of the combustion gases in the stack as by measuring the area under the time–temperature curve. In the Factory Mutual test [117], the total heat during pyrolysis is determined by actually burning the sample completely in a calorimeter and quantitatively measuring the fuel contribution.

9.4.4.2 Smoke

Smoke density is ordinarily measured as in the tunnel tests by the reduction in intensity of a beam of light passing horizontally through the stack to a photoelectric cell. Brenden [15] has reported a new optical test procedure using a closed instrumented chamber in which all the smoke formed during combustion is trapped.

Advantages of the new system are that the smoke-density parameter is dimensionless, allowing application to a variety of room situations, burning areas, and light-path lengths; the exposure conditions are carefully controlled and uniform; and flaming and nonflaming combustion measurements can be made separately and independently.

9.5 The Ideal Fire-Retardant Chemical

The ideal fire-retardant chemical should not only be effective and reasonable in cost but should also not cause any adverse changes in the properties of the wood [55]. If improvements in some of the natural deficiencies of wood such as its lack of decay resistance and dimensional stability were also to result from the treatment, this would be a bonus.

Unfortunately the auxiliary effects of fire-retardant chemicals have generally been deleterious, as discussed by Gardner [35] and Eickner [29]. These related properties are also important in the acceptance of fire-retardant wood. They include hygroscopicity, strength, corrosivity, dimensional stability, paintability, machinability, gluability, leach resistance, and resistance to decay and insects.

9.5.1 Hygroscopicity

Many inorganic salts are hygroscopic—that is, they take up and retain moisture from the air, especially at high relative humidities. At the low retentions used to protect wood against decay and insect attack, the effect of the salts on the moisture content of the wood is not great. However, at the high concentrations needed for fire retardance—10 percent of the weight of the wood and greater—the moisture picked up by the salts can significantly affect the moisture content and properties of the wood.

At high relative humidities it is not uncommon for the fiber-saturation point of the wood to be exceeded and the absorbed water to actually exude from the wood. The severity of this problem depends on the individual chemicals as well as their retention. Zinc chloride makes the treated wood more hygroscopic than untreated wood at relative humidities as low as 30 percent. Ammonium sulfate first becomes more hygroscopic than wood at about 80 percent relative humidity, while monoammonium phosphate reaches this point at 95 percent. The latter two salts pick up water very rapidly above their threshold humidity value, causing the wood to reach moisture contents of over 50 percent [44].

The effect of high moisture content from hygroscopic salts is observed in such important wood properties as strength, dimensional stability, paintability, corrosivity, and the loss of chemicals through leaching.

9.5.2 Strength

Since most of the strength properties of wood decrease with increasing moisture content, the presence of hygroscopic salts will obviously reduce the strength of wood below that of untreated wood exposed to the same conditions of humidity. These strength losses will not be severe under normal conditions, but can become serious under prolonged exposure to high humidities.

Allowable design stresses for fire-retardant-treated lumber are reduced by 10 percent from those for untreated wood [84]. The allowable loads for fastenings used in fire-retardant-treated wood which has been kiln dried after treatment are also reduced to 90 percent of the loads allowed in untreated wood [109]. However, for undried treated wood, whose moisture content can be equaled by once-dried hygroscopic treated wood exposed to high humidities, the allowable loads are reduced to as low as 25 percent of untreated for withdrawal loads on nails and spikes, 40 percent of untreated for lag screws, and 75 percent of untreated for wood screws and lateral loads.

Brink [16] states that beams should be designed for use under wet conditions because of the hygroscopic nature of treated lumber. This is probably an extreme view, and should be tempered by the realization that penetration of the fire retardant in wood of structural dimensions may not be complete and strength loss would consequently be restricted to only the outer regions. Nonetheless, the deleterious effect of hygroscopic fire-retardant chemicals on the strength of the wood cannot be overlooked.

Of equal concern is loss of strength properties caused by degradation of the wood from the chemical action of the fire retardant. Acids cause hydrolysis of the cellulose component of wood, with resultant loss in impact resistance. Alkalis, on the other hand, dissolve hemicelluloses and lignin and reduce the hardness and stiffness of wood. It is obvious that strongly acidic or alkaline fire retardants can cause severe damage to the wood. The possibility of chemical degradation by fire-retardant chemicals is enhanced by the kiln-drying step required with waterborne salts. Even weakly acidic or alkaline salts can become very destructive during long and harsh drying cycles. In order to minimize loss of strength from chemical attack, care should be taken that the treating solutions are essentially neutral and the drying schedules are mild. Formulations containing sulfates cause a greater decrease in strength than those containing borates alone [82].

Eickner [29] has reported that tests at the U.S. Forest Products Laboratory on specimens treated by current fire-retardant treating methods showed 5–8 percent decrease in modulus of elasticity, 10–17 percent decrease in modulus of rupture, and up to 32 percent decrease in work to maximum load, an index of impact resistance.

Graham [48] found that treated wood stored at normal and above-normal temperatures for one year behaved similarly to untreated controls in loads to cause failure and in moduli of rupture and elasticity. However, it was significantly lower in work to maximum load. Graham's failure to observe the other strength losses noted by Eickner might stem either from the known difficult permeability of Douglas-fir or from milder drying cycles. The lack of a time effect on degradation during extended storage is reassuring, and indicates that fire-retardant-treated wood will not undergo continued degradation on aging at normal exposure conditions.

The reduction of the mechanical properties of plywood in shear after fire-retardant treatment has been observed by Brink [16] and by Percival and Suddarth [88]. Brink showed that this reduction was proportional to the amount of salt in the wood, which could be a physical effect of the salt, or reflect the higher moisture contents observed at higher retentions of hygroscopic salts, or actually represent chemical attack by the fire-retardant treatments.

In Percival and Suddarth's work, the treated and untreated wood were tested at the same moisture content. Reductions of rolling shear strength in treated Douglas-fir and southern pine plywood truss plate assemblies ranged from 4 to 18 percent. There is also the possibility of effects of the treatment chemicals on the metal connectors.

Gerhard [38] has summarized the results of several studies at the Forest Products Laboratory, and concluded that modulus of rupture and work to maximum load in bending were reduced by varying amounts, depending on species and type of fire retardant. The 10 percent reduction in design stresses recommended for fire-retardant-treated lumber is supported by these data.

9.5.3 Dimensional stability

The dimensional stability of fire-retardant-treated wood is also dependent on the hygroscopicity of the chemicals used. The higher moisture contents in the treated wood at a given exposure condition will result in increased swelling, and at high humidities the increase in dimension of up to 10 percent could present a serious problem.

Although hygroscopic treated wood reaches its fiber-saturation point and maximum swelling at relative humidities below 100 percent, there is an offsetting factor which may have an ameliorating effect on total swelling. All the salts cause some reduction in the total swelling of the wood between measurements when ovendry and at fiber saturation because of their bulking effect at the dry dimension. For nonhygroscopic salts, the net result may be to reduce the swelling of wood by up to 40 percent [44]. For salts hygroscopic only at very high humidities, such as monoammonium phosphate, the net result is a slight reduction in swelling over that of untreated wood, even at 100 percent relative humidity.

Still another aspect of the dimensional stability of treated wood relates to the distortion caused by treatments with aqueous solutions and the subsequent kiln drying. Warping, twisting, and grain-raising are inherent problems encountered when wood is rewet and dried.

9.5.4 Other properties of treated wood

The corrosion of metal fittings and fasteners in contact with treated wood is also more severe under high humidity conditions when the fire retardant is hygroscopic. Under these conditions, rapid electrolytic corrosion is favored. Corrosion is also caused by acidic salts, and copper-based alloys are susceptible to ammonium salts. Corrosion inhibitors are used to minimize these problems. If they contain chromates, some promotion of glowing may be encountered.

High moisture contents associated with hygroscopic salts may also interfere with the application or adhesion of paint to fire-retardant-treated wood. Discoloration of the wood during kiln drying and sticker marks make the use of clear finishes undesirable.

Gluing of treated wood is sometimes adversely affected by high moisture contents. More important is the chemical interference of the fire retardant with the curing of the glue bond. This may take several forms, such as critical changes in pH, reaction of ammonium salts with formaldehyde hardeners, or complexing of the metal salts with the resin. It is

often necessary to develop modified gluing procedures and adhesive formulations for specific fire-retardant treatments. For example, the observation that ammonium salts react with the formaldehyde hardener for
resorcinol adhesives [104], has led to the use of hardeners with higher
formaldehyde content.

Salt treatments increase the hardness of the wood and the individual
crystals are abrasive. These properties of treated wood result in rapid
wear of normal machine tools and necessitate the use of special alloys.
Machining of treated wood is usually minimal, however, since it is not
good economics to cut away treated wood and there is always the danger
of exposing untreated wood where penetration was poor.

Water-soluble fire-retardant treatments are subject to loss of salts and
consequent loss of effectiveness. This may occur under high humidity
conditions if the salts are hygroscopic and exude in their own absorbed
moisture or when the wood is exposed to water as in roof coverings, cooling-tower components, scaffolding, etc. Sealers have been shown to reduce the loss of salts on leaching [11], but these require another operation,
are expensive, require periodic renewal, and may contribute to flammability.

Resistance to decay and insect attack in wood treated with fire retardants is often provided by the nature of the chemicals themselves, especially at the concentrations used. In other cases, it may be desirable to
supplement this resistance by the incorporation of small amounts of toxic
preservatives or mold inhibitors.

9.6 Fire-Retardant Treatments

In the preceding sections, occasional references were made to individual
fire-retardant chemicals in describing their long history of use or citing
their deleterious effect on wood properties. Efforts to improve the performance of fire retardants have led to the screening of hundreds of inorganic
salts and, more recently, to the development of formulations based on
organic compounds. A complete listing of all the many hundred fire-
retardant compositions described in the literature is beyond the scope of
this book, especially since for the most part they are not in use. Those
selected for discussion represent the most effective inorganic salts, new
types of treatments, or treatments which improve one or more auxiliary
properties in which treated wood is ordinarily deficient.

9.6.1 Inorganic fire retardants

With the development of the fire-tube test [1a], the U.S. Forest Products
Laboratory was in a position to compare the effectiveness of all the avail-

able inorganic salts as fire retardants. In a series of papers [56,57,58, 118,119], the performance of about 130 single chemicals or combinations of chemicals was evaluated.

These studies showed that diammonium phosphate, $(NH_4)_2HPO_4$, ranked first in fire-retardant effectiveness, followed closely by monoammonium phosphate, $NH_4H_2PO_4$. Ammonium chloride, NH_4Cl, ammonium sulfate, $(NH_4)_2SO_4$, borax, $Na_2B_4O_7$, and zinc chloride, $ZnCl_2$, were also found to be highly effective, with ammonium chloride somewhat less effective than the others. Only three compounds, the mono- and diammonium phosphates and orthophosphoric acid, H_3PO_4, showed a high degree of effectiveness in reducing both flaming and glowing. Boric acid, H_3BO_3, alone was very effective in preventing glowing, but only suppressed flaming when borax was mixed with it.

Considerable effort was expended by these investigators in producing compounds in the wood which were insoluble in water, such as MNH_4PO_4 where M is magnesium (Mg), zinc (Zn), barium (Ba), calcium (Ca), manganese (Mn), cobalt (Co), or nickel (Ni). Of these the magnesium salt showed the most promise, but was still much inferior to diammonium phosphate. None of the 130 compositions tested was considered to be an ideal fire retardant.

McCarthy [78], working with sawdust, confirmed the ranking of the salts by effectiveness. He found diammonium phosphate, monammonium phosphate, zinc chloride, and borax to be most effective, with ammonium chloride and ammonium sulfate somewhat less so. Of 67 chemicals tested by Hardy [52], only the mono- and diammonium phosphates, phosphoric acid, and monobasic magnesium phosphate were considered to have a really high degree of effectiveness.

Arent [3] devised a process for precipitating insoluble antimony oxychloride in wood, thereby providing leach-resistant fire retardance by impregnating the wood with antimony trichloride in amyl acetate and then treating with steam, water, or moist air to hydrolyze the trichloride to the insoluble oxychloride. The use of ammonium sulfamate $(NH_4SO_3NH_2)$ as a fire retardant was patented by Cupery [25].

Treatment of wood with an ammoniacal solution of basic zinc chloride $(0.2-4.0\,ZnO\cdot ZnCl_2\cdot 2NH_3)$ yielded a product which retained a high degree of fire resistance after exposure to leaching [90]. Hydrates of sodium oxyfluoroborate $(4NaF \cdot 5B_2O_3 \cdot 5H_2O)$ prepared by fusing NaF and B_2O_3 at 700°C were claimed to be effective flameproofing agents [21].

Halogenation of lignin-containing materials such as wood with chlorine or bromine in aqueous or organic solutions reduces their flaming tendency [74]. Wood chips chlorinated to 4 percent chlorine had a residual weight of 57 percent after ignition, and chips containing 3 percent bromine gave

55 percent residue [13]. The wood may also be brominated by treatment with bromide salts, drying, and dipping in dilute sulfuric acid.

Ammonium polyphosphate liquid fertilizer is an effective fire retardant for wood [31].

9.6.1.1 Commercial treatments

Four fire-retardant formulations make up Standard P10–65 of the American Wood-Preservers' Association [2]. They are listed in Table 9.1.

It is interesting that the most effective fire retardants, the ammonium phosphates, are barely represented in these formulations. The reason is the historically relatively higher cost of the phosphates. More recently, however, the cost of the phosphates has been reduced as phosphate production has grown with fertilizer usage and some coke-oven ammonia has been recovered as the phosphate instead of the sulfate. This improvement in relative cost, as well as the generally less desirable greater hygroscopicity of the ammonium sulfate and zinc chloride, has caused a shift to commercial use of ammonium phosphates.

In 1969 about 40 percent of the fire-retardant salts used commercially were in the form of a proprietary formulation called "Non-Com," which is not listed in the AWPA standard [39]. Its composition has not been disclosed and can be changed without AWPA approval (subject to continued certification by Underwriters' Laboratories to meet code requirements), but it is believed to contain ammonium phosphates. Another proprietary formulation called "Osmose Flame Proof" accounted for 20 percent of the 1969 usage, "Pyresote" accounted for almost 15 percent, and all other fire retardants 25 percent.

Since high retentions of salt, up to 3 lbs/cu ft, are required for effective fire retardance, and deep penetration is necessary for prolonged resistance to ignition, the wood is treated by full-cell pressure impregnation.

9.6.2 Organic fire retardants

Efforts to improve the auxiliary properties of fire-retardant-treated wood such as hygroscopicity, leach resistance, and dimensional stability have led in the past 40 years to the use of organic compounds in fire-retardant formulations. Although the carbon portion of these materials is inherently flammable, they contain a sufficient quantity of nitrogen and functional fire-retardant groups such as halogens and phosphorus derivatives to make the treated wood fire retardant. Organic fire retardants may be broadly divided into three categories, which show some blurring of lines of distinction. These include polymers and resins, formulations reactive with the lignocellulose, and other impregnants.

TABLE 9.1

American Wood-Preservers' Association Standard Fire-Retardant Formulations [2]

Formulation	Zinc Chloride ($ZnCl_2$)	Sodium Dichromate ($Na_2Cr_2O_7 \cdot 2H_2O$)	Chemical Composition, %			
			Ammonium Sulfate [$(NH_4)_2SO_4$]	Boric Acid (H_3BO_3)	Sodium Tetraborate ($Na_2B_4O_7$)	Diammonium Phosphate [$(NH_4)_2H\ PO_4$]
A. Chromated zinc chloride	81.5	18.5	—	—	—	—
B. Chromated zinc chloride (FR)	65.2	14.8	10	10	—	—
C. Minalith			60	20	10	10
D. Pyresote	35	5	35	25	—	—

9.6.2.1 Polymers and resins

The first use of resins in fire-retardant treatments was as a binder for conventional salts [59]. A salt such as diammonium phosphate was dissolved in a solution of a urea-formaldehyde condensation product. After impregnation, the resin could be cured to an insoluble state and retard the leaching of the salt. In a later development [8], the fire-retardant function was chemically combined with the resin by adding an acid such as phosphoric or boric to the condensation products of aldehydes with compounds containing carbon–nitrogen bonds, such as those of formaldehyde with cyanamide, dicyandiamide, melan, melamine, ammeline, or ammelide.

A similar variation [10] involves the condensation of pyrophosphoric acid and urea, mixing with a melamine–formaldehyde soluble condensation product and impregnating wood with the aqueous solution. After curing at 70–160°C, the treated wood does not support burning and does not glow. Guanidine, formaldehyde, and phosphoric acid may also be reacted to form an impregnating solution [110].

Wood may be impregnated with a partially polymerized reaction product of a tetrakis (hydroxymethyl) phosphonium salt and/or a tris (hydroxymethyl) phosphine oxide with a compound containing polyfunctional nitrogen such as urea, melamine, guanidine, or acrylamide in the presence of a dissolved alkyd resin. The wood is heated to polymerize the resin [97].

Leach-resistant flame-retardant properties are obtained by polymerizing in the wood the reaction products of organophosphorus halides with allylamine, diallylamine, or m-aminostyrene. Polymerization can be initiated by heat, chemical free radical generators, or irradiation [4]. Other unsaturated organophosphorus monomers such as bis (2-chloroethyl) vinyl phosphate, dimethylmethallyl phosphonate, triallyl phosphate, trimethallyl phosphite, etc., may be polymerized within wood by irradiation [93].

An undisclosed water-soluble monomer which becomes polymerized to an insoluble resin of high molecular weight on kiln drying provides nonhygroscopic leach-resistant fire retardance [101]. It is commercially available under the trade name "Non-Com Exterior."

9.6.2.2 Reactive compounds

Impregnation of wood with aqueous solutions containing equimolar quantities of dicyandiamide and phosphoric acid followed by curing at 70–100°C brings about a reaction between the impregnants and the cellulose of the wood [43,44]. Fire-retardant properties are similar to those reported for the ammonium phosphates, but the wood is nonhygroscopic, has increased shear strength, and its swelling has been reduced by up to 40 percent. Some leach resistance is observed, but prolonged exposure to water apparently causes hydrolysis of the reaction product. With less than 0.15 moles formaldehyde added, the solubility of the impregnants is improved and blooming is prevented without change in the beneficial properties [45].

Juneja [63] has shown that excellent leach resistance without sacrifice of fire retardance can be attained by using melamine as a cross-linking agent with dicyandiamide, phosphoric acid, and formaldehyde. Stable impregsolutions which are cured after impregnation into the wood may be formulated.

By pH adjustment and heat, tetrakis (hydroxymethyl) phosphonium chloride salts unreacted with nitrogen compounds can be fixed on cellulosic materials. Subsequent treatment with ammonia imparts flameproof properties [23]. A permanent, nonleachable, nonhygroscopic treatment results from the reaction of tris (1-aziridinyl) phosphine oxide (APO) in or with the wood. The APO can self-polymerize, and can also react with the hydroxyl groups of cellulose and lignin. If the reagent diffuses into the cell wall with the help of the moisture present, dimensional stability also results [65].

A final reactive treatment to give permanent weather-resistant fire retardance involves impregnation with phosphorus oxychloride ($POCl_3$), phosphorus trichloride (PCl_3), or phosphorus thiochloride ($PSCl_3$) in an organic solvent along with vinyl acetate–vinyl chloride copolymers. A typical solution would be 2% $POCl_3$ and 5% copolymer in 93% methylene chloride [89].

9.6.2.3 Other organic impregnants

Many halogenated and organophosphorus compounds dissolved in organic solvents have been claimed to provide fire-retardant properties for wood. Solvents of low volatility would have to be nonflammable themselves to prevent enhancement of the problem. Furthermore, large organic groups in the active compound unsubstituted by halogen can also offset any positive effect of the phosphorus group. Table 9.2 lists some of these fire retardants.

A related treatment involves impregnation of the wood with an organic solvent solution of trimethyl phosphite or a diester of phosphoric or phosphorous acid, evaporation of the solvent, and treatment of the impregnated wood with gaseous ammonia to form partial ammonium salts of the phosphorus esters which provide the fire-retardant properties [46]. The reason for the *in-situ* formation of the ammonium salts rather than

TABLE 9.2

Solvent-Soluble Organic Halogenated and
Organophosphorus Fire Retardants

Bis (2-bromoethyl) 2-bromoethanephosphonate [66]

Bis (2-halo-alkyl) alkenylphosphonates [34]

Chlorinated alkyl phosphates [76]

Chlorinated aryl phosphates [76]

Chlorinated diesters of phosphoric and phosphorous acids [47]

Chlorinated naphthalenes [33]

Phosphate triesters [102]

Solid chlorinated hydrocarbon (40% Cl) [102]

Triaryl phosphates [7]

---

the use of an aqueous impregnating solution is to retain the nonswelling, nondistorting character of the organic solvent treatments while utilizing the high fire-retardant effectiveness of ammonia-phosphorus compounds.

W ater-soluble organic compounds used as fire retardants are listed in Table 9.3.

TABLE 9.3

Water-Soluble Organic Fire Retardants

Aliphatic carboxylic acids containing over
   50% organically bound bromine [62]

Alkyl sulfamates [25]

Ammonium alkyl phosphates [24]

Antimony trichloride with tertiary amines
   (ethanolamines) [115]

Boric or a condensed phosphoric acid reacted with
   monoethanolamine [20]

Dicyandiamide with ammonium sulfate or phosphate [108]

Dicyandiamide with neutral complex from phosphorus
   pentoxide and ammonia at 150°C [32]

Dicyanodiamidine (guanylurea) phosphate [99]

Potassium esters and polyesters of bis (phosphonomethyl)
   chloromethylphosphorate [116]

Urea with ammonium phosphate [12]

Urea and sulfamic acid [26]

9.7 Fire-Retardant Coatings

Surface coatings can reduce the flammability of wood by insulating the wood from heat, thereby preventing its decomposition to flammable gases, and by restricting access of oxygen to the wood. The first mechanism seems more important, since gaseous pyrolysis products escaping through the coating could still flame above the wood.

According to Hindersinn and Wagner [54], fire-retardant coatings should be incombustible, maintain their integrity in fire, and seal off the substrate while at the same time being decorative, easily applied, weather resistant, washable, recoatable, and inexpensive. Such paragons are not available. Existing formulations, on the contrary, are usually sensitive to water and high humidity, have poor brushing characteristics, are inferior in appearance, and have poor storage stability. Despite these drawbacks, they find considerable utility—especially in improving the fire-retarding behavior of existing construction.

Fire-retardant coatings may be divided into distinct categories based on both composition and chronology. Those described until the middle 1930s were mainly inorganic, while those described since then have an organic base. Only representative formulations of the dozens developed are discussed here.

9.7.1 Inorganic coatings

Water glass, sodium silicate, is the base for many inorganic fire retardant coatings. However, it "blooms" and effloresces so the more expensive potassium silicate is used where blooming is objectionable. When heated, the silicates form a stable, frothy crust which insulates the wood. Commonly added to the silicates as fillers are asbestos, kieselguhr, magnesite, portland cement and quartz powder [85], or chalk and talcum [60].

Alkaline magnesium salts also serve as binders. Asbestos and magnesite may be mixed with an alkaline solution of magnesium chloride and used to cover wood [70], or a mixture of a solution of magnesium oxide and magnesium chloride or magnesium sulfate may be applied [64]. Lime and gypsum cement are effective when applied in sufficient thickness [60].

9.7.2 Organic coatings

Organic fire-retardant coatings may be further subdivided into those which intumesce or swell and bubble up when heated to form a cellular char and those which merely rely on their natural incombustibility and low heat conductivity.

Three types of components are necessary for the most effective intu-

mescent action. The carbon-producing ingredient is typically a carbohydrate such as starch or a polyfunctional alcohol such as pentaeryth-
ritol. The carbon is produced by dehydration when heat is applied in
the presence of a Lewis acid such as phosphorus compounds. Foaming of
the carbon is caused by the water evolved, as well as the gaseous pyrolysis
products of nitrogen compounds such as urea, guanidine, and dicyandiamide. The intumescing components are mixed with a binder which
might also be gas-producing.

A typical formulation might consist of: a urea-formaldehyde condensation product, 13% (binder and gas producer); water-insoluble reaction
product of phosphorus pentoxide and ammonia, 5% (carbonization catalyst); unhydrolyzed corn starch, 23% (carbon generator); arylsul-
fonamides, 3% (nonflammable plasticizers); wool flock, 2% (fortifier);
titanium dioxide, 4% (pigment); and water, 50% [122].

Other catalysts which have been used to carbonize the polyhydric alcohol or carbohydrate are the familiar fire-retardant chemicals; ammonium phosphates; phosphoric, boric, and sulfamic acids; ammonium
sulfate; ammonium sulfamate; ammonium bromide; and borax [61]. Variations in the binder include phenol-formaldehyde resins [79], amine-
aldehyde resins [123], latices [92], and melamine-alkyd resins [27].

Examples of nonintumescing coatings are those based on chlorinated
rubber [22], or chlorinated isobutylene polymer [41]. Mixtures of finely
divided asbestos and urea-formaldehyde adhesives can be sprinkled with
more pulverized asbestos after application, but before hardening [51].
Alginate gels containing borax and boric acid or other fire-retardant salts
have also been described [121].

9.8 Conclusion

As an organic material, wood is inherently subject to thermal decomposition. However, by suitable chemical treatment of the wood, this
decomposition can be restricted to the locus of heat application. The low
thermal conductivity of wood and its carbonaceous decomposition product also limit penetration and spread of the decomposition process, with
the result that treated wooden structural members can maintain their
function even longer than metals (which soften) or concrete (which spalls)
in heat.

Commercial treatment of wood to impart fire-retardant properties
utilizes effective inexpensive salts which do cause some undesirable
changes in other properties of the wood. Although treatments have been
devised which provide excellent fire retardance without sacrifice of other
properties, economic considerations will limit their application to special
cases if they are used at all. The cheap fire-retardant treatment without
negative side effects is yet to be discovered.

REFERENCES

1. American Society for Testing and Materials. 1970. *ASTM Standards.* Part 14 (November), Philadelphia.
   a. "Test for combustible properties of treated wood by the fire-tube apparatus." Standard E69–50 (1969). 379–84.
   b. "Test for surface burning characteristics of building materials." Standard E84–68. 412–21.
   c. "Fire tests of roof coverings." Standard E108–58. 442–50.
   d. "Fire tests of building construction and materials." Standard E119–69. 451–69.
   e. "Fire tests of door assemblies." Standard E152–66. 483–87.
   f. "Test for combustible properties of treated wood by the crib test." Standard E160–50 (1969). 459–99.
   g. "Test for surface flammability of materials using a radiant heat energy source." Standard E162–67. 500–11.
   h. "Fire tests of window assemblies." Standard E163–65. 512–14.
   i. "Test for surface flammability of building materials using an 8 ft. tunnel furnace." Standard E286–69. 531–37.
2. American Wood-Preservers' Association. 1965. AWPA Standard P10–65. *Proc., Am. Wood-Preservers' Assoc.* 61:24.
3. Arent, A. 1920. British patent 138,641.
4. Arni, P.C. and Jones, E. 1964. "Preparation of N-alkenyl- and N-m-styryl-phosphoramidates and their application as flame retardants for wood." *J. Appl. Chem.* 14:221–28.
5. Arseneau, D.F. 1961. "The differential thermal analysis of wood." *Can. J. Chem.* 39:1915–19.
6. Bains, M.S. and Barker, R.H. 1971. "An ESR study of the thermal reactions of cellulose in the presence of inorganic flame retardants." Division of Cellulose, Wood and Fiber Chemistry, 161st Meeting of American Chemical Society, Los Angeles, Calif. Mar. 29–Apr. 2.
7. Bass, S.L. 1937. "Triaryl phosphates (combustibility reducing substances for impregnating wood)." U.S. patent 2,071,323.
8. Bayerische Stickstoff-Werke, A.G. 1936. "Fireproofing materials." French patent 805,285.
9. Beall, F.C. and Eickner, H.W. 1970. "Thermal degradation of wood components." U.S. Forest Serv., Forest Prod. Lab. Rept. No. 130.
10. Berger, A., During, G. and Schurch, A. 1957. "Flameproofing of cellulosic materials." Swiss patent 321,212.
11. Bescher, R.H., Henry, W.T. and Dreher, W.A. 1948. "Permanence of commercial fire retardants." *Proc., Am. Wood-Preservers' Assoc.* 44:369–77.
12. Boller, E.R. 1937. "Fireproofing pine wood." U.S. patent 2,097,509.
13. Brandts, T.B. 1963. "Flameproofing of organic materials." U.S. patent 3,092,537.
14. Brenden, J.J. 1967. "Effect of fire retardant and other inorganic salts on pyrolysis products of ponderosa pine at 250 and 350°C." U.S. Forest Serv., Forest Prod. Lab. Rept. No. 80.
15. Brenden, J.J. 1970. "Determining the utility of new optical test procedure for measuring smoke from various wood products." U.S. Forest Serv., Forest Prod. Lab. Rept. No. 137.
16. Brink, F.E. 1966. "Static and dynamic properties of fire resistant wooden structural elements." U.S. Govt. Res. Develop. Rept. 41(23):104–105.

17. Browne, F.L. 1958. "Theories of the combustion of wood and its control." U.S. Forest Serv., Forest Prod. Lab. Rept. No. 2136.

18. Browne, F.L. and Brenden, J.J. 1964. "Heat of combustion of the volatile pyrolysis products of fire retardant treated ponderosa pine." U.S. Forest Serv., Forest Prod. Lab. Rept. No. 19.

19. Browne, F.L. and Tang, W.K. 1963. "Effect of various chemicals on thermogravimetric analysis of ponderosa pine." U.S. Forest Serv., Forest Prod. Lab. Rept. No. 6.

20. Chem. Werke Albert. 1965. "Fire retardants." Belgian patent 665,047.

21. Clare, N.D. and Deyrup, A.J. 1958. "Flameproofing with alkali metal fluoride and boric acid or boric anhydride." U.S. patent 2,823,145.

22. Clayton, E.C. and Heffner, L.L. 1940. "Painting compositions." U.S. patent 2,194,690.

23. Coates, H. and Chalkley, B. 1966. "Flameproofing of cellulosic materials." U.S. patent 3,236,676.

24. Cobbs, W.W. 1941. "Rendering flammable materials fire resistant." U.S. patent 2,262,634.

25. Cupery, M.E. 1939. "Rendering materials less readily combustible." U.S. patent 2,142,115.

26. Cupery, M.E. 1940. "Rendering materials resistant to fire." U.S. patent 2,212,152.

27. Deutsche Solvay Werke. 1963. "Water-resistant fireproofing compositions." French patent 1,319,734.

28. Eickner, H.W. 1962. "Basic research on the pyrolysis and combustion of wood." *Forest Prod. J.* 12:(4) 194–99.

29. Eickner, H.W. 1966. "Fire retardant treated wood." *J. Mat.* 1:625–44.

30. Eickner, H.W. and Schaffer, E.L. 1967. "Fire retardant effects of individual chemicals on Douglas-fir plywood." *Fire Technol.* 3:90–104.

31. Eickner, H.W., Stinson, J.M. and Jordan, J.E. 1969. "Ammonium polyphosphate liquid fertilizer as fire retardant for wood." *Proc., Am. Wood-Preservers' Assoc.* 65:260–71.

32. Ellis, R.E. 1963. "Fire retardant compositions." U.S. patent 3,102,821.

33. Englehardt, R. and Heuck, C. 1941. "Wax-like composition for fireproofing wood." U.S. patent 2,248,749.

34. Erbel, A.J. and Kenaga, D.L. 1957. "Flameproofing of wood." U.S. patent 2,803,562.

35. Gardner, R.E. 1965. "The auxiliary properties of fire retardant wood." *Forest Prod. J.* 15(9):365–68.

36. Gaskill, J.R. and Veith, C.R. 1968. "Smoke opacity from certain woods and plastics." *Fire Technol.* 4:185–95.

37. Gay-Lussac, J.L. 1821. "Note on the properties of salts for making fabrics incombustible." *Ann. Chim.* 2(18):211–17.

38. Gerhard, C.C. 1970. "Effect of fire retardant treatment on bending strength of wood." U.S. Forest Serv., Forest Prod. Lab. Rept. No. 145.

39. Gill, T.G. and Phelp, R.B. 1970. "Preliminary wood preserving statistics for 1969." Div. of Forest Economics and Marketing Res. U.S. Forest Service, Washington, D.C.

40. Gillet, A. 1931. *Chimie et Industrie.* Special No. March. 302–309.

41. Gleason, A.H. and Rosen, R. 1942. "Chlorinating olefin resins." U.S. patent 2,291,574.

42. Goldstein, I.S. 1969. "Method of flameproofing cellulosic materials." U.S. patent 3,479,211.

43. Goldstein, I.S. and Dreher, W.A. 1959. "Method of imparting flame retardance to wood." U.S. patent 2,917,408.

44. Goldstein, I.S. and Dreher, W.A. 1961. "A non-hygroscopic fire retardant treatment for wood." *Forest Prod. J.* 11(5):235–37.

45. Goldstein, I.S. and Dreher, W.A. 1964. "Method of imparting fire retardance to wood and the resulting product." U.S. patent 3,159,503.

46. Goldstein, I.S. and Oberley, W.J. 1964. "Method of treating wood with an improved fire retardant composition." U.S. patent 3,160,515.

47. Goldstein, I.S. and Oberley, W.J. 1966. "Method of treating wood with an organic solvent-soluble fire retardant." U.S. patent 3,285,774.

48. Graham, R.D. 1964. "Strength of small Douglas-fir beams treated with fire retardants." *Proc., Am. Wood-Preservers' Assoc.* 60:172–76.

49. Greenman, N.L., Knudson, H.W. and Leslie, J.C. 1959. Proc. Elec. Insul. Conf., New York.

50. Gross, D. 1960. "Flame spread measurement by radiant panel flame spread method." *Forest Prod. J.* 10(1):33–36.

51. Hall, H.W. 1944. "Fireproofing of wood surfaces." U.S. patent 2,366,025.

52. Hardy, E. 1942. "Timber in mines." *Mining Mag.* 66:265–67.

53. Heinrich, H.J. and Kaesche-Krischer, B. 1962. "Spontaneous ignition of wood." *Brennstoff-Chem.* 43:142–48.

54. Hindersinn, R.R. and Wagner, G.M. 1967. "Fire retardancy." In *Encyclopedia of Polymer Science and Technology* vol. 7. Interscience, N.Y. 1–64.

55. Hunt, G.M. and Garratt, G.A. 1967. "Fire retarding treatments." In *Wood Preservation.* 3d ed. McGraw-Hill Book Co., N.Y. 377–400.

56. Hunt, G.M., Truax, T.R. and Harrison, C.R. 1930. "Fire resistance of wood treated with zinc chloride and diammonium phosphate." *Proc., Am. Wood-Preservers' Assoc.* 26:130–59.

57. Hunt, G.M., Truax, T.R. and Harrison, C.A. 1931. "Additional experiments in fireproofing wood." *Proc., Am. Wood-Preservers' Assoc.* 27:104–28.

58. Hunt, G.M., Truax, T.R. and Harrison, C.A. 1932. "Experiments in fire-proofing wood, 3rd progress report." *Proc., Am. Wood-Preservers' Assoc.* 28:71–93.

59. I.G. Farbenindustrie, A.G. 1929. "Fireproofing." German patent 532,578.

60. Ille, R. 1936. "Decreasing flammability of wood by chemical treatment." *Lesnicka Prace* 15:73–85.

61. Jones, G. and Soll, S. 1948. "Fire retardant compositions." U.S. patent 2,452,054.

62. Joos, W. and Luck, E. 1961. "Flameproofing combustible substances." German patent 1,105,705.

63. Juneja, S.C. 1972. "Stable and leach-resistant fire retardants for wood." *Forest Prod. J.* 22(6):17–23.

64. Kali Forschungs Anstalt. 1937. "Fireproofing wood." French patent 818,591.

65. Kenaga, D.L. 1966. "Unusual chemical improves wood properties." *Forest Prod. J.* 16(12):21–26.

66. Kenaga, D.L. and Erbel, A.J. 1955. "Flameproofing of cellulosic materials." U.S. patent 2,725,311.

67. Knudson, R.M. and Williamson, R.B. 1971. "Influence of temperature and time upon pyrolysis of untreated and fire retardant treated wood." *Wood Sci. Tech.* 5:176–89.

68. Kollmann, F. 1960. "Occurrence of exothermic reactions in wood." *Holz als Roh- und Werkstoff* 18:193–200.

69. Koritnig. 1939. "Fireproofing wood." Arbeitsschutz No. 2.130–31.

70. Kramas, L. 1930. "Fireproof coating for wood." Hungarian patent 102,736.

71. Kudo, K. and Yoshida, E. 1960. "Decomposition process of wood constituents in the course of carbonization." *Nippon Mokuzai Gakkaishi* 6:85–89.

72. Kuerschner, K. and Melcerova, A. 1965. "Chemical changes in sawdust during 1–28 day heating at 80–160°." *Holzforschung* 19:161–71.
73. Kurita, Y. and Inoue, Y. 1967. "Studies on flame-retardant chemicals." *Ann. Sankyo Res. Lab.* 19:104–109.
74. Lewin, M. 1963. "Flameproofing lignocellulosic articles." Israeli patent 15,481.
75. Little, R.W. 1951. "Fundamentals of flame retardancy." *Text. Res. J.* 21:901–908.
76. Lorenz, V. 1957. "Flame retarding agents especially for wood." German patent 1,013,863.
77. MacLean, J.D. 1951. "Rate of disintegration of wood under different heating conditions." *Proc. Am. Wood-Preservers' Assoc.* 47:155–68.
78. McCarthy, J.L. 1940. "Decreasing combustion of sawdust." *Ind. Eng. Chem.* 32:1494–96.
79. Marotta, R. 1954. "Fire retardant intumescent coating." U.S. patent 2,676,162.
80. Metz, L. 1936. "Fire protection of wood." *Z. Ver. Deut. Ing.* 80:660–62.
81. Metz, L. 1937. "Experiments in fireproofing wood." *Holz als Roh- und Werkstoff* 1:217–25.
82. Middleton, J.C., Dragonov, S.M. and Winters, F.T. Jr. 1965. "Evaluation of borates and other inorganic salts as fire retardants for wood products." *Forest Prod. J.* 15(12):463–67.
83. National Fire Protection Association. 1971. Press release. Boston, Mass. January 5.
84. National Forest Products Association. 1968. "National design specifications for stress-grade lumber and its fastenings." Washington, D.C.
85. Ohl, F. 1935. "Fire proofing of wood by means of paint." *Paint Manuf.* 5:192–96.
86. Paden, J.H. and MacLean, A.F. 1950. "Dicyandiamide acid sulfate." U.S. patent 2,512,037.
87. Parks, W.G., Erhardt, J.G. Jr. and Roberts, D.R. 1950. "Catalytic degradation and oxidation of cellulose." *Am. Dyestuff Reporter* 39:P294–300.
88. Percival, D.H. and Suddarth, S.K. 1971. "An investigation of the mechanical characteristics of truss plates on fire retardant treated wood." *Forest Prod. J.* 21(1):17–22.
89. Perizzolo, C.F. 1968. "Wood fire retardant." U.S. patent 3,371,058.
90. Pershall, E.E. 1953. "Wood preservative." U.S. patent 2,637,691.
91. Peschek, K. 1938. "Treatment of wood to render it fire resistant." *Osterr. Chemiker Ztg.* 41:179–87.
92. Peterson, N.R. and Cummings, I.J. 1959. "Latex-based intumescent coatings." U.S. patent 2,917,476.
93. Raff, R.A.V., Herrick, I.W. and Adams, M.F. 1966. "Flame retardant wood." *Forest Prod. J.* 16(2):43–47.
94. Ramiah, M.V. 1970. "Thermogravimetric and differential thermal analysis of cellulose, hemicellulose and lignin." *J. Appl. Polymer Sci.* 14:1323–37.
95. Ramiah, M.V. and Goring, D.A.I. 1967. "Some dilatometric measurements of the thermal decomposition of cellulose, hemicellulose and lignin." *Cell. Chem. Technol.* 1:277–85.
96. Ramiah, M.V. and Pickles, K.J. 1969. "Effect of diammonium phosphate and sodium tetraborate decahydrate on the thermal degradation and combustion of some western Canadian wood species." Canadian Forest Products Lab. Information Report VP–X–49. Vancouver, B.C.
97. Reeves, W.A. and Guthrie, J.D. 1960. "Flameproofing of wood." U.S. patent 2,927,050.
98. Richardson, N.A. 1937. "New aspect of action of timber fireproofing compounds." *J. Soc. Chem. Ind.* 56:202–205T.
99. Ruhrchemie A.G. 1937. "Fireproofing materials." French patent 811,887.

100. Sadovnikova, V.I., Usmanov, Kh.U. and Koz'mina, O.P. 1963. "Increasing the heat resistance of cotton fibers by means of partial cyanoethylation." *Zhur. Priklad. Khim.* 36(11):2522–26.

101. St. Clair, W.E. 1969. "Leach resistant fire retardant treated wood for outdoor exposure." *Proc., Am. Wood-Preservers' Assoc.* 65:250–59.

102. Sakornbut, S.S. 1959. "Impregnating preservative for cellulosic materials." U.S. patent 2,893,881.

103. Sandermann, W. and Augustin, H. 1963. "Chemical investigation on the thermal degradation of wood. II. Investigation by DTA." *Holz als Roh- und Werkstoff* 21:305–15.

104. Schaeffer, R.E., Gillespie, R.H. and Blomquist, R.F. 1966. "Chemical interaction of ammonium salt fire retardants and resorcinol resin adhesives." *Forest Prod. J.* 16(15):23–30.

105. Schaffer, E.L. 1966. "Review of Information Related to the Charring Rate of Wood." U.S. Forest Serv., Forest Prod. Lab. Rept. No. 0145.

106. Schuler, L. 1893. U.S. patent 502,867.

107. Schuyten, H.A., Weaver, J.W. and Reid, J.D. 1954. "Theoretical aspects of the flameproofing of cellulose." In *Advances in Chemistry Series* No. 9. American Chemical Society, Washington, D.C. 7–20.

108. Shimoto, G. 1949. "Fire resistant treatment." Japanese patent 177,477.

109. Southern Pine Association. 1964. "Architects Bulletin #7." American Institute of Architecture 19–A–1.

110. Tagachi, N., Oishi, U. and Fujimoto, M. 1960. "Fireproofing solutions for wood." Japanese patent 12,750 ('60).

111. Tamaru, S., Inai, Y. and Momma, S. 1934. "Physicochemical studies of wood." *J. Chem. Soc. Japan* 55:30–52.

112. Tang, W.K. 1967. "Effect of inorganic salts on pyrolysis of wood, alpha-cellulose and lignin determined by dynamic thermogravimetry." U.S. Forest Serv., Forest Prod. Lab. Rept. No. 71.

113. Tang, W.K. and Eickner, H.W. 1968. "Effect of inorganic salts on pyrolysis of wood, cellulose and lignin determined by differential thermal analysis." U.S. Forest Serv., Forest Prod. Lab. Rept. No. 82.

114. Tang, W.K. and Neill, W.K. 1964. "Effect of flame retardants on pyrolysis and combustion of alpha-cellulose." *J. Polymer Sci.* Part C, No. 6. 65–81.

115. Tassel, E. and Vallette, P. 1954. "Flameproofing of fibrous materials with antimony compounds." French patent 1,063,983.

116. Temin, S.C. 1965. "Flame retardant organic phosphorus esters and polyesters." U.S. patent 3,179,522.

117. Thompson, N.C. and Cousins, E.W. 1959. "The Factory Mutual construction materials calorimeter." *Quart. Natl. Fire Protect. Assoc.* Jan. 19.

118. Truax, T.R., Harrison, C.A. and Baechler, R.H. 1933. "Experiments in fireproofing wood, 4th progress report." *Proc., Am. Wood-Preservers' Assoc.* 29:107–24.

119. Truax, T.R., Harrison, C.A. and Baechler, R.H. 1935. "Experiments in fireproofing wood, 5th progress report." *Proc., Am. Wood-Preservers' Assoc.* 31:231–45.

120. Tyul'panov, R.S. 1957. "Study of thermal decomposition of wood." *Gidroliz. i Lesokhim. Prom.* 10(6):13–14.

121. Van Kleeck, A. 1945. "Fire retardant coating." U.S. patent 2,387,865.

122. Wilson, I.V. and Marotta, R. 1952. "Fire retardant compositions." U.S. patent 2,600,455.

123. Wilson, I.V. and Marotta, R. 1955. "Fire retardant coatings." U.S. patent 2,702,283.

10. Special Treatments

IRVING S. GOLDSTEIN
School of Forest Resources
North Carolina State University, Raleigh, North Carolina

WESLEY E. LOOS
Atom Manufacturing Co., Inc., Altavista, Virginia

10.1 Introduction

The biological deterioration of wood has received considerable attention and its prevention has assumed great commercial importance. Wood is also vulnerable to other forms of deterioration, such as thermal and chemical degradation. Furthermore, the dimensional stability, plasticity, and other physical and mechanical properties are important in many applications.

The purpose of this chapter is to describe treatments which improve the chemical resistance, dimensional stability, plasticity, and physical and mechanical properties of wood. Many of these treatments are practical commercially, although their total volume is relatively small because of the high cost. Thermal degradation has been discussed extensively in Chapter 9 and will not be repeated here.

Modification of the chemical nature of the wood by reaction with chemical reagents and modification of the structure by impregnation with polymers (resins) and monomers followed by *in-situ* polymerization often cause changes in several properties at once. For this reason, the discussions which follow are arranged by property being considered rather than by process.

10.2 Protection from Chemical Attack

Some species of wood show a fairly high degree of resistance to degradation by various kinds of chemicals. Consequently, wood has found wide application in the chemical processing industries for such types of equipment as vats, tanks, filter press components, ducts, etc. Treatment of wood for protection against chemical attack has broadened the range of environments in which wood can serve, lengthened the service life where untreated wood was previously used, and allowed the use of wood which is not naturally resistant. The chemical resistance of wood has been reviewed by Thompson [100].

10.2.1 Chemical deterioration of wood

The structural components of the wood cell wall consist of cellulose in a matrix of hemicelluloses and lignin. Cellulose and the hemicelluloses are carbohydrate polymers which are easily hydrolyzed to shorter chain polymers and sugars by dilute mineral acids. The macroscopic effect of this hydrolysis of these carbohydrate polymers at the molecular level is embrittlement of the wood with severe loss of tensile and impact strength or toughness. Tensile strength is markedly reduced by only small reductions in the degree of polymerization (a measure of polymer chain length) of the cellulose [37].

Alkalis attack the hemicelluloses and lignin, removing them by solubilization, and thereby reduce the stiffness, bending strength, and crushing resistance of the wood. Organic solvents weaken wood in proportion to their ability to swell the wood structure, and oxidizing agents attack all cell-wall components.

Wangaard [104] concluded that resistance of wood to chemical degradation is a function of the degree of molecular compactness in the cell wall. The accessibility of the reagents to the cell-wall components is probably the controlling factor. It will be shown in the next section that all treatments for enhancing the chemical resistance of wood depend on preventing access of the reagents to the wood fibers by means of barriers.

10.2.2 Treatments for chemical resistance

Filling the pores of wood with resistant materials such as paraffin, beeswax, tar, ozokerite, resin, or asphalt for protection against acids and alkalis was patented by Roberts [140]. Impregnation of wood with coke-oven coal tar was reported by Guy [33] to be more effective than paraffin in providing resistance to strong hydrochloric and sulfuric acids. This treatment is commercially available under the trade name "Asidbar" [49]. Its limitations are the 130°F softening point and the organic solvent solubility of the impregnant.

Molten sulfur may also be used as an impregnating agent. Pressure treatment at 150°C yields retentions of 40–76 percent of the weight of the wood, and some of the inertness to chemical attack of the sulfur is imparted to the wood [47]. Comparative tests of wood impregnated with paraffin, pitch, sulfur, and Bakelite showed an increasing resistance to the corrosive action of hydrochloric acid and aluminum chloride in the order given [45].

The use of thermosetting phenol-formaldehyde resins (Bakelite) polymerized within the wood expanded the applications of chemically resistant wood to higher temperatures, and allowed its use in the presence of organic solvents. Resistance to strong acids was also improved [70,46]. The diversity of specific applications of a proprietary phenol-formaldehyde resin treated wood in chemical plants and the chemical resistance of this product have been described [47].

Although offering good resistance to sulfuric acid as strong as 90 percent, phenol-formaldehyde resin impregnated wood does not resist attack by caustic alkali solutions since the resin itself is not resistant. Formation within the wood of an acid- and alkali-resistant resin by polymerization of furfuryl alcohol provides broad-spectrum chemical resistance to everything but oxidizing agents [26,27]. After exposure to boiling 10 percent sulfuric acid for 8 days, pine containing 35 percent furfuryl alcohol resin had a wet crushing strength of 700 psi, compared to 500 psi for untreated unexposed wood and 180 psi for untreated wood exposed to the same conditions. After exposure to boiling 5 percent sodium hydroxide for 8 days, the treated wood had a crushing strength of 450 psi compared to 100 psi for untreated wood.

The chemical resistance of wood impregnated with synthetic resins is enhanced when the resin is formed by polymerization of low-molecular-weight polymers or monomers within the cell wall rather than by polymerization of more viscous prepolymers within the lumen. The resin treatments adversely affect the impact strength, decreasing it to about half that of untreated wood.

The chemical resistance of maple-polymethylmethacrylate wood–plastic composite (WPC) was assessed by Galliger [25]. Samples of untreated and treated maple were soaked in water, toluene, ethanol, aqueous solutions of NaCl (3 percent), HCl (2 and 10 percent), and NaOH (2 and 10 percent). The WPC offered little or no protection against water, toluene, ethanol, or aqueous NaCl. A moderate amount of protection against acids and bases was found.

10.3 Dimensional Stabilization

One of the most troublesome properties of wood is its relatively large change in dimensions with changing relative humidity and, therefore, moisture content. This shrinking and swelling is generally nonuniform, so in addition to loosely fitting or stuck moving parts such as doors, drawers, and windows, and cracks or bulges in flooring and paneling, there is often considerable distortion caused by warping and cupping.

This problem has attracted considerable research effort, which has provided a number of technically, but not economically, feasible processes for reducing dimensional changes significantly. The notable exception is the control of dimensional change by cross-lamination of anisotropic sheets as in plywood. This dimensional stabilization by mechanical restraint will not be discussed here, but rather attention will be directed at chemical and physical processes which reduce shrinking and swelling. Many reviews have been devoted to this subject [9,22,58,80,90,97].

10.3.1 Shrinking and swelling of wood

The basic cause of shrinking and swelling of wood is the hygroscopic nature of cellulose, the chief component of wood. Cellulose is a long-chain polymer of glucose with each unit in the chain retaining three free hydroxyl groups which exhibit strong attractive forces for water. The cellulose chains are arranged in bundles called microfibrils, which are embedded in a matrix of hemicelluloses and then permeated with lignin to form the bulk of the cell wall.

Portions of these cellulose bundles are arranged in a dense, highly ordered manner, with the free hydroxyl groups on each chain interacting with their counterparts on neighboring chains to form strong hydrogen bonds. Such ordered or crystalline areas do not adsorb water. Interspersing of the bulky, multiple-side-chained polymeric hemicelluloses between cellulose chains prevents this hydrogen bonding, producing disordered or amorphous regions in the cellulose bundles. All of the water that enters the cellulose structure enters this disordered region, thus causing swelling of the wood.

From the ovendry condition to a relative humidity of about 20 percent, the water adsorbed by the wood is held as a monomolecular layer. At higher humidities, the increasing quantity of water adsorbed is held polymolecularly in solid solution. This water has also been referred to as capillary-condensed water but, since it is found in transient capillaries that exist only when water is adsorbed by the wood, the concept of polymolecular adsorption in solid solution is more precise. The enlargement of these transient capillaries causes the cell wall to swell.

True capillary condensation in preexisting capillaries mainly occurs at relative humidities above 99 percent. A maximum swelling of the cell walls by the adsorbed water in the transient capillaries is defined by the limited dispersion of disordered regions of the cellulose which are tied together by the nonswelling ordered regions because of the common cellulose chains which pass through them. This maximum swelling and its attendant moisture content are termed the fiber-saturation point. Higher moisture contents represent water condensed in the gross capillaries and lumina of the wood.

Swelling of wood is caused by the increased volume associated with adsorbed water which spreads the disordered cellulose structure apart. Conversely, shrinkage of wood is caused by the loss of this volume as water is removed and the disordered cellulose structure contracts. It should be remembered that in its original natural state, wood exists in the swollen condition, so its return to this condition when exposed to water is not surprising. The shrinking and swelling may not be completely reversible, because formation of new water-resistant hydrogen bonds upon drying limits future swelling. Unfortunately, this effect is not large enough to be of practical value.

The macroscopic effect of these volume changes at the molecular level is the resultant of the modification of the basic swelling as a function of the various fiber compositions, fiber orientations, densities, and anatomical differences found within and between species. The external shrinkage of wood from the fiber-saturation point to the ovendry condition ranges from 4–14 percent tangentially, 2–8 percent radially, and 0.1–0.2 percent longitudinally. On a volumetric basis, the cumulative value ranges from 7–21 percent. The fiber-saturation point for most species falls within the range of 25–30 percent moisture content, but values as low as 18 percent and as high as 33 percent have been observed.

Detailed discussions of the shrinking and swelling of wood and wood–water relationship have been provided by Browning [8] and Stamm [88].

10.3.2 Measurement of stabilization

Since wood shrinks and swells to a greater extent in the tangential direction, about twice as much as in the radial direction, the measurement of dimensional changes is easier and more accurate when specimens are used which are cut to provide a large tangential dimension.

Swelling may be measured from the ovendry condition to the dimension attained after equilibration at any desired relative humidity up to the completely swollen state resulting from exposure to liquid water. It is expressed in percent of the ovendry dimension. Conversely, shrinking may be measured from the swollen or green condition to the ovendry, and is expressed in percent of the swollen dimension.

These absolute swelling or shrinking values may be converted to relative values, indicating the degree of reduction of swelling or shrinking imparted by a treatment, by comparison with the dimensional changes exhibited by untreated control specimens. The relative value has been termed dimensional stabilization efficiency, percent reduction in swelling, antishrink efficiency or antiswelling efficiency (ASE), and may be calculated as follows:

$$\text{ASE (\%)} = \frac{S_C - S_T}{S_C} \times 100$$

where

S_T = shrinkage or swelling of treated wood, %
S_C = shrinkage or swelling of control or untreated wood, %

The following mathematical identity may be used to simplify calculations:

$$\text{ASE (\%)} = 1 - \frac{S_T}{S_C} \times 100$$

Palka [63] points out in his review of dimensional stabilization of wood that there is no consistency in sample sizes used by various investigators. He indicates that sample size does have an effect: the larger the sample, the greater the dimensional stability. A sample of relatively large dimensions in the radial and tangential direction (1–2 inches) compared to longitudinal direction ($\frac{1}{8}$–$\frac{1}{4}$ inch) is a convenient size to obtain rapid results. Care must be taken that the polymer in this cross section is uniform. This is especially important in studying wood–plastic composites which are impregnated with low-molecular-weight, highly volatile monomers. For practical applications, samples as close in size as possible to the stabilized end-product should be used.

Although values of ASE as high as 90 percent have been reported for some treatments, complete stabilization of the wood (100 percent ASE) has not been attained. The water molecule is smaller than any molecule used up until now in wood-stabilization treatments. Consequently, complete stabilization of the wood has not been possible, since water can always reach regions of the wood structure which were inaccessible to the larger treating reagents and these areas remain untreated.

10.3.3 Methods of stabilization

Stamm [90] has classified all methods for attaining improved dimensional stability of wood into five types. The first of these involves mechanical restraint by lamination, as in plywood, and will not be considered further. The remaining four classes, enumerated below, are discussed in detail in this section:

1. Water-resistant surface and internal coatings which act as barriers to retard moisture movement.

2. Bulking agents which preswell the wood and prevent it from shrinking.

3. Reduction of the hygroscopicity of the cellulose.

4. Cross-linking agents which provide internal mechanical restraint at the molecular level.

Some treatments improve dimensional stability by more than one of these mechanisms.

10.3.3.1 Moisture barriers

Inasmuch as the dimensional changes in wood are caused by changes in its moisture content, it would seem at first glance that it is only necessary to seal the wood against moisture adsorption or loss to stabilize it completely. Many coatings are impervious to liquid water, but only a continuous metal-foil coating will prevent the passage of water vapor.

In practice, then, coatings can reduce the rate of moisture transmission and thus significantly retard the rate at which wood adsorbs or desorbs water and swells or shrinks. The equilibrium moisture content is unaffected, however, and the maximum shrinking or swelling will be unchanged on long exposure to the extreme conditions. This occurs quite often with wood–plastic composites. Surface applications of water repellents are even less effective, serving only to shed liquid water temporarily.

Nevertheless, almost every hydrophobic material which is capable of being impregnated into wood or forming a coating on it has been suggested, especially in the patent literature, as a treatment for making wood waterproof, impermeable, or water repellent. Among these have been asphalt and paraffin [147], rubber latex [16], higher esters of carbohydrates such as cellulose or starch laurates [115], sulfur [146], insoluble soaps [114], petroleum resins [117], alkyl, aryl, aralkyl, or alkaryl silicon halides [65], organosilicon esters [110], polymeric mixed titanium esters [131], polyorganosiloxanols [101], sulfur tetrafluoride [142], and cellulose acetate [56].

10.3.3.2 Bulking

The principle which underlies dimensional stabilization of wood by bulking is in the introduction of nonvolatile materials into the swollen disordered regions of the cell wall, where they remain. The volume of the bulking agent occupies space and prevents the cell wall from shrinking. In effect, the wood has been preswollen and is used in this condition.

Since the bulking agents are usually larger molecules than the swelling agent, which is usually water, they can only penetrate part of the cell-wall structure and the extent of penetration decreases with increasing molecular size. Consequently, the degree of stabilization imparted by a bulking agent decreases with increasing size of the impregnated molecule.

Some swelling agents such as furfuryl alcohol swell wood more than water does, and it is possible to obtain treated wood which has been permanently swollen to a larger dimension than water itself is capable of doing. Despite this phenomenon, the treated wood will swell further upon exposure to high humidity or saturation with water [26]. It appears as though some previously ordered regions of the wood cellulose were made accessible to water by the furfuryl alcohol. This behavior is another demonstration that complete stabilization of wood (100 percent ASE) is not attainable.

Bulking agents will be discussed in greater detail under the categories of soluble materials, insoluble materials, and chemical modification.

10.3.3.2.1 Soluble bulking agents

The simplest means of stabilizing wood by bulking is to impregnate it with aqueous solutions of nonvolatile materials and then dry the wood. The solute is left behind in the cell wall, stabilizing the wood in proportion to its concentration which is dependent on its solubility.

Inorganic salts can stabilize wood not only by virtue of the bulking mechanism but also by maintaining the wood in a completely swollen wet condition above humidities as low as 30 percent, because of the hygroscopic nature of these salts. The effect of inorganic salts upon the swelling and the shrinkage of wood has been reviewed by Stamm [85]. Potassium thiocyanate, which is one of the most soluble salts, reduces the shrinkage by only about 50 percent.

Other shortcomings of inorganic salts as bulking agents, besides insufficient solubility, are their corrosivity and the hygroscopicity which reduces the strength of the wood and makes gluing and finishing difficult. The latter disadvantages are not encountered with a mixture of dicyandiamide and phosphoric acid, which reduces swelling by up to 40 percent [28].

Water-soluble organic compounds are also effective bulking agents. The simplest of these are glycerol [121] and sugar [36]. Fir and pine showed 40 percent reduction in swelling and birch 50 percent after absorption of 15 percent glucose or 55 percent sucrose. The absorption of water was 20 percent less for glucose-treated than sucrose-treated wood [31]. Terpin hydrate also imparts partial dimensional stability to wood [1].

The most effective water-soluble bulking agents are the polyethylene glycols [88]. At low molecular weights they are miscible with water in all proportions and can almost completely replace the water in swollen wood, giving reductions in shrinkage of almost 100 percent. Polyethylene glycol with a molecular weight of 1000 has been studied most because it does not become as damp at high humidities. It can be applied to green wood by diffusion, and has found applications for gunstocks, carvings, and turnings [62].

The hygroscopic nature of the water-soluble bulking agents causes finishing problems and reduction in strength. Consequently, the use of solvent-soluble materials which are water-insoluble was investigated. It was found that cellosolve (ethylene glycol monoethyl ether) could be used as an intermediary because it is soluble in water in all proportions and also is a solvent for waxes, oils, and resins. Replacement of the water in swollen wood by cellosolve followed by replacement of the cellosolve with molten waxes or oils affords reductions in swelling of up to 80 percent [92]. The process is too slow for wide application, however, and much more wax is introduced into the wood than is required for the stabilizing action.

10.3.3.2.2 Insoluble polymeric materials

Direct impregnation of wood with polymers has been practiced for 50 years. Phenol-formaldehyde resins dissolved in low-boiling solvents were used by Plauson and Vielle [137] and urea-formaldehyde resins in liquid form or as aqueous solutions for wood impregnation were patented by Pollak in 1921 [138].

It was recognized by Stamm and Seborg [94] that the formation of the synthetic resins within the fine capillary structures of the wood was desirable for high ASE values, and that prepolymerization of the resins before treatment decreases ASE. The appearance and subsequent disappearance by condensation of the monomeric methylolphenols in a phenol-formaldehyde resin solution was later correlated with the ability of the solution to impart dimensional stability to impregnated wood [29]. The decrease in dimension-stabilizing power as the methylolphenols disappeared was more marked in a high-humidity atmosphere than in liquid water. However, as long as the resin was water-soluble, good stabilization could be obtained.

Although the use of light-colored, low-molecular-weight urea-formaldehyde condensates or dimethylolurea as impregnants for wood stabilization received much attention in the 1940s [5], they were displaced by dark-colored phenolics for the manufacture of "Impreg" (resin-impregnated wood), and "Compreg" (compressed resin-impregnated wood) because of the much greater dimensional stability of the phenolic-resin-treated wood [60].

Other condensation polymers used to stabilize wood have been furfuryl alcohol resins [26] and tris (1-aziridinyl) phosphine oxide polymers [40].

Recent emphasis on wood-polymer combinations has been on the use of addition polymers such as those formed by either thermocatalytic or radiation polymerization, or copolymerization of vinyl monomers such as methyl methacrylate-styrene, acrylonitrile, vinyl chloride, etc. In these systems, a high proportion of the polymer is deposited in the lumen and is extractable by solvents.

The dimensional stability, as measured by ASE, for wood impregnated with styrene-acrylonitrile gives values which increase with an increase in polymer loading [52,20]. The maximum values ranged from 60–70 percent for fully loaded specimens. This maximum is dependent on the species of wood used and also the moisture content at which the wood is converted [54]. The lower the initial MC, the greater the bulking of the WPC and the higher the ASE value obtained. Much lower values are obtained for "nonswelling" monomers such as methyl methacrylate (MMA) and styrene. The ASE values measured for WPC made with Poly(methyl methacrylate) (PMMA) range from 20–40 percent, depending on polymer loading and species of wood [52,20]. Loos [52] observed that when polymer loading was plotted against ASE, the ASE values went through a maximum at about 40–50 percent of theoretical maximum polymer loading. The decrease in ASE values at high polymer loadings was attributed to the contraction of the polymer matrix upon polymerization. At high polymer loadings, this matrix is highly interconnected; therefore, when the impregnant shrinks during polymerization, it shrinks the whole matrix. The relief of this stress during soaking in water causes the wood in the WPC to swell first to its original dimensions and then to continue to swell as it normally would, giving a lower ASE value than expected.

Improved dimensional stability may be obtained if the polymer is deposited within the cell wall. This may also be accomplished by swelling the wood first with an organic solvent such as acetone, dioxane, or ethanol and then exchanging with the desired monomer. By this technique, ASE values as high as those attained with phenolic resins (70 percent) have been observed with wood treated with styrene and styrene-acrylonitrile mixtures that were polymerized by both radiation and thermo-catalytic methods [41,83,39].

10.3.3.2.3 Chemical modification

Another method of bulking which is permanent, nonleachable and non-hygroscopic, involves reaction of the cellulosic hydroxyl groups to form substituted cellulose derivatives. The substituent groups stabilize the wood by occupying space within the cell wall and are permanently attached to the wood structure. They also reduce the hygroscopicity of the cellulose in the wood structure.

One of the simplest and most studied chemical treatments is the esterification of wood with acetic anhydride to form acetylated wood. This treatment was first applied to whole wood by Suida [145] in the form of sheets which were superficially acetylated, and made the wood more resistant to light, water, and checking. The high degree of dimensional stability imparted by acetylation (70 percent ASE) was recognized by Stamm and Tarkow [95,143], who devised a vapor-phase acetylation treatment method using pyridine as a catalyst; this method was effective on veneer up to $\frac{1}{8}$ inch in thickness.

Other acetylation studies were performed by Clermont and Bender [13], who used urea-ammonium sulfate as a catalyst and dimethylformamide as a swelling agent; Risi and Arseneau [67], who also used dimethylformamide as well as an acetic anhydride (boron trifluoride complex); Arni et al. [2], who used trifluoroacetic acid as a catalyst; and Baird [4], who studied vapor-phase acetylation with acetic anhydride and dimethylformamide.

The acetylation of wood in lumber thickness has been achieved by the use of uncatalyzed acetic anhydride, thereby eliminating problems of degradation and catalyst recovery [30]. In this process, the quantity of acetic anhydride injected into the wood was controlled by dilution with nonswelling solvents such as aromatic or chlorinated hydrocarbons. By metering the amount of acetic anhydride into the wood, the recovery problems after treatment were simplified.

By using the above process, it was possible to achieve a 70–80 percent reduction in swelling when the wood was exposed to moisture. Furthermore, tests indicated that the acetylated wood exhibited excellent decay and termite resistance at a weight gain of about 18 percent. The impact strength was not decreased, and the wet compressive strength was doubled.

Other methods of chemically modifying wood to impart dimensional stability through bulking have been studied, but offer no advantage over acetylation. Some of these carry the risk of degradation of the wood by acids or alkalis used as catalysts or liberated in the reaction. The cost of most of the alternative reagents is also much greater than that of acetic anhydride.

Among these other reagents are halogenated ethers such as chloromethyl or dichloromethyl ether [125]; phthalaldehydic acid and its chloroderivatives [129]; phthalic anhydride [68]; beta-propiolactone, which forms grafted polyester side chains on the cellulose; acrylonitrile, which forms cyanoethyl ethers [29]; ethylene oxide [55]; and butyl isocyanate [4].

10.3.3.3 Hygroscopic group inactivation

Since the hygroscopic nature of cellulose is the reason for its dimensional instability, any treatment which will reduce the hygroscopicity will increase dimensional stability. For example, the chemical modification of wood by acetylation converts hygroscopic hydroxyl groups into nonhygroscopic acetyl groups. This process lowers the equilibrium moisture content of the wood and thus improves stability. The bulking action of the voluminous acetyl groups exerts an even greater stabilizing effect, however, which is why acetylation was also discussed as a bulking treatment. Phenolic resins polymerized within the wood fibers also reduce hygroscopicity as well as bulk the wood.

Thermal treatments of wood have been shown to reduce hygroscopicity and improve dimensional stability, presumably by chemical reactions such as cross linking, oxidation, or dehydration which involve the hydroxyl groups. Conversion of hemicelluloses to less hygroscopic polymers may also occur. Falck [21] observed that heating dry wood in air at or over a critical temperature (125°C for beech) reduced the tendency of the wood to swell and shrink by up to 50 percent. Drying at 105°C for 48 hours decreased the water absorption of spruce and pine [75].

Stamm and co-workers have extensively studied the stabilization of wood by heating in various gases or under molten salts or metals. This results in a reduction in hygroscopicity and ASE values may exceed 50 percent, but such levels of treatment are accompanied by significant losses in strength. The treated wood has been called "Staybwood." Compression of the wood after heating gives a heat-stabilized compressed wood termed "Staypak" [93,91,79,76].

10.3.3.4 Cross linking

The final method of stabilization to be discussed is based on mechanical restraint at the molecular level by the formation of cross links between cellulose chains or microfibrils which prevent the spreading and swelling of the cellulose structure by water. The most effective cross-linking agent is formaldehyde, which is a small enough molecule to enter the ultrafine structure of the cell wall. As little as 7 percent bound formaldehyde can provide ASE values of 90 percent. However, the mineral acid catalyst and heat required for the formation of the acetal bridges cause severe embrittlement of the wood [98,87].

Milder catalysts which do not degrade the wood as severely do not provide good dimensional stability. The search for other cross-linking reagents has not been particularly successful. Sixteen aldehydes or closely related compounds, some used successfully in treating cellulosic fabrics for crease resistance, were investigated as possible cross-linking reagents for the cellulose in the whole wood [106]. The dialdehydes—glyoxal, glutaraldehyde, and alpha-hydroxyadipaldehyde—gave substantial reaction with pine when catalyzed with strong acids, but the resulting reductions in swelling were less than 50 percent. The high weight gains required for even moderate stabilization efficiencies indicated bulking rather than cross linking as the stabilization mechanism.

10.3.4 Evaluation of stabilization methods

Three factors require consideration in the comparative evaluation of stabilization methods. These are degree of stabilization attainable, effect on other wood properties, and relative cost.

The necessary condition, of course, is high stabilization efficiency. ASE values of over 70 percent can be attained by any of the three types of bulking as well as by cross linking. When other wood properties are considered, cross linking is immediately eliminated because of the serious embrittlement of the wood as well as loss of abrasion resistance. Considerable embrittlement of the wood also takes place by treatment with polymers which embed the disordered regions of the cellulose chains in a rigid matrix, restricting the motion of the chains and causing failure at lower levels of absorbed energy. In chemical modification, the cellulose chains are still free to absorb energy by vibration without chain failure occurring at low impact stresses. The soluble bulking agents may be hygroscopic at high humidities and can be leached out with water.

For bulking agents, as much as 25–30 percent of the weight of the wood must be added in the form of impregnants or substituents. The price of bulking agents ranges from 10 cents to $1 per pound. Since the cost of wood is only 3–6 cents per pound, it is readily apparent that the cost of such treatments can significantly exceed the value of the wood. The resultant high cost, as well as the altered properties associated with resin treatments and soluble bulking agents, have precluded the wide use of stabilizing treatments.

Acetylated wood, despite its lack of undesirable properties, has not even found the limited use accorded resin treatments and polyethylene glycol because the corrosive reagent requires corrosion-resistant treating facilities which are not available at commercial treating plants.

10.4 Weathering Resistance

When untreated wood is exposed to normal weathering conditions, the wood undergoes changes in color and texture and suffers erosion. Since weathering is a surface phenomenon, these changes can be minimized by suitable surface treatments.

10.4.1 Weathering of wood

The first change in wood caused by weathering is its color. Dark woods become lighter and light woods become darker. Upon further breakdown and leaching of the colorants, wood passes through shades of brown to a final silver-grey color. (In urban environments, this final color may be almost black from soot particles.) Oxidation of the wood surface catalyzed by ultraviolet (UV) light causes decomposition of the lignin-cellulose matrix, which is followed by leaching of the degradation products by rain.

Intermittent wetting and drying of the wood surface, with its attendant shrinking and swelling, cause grain raising followed by checking and cracking, as well as cupping, warping, and nail-pulling. Detailed descriptions of how wood weathers have been published [7,23].

Microscopic examinations of unfinished and clear-coated wood exposed to UV radiation and weathering are very informative [61,10]. These photomicrographs show severe microchecking of the cell walls and removal of exposed cell-wall material, especially in the pit areas.

10.4.2 Treatments

Since the weathering of wood is caused by the interaction of UV light and water with the wood surface, it is apparent that weathering can be prevented by protecting it from these agents. The time-honored method, of course, is by the use of pigmented coatings in the form of paint. Penetrating finishes containing some pigments in addition to a preservative such as pentachlorophenol and a water repellent have also proven effective. Clear finishes containing UV-absorbing components have not been fully developed as yet, but show future promise.

Work by Black [6] indicates that treatment of wood with heavy metal salts, such as those used in CCA treatments, in combination with a clear UV-transparent coating offer excellent weather resistance. Wood panels treated in this manner have now been exposed for as long as five years with no deterioration.

The physical changes associated with weathering are to a great extent caused by the dimensional instability of the wood to moisture-content changes. Wood which has been stabilized by such treatments as acetylation or impregnation with phenolic resins shows very little deterioration on prolonged weathering. The service life of coatings on stabilized wood is also prolonged. Wood pretreated with polyethylene glycol and coated with several different clear finishes showed improved exterior performance [10]. However, this improvement was not sufficient for satisfactory performance of clear coatings.

Unpublished studies were conducted by Loos at West Virginia University on the outdoor exposure of WPC in Florida. The material tested was southern pine and sugar maple treated with PMMA, Poly(styrene + acrylonitrile) [P(ST-AN)], and Poly(ethyl acrylate + acrylonitrile) [P(EA-AN)]. None of the combinations gave much weather resistance. The hard polymer [PMMA and P(ST-AN)] WPC lost its gloss rapidly and started checking soon after exposure was started. The rubbery polymer P(EA-AN) WPC had a low gloss to begin with, so the gloss level did not decrease as rapidly as that of the hard polymers. It also showed better checking resistance than the hard polymers. This indicates that a rubbery polymer may be feasible for a weather-resistant WPC if the UV light degradation problem can be solved.

10.5 Plasticization of Wood

While the plasticization of wood is essentially a modification of the mechanical properties of the wood, it will be discussed separately from the major topic of mechanical properties since it is a temporary treatment. The objective may be merely to allow bending or shaping the wood with less energy and fewer failures, or to allow compression of the wood into a densified form. In either case, the increase in plasticity is desired only during the processing step.

Traditionally, the bending or twisting of wood has been accomplished by subjecting the wood to steam before applying force. Both the heat and moisture have a plasticizing effect and reduce the pressure at which plastic yield occurs [77]. The softening induced by saturated steam in a pressure range from 25 to 100 psi is roughly proportional to the steam pressure. Recovery after release of steam pressure is very rapid, with 30–50 percent of the loss in hardness regained during the first 10 minutes [71].

Frost recommended treating wood for bending by impregnating it with a boiling sodium silicofluoride solution [118], or heating it in tar oils, phenols, or cresols [119]. Other materials claimed to render wood supple and flexible are neatsfoot oil, paraffin oil and glycerol butyrate [134], and hot alkali followed by glycerol [124]. Tanning agents such as bark extracts, aldehydes, and quinones can also make wood pliable [24].

The flexibility and plasticity of wood are increased by heating the wood with solutions of urea or thiourea and bending while hot. These processes have been described by several workers [132,96,122], although others claim they provide no advantage over traditional steam bending of white ash despite decreasing bending loads [35]. Other agents applied with heat which improve the plastic properties of wood are sulfur, carbon disulfide, thiophenol, diphenyl sulfide [34], and sodium thiosulfate [139]. In comparison with urea, only about two-thirds as much sodium thiosulfate is required for plasticizing wood to the same degree.

Ammonia has been found to exert a strong plasticizing effect on wood. Stamm [86] reported that liquid ammonia swells wood faster and to a greater extent than does water. He observed that the cell walls were plasticized to such a degree that severe collapse occurred on subsequent drying.

Schuerch [72] also studied the treatment of wood with liquid ammonia and discovered that the wood was so highly plasticized that it could be bent, twisted, and literally tied into knots without breaking. The hydrogen bonding of the polysaccharides in the cell walls is disrupted and the lignin in the matrix is made slightly soluble by the treatment, allowing the macromolecules to slip and flow under stress. New hydrogen bonds form and the lignin hardens when the ammonia evaporates, locking the sample in the new configuration. Aqueous and gaseous ammonia at room temperature were not nearly as effective as liquid ammonia.

In further studies, Schuerch and co-workers [74] found little chemical change in the treated wood. Physical changes included relaxation of the crystal lattice and hydrogen bonding. The addition of nonhydroxylic additives to the liquid ammonia controlled swelling and warping during treatment, as well as shrinking and checking during drying.

Pentoney [64] reported that after drying, the ammonia-treated wood is more dense, flexible, and hygroscopic than dry untreated wood. Tensile strength and dielectric constant were also increased.

Davidson [15] later showed it was possible to plasticize wood with gaseous anhydrous ammonia at room temperature at a pressure of 145 psi. Woods which exhibit the least amount of damage during bending after steam conditioning also appear to be the best species for ammonia treatment and permit the use of lower-grade material. Maple, with a green condition modulus of elasticity (MOE) of about 15×10^5, exhibited a reduction in MOE to 7×10^5 at 0 percent moisture and 2×10^5 at 10–20 percent moisture after treatment.

Sadoh [69] has reported that tetramethylenepentamine remains in the wood structure and acts as a permanent plasticizer after impregnation with water, butyl amine, and glycerol.

10.6 Aesthetic Properties of Wood

The aesthetic properties of wood which have been improved by treatments include color, gloss or luster, and whiteness. Complete discussions of bleaching and staining are beyond the scope of this work.

Special problems exist in dyeing wood with mixtures of dyes because of different diffusion rates in the wood. Despite this reservation, wood has been colored with hundreds of materials ranging from inorganic salts through natural dyes to synthetic dyestuffs. Wood coloring draws on the arts of both wood impregnation and textile and plastic dyeing. Immersion, spray, and pressure-dyeing processes for wood have been described by Courser [14], and Jones [38] has also summarized the coloring of wood. Wood–plastic composites are readily dyed by dissolving dyes in the monomer prior to impregnation [43].

The bleaching of wood has been accomplished by use of hydrogen peroxide and potassium permanganate [116], nitric acid and potassium chlorate [111], hypochlorous acid and hydrogen peroxide [130], hypochlorite and hydrogen peroxide [148], alkaline hydrogen peroxide [11], hydrogen and sodium peroxides [133], and by oxalic acid. Downs [17] has discussed the best practices employed in bleaching wood.

The luster of wood has been improved by impregnating the surface with various polymeric materials. Metallic surfaces have been applied by electrolytic deposition of any metal desired on a coating containing graphite. Finally, a rough surface imitating driftwood or other aged or weathered wood may be obtained by the selective solvent action of such reagents as zinc chloride, which cause superficial pitting of the wood [141].

One of the biggest advantages of WPC is the improvement of the surface luster of this material. With the proper selection of impregnants, almost any luster from flat low gloss to a very high gloss may be obtained.

10.7 Improvement of Other Physical Properties

Two other physical properties of wood which are utilized only to a minor extent are its self-lubricating behavior and electrical conductivity. Both are subject to improvement over the natural state by treatments.

Certain species of wood with high-extractive contents of the right kind have been used for bearings. *Lignum vitae* had at one time been used extensively as a self-lubricating bearing material under the heavy loads of marine propulsion drives. This has since been replaced by other more readily available materials. The self-lubricating properties of more common species have been enhanced by impregnation with oils and beeswax [113], paraffin, carnauba wax and rosin [108], lubricating oils [44], sulfur and lubricating oil [127], and sulfur and chloronaphthalene [128].

Internal lubricity improves machinability. Wood impregnated with paraffin is easily worked with tools, even those poorly sharpened [123]. The cutting properties of cedar pencil stock are improved by impregnation of the earlywood with paraffin and of the latewood with polyethylene glycol [136].

Wood is an excellent electrical insulator when dry. The electrical resistance of the wood decreases markedly with increasing moisture content. Treatment of the wood with nonhygroscopic, nonconducting materials assists in the maintenance of a low moisture content and consequently a low electrical conductivity. Materials used include paraffin and asphalt [144] and phenolic resins, with and without compression and lamination [112,105]. Wood chemically modified to reduce hygroscopicity will also maintain low conductivity despite humidity increases. Because of its low electrical conductivity and high tensile strength, over a million pounds a year of Compreg insulation material is manufactured in this country [19]. This Compreg is made from 1- and 2-mm-thick European beech veneer impregnated with phenol-formaldehyde. Most of this material goes into the manufacture of tie rods for power circuit breakers.

The conductivity of wood may be increased by impregnation with electrolytes. In addition, an electrically conductive material may be produced by impregnation with liquid metals or alloys [101,126].

10.8 Modification of Mechanical Properties

Among the most important factors affecting the mechanical properties of wood are density and moisture content [103]. Both factors are readily subject to modification by appropriate treatments which result in modification of the mechanical properties of wood. In addition, treatments may possibly influence mechanical properties by interaction with the cell-wall ligno-cellulose matrix at the molecular level.

10.8.1 Surface properties

Hardness and abrasion resistance are the surface mechanical properties of wood of greatest importance. Hardness is measured by resistance to indentation. Abrasion resistance is the resistance to wear and is measured by the wear caused by rubbing with sandpaper or other abrasive materials. Abrasion resistance depends not only on the hardness of the wood, but also on the resilience and the cohesion and orientation of the fibers.

The hardness of wood has been increased by up to 60 percent by impregnation with metals [101]. Phenol-formaldehyde resin impregnation has been reported to increase the hardness of sugar pine by 85 percent [78], although Campredon [12] has claimed three- to fourfold increases in hardness from such treatments. The degree of improvement of hardness depends on the polymer content and also on the species involved. Low-density species, e.g., white pine, show the greatest increase in hardness because they are so soft to begin with. They also have a greater void volume than high-density species, e.g., sugar maple, and therefore can hold more polymer.

Bryant [9] explains the increase in hardness caused by resin treatments in terms of a pipe analogy. An increase in the stiffness of the cell walls, as in pipe walls, makes them resistant to deformation. Deposition of polymer in the cavities will also prevent collapse of the pipes. Another factor contributing to the increase in hardness is the reduction of the moisture content of the wood. This mechanism is of less importance in resin-treated wood since the side-grain hardness of untreated wood only increases by 2.5 percent for each 1 percent reduction in moisture content [103]. This means that a decrease in moisture content of 10 percent would only increase hardness by about 25 percent. However, the observed increases in hardness of acetylated wood—23 percent for ponderosa pine, 22 percent for oak, and 31 percent for maple [18]—are probably mainly caused by reductions in moisture content, with some contribution from density increase.

For wood impregnated with vinyl monomers which are polymerized within the wood to form wood–polymer combinations, the resultant increase in hardness is extremely variable. It is dependent on the nature and content of the polymer, its degree of polymerization and cross linking, and its location within the wood cavities or cell wall. Reported increases in hardness range from a 100 percent increase in spruce containing 80 percent PMMA [59], through two- to threefold increases [43] and six- to sevenfold increases in birch with PMMA and polyester-styrene [3]. A ninefold increase in spruce with 120 percent PMMA was observed by Proksch [66].

Hardness increases with increasing polymer content have been reported for PMMA, polystyrene (PS), poly(vinyl acetate) (PVA), P(EA-AN) and P(ST-AN) [42,43,20]. An even greater increase in hardness was observed when the polymer was highly cross linked [51]. Additional work using cross linkers with PMMA was performed by Taylor [99], and a slight decrease in hardness was observed with highly cross-linked PMMA. Sapwood has a higher polymer retention and therefore a greater increase in hardness than does heartwood [107]. Also, radiation-polymerized materials show a surface hardness about 25 percent greater than heat-catalyst polymerized material [82]. This difference in hardness is attributed to surface evaporation of monomer during the thermal polymerization. All other properties appear to be independent of polymerization method.

In comparison with normal wood, significantly higher abrasion resistance has been observed with Compreg. The high abrasion resistance has been chiefly attributed to the compression of the wood [80]. Because of the increased abrasion resistance, several million pounds per year of this material are used in textile loom parts, *e.g.*, shuttle faces, and decorative handles for items such as refrigerators and knives [84].

Abrasion-resistant bobbins have been prepared by impregnating wood with polyester-styrene formulations which are subsequently polymerized [135]. Improved abrasion resistance has been observed with various wood–plastic combinations, containing poly(vinyl chloride) (PVC), PMMA, PVA, and P(ST-AN) [32]. Doubling or tripling of abrasion resistance can be produced [43]. An extensive study was performed in which four woods—loblolly pine, white pine, red oak and yellow poplar—were converted into wood–plastic combinations using PMMA, P(ST-AN), and P(EA-AN) at various polymer loadings [20]. The abrasion resistance increased with polymer loading in all cases but most dramatically when using the rubbery P(EA-AN) co-polymer. The undesirable loading of sandpaper with melted polymer during sanding can possibly be avoided by cross linking the polymer and thereby increasing abrasion resistance [75]. Taylor [99] did not find this to be true in similar experiments.

10.8.2 Internal properties

In discussing bulk properties of modified woods it should be borne in mind that for those treatments which swell the wood structure, a given volume of modified wood contains fewer individual wood fibers per unit volume and less ligno-cellulose material than the same volume of untreated wood. The reverse is true for Compreg. This becomes significant in comparing properties which are determined on samples of equal volume. For example, when equilibrated samples were machined to the same volume before testing, bulked acetylated wood lost 7.5 percent of its original wood structure in the case of ponderosa pine, and 10.5 percent in the case of sugar maple [18]. Conversely, the tensile strength of Compreg is increased over the original wood because the converted material has more fibers per unit volume than the unconverted wood.

10.8.2.1 Static properties

By static properties is meant the behavior of the material when subjected to a slow enough rate of loading so that there is no 'appreciable momentum in the moving parts. Slow loading in ordinary testing machines fits this definition.

10.8.2.1.1 Bending

Static-bending tests allow the calculation of four values: fiber stress at proportional limit (FSPL), modulus of elasticity (MOE), modulus of rupture (MOR), and work (expressed either at proportional limit or at maximum load) [103]. For phenolic-resin-impregnated poplar, the FSPL was increased by 91 percent to 102 percent, with a lower molecular weight resin giving the higher value [9]. Acetylated wood showed increases in FSPL of 21 percent for pine, 7 percent for oak, and 10 percent for maple. In a maple WPC which contained 50 percent P(ST-AN), an increase in FSPL of 36 percent has been observed [43]. An increased FSPL of 81 percent was observed in basswood, with a maximum retention of PMMA [50]. Other workers have reported a doubling of the bending strength of spruce containing 120 percent PMMA [66], and a doubling of the flexural strength of birch containing 100 percent PMMA [59]. In the extensive study outlined in Section 10.8.1 [20], the effect on FSPL was variable. For example, a 147 percent increase in FSPL was noted for yellow poplar fully loaded with PMMA, whereas a 25-percent decrease in FSPL was found for a white pine–P(EA-AN) combination.

The MOE for poplar phenolic Impreg was increased by 35–40 percent over that for the untreated controls. In acetylated wood there was very little difference in this property. For WPC there was less than a 10 percent increase in MOE for the maple–P(ST-AN) combination, and a 25-percent increase for basswood–PMMA combination. In the N.C. State University study [20], an increased MOE of 34 percent for the yellow-poplar–PMMA combination was typical for all the other combinations of rigid polymers and species of wood. The rubbery co-polymer, P(EA-AN), generally showed low to negative increases in MOE.

In poplar phenolic Impreg, an increase of 27 percent and 43 percent in MOR has been obtained, with the larger value representing the less penetrating resin. In acetylated wood, the MOR of pine was increased about 10 percent by the treatment, while the values for oak and maple showed slight decreases. For WPC, the MOR values showed increases of 25 percent for P(ST-AN) in maple and 78 percent for PMMA in basswood [43]. In the N.C. State University study the maximum MOR increase attained was 87 percent for the loblolly pine–P(ST-AN) combination; lesser values were obtained for the other combinations.

Work to maximum load was decreased by 30 percent for high-molecular-weight phenolic resin in poplar and by 47 percent for the cell-wall-penetrating low-molecular-weight resin. In contrast, the resilience of acetylated wood was significantly increased, to the extent of 38 percent in work to proportional limit for pine, 25 percent for oak, and 27 percent for maple. The WPC also showed greater resilience with a 154 percent increase in work to proportional limit and 77 percent increase in work to maximum load for PMMA in basswood.

In bending-strength determinations, the upper part of the beam is under compressive stress while the lower part is under tensile stress. The presence of resins in the cell wall or the lower moisture content of acetylated wood prevents the buckling of the cellulose fibers under compressive stress, thereby improving FSPL. The modified woods do not fail first in compression on the upper surface as is so often true of untreated wood.

For acetylated ponderosa pine, failure did not occur by compression as in untreated wood but in tension at the lower surface, thus allowing higher values of FSPL and MOR. Untreated oak and maple do not suffer compressive failure first, so enhancement of compressive strength by the treatment did not increase MOR.

In the plastic-impregnated wood, the greater increases in compressive strength accompanied by only modest, if any, reductions in tensile strength lead to significant increases in FSPL and MOR values. However, the increases are greater for less dense woods and less important for the denser woods, which already have a relatively high compressive strength.

10.8.2.1.2 Compression

As has already been indicated in the preceding discussion in Section 10.8.2.1.1, the compressive strength of modified woods is markedly improved. The mechanisms involve reduction in moisture content (compressive strength more than doubles between green and ovendry) [103], and bracing of the cell-wall structure by the polymer.

In phenolic-resin-impregnated poplar, the maximum crushing strength parallel to the grain was increased by 105 percent for high-molecular-weight resin and by 130 percent for a low-molecular-weight resin. In acetylated wood, compressive strength perpendicular to the grain was increased by 39 percent for pine, 6 percent for oak, and 29 percent for maple. In WPC, about a 50 percent increase in maximum crushing strength parallel to the grain was observed in maple and basswood [43,50], but a doubling has been claimed in birch and spruce at 70 percent and 120 percent polymer loadings, respectively [59,66]. For rigid polymer WPC in the N.C. State University study [20], the compressive strength perpendicular to the grain was increased sixfold using white pine, fivefold using yellow-poplar, threefold using loblolly pine, and 160 percent using red oak. In the rubbery polymer WPC, the crushing-strength values ranged from an increase of 143 percent to a decrease of 15 percent.

The compressive strength of veneer, as measured by the pressure required to produce a given reduction in thickness or the reduction in thickness caused by a given pressure, is significantly increased by impregnation of the veneer with salts. Preservative or fire-retardant formulations provide increases in the crushing strength at the proportional limit of 50–100 percent [120].

10.8.2.1.3 Shear

The shear strength parallel to the grain of acetylated wood shows reductions of 21 percent for pine, 12 percent for oak, and 24 percent for maple. Since these values are greater than the reduction in number of fibers per unit of area, it appears that some deterioration of the fiber bond occurred during the treatment.

The shear strength of WPC is higher than untreated wood. Yellow poplar that was fully loaded with PMMA exhibited a two-thirds increase in shear stress, while half-loaded specimens showed a one-third increase. The amount, and also the type, of polymer used affects the shear strength [53].

10.8.2.1.4 Tensile

For those treatments which swell the wood, there are fewer fibrils of cellulose per unit of cross section than in the untreated wood. Tensile strength is consequently decreased in proportion to the swelling unless the impregnated material can contribute to tensile strength.

In the case of uncompressed phenolic-resin-impregnated wood, the discontinuous brittle polymer does not offset the reduction in amount of wood fiber. Consequently, observed reductions in tensile strength of approximately 10 percent are not surprising.

Compressed phenolic-impregnated wood such as Compreg exhibits a tensile strength parallel to the grain which is substantially greater than that in the untreated wood. At one time the Westinghouse Electric Corporation insulator specifications required a tensile strength greater than 24,000 psi for beech Compreg. This means that this material is about $1\frac{1}{2}$ times stronger in tension than the untreated wood.

Acetylated wood contains no additional material which can contribute to tensile strength. The reductions in MOR of 8 percent for oak and maple probably reflect comparable losses in tensile strength showing up in bending failure in tension on the lower surface of the sample.

Proksch [66] has reported an approximately 45 percent increase in tensile strength of spruce containing 120 percent PMMA. It would appear that in his samples the polymer exists in a continuous matrix, thereby contributing to the tensile strength. Also, this polymer matrix possibly reduces slippage between microfibrils in the amorphous regions and at the chain ends.

In the N.C. State University study the tensile strength perpendicular to the grain was more than doubled in the white pine–PMMA composite; the other softwood studied (loblolly pine) showed an approximate 75 percent increase. Less increase in strength was observed for the two hardwoods studied. This was attributed to the greater susceptibility to radiation damage of the hardwoods.

10.8.2.2 Dynamic properties

Although static mechanical properties are readily measured in the laboratory and so make up the major part of any characterization, stress is to a certain degree dynamically applied in most practical situations. Consequently, the ability of the wood to absorb a relatively large amount of energy also is important. This is evaluated by toughness or impact tests.

The toughness or impact strength of phenolic-resin-impregnated wood is seriously reduced by the treatment. In poplar, a high-molecular-weight resin caused a reduction of 18 percent and a cell-wall penetrating low-molecular-weight resin caused a reduction of 60 percent. The low-molecular-weight resins embed the amorphous regions of the cellulose in a rigid matrix. As the motion of the chains is restricted by the resin matrix, less energy can be absorbed and stress concentrations can occur, leading to failure at lower impact stresses.

In acetylated wood, pine shows an increase in toughness of 17 percent, while oak and maple have essentially the same toughness for acetylated and untreated wood. It might have been expected that the reduced cellulose content of the acetylated specimens would have resulted in a loss in toughness. Perhaps the increased density compensates for this.

Wood–plastic combinations have been termed brittle by some investigators, but there is strong evidence that toughness—as measured by energy absorbed—is increased, even though the type of fracture may be called brittle. The shock resistance of quills and shuttles used in textile processing is increased by impregnation with polymers [135]. The WPC using a rigid polymer at high loadings tends to shatter, but the actual impact strength of birch containing PMMA is increased by 50 percent and that containing polyester-styrene by 100 percent [3]. Toughness increases as great as 100 percent have also been observed in white pine with 144 percent PMMA, although high polymer loadings (109 percent) of PVA showed no increase [43]. Basswood fully impregnated with PMMA increased in toughness by 50 percent [50].

10.9 Conclusions

A few million pounds of phenolic-impregnated wood is still used for decorative purposes such as knife and refrigerator handles and for its mechanical strength in various applications in the textile industry [84]. Another million pounds is used for high-tensile electrical insulators [19].

Autio and Miettinen [3], writing in Finland where 8,000 square meters of birch WPC parquetry was installed in the Helsinki air terminal in 1969, state that WPC will not have a broad spectrum of applications as a construction material. Except for hardness, the strength–weight relationships of wood are not significantly improved. The WPC seems most suitable for flooring, special surface-treated veneers, and wall paneling. According to Taylor [99], the greatest drawback of WPC's general acceptance as a flooring material is its water spotting. In all commercial WPC, the polymer does not enter the cell walls; therefore, raw wood is exposed when it is polished. When the polished surface is exposed to water, grain raising occurs, leaving dull spots. These are quite difficult to polish out. Until this difficulty is overcome, WPC will never become a major factor as a floor covering.

Schuerch [73] observes that wood modification by chemical agents is still in its infancy. Future research including such novel techniques as the use of gaseous reagents may expand the use of modified woods, especially as economic considerations change.

REFERENCES

1. Aries, R.S. and Malary, R. 1947. "Impregnation of wood with terpin hydrate." *Northeastern Wood Util. Council Bull.* 18:97–103.
2. Arni, P.C., Gray, J.D. and Scougall, R.K. 1961. "Chemical modification of wood. II. Use of trifluoroacetic acid as catalyst for acetylation." *J. Appl. Chem.* 11:163–70.

3. Autio, T. and Miettinen, J.K. 1970. "Experiments in Finland on properties of wood-polymer combinations." *Forest Prod. J.* 20(3):36–42.

4. Baird, B.R. 1969. "Dimenstional stabilization of wood by vapor phase chemical treatments." *Wood and Fiber* 1(1)54–63.

5. Berliner, J.F.T. 1944. "Methylolurea treated wood." *Wood Products* 49(1):27–8; *Chem. Industries* 54:680–82; *J. Forestry* 42:657–63.

6. Black, J.M. 1971. Private communication. Forest Products Laboratory, Madison, Wis.

7. Browne, F.L. 1960. "Wood siding left to weather naturally." *Southern Lumberman* 141–43.

8. Browning, B.L. 1963. "The wood-water relationship." In *The Chemistry of Wood* Interscience, N.Y. 405–39.

9. Bryant, B.S. 1966. "The chemical modification of wood from the point of view of wood science and economy." *Forest Prod. J.* 16(2):20–7.

10. Campbell, G.G. 1970. "The effect of weathering on the adhesion of selected exterior coatings of wood." Ph.D. Dissertation, School of Forestry, North Carolina State Univ. Raleigh, N.C.

11. Campbell, W.G. and Swann, G. 1938. "The bleaching action of alkaline hydrogen peroxide on wood." *Biochem. J.* 32:702–707.

12. Campredon, J. 1931. "Mechanical resistance of wood impregnated with artificial resins." *Genie Civil* 98:426–29.

13. Clermont, L.P. and Bender, F. 1957. "The effect of swelling agents and catalysts on acetylation of wood." *Forest Prod. J.* 7(5):167–70.

14. Courser, K.S. 1936. "Notes on dyeing wood." *Textile Colorist* 58:268–70.

15. Davidson, R.W. and Baumgardt, W.G. 1970. "Plasticizing wood with ammonia—a progress report." *Forest Prod. J.* 20(3):19–24.

16. Ditmar, R. 1923. "Further possible uses of rubber latex." *Chem. Ztg.* 47:793–94.

17. Downs, L.E. 1948. "A discussion of some of the best practices employed in bleaching wood." *Wood Products* 53(8):33–34,36.

18. Dreher, W.A., Goldstein, I.S. and Cramer, G.R. 1964. "Mechanical properties of acetylated wood." *Forest Prod. J.* 14(2):66–68.

19. Dwyer, J.D. 1971. Private communication. Permali Inc., Mount Pleasant, Pa.

20. Ellwood, E., Gilmore, R., Merrill, J.A. and Poole, W.K. 1969. "An investigation of certain physical and mechanical properties of wood-plastic combinations." DID, U.S. AEC ORO–638.

21. Falck, R. 1930. "How can processes for reducing the swelling of wood be improved?" *Chem. Ztg.* 54:569–71.

22. Forest Products Laboratory. 1959. "Report of dimensional stabilization seminar." U.S. Forest Service Prod. Lab. Rept. No. 2145.

23. Forest Products Laboratory. 1966. "Weathering of wood." U.S. Forest Serv., Forest Prod. Lab. Rept. No. 0135.

24. Friedlander, C.J. 1940. "New method of bending wood." *Wood* 5:137–38.

25. Galliger, G. 1966. "A chemical resistance test on plastic treated wood." Unpublished report. School of Forestry, West Virginia State Univ., Morgantown, W.Va.

26. Goldstein, I.S. 1955. "The impregnation of wood to impart resistance to alkali and acid." *Forest Prod. J.* 5(4):265–67.

27. Goldstein, I.S. and Dreher, W.A. 1960. "Stable furfuryl alcohol impregnating solutions." *Ind. Eng. Chem.* 52:57–58.

28. Goldstein, I.S. and Dreher, W.A. 1961. "A non-hygroscopic fire retardant treatment for wood." *Forest Prod. J.* 11(5):235–37.

29. Goldstein, I.S., Dreher, W.A., Jeroski, E.B., Nielson, J.F., Oberley, W.J. and Weaver,

J.W. 1959. "Wood processing. Inhibiting against swelling and decay." *Ind. Eng. Chem.* 51:1313–17.

30. Goldstein, I.S., Jeroski, E.B., Lund, A.E., Nielson, J.F. and Weaver, J.W. 1961. "Acetylation of wood in lumber thickness." *Forest Prod. J.* 11(8):363–70.

31. Grachev, I.D. and Kovalenko, A.G. 1940. "Impregnation of wood with sugars in order to increase its waterproofness." *Gidroliz. i Lesokhim. Prom.* 3(9):29–33.

32. Guetlbauer, F., Proksch, E. and Bildstein, H. 1966. "Wood-plastic combinations cured by radiation." *Oesterr. Chemiker Ztg.* 67(10):349–61.

33. Guy, H.G. 1946. "Use of treated wood under exposure to chemical attack." *Proc., Am. Wood-Preservers' Assoc.* 42:256–62.

34. Hallonquist, E.G. 1950. "Plastic properties in wood." *Modern Plastics.* 27(12):100, 152.

35. Howes, D.E. and Howes D.E. Jr. 1946. "Chemical and mechanical aids in wood bending." *Rept. Vermont Wood Products Conf.* 6:24–38.

36. Hunt, G.M. 1930. "Effectiveness of moisture-excluding coatings on wood." USDA Circular No. 128.

37. Ifju, G. 1964. "Tensile strength behavior as a function of cellulose in wood." *Forest Prod. J.* 14(8):366–72.

38. Jones, H. 1937. "Coloring Nontextile Products." *J. Soc. Dyers and Colorists* 53:465–68.

39. Juneja, S.C. and Hodgins, J.W. 1970. "The properties of thermo-catalytically prepared wood-polymer composites." *Forest Prod. J.* 20(12):24–28.

40. Kenaga, D.L. 1966. "Unusual chemical improves wood properties." *Forest Prod. J.* 16(12):21–26.

41. Kenaga, D.L., Fennessey, J.P. and Stannett, V.T. 1962. "Radiation grafting of vinyl monomers to wood." *Forest Prod. J.* 12(4):161–68.

42. Kent, J.A., Winston, A. and Boyle, W. 1963. "Preparation of wood-plastic combinations using gamma radiation to induce polymerization; effects of gamma radiation on wood." DID U.S. AEC ORO–600.

43. Kent, J.A., Winston, A., Boyle, W.R., Loos, W.E. and Ayres, J.E. 1965. "Preparation of wood-plastic combinations by using gamma radiation to induce polymerization." DID U.S. AEC ORO–628.

44. Khukhryanskii, P.M. 1939. "Impregnation of wood with lubricating oils." *Gidroliz. i Lesokhim. Prom.* 2(9):56–58.

45. Klinov, I.Y. 1933. "Application of wood in chemical equipment." *Khimstroi* 5:2310–16.

46. Klinov, I.Y. and Shishkov, V.P. 1934. "Wood in chemical apparatus construction." *Khim. Mashinostroenie* 3:32–6.

47. Kobbe, W.H. 1926. "Indurating wood with sulfur." *Chem. Met. Eng.* 33:354–56.

48. Koppers Co., Inc. 1967. "KP resin impregnated wood." Booklet W–567. Pittsburgh, Pa.

49. Koppers Co., Inc. 1969. "Asidbar, the pressure-treated super wood for corrosive industrial applications." Pittsburgh, Pa.

50. Langwig, J.E., Meyer, J.A. and Davidson, R.W. 1968. "Influence of polymer impregnation on mechanical properties of basswood." *Forest Prod. J.* 18(7):33–36.

51. Langwig, J.E., Meyer, J.A. and Davidson, R.W. 1969. "New monomers used in making wood-plastics." *Forest Prod. J.* 19(11):57–61.

52. Loos, W.E. 1968. "Dimensional stability of wood-plastic combinations to moisture change." *Wood Sci. Tech.* 2:308–12.

53. Loos, W.E. and Kent, J.A. 1968. "Shear strength of radiation produced wood-plastic combinations." *Wood Science* 1(1):23–28.

54. Loos, W.E. and Robinson, G.L. 1968. "Rates of swelling of wood in vinyl mono-mers." *Forest Prod. J.* 18(9):109–12.

55. McMillin, C.W. 1963. "Chemical treatment of wood—dimensional stabilization with polymerizable vapor of ethylene oxide." *Forest Prod. J.* 13(2):56–61.

56. Masiulanis, B. and Dutkowski, W. 1967. "Modification of wood with cellulose acetate." *Zesg. Nauk. Politech Gdansk, Chem.* 17:39–52.

57. Meyer, J.A. 1968. "Crosslinking affects sanding properties of wood-plastic." *Forest Prod. J.* 18(5):89.

58. Meyer, J.A. and Loos, W.E. 1969. "Processes of and products from treating southern pine wood for modification of properties." *Forest Prod. J.* 19(12):32–8.

59. Miettinen, J.K. 1966. "Wood plastic composites." *Kem. Teollisuus* 23(12):1084–88.

60. Millett, M.A. and Stamm, A.J. 1947. "Wood treatment with resin forming systems." *Modern Plastics* 24(6):159–60, 208,210,212; 25(1):125–27.

61. Miniutti, V.P. 1967. "Microscopic observation of ultraviolet irradiation and weathered softwood surfaces and clear coatings." U.S. Forest Serv., Forest Prod. Lab. Rept. No. 74.

62. Mitchell, H.L. and Wahlgren, H.E. 1959. "New chemical treatment curbs swelling and shrinking of walnut gunstocks." *Forest Prod. J.* 9(12):437–41.

63. Palka, L.C. 1970. "Current trends in dimensional stabilization of wood." Forest Prod. Lab. Canadian Forest Serv. Inf. Rept. VP–X–63.

64. Pentoney, R.E. 1966. "Liquid ammonia-solvent combinations in wood plasticization. Properties of treated wood." *Ind. Eng. Chem. Prod. Res. and Dev.* 5(2):105–10.

65. Prigozhin, B.S. 1946. "Waterproofing of fabrics." *Legkaya Prom.* 9/10:29.

66. Proksch, E. 1968. "Radiochemical modification of Austrian woods." *Allg. Prakt. Chem.* 19(8):267–71.

67. Risi, J. and Arseneau, D.F. 1957. "Dimensional stabilization of wood: Introduction and Part I. Acetylation." *Forest Prod. J.* 7(6):210–13.

68. Risi, J. and Arseneau, D.F. 1958. "Dimensional stabilization of wood. V. Phthaloyla-tion." *Forest Prod. J.* 8(9):252–55.

69. Sadoh, T. 1968. "Plasticization of wood using tetraethylenepentamine." *Nippon Mokuzai Gakkaishi* 14(3):175.

70. Schmidt, H. 1931. "Properties of wood impregnated with artificial resins." *Kunstoffe* 21:251–52.

71. Schrader, O.H. 1943. "The softening effect of saturated steam on western hemlock and sitka spruce." *Pacific Pulp and Paper Ind.* 17(2):16–20.

72. Schuerch, C. 1963. "Plasticizing wood with liquid ammonia." *Ind. Eng. Chem.* 55(10):39.

73. Schuerch, C. 1968. "Treatment of wood with gaseous reagents." *Forest Prod. J.* 18(3):47–53.

74. Schuerch, C., Burdick, M.P. and Mahdalik, M. 1966. "Liquid ammonia-solvent combinations in wood plasticization. Chemical treatments." *Ind. Eng. Chem. Prod. Res. and Dev.* 5(2):101–105.

75. Schwalbe, C.G. and Berndt, K. 1931. "Hygroscopicity of woods after different kinds of drying." *Kolloid Z.* 54:314–26.

76. Seborg, R.M., Millett, M.A. and Stamm, A.J. 1956. "Heat stabilization compressed wood (Staypak)." U.S. Forest Serv., Forest Prod. Lab. Rept. No. 1580. Revised.

77. Seborg, R.M. and Stamm, A.J. 1941. "The compression of wood." *Mech. Eng.* 63:211.

78. Seborg, R.M. and Stamm, A.J. 1956. "Effect of resin treatment and compression upon the properties of wood." U.S. Forest Serv., Forest Prod. Lab. Rept. No. 1383. Revised.

79. Seborg, R.M., Tarkow, H. and Stamm, A.J. 1953. "Effect of heat upon the dimensional stabilization of wood." *Forest Prod. J.* 3(3):59–67.

80. Seborg, R.M., Tarkow, H. and Stamm, A.J. 1962. "Modified woods." U.S. Forest Serv., Forest Prod. Lab. Rept. No. 2192. Revised.

81. Siau, J.F. 1968. "The physical properties of wood-plastic composites." Ph.D. dissertation, State Univ. College of Forestry at Syracuse Univ., Syracuse, N.Y.

82. Siau, J.F. and Meyer, J.A. 1966. "Comparison of the properties of heat and radiation cured wood-polymer combinations." *Forest Prod. J.* 16(8):47–56.

83. Siau, J.F., Meyer, J.A. and Skaar, C. 1965. "Wood polymer combinations using radiation techniques." *Forest Prod. J.* 15(10):426–34.

84. Smith, J. 1971. Private communication. Fibron Products, Inc., Buffalo, N.Y.

85. Stamm, A.J. 1934. "The effect of inorganic salts upon the swelling and the shrinkage of wood." *J. Am. Chem. Soc.* 56:1195–1204.

86. Stamm, A.J. 1955. Swelling of wood and fiberboards in liquid ammonia." *Forest Prod. J.* 5(6):413–16.

87. Stamm, A.J. 1959a. "Dimensional stabilization of wood by thermal reactions and formaldehyde crosslinking." *Tappi* 42:39–44.

88. Stamm, A.J. 1959b. "Effect of polyethylene glycol on the dimensional stabilization of wood." *Forest Prod. J.* 9(10):375–81.

89. Stamm, A.J. 1964a. "Shrinking and swelling of wood." In *Wood and Cellulose Science,* Ronald Press, N.Y. 215–35.

90. Stamm, A.J. 1964b. "Dimensional stabilization." In *Wood and Cellulose Science,* Ronald Press, N.Y. 312–42.

91. Stamm, A.J., Burr, H.K. and Kline, A.A. 1946. "Staybwood ... heat stabilized wood." *Ind. Eng. Chem.* 38:630–34.

92. Stamm, A.J. and Hansen, L.A. 1935. "Minimizing wood shrinkage and swelling." *Ind. Eng. Chem.* 27:1480–84.

93. Stamm, A.J. and Hansen, L.A. 1937. "Minimizing wood shrinkage and swelling— effect of heating in various gases." *Ind. Eng. Chem.* 29:831–33.

94. Stamm, A.J. and Seborg, R.M. 1936. "Minimizing wood shrinkage and swelling." *Ind. Eng. Chem.* 28:1164–69.

95. Stamm, A.J. and Tarkow, H. 1947. "Dimensional stabilization of wood." *J. Phys. and Colloid Chem.* 51:493–505.

96. Stevens, W.C. and Turner, N. 1942. "Chemical bending of wood." *Wood* 7:123–26.

97. Tarkow, H. 1966. "Dimensional stability." In *Encyclopedia of Polymer Science and Technology,* Vol. 5, Interscience, N.Y. 98–121.

98. Tarkow, H. and Stamm, A.J. 1953. "Effect of formaldehyde treatments upon dimensional stabilization of wood." *Forest Prod. J.* 3(2):33–37.

99. Taylor, G.B. 1971. Private communication. Radiation Machinery Corp., Parsippany, N.J.

100. Thompson, W.S. 1969. "Effect of chemicals, chemical atmospheres and contact with metals on southern pine wood: a review." Mississippi State Univ. Forest Prod. Utilization Lab. Res. Report No. 6.

101. Vogel, F.H. 1950. "Impregnation of wood with solid metal alloys." *Proc. Forest Prod. Res. Soc.* 4:199–201.

102. Voronkov, M.G., Dolgov, B.N. and Shebarova, Z.I. 1957. "Polyorganosiloxanols for waterproofing structural materials." *Zhur. Priklad. Khim.* 30:1221–27.

103. Wangaard, F.F. 1950. *The Mechanical Properties of Wood.* John Wiley & Sons, N.Y. 152–88.

104. Wangaard, F.F. 1966. "Resistance of wood to chemical degradation." *Forest Prod. J.* 16(2):53–64.

105. Weatherwax, R.C. and Stamm, A.J. 1945. "The electrical resistivity of resin-treated wood." *Elec. Eng.* 64:833.
106. Weaver, J.W., Nielson, J.F. and Goldstein, I.S. 1960. "Dimensional stabilization of wood with aldehydes and related compounds." *Forest Prod. J.* 10(6):306–10.
107. Young, R.A. and Meyer, J.A. 1968. "Heartwood and sapwood impregnation with vinyl monomers." *Forest Prod. J.* 18(4):66–68.
108. Bache, L.S. 1913. "Self-Lubricating wood." U.S. patent 1,076,941.
109. Bache, L.S. 1916. "Wood for use in making bearings." U.S. patent 1,197,428.
110. Barry, A.J. 1952. "Rendering water-wettable solid materials water repellent." U.S. patent 2,608,495.
111. Bateman, E. 1920. "Bleaching wood." U.S. patent 1,329,284.
112. Brossman, J.R. 1931. "Laminated wood product." U.S. patent 1,834,895.
113. Cardell, C.O.L. 1912. "Wood for bearings." U.S. patent 1,041,427.
114. Delorme-Cebrian, J. 1935. "Waterproofing wood." French patent 790,198.
115. Farbenind, I.G. 1927. "Preserving and waterproofing wood." British patent 302,698.
116. Franck-Philipson, A. 1914. "Bleaching wood." British patent 3,467.
117. Frolich, P.K. 1936. "Wood impregnation." U.S. patent 2,052,172.
118. Frost, E. 1909. German patent 233,236.
119. Frost, E. 1910. German patent 238,889.
120. Goldstein, I.S. and Oberly, W.J. 1964. "Process for making plywood." U.S. patent 3,137,607.
121. Griffin, H.H. and Burgeni, A. 1936. "Reducing the shrinkage of wood." U.S. patent 2,045,350.
122. Harnill, R.E. 1947. "Urea Treatment of Wood." U.S. patent 2,414,808.
123. Herhein, G.W. 1918. "Modifying the properties of wood." French patent 458,771.
124. Herzog, R.O. and Burgeni, A. 1931. "Flexible wood." French patent 713,476.
125. Hudson, M.S. 1955. "Dimensional stabilization of wood by treatment with halogenated ethers." U.S. patent 2,726,169.
126. Kaiser Wilhelm Institut fur Eisenforschung. 1927. "Permeating wood with metallic substances." British patent 296, 986.
127. Kawasaki, M. 1950. "Treatment of wood to be used for lubricating parts." Japanese patent 877.
128. Kawasaki, M. 1954. "Wooden bearings for use in water." Japanese patent 2096.
129. Kenaga, D.L. 1957. "Stabilized wood." U.S. patent 2,811,470.
130. Korte, H. 1927. "Bleaching wood." German patent 479,801.
131. LaBerge, R.W. 1956. "Retarding transmission of moisture through masonry and wood." U.S. patent 2,750,307.
132. Loughborough, W.K. 1942. "Impregnating and plasticizing wood." U.S. patent 2,298,017.
133. MacBean, N.A. 1943. "Bleaching wood." U.S. patent 2,312,218.
134. Ninin, G. and Thiebaud, L. 1930. "Treating wood." French patent 706,646.
135. Parks, R.F. 1964. "Wood impregnation." Belgian patent 650,150.
136. Partansky, A.M. 1959. "Impregnating wood with paraffin wax and with polyethylene glycol to improve its cutting qualities." U.S. patent 2,907,684.
137. Plauson, H. and Vielle, J.A. 1920. "Synthetic resins." British patent 156,151.
138. Pollak, F. 1921. British patent 171,096.
139. Ramsey, R.R. 1950. "Sodium thiosulfate as an aid in bending wood." U.S. patent 2,532,193.
140. Roberts, I.L. 1911. U.S. patent 992,256.
141. Schmidt, C.E. 1927. "Imitation of driftwood." U.S. patent 1,628,918.

142. Schneider, A.K. and Thomas, J.C. 1961. "Sulfur tetrafluoride for increasing the water resistance of polymeric materials." U.S. patent 2,983,626.
143. Stamm, A.J. and Tarkow, H. 1947b. "Acetylation of wood and boards." U.S. patent 2,417,995.
144. Stewart, O.V. 1926. "Impregnating wood." U.S. patent 1,572,905.
145. Suida, H. (I.G. Farbenindustrie). 1929. "Esterification of wood." British patent 336,969.
146. Tillotson, E.W. 1933. "Impregnating wood foundry pattern with sulfur." U.S. patent 1,927,076.
147. Twombly, A.H., Lundin, A.P. and Marr, R.A. 1921. "Steaming and waterproofing wood." U.S. patent 1,396,899.
148. Weigert, W. 1931. "Bleaching wood." French patent 726,350.

Index